Teaching in Lifelong Learning

Teaching in Lifelong Learning

A GUIDE TO THEORY AND PRACTICE

Second edition

Edited by James Avis, Roy Fisher and Ron Thompson

Open University Press

Open University Press
McGraw-Hill Education
McGraw-Hill House
Shoppenhangers Road
Maidenhead
Berkshire
England
SL6 2QL

email: enquiries@openup.co.uk
world wide web: www.openup.co.uk

and Two Penn Plaza, New York, NY 10121–2289, USA

First published 2015

A catalogue record of this book is available from the British Library

ISBN-13: 978-0-33-526332-5 (pb)
ISBN-10: 0-33-526332-1 (pb)
eISBN: 978-0-33-526333-2

Library of Congress Cataloging-in-Publication Data
CIP data applied for

Typesetting and e-book compilations by
RefineCatch Limited, Bungay, Suffolk

Praise for this book

"This second edition of Teaching in Lifelong Learning has been carefully updated to incorporate the recent changes that the Post Compulsory Education sector has undergone. It remains an essential textbook for both in-service and intending teachers-in-training in the Lifelong Learning Sector who are studying towards Certificates, Diplomas and Degrees in Education and Training. The book has been carefully edited to ensure that the variety of expert contributions employ an intelligently accessible style; this will enable a wide range of students and teachers to achieve practical results whilst improving their confidence to articulate the theories underpinning their approaches. The text incorporates all the latest information concerning the de-regulation and management of this vital sector, and ensures that the new Professional Standards are subjected to a balanced consideration in keeping with the critical stance which this book encourages. This remains a valuable starter text, helping new teachers to implement and justify thoughtful, student-centred approaches, whilst providing the latest references to further reading which will help assure their emerging professional status."

Dr. Andrew Convery, Senior Lecturer in Education at University of Sunderland, UK

"This book will be invaluable for both new and experienced teachers in lifelong learning. It provides comprehensive and informed account in an accessible, whilst challenging way with each chapter exploring different aspects of teaching in lifelong learning. It examines the various influences of internal and external factors such as government policy on teaching practitioners and the wider sector encouraging reflection and understanding of teaching and lifelong learning."

Dr. Cheryl Bolton, Senior Lecturer in the Education Academic Group at
Staffordshire University, UK

Contents

List of boxes	xiii
List of figures	xiv
List of tables	xv
Notes on the contributors	xvi
Preface	xviii
Acknowledgements	xix
Abbreviations and acronyms	xx
Professional Standards for Teachers and Trainers in Education and Training – England	xxvii

Part 1

Introduction to lifelong learning   1

1 Introduction to the lifelong learning sector   3
Roy Fisher, Robin Simmons and Ron Thompson

Education, the market and globalization	3
Reform and the LLS	5
Development of the LLS	6
Autonomous learning	9
Further education	9
Local authorities	10
Lifelong learning in the public services	11
Private training providers	11
Higher education	11
Some key institutions	12
The need for perspective	16

2 Teacher education for lifelong learning   18
Amanda Fulford, Denise Robinson and Ron Thompson

The growth of teacher education for lifelong learning	19
Professional standards for teaching in lifelong learning	21

A framework of teaching qualifications   24
Reviewing the framework: Lingfield and after   25
Mentoring and the work-based learning of teachers   26
The former Institute for Learning *and the* Higher Education
    Academy   27

3 Theory and practice   29
James Avis and Kevin Orr

Policy science and policy scholarship   29
Theorizing education: socio-economic and political
    context   31
Theorizing education: contingency and complexity   33
Expansive practice   36
Conclusion: what about practice?   38

4 Professionalism   40
James Avis, Roy Fisher and Ros Ollin

The professional teacher   40
Professional values and codes of conduct   43
Inter-professionality in the LLS   45
Research and scholarship   46
Conclusion   47

5 Theorizing the work-based learning of teachers   48
James Avis, Kevin Orr and Jonathan Tummons

Theories of work-based learning   48
Socially situated practice   48
Bourdieu's field and habitus   51
Communities of practice and WBL   53
Communities of practice in FE   54
Conclusion   57

6 Equality and diversity   58
Lyn Ashmore, James Avis, Julie Dalton, Penny Noel, Sandra Rennie,
Emma Salter, Dave Swindells and Paul Thomas

Equality and diversity in lifelong learning   59
Faith and religion   64
Anti-racism   66
Anti-sexism   70
Lesbian, gay, bisexual and transgender issues   71
Mental health   72
Equal opportunity in practice   73
Social class   75
Conclusion   76

Part 2

Teaching in the lifelong learning sector   77

7   Learning and learners   79
Margaret McLay, Louise Mycroft, Penny Noel, Kevin Orr,
Ron Thompson, Jonathan Tummons and Jane Weatherby

What is learning?   79
Classifying types of learning   82
Deep, surface and strategic learning   84
Factors influencing learning   85
Theories of the learning process   87
The learning styles debate   99
Widening participation   100
Adult learners and 'adult learning'   101
Learners from other countries   103
Students with learning difficulties or disabilities   104
'Academically more able learners'   105
Learners aged 14–16   106
Young people not in education, employment or training   107

8   The curriculum in the lifelong learning sector   109
Roy Fisher, Amanda Fulford, Bernard McNicholas and
Ron Thompson

What is the curriculum?   109
Curriculum theory and models   110
Curriculum design and development   116
Creativity and the curriculum   118
Vocationalism and parity of esteem   119
14–19 education and training   121
Apprenticeships and higher apprenticeships   122
College higher education   123
Literacy, numeracy and ESOL: some background   123
Skills for Life (and after)   125

9   Practical teaching   127
Liz Dixon, Josie Harvey, David Powell, Ron Thompson and
Sarah Williamson

Planning learning sessions   127
Aims and objectives   129
Learning activities   132
Using questions to promote learning   135
Learning resources   138
Whiteboards   139
Differentiation   142
Lesson plans and schemes of work   143
Modelling good practice   147

Teaching groups of learners   148
Managing learner behaviour   149
Tutorials and pastoral support   152

10 Learning and teaching with technology   155
Liz Bennett, Steve Burton, Alison Iredale, Cheryl Reynolds and
Andrew Youde

The value of learning with technology   156
Developing teachers' e-learning practices   157
Concepts of learning with technology   159
Technologies for learning   160
Teacher-led or student-initiated?   162
Designing for learning with technology   164
The potential of digital tools for social, moral and personal harm   168
Conclusion   169

11 Assessment   171
Ros Ollin, Ron Thompson and Jonathan Tummons

The nature and purpose of assessment   171
Assessment tasks   172
Planning and designing assessment   173
Summative, formative and ipsative assessment   178
Providing feedback   179
Norm-referenced and criterion-referenced assessment   182
Validity and reliability   183
Example: a test on food hygiene   184
Recognizing and accrediting prior learning   186
Moderation and standardization   188
Double marking   188

12 Subject specialist pedagogy   190
Steve Burton, Roy Fisher and David Lord

Subject specialist pedagogy in lifelong learning   190
The subject specialist dimension   194
Some wider considerations   196

13 Reflective practice   198
Barbara Reynolds and Martin Suter

What is reflection?   198
The process of reflective practice   199
Levels of reflection   200
Theories of reflective practice   202
Criticisms of reflective practice   206

14 **Coaching and mentoring**   208
    Wayne Bailey, Chris Blamires, Liz Dixon, Alison Iredale,
    Denise Robinson and Judith Schoch

        What are coaching and mentoring?   208
        Experiental learning and coaching   210
        Social and situated theories of learning and coaching   211
        Getting the best from the coaching relationship   212
        Mentoring teachers in lifelong learning   215
        The role of the mentee   218
        Being observed in the classroom   218
        Conclusion   221

Part 3

Working in the lifelong learning sector   **223**

15 **Getting to know the organization**   225
    James Avis, Julie Dalton, Liz Dixon, Ann Jennings, Kevin Orr and
    Jonathan Tummons

        Your first visit   225
        Structures and hierarchies   226
        Informal networks   227
        Managerialism and performativity   227
        The staffroom   228

16 **Health, safety and well-being**   231
    Julie Dalton, Roy Fisher and David Neve

        Risk   231
        Legal responsibilities   231
        Health and safety in the workplace   232
        Who is responsible for risk assessments?   234
        Bullying and harassment   235
        The Disclosure and Barring Service   235
        Security   236
        From Every Child Matters *to* Help Children Achieve More   237

17 **Course management and administration**   240
    Frances Marsden and Andrew Youde

        Maintaining records   240
        Managing a course   241
        Marketing   244
        Working with administrative staff   245
        Awarding bodies   245
        Committee membership   246
        Conclusion   247

18 Evaluation and quality assurance   248
Roy Fisher, Alison Iredale, Ros Ollin and Denise Robinson

The audit culture and professional autonomy   248
Evaluating teaching and learning   250
Methods of evaluating teaching   251
Evaluating the curriculum   252
Retention   254
Ofsted   255
QAA Higher Education Review   257
Conclusion   257

19 Career planning and continuing professional development   259
Robin Simmons and Martyn Walker

The FE context   259
Employment and roles in FE colleges   260
Job applications   261
The interview   262
The first post and career progression   264
Part-time teaching and agencies   264
Creating and maintaining a curriculum vitae   265
Staff appraisal and planning CPD   266
Trade unions   267
Getting promotion   267
In transition   268

References   270
Index   294

Boxes

2.1   The LLUK teaching standards 2007–14. Professional values
for domain D: planning for learning   22

2.2   The LLUK teaching standards 2007–14. Professional knowledge
and practice for domain D: planning for learning   23

7.1   Levels of learning in the cognitive domain   83

7.2   Levels of learning in the affective domain   83

7.3   Levels of learning in the psychomotor domain   84

7.4   Some key themes of cognitivism   91

7.5   Characteristics of experiential learning   96

8.1   Tyler's (1949) four fundamental questions for curriculum
development   112

9.1   Features of 'outstanding' teaching and learning selected from
post-16 inspection criteria   130

9.2   Examples of general and specific behavioural objectives   132

9.3   Prompts for learners to formulate their own questions   138

10.1   Definitions of terms relating to learning with technology   159

10.2   Case study: flipped classroom   165

10.3   Case study: contributing student model   166

10.4   Case study: supporting learners through email   167

10.5   Case study: social networking   168

11.1   Examples of selection-type questions   173

11.2   Design of written assessment tasks: some guidelines   177

11.3   Useful questions when considering accreditation of prior learning   187

13.1   Example of reflection (1)   200

13.2   Example of reflection (2)   201

13.3   Example of technical reflection   202

13.4   Critical-organizational reflection   203

Figures

7.1	Maslow's hierarchy of human needs	86
7.2	Pavlov's conditioning experiment	88
7.3	Vygotski's zone of proximal development	93
7.4	Kolb's experiential learning cycle	97
7.5	Three-stage model of reflective processes and their role in reflective learning	98
8.1	The National Qualification Framework/The Qualifications and Credit Framework/The Framework for Higher Education Qualifications	111
9.1	Factors influencing decisions in lesson planning	128
9.2	Cyclic structure for the development phase of a learning session	129
9.3	Minton's Matrix of Control	134
9.4	Sample cover sheet of a lesson plan for a childcare class	144
9.5	Extract from a lesson plan for a childcare class	145
9.6	Extract from a scheme of work for a Certificate in Education class	146
10.1	Digital literacy anatomized	164
11.1	The assessment process	174
11.2	Assessment strategy for National Vocational Qualifications	176
13.1	Basic model of reflecting on practice	199
14.1	The coaching-mentoring continuum	209
14.2	Components of a social theory of learning	212
14.3	The coaching process	213
14.4	Support and challenge in mentoring novice trainees	217
14.5	Protocols for mentees	219

Tables

6.1   Learners by gender on LSC-funded FE provision 2006–07   62
7.1   Comparisons between metaphors of learning   80
8.1   Dimensions of traditional and liberal-progressive education   114
9.1   Effect sizes of selected teaching/learning methods   133
9.2   Effect sizes of factors not related to teaching method   134
9.3   Positive and negative approaches to motivating learners   152
10.1   Web-based tools available for teaching and learning   161
10.2   Collaborative tools available for learning   162
10.3   Mapping technologies against approaches to teaching and learning   162
11.1   Table of specifications for a unit on food hygiene   185

Notes on the contributors

The editors and all contributors are currently at the School of Education and Professional Development at the University of Huddersfield except as indicated below:

Chris Blamires, formerly School of Education and Professional Development, University of Huddersfield

Steve Burton, School of Education and Childhood, Leeds Beckett University, formerly School of Education and Professional Development, University of Huddersfield

Amanda Fulford, Leeds Trinity University, formerly School of Education and Professional Development, University of Huddersfield

Josie Harvey, formerly School of Education and Professional Development, University of Huddersfield

Alison Iredale, University Campus Oldham, formerly School of Education and Professional Development, University of Huddersfield

Ann Jennings, Leeds City College

Bernard McNicholas, formerly School of Education and Professional Development, University of Huddersfield

Louise Mycroft, Northern College

David Neve, formerly School of Education and Professional Development, University of Huddersfield

Sandra Rennie, educational consultant

Barbara Reynolds, formerly Harrogate College

Judith Schoch, University Campus Barnsley, formerly School of Education and Professional Development, University of Huddersfield

Martin Suter, formerly School of Education and Professional Development, University of Huddersfield

Dave Swindells, formerly School of Education and Professional Development, University of Huddersfield

Jonathan Tummons, University of Durham

Jane Weatherby, Northern College

Preface

This book is aimed primarily at teachers and trainee teachers working in the lifelong learning sector (LLS); nevertheless, it seeks to address its subject matter broadly. Many readers will be following courses such as the Certificate in Education, Professional Graduate Certificate in Education or Postgraduate Certificate/Diploma in Education. Others may be undertaking awards such as the Diploma in Education and Training. As with the first edition, we have intended the book to be useful to a wider readership, including qualified teachers and those following education degree courses.

This book is subtitled 'A guide to theory and practice'. It has been our ambition to address practical aspects of teaching and training. These, however, do not take place in an atheoretical vacuum, but are contextualized by social and political relations. The book critically engages with theory and recognizes that education as a system and teaching as an activity are complex and demanding processes, resistant to simple analysis and 'quick fix' solutions. A commitment to social justice and inclusion is fundamental to our thinking.

The book has three sections. In Part 1, we set out the scope of the LLS and some key concepts. Part 2 is concerned with learning, the curriculum, teaching, assessment and associated issues. In Part 3 we deal with organizational and career factors that constitute the environment in which teachers work. There is, of course, some overlap between sections. We have provided a linear order of subjects which lends itself to progression from this point to the end. Many readers, however, will steer around the chapters in ways that suit themselves. Although we have aimed to be comprehensive in our coverage, this book should not be used in isolation from other texts. The ideas presented should be examined in the light of the reader's experiences as a teacher and as a learner.

We hope that you enjoy this book. We and our contributors would be grateful for comments that might be helpful to us in developing our ideas.

James Avis, Roy Fisher and Ron Thompson

Acknowledgements

This book involves contributions from a range of institutions and people, too many to list individually. Our thinking has been informed by teacher education colleagues, trainee teachers and others in the member colleges of the Education and Training Consortium (ETC), together with the many institutions and individuals in the sector who provide placements and other support to our students. We thank ETC for encouragement and support. Similarly, we acknowledge the Huddersfield University Distributed Centre for Excellence in Teacher Training (HUDCETT) and its constituent organizations.

Colleagues at the Bath Spa University, the University of Greenwich and the University of Wolverhampton have informed our thinking. Professor Terry Hyland, a visiting professor at Huddersfield, formerly of the University of Bolton, was a member of the University of Huddersfield-funded research project *The College Experience – Work Based Learning and Pre-service PCET Trainee Teachers*, which was the genesis of this book.

We are also grateful to Dalia Dasgupta, South East Essex College; Lorraine Higham, Accrington and Rossendale College; Emma Richardson at Nelson and Colne College and to Laurence Smith of the 'What Next?' Project.

We thank Angela Johnson, a former PGCE student at the University of Huddersfield, who kindly agreed to the use of her lesson plan in Chapter 9.

We are grateful to Taylor and Francis publishers for permission to adapt Fisher, R. and Webb, K. (2006) Subject specialist pedagogy and initial teacher training for the learning and skills sector in England: the context, a response and some critical issues, *The Journal of Further and Higher Education*, 30(4): 337–49. An abridged and amended version formed the basis of Chapter 12. The website for *The Journal of Further and Higher Education* can be found at http://www.tandf.co.uk/journals/carfax/0309877X.html

Figure 8.1 was kindly provided by Ofqual.

The editors would like to thank our partners for their forbearance during the preparation of this book.

Finally, we wish to express our appreciation to Fiona Richman, Richard Townrow, Nicky Whiteley and their colleagues at McGraw-Hill, and our copy editor, Maureen Cox, for their patience and guidance.

Abbreviations and acronyms

Please note that not all these refer to current concepts/organizations, or to ones which are exclusive to the lifelong learning sector, and that not all entries appear in the body of this book. In some cases, dates in square brackets indicate the active period of defunct bodies. We have tried to supply a guide to the bewildering range of abbreviations and acronyms that a reader might meet elsewhere.

AB	awarding body
ABE	Adult Basic Education
ACL	adult and community learning
AD(H)D	Attention Deficit (Hyperactivity) Disorder
AE	adult education
A Level	General Certificate of Education at Advanced Level
ALI	Adult Learning Inspectorate [2000–2007, when it became part of Ofsted]
ALLaN	Adult Literacy, Language and Numeracy
ALP	Association of Learning Providers
AoC	Association of Colleges
APEL	accreditation of prior experiential learning
APL	accreditation of prior learning
APLA	accreditation of prior learning achievement
ARG	Assessment Reform Group
AS	General Certificate of Education at Advanced Subsidiary Level
ASD	autistic spectrum disorder
ATL	Association of Teachers and Lecturers
ATLS	Associate Teacher Learning and Skills
BEC	Business Education Council [1974–1983, when it became the Business and Technology Education Council]
Becta	British Educational Communications and Technology Agency [1998–2011]
BERA	British Educational Research Association
BESD	behavioural, emotional and social difficulties
BIS	Department for Business, Innovation and Skills

BME	Black and Minority Ethnic
BNP	British National Party
BSA	Basic Skills Agency [1975–2007, when it merged with NIACE]
BSL	British Sign Language
BTEC	Business and Technology Education Council
CAL	computer aided learning
CATs	credit accumulation and transfer scheme
CBET	Competence Based Education and Training
CBL	computer based learning
CBT	computer based training
CEL	Centre for Excellence in Leadership
Cert Ed	Certificate in Education
CETL	Centre for Excellence in Teaching and Learning [a HEFCE initiative from 2005–2010]
CETT	Centre for Excellence in Teacher Training
CGLI	City and Guilds of London Institute
CIF	Common Inspection Framework
CLS	Centre for Longitudinal Studies
CNAA	Council for National Academic Awards [1965–1992]
CoVE	Centre of Vocational Excellence
CPD	continuing professional development
CRB	Criminal Records Bureau [2002–2012, replaced by DBS]
CSCI	Commission for Social Care Inspection
CTLLS	Certificate in Teaching in the Lifelong Learning Sector
CYP	Commonwealth Youth Programme
DBERR	Department for Business, Enterprise and Regulatory Reform [2007–2009, when it became the Department for Business, Innovation and Skills]
DBS	Disclosure and Barring Service
DCSF	Department for Children, Schools and Families [replaced by the DfE in 2010]
DDA	Disability Discrimination Act, 1995
DES	Department of Education and Science [1964–1992 now DfE]
DfE	Department for Education [established 2010, previously used 1992–1995]
DFEE	Department for Education and Employment [1995–2001 now DfE]
DfES	Department for Education and Skills [2001–2007 now DfE]
DIUS	Department for Innovation, Universities and Skills [2007–2009, now BIS]
DPA	Data Protection Act, 1998
DTLLS	Diploma in Teaching in the Lifelong Learning Sector
E2E	Entry to Employment
E2L	English as a Second Language
E and D	Equality and Diversity
EAL	English as an Additional Language
EAP	English for Academic Purposes

EBacc	English Baccalaureate
EBC	English Baccalaureate Certificate
EBD	emotional and behavioural difficulties
ECM	Every Child Matters
ECRE	European Council for Refugees and Exiles
EDL	English Defence League
EFA	Education Funding Agency
EFL	English as a foreign language
EIA	Equality Impact Assessment
EMA	Education Maintenance Allowance
ENTO	Employment National Training Organisation
EQF	European Qualifications Framework
ERIC	Educational Resources Information Centre
ESOL	English for speakers of other languages
ESRC	Economic and Social Research Council
ETC	Education and Training Consortium
ETF	Education and Training Foundation [known as 'The Foundation']
EYM	Every Youth Matters
FdA	Foundation Degree Arts
FDL	flexible distributed learning
FE	further education
FEDA	Further Education Development Agency [1995–2000, became LSDA]
FEFCE	Further Education Funding Council for England [1992–2000]
FEFCW	Further Education Funding Council for Wales [1992–2001]
FEI	further education institution
FELTAG	Further Education Learning Technology Action Group
FENTO	Further Education National Training Organization [1998–2005]
FETT	Further Education Teacher Training
FEU	Further Education Unit [1977–1995, replaced by FEDA]
FfE	Framework for Excellence
FHEA	Further and Higher Education Act, 1992
FHEQ	Framework for Higher Education Qualifications
FLC	Foundation Learning Curriculum
FLLN	family literacy, language and numeracy
FOI	Freedom of Information
FTE	full-time equivalent
GCE	General Certificate of Education
GCE A	General Certificate of Education Advanced Level
GCE AS	General Certificate of Education Advanced Supplementary
GCSE	General Certificate of Secondary Education
GFE	General Further Education
GLH	guided learning hours
GNVQ	General National Vocational Qualification
GTC	General Teaching Council for England [1998–2012, abolished]
HE	higher education
HEA	Higher Education Academy

HEFCE	Higher Education Funding Council for England
HEI	higher education institution
HESA	Higher Education Statistics Agency
HER	Higher Education Review
HMI	Her Majesty's Inspector
HMIC A	Her Majesty's Inspectorate of Court Administration
HNC/D/Q	higher national certificate/diploma/qualification
HRM	human resource management
HSE	Health and Safety Executive
HUDCETT	The Huddersfield University Distributed Centre for Excellence in Teacher Training
IAG	Information, Advice and Guidance
IALS	International Adult Literacy Survey
ICT	information and communication technology
IfL	Institute for Learning [2002–2014, dissolved into the ETF]
ILB	industry lead body
ILO	International Labour Organization
ILP	individual learning plan
ILT	information and learning technology
ILTHE	Institute for Learning and Teaching in Higher Education [HEA from 2004]
IQER	integrated quality and enhancement review [replaced by RCHE in 2012]
ISA	Independent Safeguarding Authority
IT	information technology
ITB	Industrial Training Board
ITE	initial teacher education
ITT	initial teacher training
JANET	Joint Academic Network
JISC	Joint Information Systems Committee
JISC CETIS	JISC Centre for Educational Technology Interoperability Standards
JVET	Journal of Vocational Education and Training
KIS	Key Information Set
LA	local authority
LEA	local education authority
LGBT	lesbian, gay, bisexual and transgender
LLL	lifelong learning
LLN	literacy, language and numeracy
LLS	lifelong learning sector
LLUK	Lifelong Learning UK [2005–2011]
LSC	Learning and Skills Council [2001–2010]
LSDA	Learning and Skills Development Agency [2000–2006, replaced by QIA and LSN]
LSI	Learning Style Inventory
LSIS	Learning and Skills Improvement Service [2008–2013]
LSN	Learning and Skills Network [2006–2008, replaced by LSIS]

LSS	learning and skills sector
LSRN	Learning and Skills Research Network
LTSN	Learning and Teaching Support Network
MHF	Mental Health Foundation
MIS	Management Information System
MoE	Ministry of Education [1944–1964, replaced by Department of Education and Science, now DfE]
MSC	Manpower Services Commission [1973–1988]
NAS	National Apprenticeship Service
NATFHE	National Association of Teachers in Further and Higher Education (now UCU)
NCE	National Commission on Education [1991–1995]
NCF	National Curriculum Framework
NCTL	National College for Teaching and Leadership [formerly The Teaching Agency]
NCVQ	National Council for Vocational Qualifications (1989–1992)
NEET	not in education, employment or training
NFER	National Foundation for Educational Research
NGfL	National Grid for Learning
NIACE	National Institute of Adult Continuing Education
NILTA	National Information and Learning Technologies Association
NOCN	National Open College Network
NOS	National Occupational Standards
NQF	National Qualifications Framework
NRDC	National Research and Development Centre for Adult Literacy and Numeracy
NSA	National Skills Academies
NUT	National Union of Teachers
NVQ	National Vocational Qualification
OCR	Oxford, Cambridge and RSA Examinations
OECD	Organisation for Economic Co-operation and Development
Ofqual	Office of the Qualifications and Examinations Regulator
Ofsted	Office for Standards in Education, Children's Services and Skills
OLASS	Offender Learning and Skills Service
PCET	Post-Compulsory Education and Training
PDP	personal development plan
PGCE	Professional Graduate Certificate in Education *or* Postgraduate Certificate in Education
PLE	Personal Learning Environment
PLN	Personal Learning Network
PTLLS	Preparing to Teach in the Lifelong Learning Sector
PSRB	Professional, Statutory and Regulatory Bodies
QA	Quality assurance
QAA	Quality Assurance Agency for Higher Education
QCA	Qualifications and Curriculum Authority [1997–2010, replaced by QCDA]

QCDA	Qualifications and Curriculum Development Agency [2010–2012, replaced by STA]
QCF	Qualifications and Credit Framework
QE	Quality enhancement
QIA	Quality Improvement Agency [2006–2008, replaced by LSIS]
QTLS	Qualified Teacher Learning and Skills
QTS	Qualified Teacher Status [in relation to schools]
RACs	Regional Advisory Councils
RAPAL	Research and Practice in Adult Literacy
RCHE	Review of College Higher Education [replaced by HER in 2013]
RPA	Recognition of Prior Achievement
RPL	Recognition of Prior Learning
RSA	Royal Society for the Encouragement of Arts, Manufactures and Commerce
S4L	Skills for Life
SATs	Standard Assessment Tests
SCAA	School Curriculum and Assessment Authority
SEN	special educational needs
SENDA	Special Educational Needs and Disability Act 2001
SFA	Skills Funding Agency
SLD	Severe Learning Difficulties
SLDD	Students with Learning Difficulties and Disabilities
SMT	senior management team
SpLD	Specific Learning Difficulties
SSC	Sector Skills Councils
SSR	staff-student ratio
STA	Standards and Testing Agency
SVUK	Standards Verification UK [2005–2011]
TA	The Teaching Agency (2012–2013, replaced by NCTL]
T2G	Train to Gain
TDA	The Training and Development Agency for Schools [2005–2012, became TA]
TDLB	Training and Development Lead Body
TEC	Training and Enterprise Council [1990–2001]
TechBacc	Technical Baccalaureate
TEFL	Teaching English as a Foreign Language
TERG	Technical Education Resource Group
TESL	Teaching English as a Second Language
TLC	Transforming Learning Cultures
TP	teaching practice
TQEF	Teaching Quality Enhancement Fund
TQM	Total Quality Management
TTA	The Teacher Training Agency [1995–2005, replaced by TDA]
TTG	Train to Gain
TtT	Troops to Teachers
TVEI	Technical and Vocational Initiative [1983–1997]

UCAS	Universities and Colleges Admissions Service
UCET	Universities Council for the Education of Teachers
UCU	University and College Union
UfI	University for Industry
UKCCIS	UK Council for Child Internet Safety
UNESCO	United Nations Educational, Scientific and Cultural Organisation
UTC	University Technical College
VAK	visual, auditory, kinaesthetic
VET	vocational education and training
VLE	virtual learning environment
VQ	Vocational Qualification
VRQ	Vocational Related Qualification
VTC	Virtual Teacher Centre
WBL	work-based learning
WEA	Workers' Educational Association
YCW	Youth and Community Work
YOI	Young Offender Institution
YPLA	Young People's Learning Agency [2010–2012]
YTS	Youth Training Scheme [1983–1989]

Mapping the chapters to the Professional Standards for Teachers and Trainers in Education and Training – England

The Professional Standards for Teachers and Trainers in Education and Training – England (ETF 2014) are structured within three sections (see below and Chapter 2). These sections are: professional values and attributes; professional knowledge and understanding; and professional skills. The mapping below indicates the chapters of most direct relevance to each section and standard; however, the nature of teaching and learning within the lifelong learning sector means that there are many inter-relationships between chapters and between different standards. Readers are advised to think broadly about the standards so that they can identify chapters in the book of particular value in developing their practice in relation to specific standards.

Professional standards

As a professional teacher or trainer you should demonstrate commitment to the following in your professional practice.

Professional Values and Attributes

Develop your own judgement of what works and does not work in your teaching and training	Chapters
1. Reflect on what works best in your teaching and learning to meet the diverse needs of learners	6–14
2. Evaluate and challenge your practice, values and beliefs	2–6, 13, 18
3. Inspire, motivate and raise aspirations of learners through your enthusiasm and knowledge	4, 6–7, 9–12
4. Be creative and innovative in selecting and adapting strategies to help learners to learn	7–12, 14
5. Value and promote social and cultural diversity, equality of opportunity and inclusion	4, 6–7, 16
6. Build positive and collaborative relationships with colleagues and learners	4–6, 9, 12, 15–17

Professional Knowledge and Understanding

Develop deep and critically informed knowledge and understanding in theory and practice

7.	Maintain and update knowledge of your subject and/or vocational area	3–4, 12–13
8.	Maintain and update your knowledge of educational research to develop evidence-based practice	3–5, 7, 9
9.	Apply theoretical understanding of effective practice in teaching, learning and assessment drawing on research and other evidence	3, 7–12
10.	Evaluate your practice with others and assess its impact on learning	11, 17–19
11.	Manage and promote positive learner behaviour	6–7, 9, 13, 16
12.	Understand the teaching and professional role and your responsibilities	2, 4, 16–17

Professional Skills

Develop your expertise and skills to ensure the best outcomes for learners

13.	Motivate and inspire learners to promote achievement and develop their skills to enable progression	6–7, 9–12, 14, 16
14.	Plan and deliver effective learning programmes for diverse groups or individuals in a safe and inclusive environment	6–12, 14, 16
15.	Promote the benefits of technology and support learners in its use	9–10
16.	Address the mathematics and English needs of learners and work creatively to overcome individual barriers to learning	6–9, 11
17.	Enable learners to share responsibility for their own learning and assessment, setting goals that stretch and challenge	7–11, 14
18.	Apply appropriate and fair methods of assessment and provide constructive and timely feedback to support progression and achievement	6–7, 9, 11
19.	Maintain and update your teaching and training expertise and vocational skills through collaboration with employers	12, 14, 19
20.	Contribute to organisational development and quality improvement through collaboration with others	17–18

Initial Guidance for Users of the Professional Standards which provides further information regarding the purposes and use of the standards can be found on the Education and Training Foundation website at www.et-foundation.co.uk

PART 1
Introduction to lifelong learning

1

Introduction to the lifelong learning sector

Roy Fisher, Robin Simmons and
Ron Thompson

In this chapter

- Education, the market and globalization
- Reform and the LLS
- Development of the LLS
- Autonomous learning
- Further education
- Local authorities
- Lifelong learning in the public services
- Private training providers
- Higher education
- Some key institutions
- The need for perspective

Education, the market and globalization

Educational institutions exist in wider economic and political systems, which both facilitate and limit the ways in which they respond to individual and societal needs. Throughout the modern era education has been seen as a process with huge potential to transform lives and to build positive futures, and this vision of education as an engine of progressive social change has been adopted by ideologies across the political spectrum. There has, however, been recognition that the progressive potential of education is circumscribed. Indeed, a number of authors have argued that education is a vehicle for the reproduction of social and economic structures rather than for social mobility. For example, Bourdieu (1974: 32) suggested that 'It is probably cultural inertia which still makes us see education in terms of the ideology of the school as a liberating force ... even when the indications tend to be that it is in fact one of the most effective means of perpetuating the existing social pattern'. Bowles and Gintis (1976: 265) expressed this more starkly: 'The education system ... neither adds to nor subtracts from the degree of inequality and repression originating in the economic sphere. Rather, it reproduces and legitimates a pre-existing pattern in the process of training and stratifying the workforce.'

In other analyses, education has been seen as perpetuating repressive political structures. Louis Althusser (1918–90), in 'Ideology and ideological state apparatuses', (1971) outlined his model of how 'Ideological State Apparatuses' and 'Repressive State Apparatuses' contrive to cement capitalistic power relations. He stated: 'I believe that the ideological State apparatus which has been installed in the *dominant* position in mature capitalist social formations ... is the *educational ideological apparatus*' (Althusser 1971: 144–5).

The determinism of Althusser or Bowles and Gintis is at odds with more recent postmodern conceptions of a relatively fluid and unpredictable social world. Jean-François Lyotard (1924–98), in *The Postmodern Condition* (1984), contended that modernist science employed grand narratives (or 'metanarratives') as a means of legitimating scientific knowledge (see Chapter 8). The positioning of science as the key to progress means the State can control education in the name of freedom and economic development. This displaces the traditional role of the universities and applies particularly to the field of teacher education and training which, in the UK, is now heavily regulated and increasingly located in schools and colleges.

The later decades of the twentieth century were said to witness not only the collapse of the 'socialist bloc' countries, but a concomitant triumph of neo-liberal capitalism (Fukuyama 1992). This claim is now recognized as premature, but capitalist economies have grown in power and influence, and large corporations have become internationalized. The globalization of industries and technology is accompanied by the globalization of culture, both through media conglomerates and the power of certain cultural forms (such as cinema, popular music and 'cybercultures'). The largely unanticipated international economic crisis of 2008/09, though deep, did not threaten capitalism as a system, and neo-liberalism remains largely unchallenged as the mainstream way of thinking about economic and social issues, including education.

The term 'globalization' is now commonly used to describe a process of transition towards global markets and the increasing power of large multinational corporations; a decline in the importance of geographical and national boundaries and greater connectivity between people arising from developments in technology; an exponential increase in global economic and cultural flows; and a compression of time and space across the planet. Undoubtedly, certain features of life in the developed world are objectively different to the way they were in the recent past, and in addition many people *feel differently* about their relationship with the rest of the globe. However, as Lauder et al. (2006: 31) point out, for some writers 'globalization is primarily an "ideological" construct that is being promulgated to support a neo-liberal agenda'. This ideological dimension is increasingly apparent in debates about education. Our only defence against global economic forces, it is argued, lies in providing the 'right kind' of education and training.

The globalization of markets and relations has had direct consequences for education. These include its increasing commodification, through which learning has come to be regarded as a product to be sold and purchased, with students positioned as consumers. The curriculum has been co-opted as a vehicle of 'economic progress', with largely unchallenged assumptions about its purpose as a means of producing efficient and pliable workers. While UK higher education (HE) has expanded through policies aimed at 'widening participation' to enhance economic competitiveness and social inclusion, this has been in the context of a rhetoric of marketization and individualism.

Neo-liberalism consists of a set of core assumptions, including a belief that economic success depends on allowing individuals to pursue their own interests and that the operation of a competitive 'free market' will lead to superior economic outcomes. At the same time, free-market approaches are not envisaged as arising of their own accord – individualized, competitive and market-driven policies are enacted by the state in order to create the 'right' environment. In addition, although neo-liberalism acknowledges that the least successful in society should be supported, this must be with the minimum of state intervention and at a level that provides an incentive for the individual to do better (see Lauder et al. 2006: 25–8). Although neo-liberalism has attained the status of orthodoxy in the UK and many other countries, its effectiveness in creating social justice is questionable.

In post-school education, neo-liberalism and globalization have led to a system which has been shaped by processes which Ritzer (2008) has called 'McDonaldization'. The largely vocational nature of the further education (FE) system means that the impact of these trends is amplified in colleges and the lifelong learning sector (LLS). Such processes have been documented in the work of Apple (2006), Brookfield (2005) and Avis (2009a) among others. For studies focusing on recent British developments, see Ball (2008) and Fisher and Simmons (2012). Teachers have found their work more scrutinized and regulated, with an associated negative impact on their autonomy leading to a crisis about their professional identity and status.

Reform and the LLS

Turbulent change within lifelong learning has affected teacher education, and teaching and learning more generally. Much of this arose from the broader agenda of successive New Labour governments and continued following the formation of the Coalition Government in 2010. This is consistent with the assumptions of a 'political era' dating back (at least) to the late 1970s and based on neo-liberal conceptions of education. The New Labour consultation document *Equipping Our Teachers for the Future* opened with 'The post-16 learning and skills sector is pivotal to our aim of bringing social justice and economic prosperity to everyone' (DfES 2004a: 3), and related proposals for a 'step-change' in initial teacher education to *Success for All* (DfES 2002a, 2002b), the New Labour Government's overarching agenda for reform in what was then being called 'the learning and skills sector' (LSS).

The New Labour 'agenda for reform' took up the theme of education as a key element in economic competitiveness and social inclusion, setting out perceived inadequacies that needed to be addressed if the UK was to prosper. It drew attention to under-funding and excessive bureaucracy, as well as variability of standards based on a neglect of pedagogy: 'While there is some excellent quality provision, this co-exists with too much poor provision. And across the system as a whole, insufficient attention has been given to improving teaching, training and learning . . . For too long, further education and training has been the forgotten sector in education' (DfES 2002b: 10). To redress this neglect of teaching and learning, two of the four elements of the reform agenda set out in *Success for All* were concerned with pedagogy and the professional development of teachers: 'putting teaching and learning at the heart of what we do' and 'developing the leaders, teachers, trainers of the future' (DfES 2002b: 5). Teacher education was at the heart of New Labour policy for the LLS.

New Labour reforms had been accompanied by increasing central control and the imposition of uniform approaches to teacher education (Simmons and Thompson 2007). May 2010, however, saw the formation of a Conservative/Liberal Democrat Coalition Government. Streamlining, simplification and deregulation became policy watchwords. *Skills for Sustainable Growth* (BIS 2010a) and *Investing in Skills for Sustainable Growth* (BIS 2010b) spoke of reducing bureaucracy and 'freeing up' colleges and other training institutions. In December 2011 *New Challenges, New Chances* (BIS 2011a) outlined the reform plan for 'FE and the skills system'. In January 2012 the Coalition Government commissioned Lord Lingfield to conduct an *Independent Review of Professionalism in Further Education*. Lingfield's final report (BIS 2012a) welcomed the already proposed (BIS 2012b) creation of 'The FE Guild', as well as advocating the introduction of an 'FE Covenant'. The prospectus for the FE Guild (BIS 2012c: 6) stated that:

> the FE sector is now moving into a new era, where there is a fundamentally different relationship with government. Our radical reform programme is freeing colleges from central government control and putting responsibility firmly on the shoulders of colleges themselves. This requires a change in thinking, where colleges will no longer look to central government for detailed steers or permissions. We now want to see the FE sector build on and increase its innovation, responsiveness and its high quality offer to students and employers.

The proposed FE Guild would change its formal title to the Education and Training Foundation (ETF), to be known as 'The Foundation', before its official launch in August 2013.

Development of the LLS

The broad field of what was until relatively recently known as post-compulsory education and training (PCET) in England has been notable for its complexity and this has been reflected in the various 'labels' placed on it. Understanding the term 'PCET' as referring to post-16 formal learning is less appropriate following the Education and Skills Act 2008, which requires young people in England to remain engaged with education or training until the end of the academic year when they reach 17 (18th birthday from 2015). This engagement can include apprenticeships, or part-time study if employed or volunteering for more than 20 hours per week. The Further Education National Training Organization (FENTO) had, when abolished in 2005, begun to employ the term 'learning and skills sector', and this is still often used. The establishment of Lifelong Learning UK (LLUK) in 2005 as the Sector Skills Council seemed to signify that the term 'lifelong learning' had arrived and this was cemented when LLUK used it in relation to the 'new professional standards' which it published in 2007. Early publications from the 2010 Coalition Government, however, indicated that 'further education and skills system' (or sometimes 'sector') was to be favoured. As suggested by the title of this book, our preference remains with lifelong learning as the term that most effectively captures the field in all its diversity, and which is most likely to withstand the vicissitudes of policy makers.

Numerous types of provider offer diverse opportunities to people beyond the age of compulsory schooling, including school sixth forms, sixth-form colleges, FE colleges, universities and adult education services. Specialist colleges cater for subjects such as art and design, performing arts and land-based studies. In 2010 the first university technical college (UTC), serving 14–19-year-olds, opened. More UTCs quickly followed. Other colleges serve learners with special needs or adult learners. Further diversity has been promoted through encouraging private companies to enter the marketplace. This landscape is governed by what has been a network of rapidly changing regulatory bodies.

A large proportion of non-advanced vocational provision takes place in FE colleges. Foster (2005: 58) points out that FE has been the poor relation of English education – 'the neglected middle child between universities and schools'. Historically, there has been little central guidance, and funding has been inadequate. Many FE institutions trace their roots to the mechanics' institutes of the mid-nineteenth century and most were established under the *laissez-faire* spirit that then characterized the English approach to education. Until the late nineteenth century, the majority of the population was without formal education (Pratt 2000).

In response to economic competition, the last quarter of the nineteenth and the early years of the twentieth centuries saw a burst of activity that encouraged the growth of technical and commercial post-school education. It was not until the 1944 Education Act that education beyond school received more attention and a statutory duty was placed on local education authorities (LEAs) to provide 'adequate facilities' for what then became known officially as 'further education' in England. The duty placed on LEAs was, however, open to interpretation and there was variation in provision. For an account of the development of English FE after the Second World War, see Richardson (2007).

Following the 1944 Education Act, LEAs were given responsibility for the 'general educational character' of colleges. How this responsibility was discharged depended on the 'local ecology' (Waitt 1980: 402). Provision was influenced by local communities and labour markets, and was also shaped by personalities, politics and culture. This affected the level of commitment towards FE within each authority – some LEAs created extensive provision, while others did not (Lucas 2004).

LEAs dominated the educational landscape for over forty years after World War Two. Since the 1980s there has been a reversal of this process; Local Authorities (LAs) have become disempowered and their role in planning education reduced (Ainley 2001). From the early 1980s a series of reports criticized the management, organization and culture of LAs. Official discourse came to characterize LEAs as pedestrian, unresponsive and divorced from the 'real world'. Subsequently, the White Paper *Education and Training for the 21st Century* (DES 1991) portrayed the sector as in need of reform. Following this, the 1992 Further and Higher Education Act removed FE, specialist and sixth-form colleges from LA control, recreating them as self-governing institutions directly accountable to the state. This was generally regarded as 'freeing' colleges from bureaucracy (a theme which would have renewed resonance after the Coalition Government formed in 2010).

The effective end of LEA control of FE in the early 1990s should be understood in the context of a belief that the use of market mechanisms is the most effective way to raise standards and reduce costs. From the 1980s onwards successive governments had viewed public sector organization as inefficient and unfairly protected from competition (Kessler and Bayliss 1998). Even before their 1997 election victory, New Labour placed 'education, education, education' at the heart of their policies as this was seen as the key to success in the global marketplace. A successful economy would contribute towards social justice, prosperity and well-being for all (Allen and Ainley 2007; Avis 2009a). In the context of 'lifelong learning' individuals would be required to continuously reinvent, 're-skill' and 'up-skill' themselves. For Brine (2006: 652), this discourse places workers in a 'state of constant becoming': a readiness to retrain for whatever employment becomes available.

Since the advent of the New Labour Government in 1997, policy towards lifelong learning has strongly emphasized its economic function (BIS 2010a, 2010b, 2011a; Foster 2005; Leitch Review of Skills 2006). This is not to argue that the role of lifelong learning and FE in facilitating social inclusion and social mobility has been unrecognized; the Coalition Government certainly saw its potential in relation to the 'Big Society' agenda (BIS 2010a). A feature of the LLS in the late twentieth century was the creation of a mixed economy of semi-privatized state sector organizations alongside a plethora of state-subsidized private sector providers (Ainley 2001). Institutions formerly having a public service ethos were expected to behave like private businesses: performance indicators were set; funding was tied to targets and managerialism was commonplace (Coffield 2006). Education is now regarded as a commodity that can be provided cheaply and efficiently by organizations imbued with an ideology of enterprise (Allen and Ainley 2007). Nevertheless, Keep (2006) has described the regulatory systems governing education and training in England as being the most complex and centrally controlled in the world, and Coffield (2006) pointed to a growing accountability framework.

The LLS is now characterized by commercialized public-sector institutions in a quasi-marketplace where private companies receive funding to deliver accredited courses. Learning takes place, not only inside the traditional structures of the education system but, increasingly, in an eclectic range of settings (Jarvis 2004).

Whilst the term 'lifelong learning' is commonplace, the concept is not a straightforward one. It can be understood as a process through which the individual continues to engage in education and/or training throughout the life course. Orr (2008) argued that, according to the then New Labour Government, all social formations but especially education, must conform to the economic stringencies of globalization. Individuals are expected to take responsibility for their learning which can be undertaken in a variety of contexts. The expression lifelong learning is often used to encompass learning that takes place in settings beyond the education system (Jarvis 2004). Below is a consideration of autonomous learning, followed by sections which provide an overview of some of the main components of the 'system' of lifelong learning.

Autonomous learning

Discussion of autonomous learning often concerns relatively independent or self-directed learning that takes place within educational institutions. The development of learner autonomy is sometimes seen as a positive consequence of student-centredness. There is, however, a more fundamental form. Learning in all parts of an individual's life course is essentially an unbounded activity, one which frequently takes place beyond institutions – this is especially the case in the twenty-first century where information technologies enable individuals and groups to freely access existing (and create new) knowledge. The idea of the 'autodidact' as a relatively solitary figure within a public library is being replaced with that of an active participant in cyber based community dialogue (Fisher and Fisher 2007). People can (and do) learn without courses and without teachers. The future of autonomous learning is rich with possibility, and it will have profound implications for the nature and structure of universities, colleges and, indeed, schools – as well as for the associated regulatory institutions.

Further education

FE colleges represent the largest institutional component within the LLS: during 2011–12 FE was serving over four million students. According to the Association of Colleges (AoC) as at January 2013 there were 219 general FE colleges and 94 sixth-form colleges in England. There were six colleges in Northern Ireland, 36 in Scotland and 19 in Wales (AoC 2013). During 2010–11, 942,900 learners aged 16–18 were enrolled on courses in general FE or sixth-form colleges or in HE (Ofsted 2012a). For almost fifty years after the end of World War Two, the majority of FE colleges were under LEA control. General FE colleges vary in size; following mergers, the largest have over 50,000 students. Most FE colleges have strong links with industry, and a tradition of teaching the theory and practice of skills used in everyday occupations; as Ainley and Bailey (1997) point out, their work has focused on vocational learning. General FE colleges, however, usually offer a broad curriculum attracting a diverse profile of students. Typically this includes basic skills and courses for those with special educational needs; English for speakers of other languages (ESOL); and work-based learning for people following apprenticeships.

Notwithstanding the vocational orientation of FE colleges, traditional academic subjects have a significant place in their provision. Many students in FE undertake degree level courses, including professional qualifications. Increasingly, foundation degrees – work-related HE qualifications designed in conjunction with employers – are offered. These cover a range of occupational areas. In combining academic and work-based learning, foundation degrees can be seen as similar to the established higher national certificate (HNC) and diploma (HND) courses. Some larger general FE colleges with substantial HE provision are now designated as 'further and higher education colleges', sometimes referred to as 'mixed economy colleges'.

General FE colleges are complex organizations, serving fragmented and diverse interests and it is difficult to describe a 'typical' general college (Ainley and Bailey 1997; Hyland and Merrill 2003). The other institutions that comprise FE are more easily defined as they concentrate mainly on particular groups of learners or subjects. Traditionally, sixth-form colleges were regarded as part of the school sector. To the surprise of many, alongside other colleges, they were removed from LA control following the 1992 Further and Higher Education Act and reclassified as part of FE. To a large extent, sixth-form colleges remained distinct from other FE institutions, mainly due to their academic curriculum and the relative social advantage of their intake (Foster 2005). The Apprenticeships, Skills, Children and Learning Act 2009 amended the Further and Higher Education Act 1992 to create a new, legally distinct sixth-form college corporation sector. Sixth-form colleges focus mainly on courses that prepare students for entry to HE and the prevailing ethos is one of examination success.

A range of FE colleges concentrate on specific subjects or vocational areas. In 2013 there were three FE arts colleges offering courses in art and design, music and performing arts; 15 land-based studies colleges focused chiefly on agriculture, horticulture and related areas; and 10 specialist colleges, some of which were residential, offered provision mainly for people with special needs (AoC 2013). This category includes those with learning, emotional and behavioural difficulties and students with physical disabilities There is a small number of adult residential colleges with a tradition of providing opportunities for adults unable to take advantage of education earlier in their lives – these include Coleg Harlech Workers' Educational Association in North Wales, Northern College (near Barnsley), and Ruskin College in Oxford. Their provision ranges from short introductory courses through to HE, and they tend to specialize in trade union studies and community regeneration.

Local authorities

The Further and Higher Education Act of 1992 ended an era of LA control for FE. Although losing responsibility for the majority of the education and training system in the early 1990s, LAs retained involvement at its margins – for example, providing non-vocational adult education classes. Indeed, a role in FE funding briefly returned to LAs in 2010 before the responsibility was shifted to the Young Peoples' Learning Agency (YPLA) which was launched in April 2010 and closed on 31 March 2012 to be replaced by the Education Funding Agency (EFA).

Whilst there is a trend towards the creation of directly funded academies, currently most schools remain under the aegis of local authorities and many provide education for adults, with classes often taking place on school premises in the evening. Nowadays, these courses are usually certificated – for example, by the National Open College Network (NOCN) – and they encompass a range of vocational courses in addition to learning orientated towards leisure and general interest. The curriculum offer can range from information technology (IT) and business administration, to courses in car maintenance, cookery, modern languages, flower arranging and yoga. In addition, LAs are involved in responding to various government-led agendas through schools. For example, the Family Learning initiative aims to give parents and carers the opportunity to find out how their children are taught at school, to share ideas and to develop their knowledge and skills, particularly in areas such as literacy, numeracy and 'healthy living'.

Lifelong learning in the public services

Public service organizations such as the NHS, police and fire and rescue services, have a tradition of providing professional development. This includes extensive 'in-house training' programmes, or can take the form of day or block release attendance at colleges or universities and, increasingly, partnerships providing recognized qualifications. Employees are expected to continuously update their knowledge and skills.

Regional police services have training schools that provide opportunities in a range of vocational areas for officers and support staff. Examples include courses in IT, management, forensic science and crime detection as well as areas of specialist policing such as public order, firearms and driver training. There are also courses for promotion examinations. These require officers to gain high levels of knowledge, skill and understanding in a range of operational and strategic competencies and to undergo a variety of assessments. Similar arrangements exist in the fire and rescue service, the ambulance service and other areas of the public services.

Private training providers

Private training organizations vary in size and expertise. It is, however, possible to identify some common characteristics. Rather than covering a range of subjects catering for a broad cross-section of students, most private training providers focus on vocational areas such as business, IT or language training. These providers also offer courses for the unemployed, or individuals who are otherwise disadvantaged or socially excluded, for example, provision aiming to support young people not in education, employment or training (see Simmons and Thompson 2011).

In recent years, private training organizations have played an increasing role in the provision of lifelong learning. This was encouraged by the New Labour White Paper *Raising Skills, Improving Life Chances* (DfES 2006), and new competitive arrangements were introduced to support such providers through development and revenue funding as well as capital incentives. The White Paper claimed this would: 'promote dynamism and innovation . . . where significant expansion of high quality provision is needed' (DfES 2006: para. 32). This indicated a belief that involving private companies in education and training would improve quality and responsiveness through increasing competition. Through the Education Act 2011 the Coalition Government sought to give colleges more freedom, including making it easier for them to set up companies or trusts and to establish partnerships with training organizations (BIS 2011a). This took the mixed economy of private and public lifelong learning providers a step further blurring the boundaries between them.

Higher education

In 2013, there were over 160 British higher education institutions (HEIs), with various institutional titles – 'university' being the most common. Although HE is normally understood to incorporate foundation degree, first degree and postgraduate provision, its detailed structure is complex. As mentioned above, a significant proportion of

HE provision is located in FE colleges, with approximately one in ten HE students studying through 'college HE'.

In general, HEIs offer a different culture to that found in FE and elsewhere in the field of Lifelong Learning. The background to English cultural attitudes towards the vocational was outlined long ago by Weiner (1981), and the strongest antipathies are found within the great English universities which have for centuries held sway over the intellectual climate. Higher education in North America lacked the legacy of medievalism which lingered in the ancient European universities, and was therefore more able to embrace technocratic knowledge. The instrumental and applied nature of vocational education is at odds with the liberal traditions of the traditional English university, and this still permeates HE.

The implicitly hierarchical division of HEIs into 'pressure groups' – such as the 'Russell Group' (founded at the Russell Hotel, London, in 1994 and currently comprising 24 research intensive universities), the 'Million+ Group', the 'University Alliance' and 'Guild HE' – underscores differences now compounded by a performative obsession with league table positions. The so-called 'modern universities' are mainly former polytechnics (redesignated as universities in 1992), which often evolved from colleges of technology. Those wishing to know more of the history of HE in Britain should consult a specialist work such as Anderson's (2006) *British Universities Past and Present*. Barnett (2003) provides a critical but accessible analysis of the trajectory of HE from an elite to a mass system. More recently, his *Imagining the University* (Barnett 2013) explores fundamental questions relating to the role of the university. Deem, et al. (2007) discuss the impact of 'audit culture' and managerialism on HE. There is no doubt that the move to mass HE has changed its nature: however, the balance of negative and positive consequences is not easily weighed. Most would agree that widening participation in HE is, on a number of levels (not least social inclusion), part of a democratizing process.

Some key institutions

The framework of institutions that manage and monitor British education has been in a state of flux ever since New Labour began to implement its reforms in the late 1990s. The Coalition Government formed in 2010 continued this. The system is littered with the remnants of superseded agencies and, for the uninitiated, baffling acronyms. We shall not provide a comprehensive overview of all these agencies here. Readers are advised to regularly check websites to monitor changing names and policies; in all probability some of the details below will have changed when this book appears.

The Department for Business, Innovation and Skills

The New Labour Government's short-lived Department for Innovation, Universities and Skills (DIUS) was, together with the Department for Children, Schools and Families (DCSF), and the Department for Business, Enterprise and Regulatory Reform (DBERR), set up on 28 June 2007. DIUS and DCSF, effectively, replaced the DfES – itself at the end of a sequence of re-brandings that can be traced back beyond the former Ministry of Education (previously known as the Board of Education). The three departments newly created in June 2007 had some closely related responsibilities and, given the increasingly overlapping curriculum boundaries of schools and FE, and of FE and HE, it was always likely that further change would follow quickly. The Department for Business, Innovation and Skills (BIS) came into being on 6 June 2009 following a merger of DIUS and DBERR. The dropping of 'Universities' from the title of the new department was seen by some as indicative of a culture whereby education was regarded as incontestably in the service of business. BIS has a wide portfolio of responsibilities in relation to economic growth, including working with providers of FE and HE.

The Department for Education

The Department for Education (DfE) was established in May 2010 following the formation of the Coalition Government. Effectively replacing DCSF, the DfE is responsible for state infant, primary and secondary education.

The National College for Teaching and Leadership

The Teaching Agency (TA), formerly the Training and Development Agency for Schools, was incorporated as an executive agency of the DfE on 1 April 2012. The National College for Teaching and Leadership (NCTL) was formed on 1 April 2013 when the TA merged with the National College for School Leadership. The NCTL is responsible for the recruitment, supply and initial training and development of school teachers, promoting high quality teaching and leadership in schools. It supports the recruitment and development of early education and childcare workers, special educational needs coordinators and education psychologists as well as having oversight of the conduct of school teachers. On 31 March 2012 the Qualifications and Curriculum Development Agency (QCDA) closed as part of the Government's reforms. Its examinations administration function is now performed by the NCTL, whilst its role in relation to National Curriculum assessments was transferred to the Standards and Testing Agency (STA).

The Education and Training Foundation

The Education and Training Foundation (initially proposed as 'the FE Guild') was formally established at the end of August 2013 as an employer led partnership which aimed to provide a 'focal point for all FE and Skills sector interests in taking forward the professionalism flowing from the Lingfield Review' (BIS 2012c:7). It was envisaged that the new organization would 'act as an overarching body with end to end responsibility for professionalism and vocational education across the sector' (2012b P. 7) Its responsibilities were to include:

- professional standards and codes of behaviour for members;
- developing appropriate qualifications for people working in the sector through which people can progress;

- supporting individual, subject specific and corporate CPD [continuning professional development];
- working at a strategic level to help bring in expertise across the sector; and
- supporting employer recognition of professionalism.

(BIS 2012c: 7).

Ofqual: the Office of the Qualifications and Examinations Regulator

In its 2008 launch document, Ofqual (2008: 2) proclaimed its role as,

> the new regulator of qualifications, exams and tests in England. We ensure that children, young people and adult learners get the results their work deserves, that standards are maintained and that qualifications count now and in the future. We also make sure that the qualifications available meet the needs of learners and employers.

A major aspect of Ofqual's operations is its accountability directly to Parliament (not to Government). Ofqual regulates by recognizing and monitoring organizations that deliver qualifications and assessments as set out in the Apprenticeship, Skills, Children and Learning Act (2009) and Education Act (2011). To achieve its goals, Ofqual holds awarding bodies to account, ensuring the standardization of qualifications. A major challenge is to enforce quality and assure the fairness of examination marking across a large and complicated system.

The Education Funding Agency

Since 1 April 2012 revenue and capital funding for the education of learners between the ages of 3 and 19, or 3 and 25 for those with learning difficulties and disabilities, has been the responsibility of the EFA, part of the DfE. The creation of the EFA brought together the roles of the YPLA and Partnerships for Schools, both of which were dissolved. The EFA funds academies directly and funds LAs so they can pay maintained schools. It also funds sixth forms, colleges and training providers in relation to 16–19-year-olds as well as for learners with learning difficulties and/or disabilities aged 19–24 who are subject to a learning difficulty assessment. The EFA also supports the delivery of building and maintenance programmes for schools, academies, free schools and sixth-form colleges (EFA 2013).

The Skills Funding Agency

In 2001 the Learning and Skills Council (LSC) took over the work of the Further Education Funding Council for England (FEFCE) and the regional Training and Enterprise Councils (TECs). The LSC would be a major presence in the planning and funding of post-compulsory education and training in England other than for universities. In February 2009, the LSC identified its 'major tasks' as raising the participation of young people and adults in education; improving skills levels; lifting the quality of education and training; and improving the effectiveness of the sector as well as access to learning for all. It would, however, be closed at the end of March 2010. The Skills Funding Agency (SFA) was created from 1 April 2010 to take on a major part of what had been the LSC's role, and subsequently became an executive agency within BIS. The SFA is concerned with funding and promoting adult FE and skills training in England (FE colleges, independent training providers and organizations with which they and colleges sub-contract). The SFA also incorporates the National Apprenticeship Service (NAS), which works to increase the take up of apprenticeship schemes. The statement announcing the birth of the SFA had also proclaimed the establishment of the YPLA, which was concerned with the funding of academies and supporting local authorities to commission education and training for all 16–19-year-olds. A short-lived agency, the YPLA closed on 31 March 2012 following the creation of the EFA (see above).

Office for Standards in Education, Children's Services and Skills (Ofsted)

Ofsted was established in 1992, quickly attracting controversy under the leadership (from 1994 to 2000) of Chris Woodhead. Its main function is to inspect and report on standards in education. In 2007, Ofsted merged with the Adult Learning Inspectorate (ALI) to provide a service which inspects all post-16 government funded education excepting HEIs which are generally inspected by the Quality Assurance Agency for Higher Education (QAA). Teacher education provision in HEIs, however, is subject to Ofsted inspection. Also, from 2007 Ofsted was given responsibility for the registration and inspection of social care services for children, and the welfare inspection of independent and maintained boarding schools. Technically, Ofsted is a non-ministerial government department of Her Majesty's Chief Inspector of Schools, from whom its powers devolve. Similar functions exist under different arrangements in Northern Ireland, Scotland and Wales.

Whatever the controversies surrounding Ofsted, it plays a major role in the education system and, many believe, serves an important purpose. Ofsted has defined its role as follows:

> to raise aspirations and contribute to the long term achievement of ambitious standards and better life chances for service users. Their educational, economic and social well-being will in turn promote England's national success. To achieve this we will report fairly and truthfully; we will listen to service users and providers; and we will communicate our findings with all who share our vision, from service providers to policy-makers. We do not report to government ministers but directly to Parliament (and to the Lord Chancellor about children and family courts administration). This independence means you can rely on us for impartial information.
>
> (Ofsted 2009)

The Quality Assurance Agency for Higher Education (QAA)

Established in 1997, the QAA provides universities and colleges with an independent service which reports on how they maintain HE standards and quality. While individual institutions retain responsibility for the quality of their courses and awards, through its external reviews the QAA encourages improvement, comments on the ability of institutions to maintain standards, offers guidance and also advises government on institutional applications for powers to award degrees or to receive the title of 'university'.

Two further key institutions, the Institute for Learning (IfL) which in 2014 was dissolved into the ETF, and the Higher Education Academy (HEA) have functioned as the professional bodies for FE and HE respectively. They are discussed in Chapter 2.

The need for perspective

The birth of the Education and Training Foundation in the summer of 2013 spelled the end for the Learning and Skills Improvement Service (LSIS) which had begun work on 1 October 2008 and closed in August 2013. LSIS had been created as a replacement for the Centre for Excellence in Leadership (CEL) and the Quality Improvement Agency (QIA). At its inception, LSIS (2008) announced that it would: 'focus on learners and on developing excellent and sustainable further education and skills provision across the sector'. Its demise was symptomatic of what has been termed 'policy hysteria' (Avis 2009b). Changing policies have littered the sector with institutional corpses. Significant amongst these were LLUK and its subsidiary Standards Verification UK (SVUK), both of which operated between 2005 and 2011. SVUK was established as an operating arm of LLUK and was primarily concerned with monitoring and endorsing generic initial teacher education (ITE) qualifications for the LLS in England and Wales, and those for Skills for Life practitioners in ESOL, literacy and numeracy in England. LLUK described itself as 'the independent employer-led sector skills council responsible for the professional development of all those working in community learning and development, further education, higher education, libraries, archives and information services, and work based learning across the UK' (LLUK 2009). LLUK set standards for occupational competence in the delivery and support of learning and was therefore, in its time, hugely influential.

The reform and successive reorganizations that were the hallmark of the New Labour Government (1997–2010) were followed by the implementation of radical changes by the Coalition Government. There is a need for a sense of perspective in relation to this turbulence. The history of the English education system has benefited from a number of significant studies which have provided a basis for understanding developments. In the important area of comparative studies, Archer (1979) still stands as a central contribution to the analysis of educational change. Green (1990), in his study of the rise of the education systems in England, France and the USA, recognized the significance of the social functions of the state and of the relationships of social classes to the state. Comparative studies of vocational education are fewer in number. Smithers (1993) incorporated an element of (unfavourable) comparison of English vocational education/training with the systems in France and Germany in what became a notable (if populist) attack on the 'new vocationalism'.

For a broad account of the history of education in England and Wales, Brian Simon's four-volume *Studies in the History of Education* (see Simon 1991) presents a classic overview. Donald (1992) examines the emergence of education as a system of control in a study that draws on postmodern perspectives. Donald argued that a grasp of the associated 'social and cultural dynamics' (p. 18) requires an investigation that focuses on educational ideologies, the routines of schooling as power mechanisms and the ways in which knowledge is organized into a curriculum. Tomlinson (2008a) provides an excellent overview of post-1945 education policy in Britain, including specific consideration of lifelong learning. It is envisaged that it may be some time before a similar study encompassing post 2005 developments appears.

Green (1991) quotes a Parliamentary Select Committee of 1818 stating that 'England is the worst educated country in Europe' before citing Balfour's 1902 claim that 'England is behind all continental rivals in education' (p. 7). Nearly a century later the National Commission on Education (NCE 1993) pronounced 'In the United Kingdom much higher achievement in education and training is needed to match world standards' (p. 43). For Green (1991) the historical reasons for Britain's relative under-development in terms of a national education system lie in religious divisions and, more importantly, deep structural obstacles in the form of economic complacency and aristocratic opposition to educational advance. Despite the reforming energies of recent UK governments, their neo-liberal reforms have done little to solve these problems.

2

Teacher education for lifelong learning
Amanda Fulford, Denise Robinson and Ron Thompson

In this chapter

- The growth of teacher education for lifelong learning
- Professional standards for teaching in lifelong learning
- A framework of teaching qualifications
- Reviewing the framework: Lingfield and after
- Mentoring and the work-based learning of teachers
- The former *Institute for Learning* and the *Higher Education Academy*

The key role of lifelong learning in government policy since the late 1990s led to an intensive focus on teacher education for the sector, in contrast to the earlier 'history of neglect' described by Lucas (2004). Following calls for a coherent, nationally recognized system of FE teacher training in both the Fryer Report on lifelong learning (Fryer 1997) and the Kennedy Report on widening participation (Kennedy 1997), reforms were introduced in the early years of New Labour government. These included national standards for FE teachers and a statutory requirement for new teachers to acquire a recognized teaching qualification. However, the impact of these reforms was limited and the FE sector continued to attract critical scrutiny in which issues of teacher professionalism were prominent. The Further Education White Paper of 2006 set out a 'vision' of a world-class system of vocational education in which teaching expertise ranked alongside subject knowledge, and more recently the Coalition Government continued this theme in its FE and Skills Reform Plan, *New Challenges, New Chances* (BIS 2011a).

The criticisms deployed by successive governments focused not only on the supply of trained teachers but on the quality of FE teacher training itself. A survey inspection conducted by Ofsted in 2003 concluded that 'The current system of FE teacher training does not provide a satisfactory foundation of professional development for FE teachers at the start of their careers' (Ofsted 2003: 2). As a result, the Labour Government promised a 'step change' in the quality of ITE for the 'learning and skills sector' – an extension of the earlier focus on FE teachers to a much wider range of contexts. Their proposals, set out in *Equipping Our Teachers for the Future* (DfES 2004a) and introduced in September 2007, effectively created a national curriculum for ITE, alongside a requirement for CPD. As with earlier reforms, the impact of this new system was limited – not least because of its internal contradictions. In any case, the political climate was changing, and the onset of the global financial crisis in 2008, followed by the formation of the Coalition Government in 2010, were accompanied by new ideological perspectives on teacher education. A review of arrangements for regulating and facilitating FE professionalism, chaired by the Conservative educationalist Lord Lingfield, was announced in *New Challenges, New Chances*. It reported in two stages, in March and October 2012 (BIS 2012b, 2012a). This chapter is largely concerned with discussing the system of teacher education implemented in 2007, and the changes introduced following the Lingfield Review. However, to understand the perceived deficiencies of teacher education for FE and the nature of the debates, we need to consider ITE in FE over a longer period.

The growth of teacher education for lifelong learning

Until 2001, FE teachers were not required to undertake ITE. Even the term *initial* is problematic, for while school teachers are normally trained prior to employment, those in FE often receive their first experience of teacher training *in* post. Indeed, for many years it was not uncommon for FE teachers to remain untrained. In FE and the wider lifelong learning sector, it is usual to distinguish between *pre-service* and *in-service* initial training, the former normally taken full time and before finding employment as a teacher, the latter taken part time and based around concurrent teaching employment.

The explanation for this situation lies partly in considerations of labour supply. The vocational nature of much of the lifelong learning curriculum means that teachers are normally required to have work experience outside teaching; employment as a teacher often develops alongside their main occupation. At the same time, the need for up-to-date practitioners has often led employers to recruit staff without teaching qualifications. Although some governments have used bursaries to encourage intending teachers to train pre-service, these are often insufficient and there has been an understandable reluctance on the part of both Government and employers to face up to the implications of compulsory pre-service training. There has also been a *cultural* tendency in lifelong learning not to fully recognize the value of ITE, particularly as a pre-service requirement. Teaching skills have been seen as something to be 'picked up' through experience. As Robson (2006: 14) notes 'The assumption has been . . . that if I know my subject, I can, by definition, teach it to others'. The in-service mode of initial training remains the norm today, and has not been challenged by recent reforms.

Participation in ITE has therefore, until quite recently, been voluntary – perhaps expected by employers, but ultimately at the discretion of the individual. Nevertheless, a number of government reports since the Second World War have attempted to improve or extend FE teacher training. The McNair Report (Board of Education 1944) was particularly significant, providing the impetus for the establishment of specialist technical teacher training institutions based in Bolton, Huddersfield and London – later expanded to four by the addition of a college in Wolverhampton following the Crowther Report (MoE 1959). These reports share both a concern to increase the number of trained teachers and reluctance to accept the cost involved. For example, the Russell Report's (DES 1966) recommendation that new teachers of 15- to

18-year-olds should be teacher trained within three years of taking up their posts was rejected. The continuing absence of clear policy into the early 1990s did little to improve the proportion of trained teachers, which increased from 43 per cent in 1975 to just 56 per cent in 1991 (Lucas 2004: 75).

The economic crises of the 1970s led to fundamental changes in FE, together with growing intervention by government. Given the political climate of the time, it was perhaps inevitable that market forces would penetrate FE. The 1992 Further and Higher Education Act created a marketized environment in which colleges competed for students. As a result, many colleges were placed under severe financial pressure – often leading to increased workloads for staff. In the period 1993–98, 20,000 teaching posts were lost while student numbers increased by over a third (Beale 2004: 469); to cope significant numbers of part-time and casual staff were recruited. Because many of these new teachers were not trained, the proportion of staff with teaching qualifications actually *declined* in those years (Lucas 2004: 86–8).

The 1990s also saw a change in the nature of teaching qualifications. Until then, the major awards had been the university-validated Certificate in Education (Cert Ed) and PGCE, together with national awarding body qualifications such as the City and Guilds 730. However, the development of competence-based National Vocational Qualifications (NVQs) was associated with the introduction of a range of specific awards, developed by the Training and Development Lead Body (TDLB) and dealing with NVQ-related training and assessment. Vocational teachers were required to gain awards relevant to their role as trainers or assessors, undermining the status of the existing generic awards and leading to a proliferation of fragmented, competence-based teaching qualifications.

Competence-based training also influenced the generic courses themselves, and many universities re-designed CertEd/PGCE courses to reflect the NVQ framework. However, there was considerable opposition to the idea of competence as a basis for teaching qualifications and universities moved away from NVQ-style approaches. Nevertheless, the formation of the employer-led FENTO in 1999 to implement new occupational standards for FE teaching meant that competence-based approaches persisted into the new century. Although intended as descriptions of the occupational competence of experienced teachers, the 'FENTO standards' (FENTO 1999) also formed the basis for recognition of initial teaching qualifications. Both university and awarding body courses were required to undergo a process of *endorsement* against the FENTO standards, providing for the first time some measure of central control over all ITE curricula in FE.

As Lucas (2007) notes, the FENTO standards and others like them encouraged a mechanistic, 'tick-box' approach – although, arguably, it is the culture of surveillance and central control now widespread in education, rather than a particular curriculum model, which has the greater responsibility for this. Whatever the reason, it became clear that the FENTO standards were not helpful to the development of trainee teachers and were 'not an appropriate tool for designing ITT courses or for judging the final attainment of newly-qualified FE teachers' (Ofsted 2003: 36).

Although substantial numbers of FE teachers had been trained, by 2004 only 47 per cent of part-time staff and 70 per cent of full-time staff were qualified (LLUK 2005) compared with 25 per cent and 66 per cent respectively in 1996/97 (Lucas 2004: 87). This increase was stimulated by the 2001 requirement for a teaching qualification, but also reflected increasing numbers of trainees from the wider learning and skills sector.

A major factor in achieving these numbers was the growth of teacher training in colleges, through partnership arrangements with universities as well as work with awarding bodies.

Several years into the new century, FE teacher training was still somewhat patchy. Although progress had been made and greater recognition of the value of teacher training achieved, the proportion of trained staff remained low. In comparison with school teaching, work in FE appeared to be of lower status and lacking a professional identity. In addition, government concerns about the quality of training, together with a growing readiness to intervene at a *curriculum* level, led to a prescriptive approach enforced by mechanisms such as occupational standards and endorsement (Simmons and Thompson 2007). This was the context of the 2007 reforms. The statutory requirements implementing these reforms were contained in two sets of regulations, governing initial qualifications and CPD respectively (HM Government 2007a, 2007b). They comprised three main strands: new teaching standards for the lifelong learning sector; a centrally specified curriculum structure, including a framework of teaching qualifications corresponding to defined teaching roles; and measures to improve workplace learning (Thompson and Robinson 2008; Thompson 2014).

Professional standards for teaching in lifelong learning

From September 2007, initial teacher training courses for the LLS (other than courses for teachers working solely in HE) were based on new 'professional' standards developed by LLUK, the successor organization to FENTO. These standards expressed the 'key purpose' of the teacher as being 'to create effective and stimulating opportunities for learning through high quality teaching that enables the development and progression of all learners' (LLUK 2007a: 2) and described the skills, knowledge and attributes required. They were divided into six areas or domains: professional values and practice; learning and teaching; specialist learning and teaching; planning for learning; assessment for learning; and access and progression. Each domain was further divided into statements relating to professional values, professional knowledge and understanding, and professional practice. Box 2.1 shows the statements of professional values for domain D, 'planning for learning'. In Box 2.2, the statements of professional knowledge and professional practice are shown for this domain.

The LLUK standards, although described as 'professional', continued the occupational-industrial approach used by FENTO, with around 150 statements describing the values, knowledge and practical abilities expected of those in a full teaching role. Unlike the FENTO standards, they underpinned a qualification framework intended for use in course design. However, although courses were aligned with the LLUK standards as a requirement, it is important to recognize the contested nature of these standards and the problematic status of some features of the teacher training curriculum, including orthodoxies which pre-dated regulation – for example the notion of 'reflective practice'. Much criticism was levelled at the over-prescriptive nature of the LLUK standards and their inadequacy as a means of conceptualizing the activity of teachers (Lucas 2007; Nasta 2007). Furthermore, the impact of the new standards on *learning* was difficult to establish, and there was little evidence that the experiences of trainee teachers had been enriched (Lucas et al. 2012). As part of the reappraisal of teaching qualifications

---

Box 2.1 The LLUK teaching standards 2007–14. Professional values for domain D: planning for learning

---

Teachers in the lifelong learning sector value:

AS1   Learners, their progress and development, their learning goals and aspirations and the experience they bring to their learning.

AS2   Learning, its potential to benefit people emotionally, intellectually, socially and economically, and its contribution to community sustainability.

AS3   Equality, diversity and inclusion in relation to learners, the workforce, and the community.

AS4   Reflection and evaluation of their own practice and their continuing professional development as teachers.

AS5   Collaboration with other individuals, groups and/or organizations with a legitimate interest in the progress and development of learners.

They are committed to:

DS1   Planning to promote equality, support diversity and to meet the aims and learning needs of learners.

DS2   Learner participation in the planning of learning.

DS3   Evaluation of own effectiveness in planning learning.

Source: LLUK (2007a: 10)

---

conducted by LSIS following the Lingfield Review (see below), a proposal to review the LLUK standards met with widespread support across the sector, particularly from Ofsted (LSIS 2013: 18). However, such a review has not yet taken place.

In May 2014 the Education and Training Foundation published its *Professional Standards for Teachers and Trainers in Education and Training – England* (ETF 2014). These new standards replace the LLUK standards as the basis of professional activity for teachers in lifelong learning; they are reproduced at the beginning of this book (see pp.xxvii–xxviii). In a similar way to the LLUK standards, which in each domain were organized into three groups of statements, the new standards are structured according to professional values and attributes, professional knowledge and understanding, and professional skills. However, these standards are much fewer in number and are not subdivided into different domains of activity. They comprise 20 descriptions of activities, attributes and abilities to which 'As a professional teacher or trainer you should demonstrate commitment . . . in your professional practice' (ETF 2014: 3).

The standards have several specific purposes, and are intended to:

- set out clear expectations of effective practice in education and training;
- enable teachers and trainers to identify areas for their own professional development;
- support initial teacher education;

- provide a national reference point that organizations can use to support the development of their staff. (ETF 2014: 2).

The standards are prefaced by a number of broad statements about the expectations for teachers and trainers. These include being a reflective and enquiring practitioner, maintaining high standards of ethical and professional behaviour, and maintaining a 'dual professionalism' in which expertise in teaching and learning is accompanied by

---

Box 2.2 The LLUK teaching standards 2007–14. Professional knowledge and practice for domain D: planning for learning

PROFESSIONAL KNOWLEDGE AND UNDERSTANDING PROFESSIONAL PRACTICE

Teachers in the lifelong learning sector know and understand:		Teachers in the lifelong learning sector:	
DK1.1	How to plan appropriate, effective, coherent and inclusive learning programmes that promote equality and engage with diversity.	DP1.1	Plan coherent and inclusive learning programmes that meet learners' needs and curriculum requirements, promote equality and engage with diversity effectively.
DK1.2	How to plan a teaching session.	DP1.2	Plan teaching sessions which meet the aims and needs of individual learners and groups, using a variety of resources, including new and emerging technologies.
DK1.3	Strategies for flexibility in planning and delivery.	DP1.3	Prepare flexible session plans to adjust to the individual needs of learners.
DK2.1	The importance of including learners in the planning process.	DP2.1	Plan for opportunities for learner feedback to inform planning and practice.
DK2.2	Ways to negotiate appropriate individual goals with learners.	DP2.2	Negotiate and record appropriate learning goals and strategies with learners.
DK3.1	Ways to evaluate own role and performance in planning learning.	DP3.1	Evaluate the success of planned learning activities.
DK3.2	Ways to evaluate own role and performance as a member of a team in planning learning.	DP3.2	Evaluate the effectiveness of own contributions to planning as a member of a team.

Source: LLUK (2007a: 10–11)

subject and/or vocational expertise. Both in these preliminary statements and in the standards themselves, teachers' knowledge of educational research figures prominently, but is related to notions of evidence-based practice which, as we shall see in Chapter 3, sound attractive but can be problematic. Broadly, the new standards appear to be an attempt to meet some of the criticisms of complexity and confusion of purpose aimed at the LLUK standards; they also appear, at least implicitly, more sympathetic to ideas about the individual and social construction of teacher knowledge to be found in literature on the work-based learning of teachers (see Chapter 5) – for example by acknowledging the contextual sensitivity of professional practice in the sector and the role of collaboration between colleagues and with learners.

A framework of teaching qualifications

The 2007 regulations identified a *full teaching role*, together with a more limited *associate teacher role* which institutionalized the increasing use of support posts (usually lower paid) under the supervision of a fully-qualified teacher. Corresponding to the full teaching role, the regulations introduced the status of Qualified Teacher Learning and Skills (QTLS), to be achieved within five years. QTLS was intended to help bridge the gap in professional status between school teaching and teaching in further education, and took over several of the elements governing entry to the school sector, although there were also important differences. A more limited status, known as Associate Teacher Learning and Skills (ATLS), was intended for those in an associate teacher role. Both QTLS and ATLS had specific qualification and professional formation requirements, contained within a new framework of awards.

QTLS is not awarded automatically on achieving an appropriate award; it requires completion of a period of 'professional formation', a post-qualification process which, until late 2014, was administered by the IfL and which requires a teacher to demonstrate competence in practice. Although it differs in some respects from Qualified Teacher Status (QTS) in schools, holders of QTLS may be employed in schools as qualified teachers (see HM Government 2012).

The 2007 qualifications framework contained three main awards:

- *Preparing to Teach in the Lifelong Learning Sector* (PTLLS), an induction to teaching to be achieved within one year of taking up a first teaching post;
- *Certificate in Teaching in the Lifelong Learning Sector* (CTLLS), intended for those in an 'associate' teaching role and comprising 24 credits at Level 3 or Level 4 in the QCF;
- *Diploma in Teaching in the Lifelong Learning Sector* (DTLLS), a full teaching qualification required for QTLS, comprising 120 credits at Level 5 in the QCF. A 'minimum core' of knowledge of language, literacy, numeracy and ICT (consisting of pedagogical knowledge as well as personal skills) was included (LLUK 2007b, 2007c).

These qualifications were largely offered by national awarding bodies such as City and Guilds, although universities were required to align their programmes with this framework and some adopted its terminology for their awards. However, the well-established university awards of Certificate in Education and PGCE continued to be offered, albeit in an increasingly competitive environment. These are full teaching qualifications leading to QTLS. A Cert Ed is worth 120 credits; in most cases this will be at Level 5 in the FHEQ but may be higher. In some institutions, the PGCE is available at two levels: a Professional Graduate Certificate at Level 6 and a Postgraduate Certificate at Master's level (Level 7 in the FHEQ). Awards in which all 120 credits are at Master's level may also be offered; the term Postgraduate Diploma in Education is normally used for such programmes.

Reviewing the framework: Lingfield and after

Although, as Avis (2011) points out, there were significant continuities in education policy between New Labour and Coalition Governments, the Lingfield Review marked a watershed for FE teacher education, signalling a period in which de-regulation and market forces were to replace a statutory national system. To some extent, the ground for this ideological shift had been prepared by the limitations of the 2007 regulations. Whilst an evaluation of the reforms published at almost the same time as the first Lingfield report was broadly positive (BIS 2012d), it was clear that difficulties had been encountered. In FE and adult learning, the proportion of new teachers either holding or working towards a teaching qualification was below 80 per cent, and only 57 per cent of all FE teachers held a teaching qualification at Level 5 or above (BIS 2012d: 7). Mentoring support, identified by Ofsted as a key weakness in 2003, continued to be variable in extent and quality, and the numbers of teachers achieving QTLS or ATLS were as yet relatively small (BIS 2012d: 9).

There were also concerns about the coherence of the system of qualifications, which had been designed to serve different purposes rather than provide smooth progression. In adult education and work-based learning, teachers were often not supported to go beyond PTLLS (see also Thompson 2010). A significant difficulty with CTLLS was the disparity in credit and level between this qualification and those appropriate to QTLS, making progression to a full teaching role problematic. The establishment of QTLS was also hampered by growing controversy over the role of the IfL. The 2007 regulations had made both CPD and IfL membership compulsory. Initially, the membership fee was government funded but in 2011 responsibility for payment was transferred to individual teachers. The resulting boycott of IfL membership by the FE teachers' union UCU further reduced the credibility of both the regulations and the professional body.

The Lingfield Review reported in two stages: an interim report largely concerned with the 2007 regulations, and a final report dealing with teacher professionalism more broadly (see Chapters 1 and 4). The interim report (BIS 2012b) largely ignored the recently-published BIS review and instead appealed directly to Government policy on de-regulation and criticisms of the regulations from across the sector. Citing the UCU boycott and the slow uptake of QTLS but failing to acknowledge the systemic under-funding that had undermined attempts to professionalize the FE workforce, the report concluded that regulation had been ineffective. It recommended that:

- the 2007 regulations should be revoked, so that CPD and teaching qualifications become once more a matter for the individual teacher and their employer;

- the category of associate teacher, generally recognized as divisive and counter-productive, be abolished;
- the qualifications framework be revised and simplified;
- qualifications at Level 7 (Master's level) should be developed 'to help form the capabilities of those who aspire to the highest professional levels'.

(BIS 2012b: 6)

These recommendations were largely accepted by the Coalition Government, although ending the statutory requirement for a teaching qualification was delayed until September 2013. LSIS was given the task of developing a new, voluntary qualifications framework – although LSIS itself was due to close shortly after the new framework was completed in 2013. A significant feature of the debates surrounding this framework was the question of the size of the Level 5 qualification – should it be reduced to 60 credits, lowering costs for individuals and also for the Government, which would have to provide student loans to support the award? In the event, it became apparent that such a reduction would diminish its credibility and a 120 credit qualification was retained. The resulting framework, like the one which preceded it, contained three distinct awards, excluding the proposed Level 7 qualification being developed for use by awarding bodies (LSIS 2013):

- *Award in Education and Training* (12 credits at Level 3): an introduction to teaching and training, primarily knowledge-based with some assessment of microteaching;
- *Certificate in Education and Training* (36 credits at Level 4): a qualification for those with 'a broad range of teaching or training responsibilities';
- *Diploma in Education and Training* (120 credits at Level 5): for those with 'an extensive range of teaching or training responsibilities, including those in more than one context'.

As before, universities were not required to adopt this framework in detail, but guidance was provided for HEIs on how to align their awards with the new framework. Unlike the highly prescriptive LLUK guidance, which specified learning outcomes and assessment criteria, the new guidance was largely concerned with broad principles and outlining mandatory course content.

Mentoring and the work-based learning of teachers

Concerns about the work-based learning of trainee teachers have been consistently expressed by Ofsted since assuming responsibility for inspecting FE teacher training in 2001. An early survey report (Ofsted 2003) found inadequacies in the integration of practical skills with the more theoretical elements of training. Comparing FE with training for schools, Ofsted concluded that this was due largely to weaknesses in mentoring and poorly developed links between teacher educators and staff in FE colleges. The survey also highlighted the often limited experience of the LLS gained by trainees. Because in-service training is the norm, 'teaching practice' is linked to the job role of individual trainees, who may therefore find it difficult to broaden their experience. Academic research, whilst paying more attention to systemic factors, also highlighted problems with mentoring and work-based learning; indeed, Lucas and Unwin (2009) propose that, in many cases, the FE workplace is a barrier to learning rather than a facilitator.

In response to these concerns, the 2007 reforms established a network of Centres for Excellence in Teacher Training (CETT). Each CETT is a partnership of organizations in the sector. Although there are different emphases, their activities focus mainly on developing and supporting ITE and CPD. The CETTs cover different areas of England, although a small number also have a national remit for certain specialist activities. However, government funding for these organizations ended in 2010, although many continue as self-sustaining networks.

Improved mentoring and access to wider networks of teachers are also relevant to another weakness identified by Ofsted – inadequate development of subject-specific teaching skills and knowledge. Due to the reliance on small-scale local delivery of in-service courses discussed earlier, subject-specific groupings are rarely viable. Some providers have developed alternative strategies based on study days or summer schools, and virtual networks have also been used. However, the belief in local mentoring arrangements as the fundamental strategy for improving the work-based learning of trainees – in particular its subject specific aspects – has become institutionalized, highlighting the need for high-quality training and support for mentors.

In spite of widespread recognition of the importance of mentoring and the integration between work-based learning and other aspects of ITE, this remains a significant weakness. Although somewhat sweeping in its generalizations, the verdict of Lord Lingfield on the state of work-based learning in the FE sector after a decade of reform is difficult to refute:

> Initial teacher training programmes appear to be largely generic and theoretical . . . mentoring continues to be weak; . . . and the commitment of FE employers to support their staff to attain excellence in pedagogy appears distinctly uneven. It is at least arguable that most of the national effort has been made in the wrong place: towards standards, regulations and compulsion, rather than towards fostering a deep and shared commitment to real 'bottom up' professionalism among FE employers and staff.
>
> (BIS 2012b: 14)

The former *Institute for Learning* and the *Higher Education Academy*

The IfL was officially recognized as the professional body for the learning and skills sector in 2004. On 1 July 2014 its closure was announced, with its legacy and assets passing to the ETF. The idea of a professional organization for FE teachers was not new, and the IfL's development over time reflects the slow move towards recognition of teaching in the sector as a professional activity. The UCU has always had a strong professional focus. Employer- or sector-based organizations – for example, the former

Further Education Development Association (FEDA) – promoted the discussion of staff and professional development issues. However, none of these organizations could be regarded as a professional body in the traditional sense as they lacked regulatory power and did not encompass all staff teaching in the sector.

The 2007 reforms gave IfL a key role in the FE system, with the responsibility to register FE teachers and award QTLS status. However, as we have seen, IfL had a troubled existence and its position was compromised by de-regulation and the end to government funding for membership fees (see above). These changes have left the status of QTLS in an anomalous position: whilst being officially recognized as enabling holders to teach in schools, it is no longer compulsory for FE teachers. Furthermore, the termination of government funding led IfL to introduce a fee for QTLS applications which may impact upon the numbers seeking this status in future.

In HE, perhaps even more so than in the FE sector, traditional views of teaching and learning have prioritized subject knowledge over pedagogy. The emphasis on research as a distinctive feature of the activity of HE teachers provides a further 'pull' away from pedagogy as a core concern for many HE teachers, and career progression in HE has often been perceived as dependent far more on scholarly output than on teaching ability. However, the emphasis on widening participation has brought about significant change in the student body, with expectations and backgrounds ranging from the purely academic to the strongly vocational. As a result, attention has focused much more urgently in recent years on issues of teaching and learning in HE.

The Dearing Report (NCIHE 1997) called for a more student-centred approach in HE, supported by greater professionalism in HE teaching. A specific recommendation, duly accepted by the Government, was to establish an Institute for Learning and Teaching in Higher Education (ILTHE), conceived as a professional body for HE teachers and intended to accredit HE teacher training programmes, commission research into teaching and learning, and stimulate innovation in teaching. The HEA was formed in 2004 by merging the ILTHE with two other organizations having a teaching and learning focus within HE, the Learning and Teaching Support Network (LTSN) and the National Co-ordination Team for the Teaching Quality Enhancement Fund (TQEF). The HEA manages a range of professional networks and offers accreditation to appropriate teacher-training courses. Individuals can apply for HEA recognition at various levels.

In the FE system, occupational standards were set by the former LLUK – essentially a government body – while regulation and support for individual teachers was provided by IfL, the professional body. The ETF now combines these roles. The HEA is responsible for both of these functions (albeit in consultation with employer bodies) in relation to HE and has developed the *UK Professional Standards Framework* (HEA 2011). In this framework, teaching is conceptualized in terms of five 'areas of activity' relating to planning, assessment and scholarship; 'core knowledge' relating to subject and pedagogy; and 'professional values'. Four descriptors are defined, corresponding to different levels of involvement and responsibility in the areas of activity. Within this broad framework, there is considerable freedom for individuals or course designers to choose how to demonstrate their abilities, knowledge and understanding in the areas of activity. The HE standards are therefore less prescriptive, and arguably more attuned to professional development, than those applying elsewhere in lifelong learning.

3

Theory and practice

James Avis and Kevin Orr

In this chapter

- Policy science and policy scholarship
- Theorizing education: socio-economic and political context
- Theorizing education: contingency and complexity
- Expansive practice
- Conclusion: what about practice?

This chapter explores the relationship between theory and practice. On one level this is self evident: how we make sense of learning and teaching informs practice. The manner in which we construct learners and understand learning will frame notions of effective teaching and what it is to be a 'good' teacher. Policy scholarship shifts understandings of practice away from a focus on classroom processes to their wider context. Educational processes are always theorized – even denying the salience of theory represents a theoretical standpoint. It is important to engage with theory, to deconstruct and interrogate it. How far can theory take us? What are its limits and possibilities? What does it say about pedagogy and social justice? Although we draw on policy to illustrate points, the debates and issues we discuss move beyond the policy orientations of any particular government.

Policy science and policy scholarship

College mission statements and teaching and learning policies frequently claim to place the learner at the centre of educational processes. Continuous improvement will enhance standards and address the needs of learners. This is the terrain of policy science which sits alongside a number of related currents: evidence informed practice, value for money, customer satisfaction, and so on. These may be drawn upon to inform and develop practice. For example, providers may call upon particular strategies to enhance the performance of learners. These activities can be placed under the remit of policy science whereby providers are deemed able to intervene in educational practices, achieving the desired outcomes.

Policy science readily folds over into interventions that focus upon individual colleges, particular classrooms or teachers, and the type of community from which learners are drawn (Grace 1995). It can veer towards an analysis that pathologizes the practices of particular teachers, colleges or communities. Paradoxically, policy science can sit alongside approaches that emphasize the possibility of intervening in practice and making a difference in a particular context. This can be seen in the case of those interventions linked to effectiveness or improvement. The difficulty is that such approaches pay scant attention to the wider socio-economic and political context of education and learners. In neglecting the political context policy science works with the status quo, securing the interests of those with power.

Policy science can become preoccupied with descriptive accounts of initiatives and questions of implementation. We could use this type of approach to think about any current policy or curriculum initiative – the development of teacher education, college based HE, and so forth. The questions with which policy science is concerned are attractive. It avoids the apparent obfuscations of theory, having a concreteness in its direct relationship to practice. In addition, its technicist orientation leads it to portray itself as offering a rational and value-free approach – a problem is identified and a solution proposed. This renders it attractive to policymakers.

Educational practice orientated towards making a difference is no bad thing, but there are costs associated with the framework within which policy science is placed. Interventions are determined elsewhere and the language of managerialism, effectiveness and efficiency has gained ascendancy. Education, and in particular the LLS, must address the needs of the economy and there is a blurring between the needs of industry and learners. While the State may suggest a parallel between the interests of learners and of capital, this is by no means the case. The necessity for economic competitiveness may be a common refrain among policymakers, but the outcomes will be unevenly distributed (Avis 2007).

Policy scholarship develops an analytic framework beyond that of policy science, placing its analyses within a wider context (Grace 1995). There is a necessity to examine the ideologies that inform policy making. Such a stance would explore how the ideas of the New Right have informed the development of educational policy, or the manner in which New Labour or the UK Coalition Government appropriated neo-liberalism. Whilst this approach may be castigated for its distance from everyday education practice, it nevertheless raises important questions about the wider socio-economic context as well as the political implications of what takes place within the LLS. It seeks to expose contradictions and tensions. Policies and practices concerned with widening participation and equal opportunities that address classed, gendered or raced educational inequalities may hold progressive possibilities. Yet not challenging the wider social structure may in the end be ameliorative – serving a deeply ideological function (Ainley 2008). They may offer benefits to those involved but do little to transform the wider social structure. A policy scholarship analysis would construe the inequalities related to race, ethnicity, class and gender as structural phenomena rather than arising out of discrimination or prejudice. To interrupt the processes through which these inequalities are generated it is necessary to address the social practices through which they reproduce.

It could be argued the dichotomy between policy science and policy scholarship is overdrawn, and that there is a continuum containing an interrelationship between agency and structure. Much social theory suggests a dialectical relationship between agency and structure. Marx (1968) suggested that while people make history, they do not do so in conditions of their own choosing. Similarly, Giddens's notion of *structuration* (Giddens and Pierson 1998) illustrates how social interactions re-produce social structures – by interacting with others we are simultaneously creating structure. Bourdieu's analyses emphasize the dialectical relationship between *habitus* and *field*:

> '[habitus] names the characteristic dispositions of the social subject. It is indicated in the bearing of the body and in deeply ingrained habits of behaviour, feeling, thought' (Lovell 2000: 27). Habitus engages with the field, which is conceptualised as 'a structured system of social relations, at micro and macro level, rather like a field of forces in which positions are defined . . . in relation to each other'
>
> (James and Bloomer 2001: 5)

Human agency can make a difference, but constraints must be recognized. Paradoxically, research and state interventions into education often play down the salience of structure, adopting individualistic and technicist positions that deny the politics of engagement. This has an affinity with policy science which operates with a consensual model of society. If we all share similar goals, as in the discourse of competitiveness, then individualistic solutions become readily available. This position denies the existence of social antagonism in which the interests of particular groups are in fundamental contradiction, as with capital and labour. This tendency can be seen in the demonization of bankers following the financial crash of 2008, rather than in the development of a critique of capitalism. The result is that systemic contradictions, patterns of exploitation and oppression become sidelined. Policy scholarship points towards a political understanding of the policy process, raising questions about the role of the State. It works with a conflict model of society and state, in which both are riven by antagonisms that are not necessarily amenable to solutions that benefit all.

Theorizing education: socio-economic and political context

The socio-economic and political context frames practices within lifelong learning. It shapes and impacts on qualification structures, models of assessment and the curriculum. This is an uneven process, accented differentially towards particular learners and educational sectors. Nevertheless there is a relationship between this wider context and educational practice. It has an influence on the skills learners should develop. It also has a bearing on what counts as the form of knowledge that education is to deliver. This derives from particular understandings of society, the economy and, somewhat tautologically, the role of the learner and what it is to be a teacher. Underpinning these ideas are theorizations of educational relations. The following, from the White Paper *Opportunity, Employment and Progression*, raises several key themes: '*Skills* are now a key driver to achieving *economic success* and *social justice* in the *new global economy*' (DIUS/DWP 2007: 30, our emphasis).

The development and enhancement of skills is seen as pivotal to economic success and the well-being of society in the 'global economy'. The pursuit of these aims also delivers social justice through opportunity, as well as providing the resources that can be used to benefit all members of society. These were key elements in New Labour's stance towards competitiveness that attributed particular roles to education, teachers and learners (Brown 2007, unnumbered), but are also a feature of Coalition rhetoric with variants on a Blairite notion of rights and responsibilities (Blair 2002).

> Skills are vital to our future and improving skills is essential to building sustainable growth and stronger communities. A skilled workforce is necessary to stimulate the private-sector growth that will bring new jobs and new prosperity for people all over this country.
> And a strong further education and skills system is fundamental to social mobility, re-opening routes for people from wherever they begin to succeed in work, become confident through becoming accomplished and play a full part in civil society.
>
> (Cable and Hayes, 2010: 3)

The way the socio-economic context is understood leads to the suggestion that there are boundless possibilities for those who avail themselves of the opportunities. This remains the case in hard times that arise in conditions of austerity (but see Standing, 2011). Indeed, we have a duty to take advantage of the opportunities that arise for the benefit of ourselves, our families and society as a whole. The State becomes an enabling body offering the opportunity to develop – it becomes the social investment state embodying social justice. This is as much a feature of Coalition politics as it was of the previous government (see Giddens 1998 and Avis 2011). This raises questions about the way in which the State seeks to manage the contradictions and tensions surrounding capitalism – a difficulty that all governments face. Underpinning these ideas is the notion that the social formation is based on consensus. These theorizations not only describe the socio-economic context but constitute it, resting alongside allied conceptualizations of the social formation and the role individuals play within it. This constitutes a *regime of truth*. 'Each society has its regime of truth, its general politics of truth: that is, the types of discourses which it accepts and makes function as true' (Foucault 1980: 131).

Such theorizations also shape the way in which we understand educational achievement. Early work in the sociology of education drew upon the notion of educability:

> This [improving the schooling of working-class children] would undoubtedly be the most effective way of eliminating the social problems of the so-called delinquent areas, a name that masks a much wider social problem – the failure to integrate the unskilled and semi-skilled working class into a society which is becoming predominantly governed by the values and standards of the professional middle class.
>
> (Vaizey 1962, cited by Education Group CCCS 1981: 78–9)

This resonates with current policy, which resurrects in various guises the deserving and undeserving working class. In some writing we confront notions of an underclass or a racialized section of the white working class who fail to take up available opportunities (Preston 2003). In some respects these debates are echoed in the current concern with those not in education, employment or training (NEET) (Simmons and Thompson 2011). Consider the following passage:

> [T]he risk of non-participation [learning or work] is higher for young people if:
> * Their parents are poor or unemployed
> * They are members of certain minority ethnic groups
> * They are in particular circumstances which create barriers to participation
>   i   They are carers
>   ii   They are teenage parents
>   iii   They are homeless
>   iv   They are or have been in care
>   v   They have a learning difficulty
>   vi   They have a disability
>   vii   They have a mental illness
>   viii They misuse drugs or alcohol
>   ix   They are involved in offending
>
> (Social Exclusion Unit 1999: 48)

While this hints at a structural explanation it also veers towards an underclass model that uses the language of cultural pathology to explain differential educational achievement. This results in an 'othering' of those who do not participate in education: they are different and we need to take steps to ensure their inclusion. Accordingly, we need to disrupt and undermine their 'irrational' culture which is antithetical to education. This stance was reflected in the Fryer Report: 'In our country today, far too many people are still locked in a culture which regards lifelong learning as either unnecessary, unappealing, uninteresting or unavailable' (NACCCE 1999: 8).

Particular forms of white working-class culture are deemed out of step with the needs of modern society. The same can be said of certain groups within the black working class. The logic is to castigate such groups for their failure to grasp the opportunities available. It views as irrational the cultural defences of these groups and renders rational the orientations of the middle class (Davies et al. 2008). Ainley (2008) suggests that the call to widen participation in HE is a 'con'; rather than promising upward mobility, it represents in effect the proletarianization of the professions. If this is the case, how should we make sense of the 'poor' who do not engage with HE? Is this irrational?

Theorizing education: contingency and complexity

Policy scholarship recognizes the complexity of educational processes. Government exhortations to 'eliminate failure' (DfES 2006: 56), or an emphasis on 'best practice' reduce the significance of contingency and over-simplify. At classroom level, what works with one group may not work with another; a student engaged by one tutor may 'switch off' with another (Hodkinson 2008). Even at the most fundamental level of what we teach, or what knowledge is, there is complexity. Young (2003: 554) wrote:

'we have a national curriculum, a post-compulsory curriculum and even a higher education curriculum, all of which take for granted the assumptions about knowledge on which they are based'. Young had earlier asserted that the idea that 'all knowledge is socially produced for particular purposes in particular contexts is by now relatively uncontentious' (1998: 1), but this may overstate the level of agreement. Young (1998: 1) asked 'does this mean that what counts as knowledge in society or what is selected to be included in the curriculum at a particular time is no more than what those in positions of power decide to be knowledge?' The answer must be, no: there is always dispute and unevenness. For example, the radical Chartist movement in the nineteenth century used the term 'really useful knowledge' to describe the type of education they promoted. Richard Johnson explains:

> 'Really useful knowledge' was a knowledge of everyday circumstances, including a knowledge of why you were poor, why you were politically oppressed and why through the force of social circumstance, you were the kind of person you were, your character misshapen by a cruel competitive world.
>
> (Education Group, CCCS 1981: 37)

Apple and Beane (2007: vii) noted 'the growing dissatisfaction on the part of educators in so many places with curricula that have little relationship with the cultures and lives of the students'. They endorse how engaged practitioners can challenge received notions of knowledge by (re)connecting it to 'the communities and biographies of real people' (2007: 151). Teachers have the autonomy, despite the constraints they face, to emphasize particular aspects of the curriculum according to their values. The curriculum is a social construct that reflects society in all its complexity, and the manner in which it is interpreted is complicated by individual biography and belief.

Even when considering practice, to describe particular objective circumstances may not adequately predict or explain what takes place or how individuals react. As an illustration, here are extracts from interviews with two trainees on a Lifelong Learning teacher training course who were asked to describe their experience of the staffroom.

Trainee A

[I]t's fantastic . . . It's really good. You've got like space to breathe . . . and everybody's friendly . . . and very cooperative . . .

I've been . . . given a desk and a computer . . . I mean, everybody has access to the computer . . . if I'm working at that desk they tend not to disturb me . . . They go and use other computers . . . which is brilliant 'cause . . . I am a student . . . but they have really valued me and I don't feel like a student sometimes.

Trainee B

Well, first of all we went into the department, the manager wasn't there so it was a case of oh, you know, everyone looking up and staring at you, and the first greeting was, 'Bring your own tea . . . bring your own coffee. You don't touch anyone else's. You can't sit anywhere that's anyone else's seat; you won't have a seat of your own . . .'

These trainees were describing the same staffroom, in the same college at the same time, which suggests that a relationship between situation and biography (including expectations) formed their contrasting reactions. Such complex relationships influence perceptions. To quote Law (2003: 3), simplicity 'won't help us to understand mess': the LLS is characterized by messy contradictions.

Even contradictory situations may seem normal to those experiencing them. Reeves, writing in the 1990s, described circumstances still recognizable today: 'The structure of further education is so immediate and enveloping that, far from seeing any absurdities or contradictions, most staff and students who work within it undertake without any question what is expected of them' (1995: 93). Bourdieu may help us to understand this apparent myopia. He explained *doxa* as 'the coincidence of the objective structures and the internalized structures which provides the illusion of immediate understanding, characteristic of the familiar universe, and which at the same time excludes from that experience any inquiry as to its own conditions of possibility' (1990: 26).

We absorb the way the world around us works so that incongruities become familiar and unnoticed. This underpins the need to delve beneath the obvious, which conscious theorization allows. Analysing education with the benefit of a coherent theoretical approach avoids a paralysing relativism that says situations are too complex to explain. If it is impossible to explain, then any explanation is equally valid, and education cannot meaningfully be changed. So, to acknowledge that many contingencies may interact within a given set of relationships is not to say that analysis is pointless. Rather, the point is to adopt an analysis that is sophisticated enough to comprehend complexity. Consider what Bourdieu wrote about the role of the teacher in France:

> Agents entrusted with acts of classification can fulfil their social function as social classifiers only because it is carried out in the guise of acts of academic classification. They do well what they have to do (objectively) because they think they are doing something other than what they are doing, because they are doing something other than what they think they are doing, and because they believe in what they think they are doing. As fools fooled, they are the primary victims of their own actions.

> (Bourdieu 1996: 39)

Bourdieu argues teachers make decisions about students that may appear impartial and based on academic progress or ability. Yet, what is happening is more nuanced because teachers do not stand outside society, and their decisions are not only shaped by the norms of society, but also perpetuate them. Teachers may think they apply objective criteria, however, those criteria reflect an unequal society where certain types of knowledge and expression are valorized and perpetuate social division. Elsewhere Bourdieu and Passeron (1990: 125–6) write:

> If the freedom the educational system allows the teacher is the best guarantee that he will serve the system, the freedom allowed to the educational system is the best guarantee that it will serve the perpetuation of the relations prevailing

between the classes, because the possibility of this re-direction of ends is inscribed in the very logic of a system which never better fulfils its social function than when it seems to be exclusively pursuing its own ends.

The education system does not need to be closely controlled by the State because in pursuing its goals it follows those of an unequal society, which it then helps to reproduce. The role of education or the teacher can only be understood in relation to the values of society, the culture of the organization and its socio-economic structure.

To extract educational practice from its context is to misrepresent it, even if we are trying to understand what works in the classroom. Coffield and Edward (2008: 2), in a critique of 'best practice', suggest that to improve teaching and learning in the LLS:

> The first task is to appreciate the implications of the complexities of teaching and learning in specific localities and only then to devise policies to respond to those implications. We need an approach that constructs policy, based on a deep under-standing of the central significance of what happens in classrooms, e.g. by first assessing the needs of learners, tutors and institutions, the demands of practice, the conditions of the labour markets and how these (and many other) factors interact differently and dynamically in particular areas.

Best, or even good practice, cannot be passed around like a handout, because successful learning is conditional on many factors, each of which differ from setting to setting. To suggest otherwise not only fails to explain, but sets up unreasonable expectations. A student who goes to an FE college because they have not succeeded at school may similarly not succeed at college. Is that because of the failings of the staff, or the failings of a society that produces teenagers who are alienated and disengaged? Apple and Beane (2007) rightly extol inspirational, engaged teachers, but the selfless commitment of individuals cannot counterbalance the weight of a complex, hierarchical and unequal society.

Classroom practice can develop through being informed by contingency, as Coffield and Edward describe above, because teachers retain some agency to affect what happens in their classroom or workshop. This, however, demands more than a perfunctory description of 'best practice'. Indeed, the 'Transforming Learning Cultures' project, which researched learning in FE, stressed that the role of the tutor is a crucial element in successful learning.

Expansive practice

The section above explored issues that bear on the complexity of educational relations, and indeed on the importance of 'happenstance' or contingency in relation to the forms of capital and habitus that learners and lecturers carry. There are no easy and straightforward answers of the type suggested by the technicization embedded in policy science. Inevitably interventions into educational relations are formed by values. However, while accepting the complexity of these processes it is important that we lodge them within a framework that can move beyond relativism. If, for example, we stop at an exploration of pedagogic relations that views these as ultimately arbitrary, in that 'what works for one learner or lecturer doesn't for another', this can become debilitating and overly individualistic. We need to locate education within the social relations of class, gender, race, sexuality, age and disability, together with the institutional and wider socio-economic context. Bourdieu's work points towards the importance of these interconnections deriving from his conceptualization of the relational in education and social processes.

One of the benefits of a relational approach that locates classroom processes in a wider context is that it can avoid the 'pathologization' of the practices of learners and teachers while constituting education as a site of struggle. Some years ago Troyna (1984) sought to contest understandings of black (predominantly male) educational underachievement. His position was that in a social context in which racist processes restricted access to the labour market, educational disengagement could not be understood through a simplistic lens of underachievement. A more complex process was taking place. We may question the political efficacy of young people's disengagement from education, nevertheless such a stance embodies a particular rationale. Ironically, when such disengagement leads to civil disturbance this may bring positive interventions for the community involved.

Much has been written about the performative context within which FE teachers work and the consequence for their morale as well as the different responses this might engender. These may mirror those of disengaged youth, or may be concerned with some sort of survival strategy, and while some of these responses may be deemed anti-educational, so is much of the associated policy context. The tendency to individualize the failing of particular teachers needs to be set within this understanding. If this prognosis is bleak the same argument could be made in relation to what constitutes 'good practice', as well as ideas about learner engagement. Successful learners may serve to sustain the illusion of meritocracy and thereby perform an important ideological role (Althusser 1971). In addition, the notion of success is a relational concept. Success within a low ranked institution will not necessarily carry the dividends associated with a high ranking one, although the abilities and potential developed may be greater in the former. It is at this juncture, and with some force, that society's inequitable social structures are encountered. Ainley's (1994) work illustrates this. In his study of HE, students from a new university found it difficult to obtain the type of graduate employment that those from prestigious universities gained. For Ainley, this reflected class processes – the recruitment 'of those like us'. For his students however, this was misrecognized and was felt to indicate their own failings in developing the types of skills required in employment.

Educational practices need to be located in their wider context, and classroom processes need to be set within their wider institutional context. The college itself needs to be related to the social relations of education, that is to say the relations between educational providers and the implicit status attached to particular qualifications. This articulates with the patterning of social relations in terms of class, race and gender. If we wish to engage in educational practices underpinned by a commitment to social justice, we need to consider a number of different sites of struggle and potential alliances. These include the classroom and practices that contribute to learning. Here we may encounter the contradictions of our own practice and its unintended consequences. Reflexivity is important at this level but has to be set within a wider context, otherwise we can exaggerate the efficacy of our teaching or alternatively blame ourselves for the underachievement of our students, with all the associated emotional costs (Colley 2006). The classroom is just one site of struggle among many and this is why an expansive understanding is important.

Conclusion: what about practice?

Earlier we argued that the way we think about what constitutes 'good practice' will be informed by how we construct knowledge, the learner and learning, the teacher and teaching, as well as the socio-economic context. These are political questions in that answers will inform our orientation to pedagogic practice and our understanding of the relationship of education to wider society. Classroom processes are a form of social practice that must be set alongside those taking place outside. It is because of this that an expansive notion of practice is important. This suggests that doing the best for our learners involves engagement with social practices beyond the classroom. This is not to deny the salience of the classroom but to place it in its relational context. At the same time it is important not to construct the teacher as a 'super hero' actively engaging in the community, professional associations, unions, as well as social movements. Such expectations are unreasonable, gendered and in the long term untenable, failing to recognize that teaching is among other things paid employment – a job.

Research that has explored the experiences of newly qualified lecturers or those undergoing FE teacher training characterizes these groups as holding an ethos of care, as well as a real desire and hope of giving something back to the community (Avis and Bathmaker 2004, 2006). However, the way in which community is conceived varies: for those rooted in occupational and vocational cultures it is the trade or profession, while for others it is to stand as a role model for those drawn from disadvantaged communities of what it is possible to achieve. Such orientations connect with an interest in doing the best for students, and in facilitating learner development to enhance life chances. This is in spite of the difficulties that derive from the socio-economic and institutional context in which teachers and learners labour. Underlying such commitments rests a particular orientation to practice. Hodkinson (2008: 11) argues that learning in college is directly influenced by:

- the positions, dispositions and actions of the students;
- the positions, dispositions and actions of the tutors;
- the location and resources of the learning site which are not neutral, but enable some approaches and attitudes, and constrain or prevent others;
- the syllabus or course specification, the assessment and qualification specifications;
- the time tutors and students spend together, their interrelationships, and the range of other learning sites students are engaged with;
- issues of college management and procedures, together with funding and inspection body procedures and regulations, and government policy;
- wider vocational and academic cultures, of which any learning site is a part;

- wider social and cultural values and practices, for example around issues of social class, gender and ethnicity, the nature of employment opportunities, social and family life, and the perceived status of further education as a sector.

Teachers' agency and social practice will be framed by these conditions. For those with a professional and vocational commitment the wider context in which learners labour frames life chances and the possibilities for social justice. The desire of these teachers to do the best for their students necessitates a consideration of the wider social context which in turn articulates with an expansive notion of practice. At the same time, the desire to do the best reflects teacher commitment and agency offering a politics of a kind – a politics of hope. Apple and Beane (2007: 12–13) suggest that what distinguishes progressive from democratic educational institutions is that the latter's vision

> extends beyond purposes such as improving the school climate or enhancing students' self-esteem. Democratic educators seek not simply to lessen the harshness of social inequities in school, but to change the conditions that create them. For this reason, they tie their understanding of undemocratic practices inside the school to larger conditions on the outside.

4

Professionalism
James Avis, Roy Fisher and Ros Ollin

In this chapter

- The professional teacher
- Professional values and codes of conduct
- Inter-professionality in the LLS
- Research and scholarship
- Conclusion

The professional teacher

'Professionalism' is a much abused term. Historically, the term 'profession' has applied to elite occupations such as medicine and the law. Today many occupations seek the appellation 'profession' for the status it accords, consequently it has become relatively meaningless. There are many ways to theorize the professional and below we comment on three approaches.

Initially, we examine the trait and functionalist approaches which take at face value the self-presentation of the professions (Barber 1963; Millerson 1964). The trait approach argues that the professions have characteristics that set them apart from other occupational groups. For example, professions are thought to possess particular skills and knowledge, acquired through training, used for the benefit of society. Because of the high levels of skill and knowledge involved, only members of the profession are able to judge whether this has been used appropriately, with conduct being governed by codes of practice. Professions are thought to be marked by altruism orientated towards meeting the needs of clients and society more widely, for which professional autonomy is a necessity. A trait approach therefore identifies characteristics of the professions as: high levels of skill and knowledge, codes of conduct and altruism and autonomy, among others. The difficulty is, why these factors and not others?

Functionalist approaches resolve this difficulty by theorizing the relationship between characteristics. If 'professional' occupations have specialized knowledge and skills that are to be used for the broad benefit of society, this claim can legitimize their autonomy. There will typically be an ethos of altruism as well as professional control through a code of practice. In other words, the high status and value accorded to professions is necessary if they are to meet the needs of society. The difficulty with this argument is that it essentially supports the status quo. Johnson (1972) presented an alternative to the trait and functionalist positions which raised questions of power. He argued that the professions are those occupations able to define their relationship with clients. He suggested those occupations that recruit from powerful social groups arc more likely to be able to do this.

Johnson's (1972) work forces us to consider power and to question the manner in which professions present themselves. Not only does Johnson remind us of historical contingency, in that in specific conditions particular occupations may be able to attain a degree of autonomy and control over their labour, but that this is pivotally related to questions of class. If members of a particular occupational group have at their disposal class power this can be used to secure professional status and influence. Witz (1992) highlighted the way in which classed processes intersect with those of gender in her discussion of occupational divisions in medicine.

The notion of professionalism and the ability of an occupational group to attain autonomy are connected to historical contingency as well as processes of class and gender. Indeed, it could be argued that the apogee of the professions is past, being a feature of the nineteenth and early twentieth century. Currently the so-called professions are increasingly located within large organizations, their work determined by managerial and institutional diktat, and forms of collegiality and professional community are undermined (see Avis and Orr 2014). Adler et al., whilst acknowledging such changes, nevertheless argue that community, and we could add collegiality, remain important despite the ascendancy of the market and hierarchy principles (2008: 360). Teachers have always had a somewhat ambivalent relationship to professionalism. It has been drawn upon as part of an occupational strategy that sought to gain autonomy and control over the labour process, and yet this claim to professionalism has rested alongside another strategy located in trade unionism. Both of these strategies have sought occupational control (Ozga and Lawn 1981), being shaped by the economic conditions of the time.

The years between the First and Second World Wars saw the development of legitimated teacher professionalism, a very particular form of professionalism. Teachers were deemed to possess expert curricular and pedagogic knowledge which was enacted in the classroom. Legitimated teacher professionalism embodied this idea, with teachers being granted autonomy in the classroom on the basis that politics were kept out of education. These ideas were developed in the socio-economic context of the 1920s and 1930s, in which the political Right was fearful of socialism. During this period, teachers were seen as a bulwark against the incursion of socialist ideas into education (Grace 1987: 207).

The outcome was the suggestion that school and education lie outside politics. This in itself is a deeply political act that served conservative interests of the time. Teachers were granted autonomy in the classroom based on the evacuation of politics from education. At this time there were a range of politics surrounding education some of which were related to class, gender and ethnicity. The significance of this argument is to acknowledge historical contingency as well as the construction of teachers as a conservative force.

Legitimated teacher professionalism was hegemonic following the Second World War. It was during this period that the curriculum was described as a 'secret garden'. Curriculum and schooling were seen to be controlled by teachers. Paradoxically two contradictory arguments were applied during this period – from the Left, teachers, curriculum and pedagogic processes were critiqued for their complicity in reproducing inequality and failing to deliver social justice (Young 1971). Initially these were raised in relation to social class but were followed by concerns about gender and ethnicity (Meighan and Siraj-Blatchford 1997). At the same time writers on the Right were becoming anxious about the apparent entryism of leftist teachers (Education Group, CCCS 1981). These teachers were critiqued for their attachment to the tenets of progressive education, as well as their 'anti-business' orientations.

The result of these critiques, particularly those from the Right, was to re-focus an interest in teacher professionalism, the ramifications of which are still being felt. The curriculum became open to view through the introduction of the National Curriculum for schools, with a focus on transparency and increasing surveillance of teachers' practice. Within FE and the LLS more generally these developments are reflected in external processes of review and inspection and are also present in moves towards self-regulation and self-assessment. The development of occupational standards reflected a particular construction of what it is to be a teacher. While such frameworks cannot completely determine what goes on in the classroom, they do set the terrain in which teachers practice.

There is an influential body of work that examines the labour process of teachers in FE. This research agrees on a number of elements:

- loss of control
- intensification of labour
- increased administrative loads
- perceived marginalisation of teaching
- stress on measurable performance indicators

(Avis 1999: 251)

Wahlberg and Gleeson (2003) in their study of FE business lecturers reflect these tensions where lecturers feel 'caught in a fast changing policy-practice dynamic in which their status has been "casualised" and deprofessionalised by a process of market, funding-led and managerialist reform' (2003: 438).

There has been a struggle over teacher professionalism and its inherent politics. Various notions have been developed that seek to move professionalism in progressive directions, the learning professional, dialogic professionalism and other models rooted in Habermassian theory (Gleeson et al. 2005). In some respects these arguments sit alongside Adler et al.'s (2008) in as much as they point towards the continued salience of community, one set within an hierarchal organization operating within an educational market place. However, models of the learning or dialogic professionalism come up against the preferred model of the state which construes the FE teacher in particular as a service provider, at the behest of the market, and as one who will acquire earned autonomy as a 'trusted servant' of the state (Avis 2003a). Ainley (2008) reminds us that state interest in professionalization often becomes a veneer for proletarianization. The dominance of performativity, target setting and technicized models of accountability illustrate this.

Professional values and codes of conduct

Much writing on professionalism moves beyond mere description of professional behaviour to discuss more fundamental values and beliefs underpinning professional action. This work locates professionalism in a broader set of relations between the practitioner and society, in which 'professionalism' indicates attitudes and responsibilities demonstrated within a specific social context. Implicit is the notion that professionalism is more than individual satisfaction, but relates to the 'common good' and that such values remain to some extent independent of government policy changes or shifts in the economy.

In the past professions operated within slow moving social contexts, with little change in public expectations or the prevailing social order. Professional values could remain constant and unchallenged, although they might also be relatively untested in a climate of self-regulation and protectionism. In contrast, the current social environment is characterized by rapid change, with the public having higher expectations of professionals and increased awareness of individual and societal rights. In this context, professionals are exposed to public scrutiny and the necessity to justify decisions and actions. The evidence required to support decisions in case of audit, inspection or legal action is one manifestation of this. It is not surprising that the tension between personal and professional values and the need to be seen to be accountable to the public are at the root of much writing on professionalism.

The potential impact on professional values of managerialist cultures operating within complex regulatory and legislative frameworks is discussed in RSA (2002), which considers whether values are context specific or whether there is an overarching set of values applicable to all professions. The 'trait' approach to professionalism has been criticized for the arbitrary nature of the traits identified, with different sociocultural contexts placing a higher value on some rather than others. If professionalism involves working towards the 'common good', then it is likely that some core values will underpin different professions, although they may be accorded more or less prominence. They may also be subject to different interpretations according to the socio-cultural-historical context in which they operate. The following examples of how different educational bodies have tackled the notion of professional values suggests these are not neutral, but reflect particular contexts, types of discourse and 'a particular ideology of experience and service' (Evans 2008: 24).

In its 'Statement of professional values and practice for teachers' (GTC 2006), the now defunct General Teaching Council for England (1998–2012) emphasized that school teachers are 'skilled practitioners', placing the learner at the heart of what they do. It also referred to the legislative framework within which school teachers must work, the value and place of the school in the community and the importance of partnership with parents, carers and colleagues. A commitment to equality of opportunity was detailed as 'challenging stereotypes, opposing prejudice and respecting individuals, regardless of age, gender, disability, colour, race, ethnicity, class, religion, marital status or sexual orientation' (GTC 2006: 2). School teachers are currently subject to 'Teachers' Standards' set out by the Department for Education in May 2012. A preamble to the Standards summarizes the 'values and behaviour that all teachers must demonstrate throughout their careers. Part 1 comprises the Standards for Teaching; Part 2 comprises the standards for Professional and Personal Conduct' (DfE 2012: 3–4). These Standards also apply to trainee school teachers and to those teachers completing their statutory induction period. It should be noted that those 'Standards relating to professional and personal conduct will be used to assess cases of serious misconduct, regardless of the sector in which the teacher works.' (DfE 2012a: 2; and see ETF 2014).

The HEA identifies the following core professional values:

1   Respect individual learners and diverse learning communities

2   Promote participation in higher education and equality of opportunity for learners

3   Use evidence-informed approaches and the outcomes from research, scholarship and continuing professional development

4   Acknowledge the wider context in which higher education operates recognising the implications for professional practice.

(HEA, 2011: 3)

The IfL, now subsumed into the ETF, developed a code of professional practice for those working in the sector (2008) which cited seven key 'behaviours'. 'Behaviours' suggests measurable actions rather than underpinning values and may indicate a bias towards public accountability rather than individual integrity. The IfL's behaviours were as follows:

Behaviour 1: Professional integrity
Behaviour 2: Respect
Behaviour 3: Reasonable care
Behaviour 4: Professional practice (providing evidence of compliance with CPD requirements)
Behaviour 5: Criminal offence disclosure
Behaviour 6: Responsibility during Institute investigations
Behaviour 7: Responsibility to the Institute

Notably, professional integrity included upholding the reputation of the 'Institute' and to 'not knowingly undermine' its views. In other words, professional integrity included not criticizing the IfL. A difference from HEA's values is that the IfL referred to behaviour in organizational contexts. Respect for the rights of learners was not only in accordance with legislation, but with 'organization requirements'.

The ETF's 2014 standards explicitly state that practice should be underpinned by a set of professional values. These values not only express what many teachers feel about the principles guiding their work, the need for reflection, innovation and enthusiasm etc., but also the importance of inclusive practices and collaborative relationships with learners and colleagues. Yet the Coalition Government which formed in 2010 sought to place FE professionalism in a context of de-regulation and privatization, replacing state regulation with an emphasis on the responsibilities of employers and individuals (see for example, the final Lingfield Report, BIS 2012). In this context the development of professionalism as well as continuous professional development (CPD) rests upon establishing a *moral* rather than statutory framework to underpin the development of professional traits. However, whether such a morality can be supported by a de-regulated market environment remains to be seen, as does the sustainability of the concurrent model of FE professionalism and CPD. The anomalous situation in which the LLUK standards continued in force after LLUK itself ceased to exist was finally rectified in May 2014 when the ETF launched in August 2013 and known as 'The Foundation' published its 'Professional Standards for Teachers and Trainers in Education and Training – England'. These appear in full on pages xxvi–xxviii at the front of this book.

Inter-professionality in the LLS

In imagining the 'lecturer of the future', two decades ago, Young et al. (1995) identified 'inter-professional knowledge' as a key requirement. The rationale was based on the ways in which the trend towards resource-based learning was bringing teachers into increasing contact with non-teaching colleagues who actively supported the new modes of learning. These might include specialists in assessment, information technologists, librarians, career guidance specialists and counsellors. It was reasoned that to be effective teachers would need to have knowledge of these roles, and how best to utilize and work with them collegially to optimize learning. In more recent years learning support workers, mentors and learning coaches have taken on a higher profile, becoming part of a range of colleagues with whom teachers need to liaise. These organizational and communication trends have clear implications for the ways in which teachers need to orientate to their work (see Robson and Bailey 2009).

Inter-professional collaboration is relatively well established in the health service. Social work has also established a tradition of 'inter-agency' working. Historically teachers have mostly worked as 'lone operators', and the culture of teaching is often premised on the idea of an individual being in sole charge of a class. It was not until the 1980s that FE teachers began to systematically 'design and deliver' the curriculum in more collaborative ways, with teams from different specialisms working in a more problem-based approach to learning. Effective inter-professionality presents challenges to institutional structures and to human resource management, but perhaps more profound are the ways in which it requires teachers to think differently about how they design, organize and implement learning cooperatively with others in supporting learners. In practical terms this involves active networking, interdepartmental planning and a spirit of inclusivity that reaches beyond traditional boundaries. It is fair to say that in many cases institutional mechanisms do not always currently facilitate such ways of working, and this is sometimes true of individual attitudes and departmental cultures. In some respects, the vision set out by Young et al. (1995) remains an aspiration, but it is one which is even more crucial now than it was at the time. Professional identities are never static, and are constantly negotiated in the context of changing technologies and relations to associated forms of labour.

Research and scholarship

Research is almost universally held in high esteem regardless of the educational sector in which it is conducted. However, the way in which research and scholarship are marshalled can reflect diametrically opposed political positions, holding divergent understandings of society and education. At its most basic level scholarship can refer to the necessity to keep up to date with one's discipline and in the case of practitioners, to acquire recent and relevant experience. Similarly, research can be construed as important in keeping the practitioner up to date with pedagogic research that can be drawn upon to inform practice. It may also point towards the importance of engaging in action research as a reflective practitioner. All of these practices sit quite comfortably with the State's interest in using research to improve educational practice and to validate evidence informed practice (Avis 2003b, 2009a).

For some time now the State has sought to promote educational research that can be used to enhance practice. The thrust of policy, however, has been to validate particular types of educational research, namely that which addresses questions of teaching and learning and that actively contribute towards the enhancement of practice. Michael Gove, the current secretary of state for education, is adamant that educational research should address this brief rather than be subject to the 'whims of ideologues' and their 'pet passions'. Such a stance technicizes research and restricts its range with resulting negative consequences.

Government policy is concerned with the production of 'useful knowledge'. As a result of the critiques of writers such as Tooley and Darby (1998), and Gorard (2001), who have questioned the validity of much qualitative educational research, there is a tendency to fall back on traditional and common-sense models that resonate with forms of positivism. Hodkinson (2004) argued that 'a new orthodoxy' validated improvement orientated research located within a spurious 'scientificity'. There is a struggle over the nature of educational research and the type of contribution it makes to society. For writers such as Pring (2000), education is an applied discipline that directly addresses pedagogic and educational questions. This means that research engaging theoretical questions that have no immediate practical implications is seen as something other than educational, being possibly socio-logical or psychological. The difficulty rests with where this particular division is drawn, and how narrowly or broadly we think about research and practice.

The interest in systematic review and 'scientifically' orientated research derives from its supposed capacity to generate findings that can be disseminated to practitioners to improve classroom practice (EPPI 2001; Evans and Benefield 2001). For some, the goal is to produce a 'crib sheet' which specifies the findings of research, the conditions in which these are operable, and the exceptions and alternative strategies that may be deployed (Davies 2000). Resting within this aspiration is the suggestion that universal solutions are possible. However, Hodkinson and James (2003) have shown that what constitutes effective learning and teaching is situationally located and cannot be straightforwardly associated with universalized models of good practice. This argument raises questions about the use of observational check lists to measure effective teaching, and calls for a nuanced approach when making judgements about learning and teaching.

Much of the ethnographic research that has examined learner experiences in further education has related these to the cultural capital and habitus that students carry into the classroom (Hodkinson and James 2003). Learners hold particular forms of cultural capital that may articulate with the educational processes encountered. Similarly their habitus will inform the dispositions carried into the classroom and will influence responses to pedagogy. A significant current in LLS and HE research is concerned with widening participation. Some of this work explores learner experience and suggests ways in which classroom encounters could be rendered relevant and accessible for such learners. Furedi (2003), Ecclestone (2004) and Hayes (Ecclestone and Hayes 2009) argue that such practices can easily slide into a form of 'therapy culture' that encourages learners to feel good about themselves rather than developing educationally.

Within educational research we find a number of ambivalent and cross-cutting currents. For example, one strand of action research may operate with a restricted understanding of pedagogic practice yet empower the practitioner; this may in turn contrast with models of action research rooted in either a positivist paradigm or in Habermassian critical theory. To conclude we consider two key issues: first, how broadly or narrowly can we view the remit of educational research and, second, its politics – is it necessarily a political practice? What goes on in the classroom, college or training organization cannot be fully understood without setting it in its wider societal context. This is particularly the case if we believe that education should hold a commitment to social justice. Such a stance validates research that seeks to relate educational relations to wider society. This position would also suggest that we cannot escape the politics of educational research – research is inevitably a political practice. Lest we are accused of naivety and of promulgating an overly simplistic argument, it is important to recognize the significance of contingency, contradiction and a general 'messiness'. While any research practice will necessarily contain a politics, its exact form will not necessarily derive from the way in which such work represents itself. The politics of research are subject to analysis and deconstruction by others.

Conclusion

We have addressed a number of issues surrounding professionalism in the LLS. The term professionalism is inherently contradictory, pointing as it does in both progressive and conservative directions. Consequently, it is a site of contestation as are the values attributable to it. Notions of professionalism may be more or less expansive, as well as dialogic. Frequently the language of professionalism has been turned back on itself being aligned with managerialism, performativity and targets. Necessarily, there is a struggle over what it is to be a professional, one which is entwined with the politics of social justice.

5

Theorizing the work-based learning of teachers

James Avis, Kevin Orr and Jonathan Tummons

In this chapter

- Theories of work-based learning
- Socially situated practice
- Bourdieu's field and habitus
- Communities of practice and WBL
- Communities of practice in FE
- Conclusion

Theories of work-based learning

Many writers have drawn upon notions of occupational socialization or entry into communities of practice (Avis et al. 2002a) but much of the analysis stops short of a full engagement with processes of learning in the workplace. This chapter seeks to critically engage with the theorization of work-based learning (WBL) and its progressive possibilities.

WBL has been central to policy since the election of New Labour in 1997 and constitutes a substantial proportion of vocational education and training (VET). It remains an element of policy with respect to the re-balancing of the economy away from financial services towards manufacturing. Teachers in lifelong learning may be involved in WBL with their students on placements, or on day-release courses, or in workplaces. WBL is also an important element of ITT and is an integral part of the FE curriculum.

Socially situated practice

Avis and Bathmaker have considered the experience of trainee FE teachers on 'teaching practice' and how this shaped their professional identity (Bathmaker and Avis 2005) and attitudes towards pedagogy (Avis et al. 2002b; Avis and Bathmaker 2004). They highlight the importance of trainee biographies and while finding evidence of commitment to teaching, there was little real integration with teachers at placements. One trainee commented, 'Sometimes I feel like I am sneaking around' (Bathmaker and Avis 2005: 54–5). Like Wallace (2002a), the studies found discrepancies between the expectations of trainees and their experience of placements. A sense of purpose and social justice had attracted a number of these trainees to teaching, which on occasion was at odds with teaching experience and the attitudes of college staff (Avis and Bathmaker 2006). Avis et al. (2002b: 187) quote one trainee, 'I think that they [existing teachers] forget that at the end of the day, these students are human beings.'

The work of Avis and Bathmaker, and of Wallace, suggests that trainees' prior experience is fundamental to understanding how FE teachers develop as well as their engagement with WBL more generally. Colley and James (2005: 11) suggest, 'There is certainly no such thing as "FE tutor" separate from the complex, wider lives that [teachers in FE] have lived and are living'. The marginalization of trainees is a recurring feature of research addressing pre-service trainees in FE and informs what is absorbed through their placement, influencing the way they cope and develop.

The definition of 'work-based learning' is disputed. Learning related to work has been divided into three elements: learning about work, or how organizations operate; learning for work, or developing skills appropriate for work; and learning through work, or using the workplace as the context for learning (Huddleston and Oh 2004: 85). We concentrate on the latter here, though to define WBL as learning that takes place in the workplace alone may be to over-simplify (see Avis and Orr 2014; Hodkinson 2009).

Conceptually, this dichotomy between college- and work-based learning can be misleading. This is especially the case where formal classes and college placements form part of the course in a blurring between on- and off-the-job learning. As Hodkinson (2005: 524) notes: 'Workplaces and educational institutions merely represent different instances of social practices in which learning occurs through participation . . . to distinguish between the two . . . [so that] one is formalised and the other informal . . . is not helpful'.

Such an approach considers learning as a process that is situated within a particular social setting, and any knowledge derived is contingent upon that. It emphasizes learning as a process of *becoming* through participation in the social practices of a group or culture. This means that 'learning a subject is now conceived as a process of becoming a member of a certain community. This entails, above all, the ability to communicate in the language of this community and act according to its particular norms' (Sfard 1998: 6).

This emphasis on participation can be useful in understanding WBL where the customs, habits and even language used by particular vocational groups are never formally taught, but are acquired by newcomers alongside established workers. This approach considers what is learnt to be situated and not transferable. However, it may also ignore the transferable knowledge and skills trainees acquire in the workplace. Arguably, some of these transferable skills, such as the use of a keyboard, may not be strictly situated nor related to a sense of 'becoming'.

Aspects of formal learning exist in the workplace as well as in educational institutions. The notion of informal learning is frequently applied to WBL; however, Billett (2002a: 457) challenges this: 'Workplace experiences are not informal. They are the product of the historical-cultural practices and situational factors that constitute the particular work practice, which in turn distributes opportunities for participation to individuals or cohorts of individuals.' For Billett a significant consideration in WBL is the opportunity (or lack of) for participation in the workplace, and the bearing this has on learning. In his investigations of learning at work Billett (2001: 209) found 'learners afforded the richest opportunities for participation reported the strongest development, and that workplace readiness was central to the quality of experiences'.

The key contributors to successful learning for the trainee were 'engagement in everyday tasks'; 'direct or close guidance of co-workers' and 'indirect guidance provided by the workplace itself and others in the workplace'. Billett (2002b: 30) argues that, 'the negotiation with and resolution of these (even if it is partial) has cognitive consequences as these activities transform individuals' knowledge'. For Billett, the workplace is understood as being defined by rule-bound structures that are only informal in so far as these rules are unwritten. These socially constructed structures pre-date any training placement and their form determines what the trainees are able to do. Billett (2002b: 36) writes that, 'Contingent workers', among whom we would include trainee teachers, 'are particularly susceptible to securing only limited workplace affordances'. Indeed, those structures can be formed to prevent the full participation of 'in-comers' and just how formal these unspoken structures are becomes clear when people threaten or go beyond them. It is important to acknowledge that knowledge is developed through socially situated practices in a particular location, and is re-contextualized when drawn upon in different sites. We could think about such re-contextualization when trainees draw upon learning that has arisen in educational contexts and apply it to workplace practices and vice versa (Hodkinson and Hodkinson 2005). In addition, the workplace as well as the training and education encountered may be expansive and/or restrictive. Hodkinson (2009) has drawn upon Fuller and Unwin's (2004) continuum of expansive-restrictive workplace learning environments applying this to teachers' labour. This encourages us to interrogate workplaces and educational provision for the affordances these offer for learning (see Evans et al. 2006).

Similarly, Beckett and Hager (2000: 300) ask, 'What do practitioners actually do at work from which they learn?' In seeking to examine what is learnt in workplaces they eschew the frequently used notion of 'tacit knowledge' (see Eraut 2000): 'In attempting to de-mystify such knowledge, the danger is that ascription of "tacitness" re-mystifies it' (Beckett and Hager 2000: 302).

More generally, their questioning of assumptions about the purpose of WBL helps to '"get beneath the surface of experience", rather than merely report it' (Beckett and Hager 2000: 303). A trainee teacher learning to navigate the social constructs of the workplace, that is learning to 'fit in', is not necessarily learning to teach well but rather to accommodate to work-based cultures. More fundamentally, Young (2003: 555) questions the value of experiential learning, 'because the world is not as we experience it, curriculum knowledge must be discontinuous, not continuous with everyday experience'.

If we only learn what we experience, we may learn little. Nevertheless, learning of one kind or another occurs in the workplace. For example, Gleeson and Shain (1999: 482) define as *strategic compliance*: 'innovative strategies for dealing with the pressures of income generation, flexibilization and work intensification while at the same time, continuing their [the FE teachers'] commitments to educational values of student care, support and collegiality'. In other words, teachers can learn how to comply with what is necessary, even if they do not value it, in order to carve out space for what they consider important. Whatever happens in the workplace, Wenger (1998: 8) suggests, 'Learning is something we can assume – whether we see it or not, whether we like the way it goes or not, whether what we are learning is to repeat the past or shake it off. Even failing to learn usually involves learning something else instead.'

What trainees learn from participation in the workplace has much to do with their biography and predispositions, which is another area of contention and dispute. How much agency do people have within a situation they have not created? How much does the situation form the individual? Questioning the relationship between person and environment echoes Marx's contention that human beings make their own history, but not in circumstances of their own choosing (Marx 1968). This relationship is at the heart of much of the discussion of WBL (see Avis 2010).

Bourdieu's field and habitus

Below we consider Bourdieu's work, followed by a discussion of Lave and Wenger's notion of communities of practice.

The Transforming Learning Cultures (TLC) research project investigated student learning in FE over a period of three years and at a variety of learning sites (James and Biesta 2007). It sought to identify what enabled successful learning so that such conditions could be encouraged and enhanced. The TLC researchers used Bourdieu's concepts of *field* and *habitus* to explain the transformations involved in learning. They describe 'learning as becoming' (Colley et al. 2003: 471) and use the term 'learning culture' (James and Biesta 2007: 4) to express the interplay between an individual student and the college environment.

Bourdieu's concepts illuminate how this dynamic process of learning, enculturation and mutual influence occurs through a series of relationships. His central concern is to overcome the dichotomy between a subjectivist emphasis on individual consciousness and an objectivist emphasis on social structures by explaining how the two are interconnected (Jenkins 1992: 66).

Bourdieu describes a person's set of dispositions and behaviour as their *habitus*. This is 'a product of the incorporation of objective necessity'; it is like having a 'feel for the game' (1990: 11). What constitutes that objective necessity or the game itself is the *field* within which a person lives and operates. Jenkins (1992: 85) defines Bourdieu's term *field* as 'the crucial mediating context between where external factors are brought to bear on individual and institutional practice'. It is the contested area where social forces interplay and struggle over resources such as capital or prestige.

Bourdieu describes how people adapt to structures and relationships, internalizing rules which they may be unaware of and which may never have been formally constituted. At an almost palpable level, in a college with no dress code, staff in one staffroom may wear suits, while those in another wear jeans. '*Habitus* contributes to constituting the field as a meaningful world, a world endowed with sense and with value, in it which is worth investing one's energy' (Wacquant 1989: 44). *Habitus* is 'essentially the internalization of the structures of that world' (Bourdieu 1989: 18) and is as much to do with physical composure as with attitude. However, people enter a *field* with their existing *habitus* formed elsewhere, which either helps or hinders their incorporation into the new *field*. This can lead to feeling out of place or unsure of how to deport oneself. The dispositions and behaviour that have status in one vocational area may be regarded as inappropriate elsewhere.

Bourdieu stresses that individuals are not controlled by the *field*, and that they maintain individual agency; indeed, the *field* will itself have emerged through social interaction. The expectations and routines on a construction site today have evolved and changed over time from those prevalent in, say, the 1970s. What exists today will feel normal to today's construction workers. Bourdieu explains how the social practices involved in any situation have an objective reality (conditions of work on building sites have altered) and a subjective reality (current conditions feel normal to those who work on today's building sites).

Applying these concepts to WBL acknowledges the dynamism of the relationship between the individual and the situation with its complexity and contingency. Bourdieu, in Wacquant (1989: 40), sets out how the *field* can be analysed. First, the *field* must be considered in relation to the external *field* of power. The divisions between academic and vocational education may be pertinent, or the relationship of a group in a company to senior management. Second, the objective structure of the relations between the individuals (or agents) competing for authority within the *field* must be described and, third, the specific *habitus* of the individual needs to be analysed.

> What must be emphasized is . . . that the external determinations that bear on agents situated in a given field (intellectuals, artists politicians, or construction companies), never apply on them directly, but only through the specific mediation of the specific forms and forces of the field . . .
>
> (Bourdieu, in Wacquant 1989: 41)

This describes a subtle, contingent process of influence that can only be understood within a specific situation. People learn to improvise according to what is around them and in so doing internalize, or learn, attitudes and behaviour. Such a conceptualization understands learning as a socially situated process that reflects the immediate situation as well as broader society.

Within a large FE college several fields will interact: the wider culture of the college and the vocational fields of departments or sections. This may be viewed, or heard, in contrasting registers of language: managers may use terms from business (audit, benchmarking, performance indicators) while teachers in a staffroom may use the language of their vocational area, or that of pedagogy. All of these *fields* sit within or alongside that of FE nationally, with its policy initiatives and hierarchies.

Bourdieu uses the terms 'cultural' and 'social capital' to describe how the knowledge and experience that people assimilate, as well as their social networks, have differing currency according to the values and mores of those around them. For example, an education system that applies the same criteria to all students may seem to be fair. However, when those criteria reflect middle-class behaviour (for example linguistic expression) and values, working-class students are disadvantaged. Their *habitus* holds different, less esteemed cultural and social capital, which also helps explain the low status of vocational education.

Bourdieu's conceptualization is valuable in analysing WBL, helping us to understand changes that take place in an individual, for example from the commencement of work to becoming established in the *field*. Moreover, it explains how conflict can arise from the relative positions of individuals in relation to the *field* according to the distribution of power. Above all, Bourdieu's approach suggests how participation within a culture shapes individual disposition and physical behaviour in relation to their situation and the *field*. Thus a person gets 'a feel for a situation' which seemingly results from rational consideration, yet it is based upon an unstated, usually unnoticed, incorporation of culture which is simultaneously shaped through individual participation.

Communities of practice and WBL

Communities of practice, as a way of thinking about what learning is and how it happens, have been interpreted differently. Indeed, Wenger has modified his conceptualization in significant ways. At the same time, other writers have drawn on complementary theories to enhance or expand the community of practice framework (Barton and Tusting 2005). In this section, the focus is on learning within the community of practice itself. We draw on the original work of Lave and Wenger (1991) and Wenger (1998), as distinct from later work that loses sight of the central role of learning within a community of practice and focuses on organizational membership and identity.

Learning is a process that takes place almost continuously, in all kinds of places and does not necessarily involve teachers. Frequently, people are shown how to do things by friends or colleagues, or work out how to do things by reading, or they experiment to see how something operates, based on experiences of a similar item. Formal educational settings, homes and workplaces are all sites of learning, and the process of learning is similar even though what is being learned will vary considerably.

What does 'learning' mean in this sense? Put simply, learning is an inevitable consequence of participation within a community of practice, which is a way of describing a collection of people engaged in any number of similar or less similar activities. Communities of practice are found in places of work and places of leisure. They might be small and local, such as a community of railway enthusiasts, or large, distributed across geographic distance, such as a community of online gamers. Groups of communities, known as constellations, might exist within large and complex organizations such as insurance offices or FE colleges. Communities can be formal, such as those found in the workplace, or informal, such as those of hobbyists. Membership of any community of practice entails learning of some kind as a consequence of that engagement. Such learning may be more or less profound, or difficult, and may be more of less transferable to other contexts.

Through participating in communities of practice, members learn how it works and communicates. Members learn about the history of the community, and how it goes about doing what it does. They learn how to engage and contribute to the practices of the community and, perhaps, how to change them. They also learn how to use the resources, tools and artefacts the community has built over time. Such engagement in the practices of a community has learning as an integral component, and is described as *legitimate peripheral participation*. A member of a community is a participant, who is engaged in legitimate, authentic and meaningful participation (actually doing the work of the community, not simply being told about it or reading about it or observing it). The new participant is in a peripheral position, and moves to fuller participation as he or she learns, through participating, more about the practice of the community.

Any community of practice, irrespective of scale, consists of three fundamental aspects. For Wenger (1998) these involve:

1   *Mutual engagement* In any community of practice people work together, in complementary and overlapping ways, at some kind of activity or activities.
2   *Joint enterprise* The work of the community is shared but need not be uniform. Participants will negotiate their understanding of the enterprise and its effect on their lives.
3   *Shared repertoire* Within a community, participants work with a shared repertoire of tools, artefacts, and ways of talking, writing and behaving.

Communities of practice in FE

In the following we focus on communities of practice in FE, however, the processes described are more widely applicable. An FE college is too large and complex to be considered a single community of practice. Rather, it consists of multiple communities arranged in a constellation, each with their own way of doing things, their own shared stories and meanings. These communities might be situated within staffrooms, workshops or classrooms. Some participants are experts and others are apprentices, while some are members of more than one community. For the trainee teacher, a staffroom or department will be a community of practice. A workshop or classroom will be another. Other communities of practice within an FE college, relating perhaps to senior management or the estates department, would not be participated in although a trainee teacher might come into contact with them. Clearly, these communities work in different ways.

A community of practice within a staffroom rests on a different kind of mutual engagement than one within a workshop or classroom. Indeed, any talk of formal educational structures is at odds with the notion of communities of practice as originally envisaged by Lave and Wenger (1991), who rejected the concept of pedagogy or formal instruction as being incompatible with a social model of learning. In later work, however, Wenger (1998) proposed the idea that an *architecture* could be created that might provide the opportunity for more formalized learning within a community. Such an architecture might include the right resources or the right people, for example, but he stresses that there will always be uncertainties between designing a learning architecture and how it will work on implementation. Drawing on this concept, a community of practice within a formal learning and teaching environment can be seen as resting on a learning architecture made up of the syllabus, the physical environment of the college workshop or classroom, the books and handouts, the equipment, and the teachers.

The staffroom

What might be termed 'the community' of the staffroom rests on engagement within an institutional architecture. A trainee teacher or new member of staff will learn about the workplace through taking part in the joint enterprise of the work that is being done and talked about: planning lessons, admissions procedures, discovering how to get photocopying done, strategies for learners late to class, obtaining passwords for the IT systems and so on. This process will be facilitated to some degree by more established members of the staffroom community. It is also a process that can be limited by the trainee teachers themselves, who may choose to engage in these practices at more or less profound levels, or to focus on some activities in preference to others. Fundamentally, however, the learning that takes place rests on trainee participation in the community. At first this is a peripheral process, but over time the trainee becomes more fluent and confident in using the shared repertoire of the community (the forms and the procedures as well as the 'in-jokes'). That is, the trainee becomes a fuller participant in the community. However, it is important to note that for a trainee on a teaching placement, this learning journey (or *trajectory*) will only be peripheral. The trainee is a temporary member of the community, and after the placement, will leave. It may only be a short time before they get a job in another college. The process of learning will have to begin again to some extent as no community of practice is the same, although some are related. The newly-qualified teacher's new staffroom may have familiar features, but many aspects of their engagement, enterprise and repertoire will be different and will need to be *negotiated* afresh.

The workshop or classroom

A classroom of basic skills students, a workshop of trainee mechanics or a classroom of trainee teachers is also a community of practice, albeit very differently constituted to the staffrooms previously discussed (Tummons 2008). Members engage in the community in a number of ways: the regular meetings of the class; the shared workload of class and assignment preparation; perhaps the use of a virtual learning environment (VLE). The efforts of the students and teachers are focused on a quite specific joint enterprise: successful negotiation of the course or programme of study, leading to the award of a certificate or other form of achievement. As the teachers and students work, they draw on a shared repertoire of artefacts: worksheets; course handbooks; PowerPoint presentations; tools; textbooks; websites; individual learning plans; and so on.

These are not communities of practice that have emerged solely as a response to localized conditions, needs or wants. Beyond the sector as a whole, a range of both political and professional interests have combined to create a need for these courses, which arrive at the college more or less fully formed. Teachers and students work with handbooks that are generated by the awarding body. Assessment activities are detailed within such documents. These materials and procedures can be seen as the conceptual architecture (Wenger 1998: 230), a collection of things that can encourage the development of a community of practice, encompassing the joint enterprise, mutual engagement and shared repertoire of the community.

For the teacher, membership of such communities can be seen as providing opportunities for participation, and hence for learning, in two distinct ways. First, teaching a course allows the teacher to learn about being a teacher in that specific college. Some of this learning will be transferable to other contexts, other communities. Second, the teacher will learn more about that specific community of practice, as indeed will the students through their engagement, though in the latter case this will be accented differently. In this sense, the learning journeys or trajectories of students are different from those of teachers. For example, on a plumbing course, the students are learning to become plumbers within a community of practice of apprentices. Eventually they will go into the world of work as qualified plumbers – encountering and becoming full participants in workplace communities of practice. These workplace communities will share some of the engagement, enterprise and repertoire of the 'trainee community'. The more successfully the plumbing course 'authentically' reflects the world of work, the more successful the transfer of learning will be. However, in the trainee community the role of the teacher is to facilitate the students' engagement with the practice and repertoire of the community.

There is one crucial difference between the community of the real world of work and that of the college course: pedagogy. A college course is a formal learning environment involving teaching and assessment. Assessment and the preparation for it, as aspects of pedagogic activity, do not sit comfortably within the community of practice model as initially posited by Lave and Wenger, who argue: 'in a community of practice, there are no special forms of discourse aimed at apprentices or crucial to their centripetal movement toward full participation that correspond to ... the lecturing of college professors' (1991: 108). However, by drawing on some of the key concepts of community construction proposed by Wenger (1998), it is possible to explain how assessment might fit into an educational community of practice situated in a formal learning environment.

Assessment demonstrates the students' fuller competence and experience in the practice of the community (Wenger 1998: 216). It can be seen as a signpost or a marker that students can successfully negotiate and travel along their learning trajectory. For some students, however, learning how to pass an assignment – about how to be a successful student for the purposes of accreditation – is all that they wish to do. It is the 'piece of paper', the end qualification, that counts. For other students, assessment can be a way of learning about the practice of the community and other communities the student is in or likely to join. This learning moves beyond the instrumental, as participation in the trainee community impacts on their identity so that they carry this learning with them as they travel through the community and into other communities of practice in their chosen work.

For some students, assessment is part of learning, whereas for others it is a mechanistic, instrumental process to be completed and shelved. As Lave and Wenger point out, there is a contrast between learning to know and learning to display knowledge for evaluation (1991: 112). If assessment is a reified form of activity within the community of practice, then it embodies the 'double edge of reification' (Wenger 1998: 62).

That is to say, it can (but need not necessarily) be reduced to a procedure, and the meanings and purposes of the procedure might be lost sight of. So where does the learning happen? Wenger (1998) draws a distinction between newcomers to a community and those who have been members for a longer time and have a greater expertise. Newcomers can learn from the longer standing members and from each other. What is important is that learning is happening in an authentic community of practice with learning through participation.

Conclusion

This chapter has drawn upon conceptual resources that can be used to explore WBL generally, and more particularly that of trainee teachers in the LLS. We have commented upon learning as a socially situated and participatory process, but set this within a wider context by drawing upon Bourdieu's notion of *field* and *habitus*. While the *field* is socially constituted it provides the context in which agency is enacted and is indicative of Bourdieu's attempt to go beyond the dichotomy of agency and structure. We drew on Lave and Wenger to explore the notion of community of practice, seeking to emphasize aspects of learning within such communities and addressing the relationship between college- and work-based processes.

We have pointed to a number of implicit tensions and have focused upon processes of 'becoming' a teacher through participating in a community of practice. This focus on 'becoming' neglects the participatory and learning processes involved when the reverse occurs – when a member of a community of practice moves from a position of centrality to the periphery and exits that particular community. Colley et al. (2007) have described this as a process of 'unbecoming'. It is important to acknowledge that this process of 'unbecoming' a teacher is as much a participatory process as becoming one, and that conceptualizations of *habitus, field* and communities of practices can help us to make sense of this (Colley et al. 2007).

We have acknowledged the constraints that frame socially situated practice and referred to the relationship between WBL and wider curriculum and assessment contexts. The tensions and contradictions surrounding work-based practices and the *habitus* of trainees, as well as their responses to the communities of practices they inhabit, first as trainees and then as practitioners, provide the context in which they can assert agency. It is important to recognize this, for otherwise analysis can present a model of unreflexive socialization into the teaching role, denying agency and change.

6

Equality and diversity

*Lyn Ashmore, James Avis, Julie Dalton,
Penny Noel, Sandra Rennie, Emma Salter,
Dave Swindells and Paul Thomas*

In this chapter

- Equality and diversity in lifelong learning
- Faith and religion
- Anti-racism
- Anti-sexism
- Lesbian, gay, bisexual and transgender issues
- Mental health
- Equal opportunity in practice
- Social class
- Conclusion

Equality and diversity are contestable concepts and can be interpreted in different and sometimes contradictory ways. In particular, the notion of equality is complex; one way to illustrate this is to consider equality of opportunity. Do we offer equality if we provide equal access to a differentiated education system that is selective on the basis of ability or interest? How are notions of ability and interest understood? Can they be treated separately from social and cultural background? Do they by default serve to reproduce inequality? One of the difficulties with equality of access is that it ignores such questions. This has partly been addressed by concerns with equality of outcome, which examines *what actually happens to people* in relation to categories such as class, race or ethnicity, gender and disability. The outcomes of particular categories are compared and if there are significant differences these suggest the presence of inequality. Often the comparison is with the white male middle class and can be used to point to discriminatory educational practices. Paradoxically, however, this category becomes the 'norm' against which others are compared, and the 'others' who 'underachieve' can implicitly be construed as in some ways inadequate. A possible response is to recognize and value diversity in relation to race/ethnicity, class, gender, sexuality, religion, age, disability and so on. Diversity becomes an all-embracing concept that nevertheless seeks to acknowledge and value difference and otherness, and calls upon us to consider the interrelationships between these categories. Such analyses are reflected in the concern to increase access and widen the participation of disadvantaged groups in FE and HE.

In the context of lifelong learning, valuing diversity means creating a learning and workplace environment that includes and respects difference and otherness. It means recognizing the unique contributions individuals can make. By nurturing, embracing and valuing diversity institutions can create an environment that maximizes the potential of all. But is this possible?

Equality and diversity in lifelong learning

'How diverse is the LLS?' This is a difficult question with only a partial answer. Although legislation requires public authorities to monitor race, gender and disability, there is no shared understanding in the sector about the importance or scope of diversity. In their assessment of barriers to increasing the diversity of the LLS workforce, Cummins et al. (2006: 10) found that 'independent providers often lack a basic understanding or any empathy with the issue of workforce diversity'. In addition, there are significant difficulties in collecting reliable data.

The concept of 'diversity' is complex and involves multiple understandings. For instance, Lumby et al. (2005: 71) found: 'The starting point is to use the term diversity to describe different "kinds" of people working or studying in the organisation. Most often it is used to designate "others" as different from themselves. Thus the term is frequently used to categorise individuals in terms of visible difference.' Discussing workforce diversity, Kandola and Fullerton (1998: 8) use an inclusive definition recognizing both 'visible and non-visible differences'. If we accept this, the question arises: which differences should be used to measure diversity? Inherent difficulties with a singular approach are suggested by Grayling (2007):

> a person is not one thing (a Muslim or a Jew only, or an Arab or an American only) but many: a parent, a mathematician, a tennis player, a Bangladeshi, a man, a feminist, a Muslim – all these things at once, and thus a multiple and overlapping complex being, whom the politics of singular identity reduces to a mere cipher and crams into a small box with a single simple label stuck on it.

Furthermore, there may be a discrepancy between self and institutional definitions of that individual as a member of a particular category (Rennie 2006). However, in relation to discrimination and inequality, not all aspects of identity carry the same import. Differing aspects of identity are highlighted within the equality and diversity policies of LLS providers. These may include; age, gender, ethnicity, race, disability, national origin, religion and belief, marital status, sexual orientation, transgender status, social class and political opinion. The focus upon certain aspects of identity involves value judgements. Embedded within the rhetoric of diversity policy are judgements about which categories should be represented proportionately. Ironically, such values will not necessarily be shared across categories. A survey undertaken for the Cabinet Office *Equalities Review* into prejudice in Britain explored how far this is rooted in relationships between specific social groups, finding 'prejudices do correspond to intergroup differences of interest or perspective' (Abrams and Houston 2006: 56).

Within the LLS a number of identity categories are monitored, often as a legal requirement, and much of the resulting data, although incomplete, is updated annually and publicly available. However, for many of the aspects of identity highlighted above there is little or no comprehensive data, and many people may not identify with the category with which they are labelled. Those who do may be uneasy about providing information, particularly if they feel prejudice exists. Awareness of this was made explicit in guidance issued by the Equality Challenge Unit:

> While general best practice suggests that staff and potential staff should be moni-
> tored on the grounds of sexual orientation, experience has proven that staff . . .
> have been reluctant to declare their orientation because they are not convinced
> that the information will be kept confidential or that it is relevant. There is also
> suspicion that any declaration will result in prejudice or will not be used in a
> constructive way.
>
> (ECU 2004: 36)

While the purpose of monitoring is to ensure the elimination of discrimination is measured and appropriate action implemented, this process is not unproblematic and diversity profiles are incomplete.

Diversity, equality and learners in the LLS

Minority ethnic young people are more likely to stay on in full-time education, and are more likely than white learners to enter FE or sixth-form college, rather than remaining in school (Connor et al. 2004). The Youth Cohort Study (2009: 18) found that

> male respondents were more likely to be attending FE institutions than female
> respondents (24% compared to 20%), as were young people from the Black African
> or Black Caribbean ethnic groups (39% and 36% respectively) when compared
> with other ethnic backgrounds . . . these particular ethnic groups tended to attain
> Level 3 later than other groups. Young people with parents from intermediate and
> lower occupational backgrounds and parents educated to below degree level
> were more likely to be in FE.

Minority ethnic young people are under-represented in apprenticeships and are less likely to gain employment on completion. Grindrod and Murray (2011) suggest that in relation to gender, ethnicity and disability there remain significant disparities. They write:

> Gender segregation remains a huge problem with only 3% of engineering appren-
> tices accounted for by female participants compared to 92% of hairdressing
> apprentices . . . Black and minority ethnic (BME) communities also face huge
> barriers. For example, while 18- to 24-year-olds from BME communities account
> for 14% of this age group in the overall population, they account for less than

8% of apprenticeship places . . . Disabled people face similar barriers, with trends suggesting a worsening of the situation. Access to apprenticeships for people declaring a learning difficulty and/or disability has fallen from 11.5% in 2005/06 to 8.2% in 2010/11.

(Grindrod and Murray 2011: 79–80)

Notably, Grindrod and Murray (2011) draw our attention to the significant differences existing between the apprenticeship system in England and other countries. We could speculate that these arise in part from the peculiarities of the English response to vocational education which has consistently been devalued (Green 1991). Grindrod and Murray (2011: 78) comment,

> Another major difference between apprenticeships in England and other countries, highlighted by Steedman, is that we have a large proportion of individuals engaged in level 2 training (roughly around two-thirds) and it appears that a large proportion of them (around two-thirds) do not progress to a level 3 apprenticeship. It is, therefore, of little surprise that Wolf (2011) noted in her review that ' the young person who follows first a level 2 course in a vocational area, then a level 3 one, and then goes on to a long-term career in that sector is the exception not the rule.'

The Commission for Black Staff in FE, while acknowledging in a 2002 report that 'major progress has been made where learners are concerned' (2002: 8), drew attention to witness concerns:

> Despite the fact that the students are predominantly Asian the syllabus does not reflect this, for example, in music technology, they study mostly European music . . . At one college, there had been 30 exclusions, 26 of whom were Black students. The reasons given were not consistent and appeared to take a stereotypical view of students . . . Muslim staff and parents emphasised the need for a separate common room for girls at the college, as well as for a prayer room for staff and students. Food to meet the specific cultural and religious dietary requirements of our community is still not provided.

(p. 64)

> The tendency to equate the dialect and accent of some Black learners with literacy or English language needs.

(p. 65)

In the first decade of the twenty-first century there was some progress in the sector. Reporting on race equality, Ofsted (2005a) found that 'Nationally, the success rates of groups of Black and minority ethnic (BME) learners of all ages have improved at an above average rate' (p. 1) and note:

> Learners identified as strengths in their colleges friendly and supportive teachers, the safe and secure environment, the respect with which they were treated as

individuals, and the support and opportunities they were provided with. The quality of teaching and learning was also important to them, as was a good atmosphere in the institution. Learners gave very few examples of problems relating to race.

(p. 4)

Ofsted drew attention to the too few colleges 'actively and systematically instigating change to improve race equality at the rate which might be expected' (p. 1).

In the LLS, approximately 56 per cent of adult learners (aged 19+) are female. Similarly, the student gender mix in former ACL provision reflects that of its teachers, with 75 per cent being female. Conversely, WBL and Train to Gain (TTG) have a higher proportion of male learners with only one in fifty apprentices being female. Throughout the sector, subject segregation by gender is pronounced. Apprenticeships in construction, plumbing and the motor industry are overwhelmingly male, whereas more than 90 per cent of hairdressing apprentices are female. The same pattern of subject segregation characterizes both FE (see Table 6.1) and HE (see Youth Cohort Study 2011: 14).

Stereotypical attitudes to subject choice post-16 are well established before school-leaving age. Tomlinson (2004) found that 'the uptake of Year 10 work experience placements is highly gender stereotypical and, instead of broadening pupils' horizons, their perceptions of the adult workplace are frequently being reinforced by work experience practice' (p. 84). The persistence of this segregation does little to reduce the gender pay gap as women continue to be disproportionately represented in low-paid employment.

In 2011–12, over 370,000 adult learners (aged 19+) across the LLS identified themselves as disabled (including students with learning difficulties), representing 11.8 per cent of total adult learner numbers (BIS 2013). As noted earlier, disclosure can create anxiety. Data was unavailable for around 5 per cent of students but the full extent of non-disclosure remains unknown. A review of disabled students in FE and HE in London (Barer 2007) identified little difference between the level of study of disabled

Table 6.1 Learners by gender on LSC-funded FE provision 2006–07

Selected sector subject areas	Women		Men	
	Thousands	%	Thousands	%
Retail and commercial enterprise	118	78	34	22
Health and public services and care	309	77	94	23
Languages, literature and culture	101	66	51.5	32
Business administration and law	113	62	67	38
Science and maths	54	60	36.5	40
ICT	191	56	149	44
Engineering and manufacturing technologies	12	10	119	90
Construction, planning and built environment	5	5	94	95

Source: LSC (2007a)

students and those with learning difficulties, with both studying at a lower level than other students, the implication being that disabled learners underachieve. Clearly, disabled students with academic potential do study at higher levels; however, there are many enrolled only at Level 1. Disabled people have drawn attention to the importance of flexibility in relation to the learning environment, highlighting a number of barriers (GLA 2006). For example, potential learners have expressed concern about the loss of benefits that learning may entail, particularly as disabled people are significantly more likely to face barriers to employment. Lack of access to appropriate support has been identified as another obstacle. Disabled learners have reported 'unhelpful and even hostile staff attitudes' (GLA 2006: 81) and teasing by other students. The lack of consistency experienced by disabled learners is illustrated below:

> I'm going to the college in October and this is only really possible because they are giving me relevant support. This whole experience for me is possible because I will be given a PA, tape recorder, a copy of notes. All the tools to be able to contribute to the course.
>
> (p. 83)

> I was taking a community care course and as soon as they realised I was disabled they took me off the course. They said that I did not have the aptitude to pass ... So I left, I was very upset. I could have done the course, if they'd helped me.
>
> (p. 85)

Notably, the 2014 *Children and Families Act* (DfE and DoH, 2014a) as well as the DfE and DoH's (2014b) *Special Educational Needs (SEN) Code of Practice: for 0 to 25 years* places particular responsibilities on FE and local authorities. The aim is to ensure that young people with LDD and their families have greater choice and control over the services they receive as well as the support they need to realise their goals. For example, a young person will be able to express a preference for a particular college with that institution having to admit them unless it could be shown to be unsuitable for their educational needs. The college would have to ensure that the young person is enrolled on a suitable course and provided with appropriate support.

Whereas HE is concerned with the representation of differing social classes this is less so within LLS, and when class is used it is associated with disadvantage and deprivation. An explanation for this derives from a perception of the LLS as predominantly working class. Thompson (2009), analysing the youth cohort study, found substantial middle-class representation in the sector. While these middle-class participants have tended to be school 'failures' they nevertheless access the more prestigious courses, whereas their working-class counterparts are less likely to attend. In other words, those working-class young people who have had some success at school are likely to attend while those who have failed are less likely to do so. In addition the class structure is mirrored by the sector's tripartitism embedded in its academic, technical and work-readying streams (Gleeson 1983).

The analysis of diversity and equality across the sector is not straightforward. Data is missing or incomplete, and the notion of diversity is elusive. However, the examination of diversity in relation to staff and learners indicates that there is some way to go in achieving proportional representation of diverse communities. Foster (2005) observed that FE 'colleges have a strong commitment to social inclusion and inclusive learning' and that 'they attract a higher proportion of disadvantaged learners than the local population average' (p. 27). He also cautioned that 'Demographic changes and an increase in local diversity will mean that the numbers of learners from under-represented groups is set to increase and colleges will need to adapt to their changing requirements' (p. 27). This is pertinent to all LLS providers. Adaptation must include improvement in staffing to reflect local communities, being better able to identify and respond to differing needs, and therefore more likely to attract and retain under-represented learners.

Faith and religion

Here we discuss why and how teachers and colleges might accommodate the religious needs of students.

What counts as religion?

The word 'religion' refers to prescribed beliefs and customs associated with generally recognized religious faiths. However, identifying the boundaries of legitimate religious observance is not straightforward. This should not fall to individual teachers, but be part of an institutional policy that ensures students and staff are not disadvantaged because of their religious beliefs. It is each teacher's responsibility to be aware of policy so that all students are treated fairly.

Why accommodate students' religious observances?

In 2004, France reinforced its secular position by banning religious symbolism in public arenas. Muslim girls were not allowed to wear the hijab [headscarf] to school. Opinions within and without the Muslim community vacillated between support for the legislation and its claim to foster citizenship, and repugnance at the ban which was perceived as racist and an infringement of human rights. In the UK, although a number of similar cases relating to religious dress in schools have resulted in court proceedings, secular liberalism is espoused rather than the secular conservatism of the French. In theory at least, we foster citizenship through inclusion by 'celebrating diversity'. In practical terms, institutional commitment to secular liberalism means enabling students to express their religious identity as far as it is reasonable without compromising other students' learning.

Educational institutions have a political incentive and, arguably, a moral duty to support students in their religious observances. There are also legal obligations. Admissions policies for FE are regulated by the Equality Act 2010 which makes it illegal to discriminate against an employee (or applicant) because of their religion or belief, or lack thereof. The University and College Union provides clear information about the Equality Act on its website (http://www.ucu.org.uk).

Religious literacy in the classroom

Here the 'classroom' is used to refer to any teaching environment. Teachers have a professional obligation to treat students fairly and equally, and to enhance the learning of all. In terms of religious literacy, this means being aware of how students' religious affiliation may affect their learning so that schemes of work can be planned accordingly. Teachers are not required to become experts in world religions, but some awareness and forward planning is good practice. The BBC Religion and Ethics website (http://www.bbc.co.uk/religion/) provides an overview. Other sources of information include *Faith Guides for Higher Education* (Blunt, series editor) and the Multifaith Centre at the University of Derby (http://www.multifaithcentre.org). Although religious literacy may be desirable for teachers, discretion is advisable. Hypersensitivity towards religious backgrounds could accentuate difference and hinder learning. It is important to avoid stereotyping; all religions have internal diversity and those who subscribe to a religion may have varying levels of observance.

A primary consideration for the teacher is planning schemes of work. The Western calendar is tailored around the main Christian festivals of Easter and Christmas; consequently those of non-Christian students often fall during term time. Significant events such as field trips, visiting speakers or examinations should not be scheduled when students may be absent due to religious observance. This may require forward planning if the class includes a range of religions. It can be useful to highlight those of relevance. Schemes of work are easier to manage where the student body is predominantly or exclusively of the same faith, for example, if a college population is largely Muslim it may choose to suspend formal teaching during Eid and provide students with independent study tasks. Or in the case of a Jewish student who cannot attend Friday afternoon classes during winter months because they must be home before sunset to observe the Sabbath, the obvious solution would be to re-timetable the class.

Another consideration is the types of activity students feel comfortable with. Physical contact between females and males such as induction 'ice-breakers' are best avoided. Some females may follow dress codes and prefer to wear an adapted PE kit, covering arms and legs. Some Muslim students may not want to draw images of people or animals, while Buddhist, Hindu and Jain students may not want to participate in animal dissection or handle meat products. The cow is sacred in Hinduism, which means devout Hindus may prefer not to handle leather goods. Jains and some Buddhists also avoid leather. Jewish and Muslim students may wish to avoid products derived from pigs. Christian, Jewish and Muslim students may be offended by blasphemy, however casually expressed. Rephrasing the exclamation, 'God!' to 'Goodness!' or something similar may avoid causing offence. Student behaviour may also be affected by particular religious observances, for example, during Ramadan Muslims refrain from eating and drinking during daylight hours, which could affect concentration.

Religious literacy in the whole college

Institutional resources may govern the extent to which religious needs can be met. Nevertheless, accommodating religious observances within reasonable limits should form part of an equality and diversity policy, and reflect the needs of its student population. It is important to recognize the difference between direct and indirect discrimination. Direct discrimination is where someone is openly disadvantaged; indirect discrimination is where an individual is disadvantaged due to official or unofficial institutional policy. This can be less apparent, particularly when the individual teacher, or college as a whole, is unaware of a student's religious observances. Offering the Jewish student no alternative to their Friday afternoon classes could be classified as indirect discrimination because the student's learning will be disadvantaged through missed lessons. Organizing timetables to accommodate religious observances would be a good example of implementing secular liberalism.

There are a variety of ways to support religious diversity. These include providing access to appropriate pastoral and chaplaincy services, as well as careers and progression advice that is culturally sensitive and relevant. Library resources could include journals, newspapers and websites that reflect students' cultural and religious backgrounds. Most colleges provide canteen facilities. While the feasibility of providing Kosher and Halal food is likely to be dependent on local stockists, the canteen menu should at least provide a range of options suitable for Muslim and Jewish students. Provision of worship facilities can be particularly contentious as colleges rarely have space, and if given to one group others may feel entitled to similar accommodation.

The thesis that religion has shifted from the public to the private sphere and is a personal matter is now questioned. Religion has re-emerged, claiming recognition in the public domain; Casanova (1994) describes this as the 'deprivatization of religion'. This presents a challenge to secular organizations who, because of equality legislation, have to consider not just one familiar religion, but a range of often unfamiliar religions each with its own internal diversity. Gilliat-Ray (2000) noted that religion is fundamental to many young people's identity, particularly among minority ethnic groups, and that 'an individual's identity becomes more sharply defined when it is not recognised by the institution' (p. 55). Combined with secular liberalism and developments in equality legislation, this means that harmonious institutional environments depend in part on accommodating religious observances to a reasonable degree. If religious identity is accepted as inextricably part of the person, then religious literacy becomes an important aspect of a teacher's ability to meet the professional obligation of employing strategies to ensure the best learning experience for students.

Anti-racism

Anti-racism, or 'political multiculturalism', became a significant policy approach following the 1981 urban disturbances that exposed systematic racial discrimination and inequality faced by non-white people in Britain (Scarman 1981; Solomos 2003). Anti-racism provides a critique of 'race relations' policies of multiculturalism that focused on sharing cultural practices and overcoming individual prejudice and ignorance. In contrast, anti-racism stresses the structural nature of racism within British society, and the role of colonialism, slavery and Empire in creating racism. Rather than focusing on individual attitudes, anti-racism is concerned with patterns of discrimination and unequal outcomes for disadvantaged ethnic groups. For anti-racists, these are non-white and share a common experience of white prejudice, discrimination and violence, as well as institutional bias. Here, the over-representation of African-Caribbean young men in school exclusions, the under-achievement of some non-white school pupils, and the over-representation of non-white young men in all aspects of the criminal justice system are not due to the prejudices of individual racist teachers or police officers, but rather to 'institutional racism' whereby assumptions, practices and inherited traditions combine to produce unequal outcomes for non-white people (Solomos 2003).

The importance of policy

The response of anti-racists has been to campaign for equal opportunities policies and procedures designed both to counter past bias and to make future practices open and transparent, with the expectation that this will eventually produce more equal outcomes (Bhavnani et al. 2005). Initially championed by left-wing LAs from the early 1980s, anti-racist and equal opportunities policies have become increasingly 'mainstream'. The development of 'ethnic monitoring data' has produced information on the experiences of different ethnicities in all aspects of society, enabling targets for improvement, such as increasing the numbers of ethnic minority police officers and fire-fighters. While British legislation specifically outlaws positive discrimination or quotas (as used in the USA), it does allow 'Positive Action' efforts to encourage more qualified candidates from underrepresented ethnic groups through processes of training, mentoring and preparation. Allied to this have been fair recruitment and selection policies, and measures against racial harassment and violence. Following the racist murder of Stephen Lawrence and the Macpherson Inquiry (1999), there have been significant improvements in the recording, acknowledgement and investigation of racial incidents and crimes. Many organizations carry out Equality Impact Assessments in order to show that they have paid due regard to the need to eliminate discrimination, as required by the Equality Act 2010. While non-white groups continue to lag behind white people on a range of socio-economic indicators, significant advances have been made as a result of these measures.

Problems with anti-racism

While many of the assumptions and priorities of anti-racism have been accepted, difficulties have emerged. One key problem has been a simplistic understanding of ethnic relations, with white people characterized as powerful and dominant and all ethnic minorities portrayed as victims of racism and inequality. While this picture carried weight in 1976 when the Race Relations Act came into force, it is less recognizable in the ethnically diverse Britain of today. Some non-white ethnic groups are academically outperforming whites and, as a result, accessing high-status jobs. Modood et al. (1997) conclude that Chinese and African-Asians (mainly Hindus and Sikhs arriving in Britain from Africa) cannot be characterized as 'disadvantaged' in any meaningful way. Education and employment data suggests the severe educational and economic disadvantage faced by other Asian groups, particularly Pakistanis and Bangladeshis, is as much to do with class, economic background and qualifications as with racial discrimination. The concentration of these communities in the Midlands and North of England where de-industrialization has occurred is relevant.

Alongside this came an unravelling of an over-arching 'Black' identity crucial to the development of anti-racism. Increasingly, Asian-origin commentators highlighted how 'Black' identity focused more on Afro-Caribbean experiences, failing to reflect the concerns and priorities of Asian communities. This came to a head with the *Satanic Verses* crisis of 1989 when anti-racist alliances fractured over Muslim demands for the banning of Rushdie's book (Modood 2005). These new demands by specific ethnic and religious communities could be seen as an inevitable outcome of LA funding of facilities and organizations aimed at specific ethnic groups in the name of 'anti-racism'. Such practices fractured previous multi-racial alliances in the fight against racism (Sivanandan 2005).

The fundamental importance of economic factors in explaining disadvantage has been downplayed by anti-racism's over-concern with ethnicity and 'race'. Some understandings of ethnicity have obscured the role of class, gender and place in creating and maintaining the identities of individuals and communities. This approach of measuring experience by ethnicity rather than income has served to obscure the severe educational and economic disadvantage faced by the poorest white working-class communities, a failing now starting to be addressed (Joseph Rowntree Foundation 2007). Alongside this have been concerns about a 'white backlash' to anti-racist policies and curriculum approaches within schools, colleges and youth work.

Attempts to challenge racist attitudes and behaviour have often been 'clumsy' and less than even handed. While this reflects the lack of confidence and clarity of practitioners (CRE 1999), it also highlights fundamental problems with anti-racism. These include a belief that 'racism' is something that only white people do to non-whites, and that incidents the other way round cannot be characterized in the same way. However, the reaction of established ethnic communities to recent migrants questions this assertion. Anti-racist educational approaches have focused unduly on white people learning about the (essentialized) 'cultures' and religions of ethnic minorities, with little concern for cultures and traditions of white communities, as shown by recurring concerns over whether public displays of St George's flag are 'racist'. Research has shown that white English-origin young people have less understanding and confidence in their own 'culture' than any other ethnic group (Nayak 1999).

Multiculturalism, integration and community cohesion

The turn of the twenty-first century saw a significant shift in the concerns and priorities of 'race relations' policies (Solomos 2003). This shift has been characterized, negatively, as a retreat from 'multiculturalism' towards 'integration', one less concerned with difference and the promotion of ethnic diversity. Rather than replacing 'multiculturalism' in general, the current policy approaches of integration or community cohesion represent a move away from one particular type of multiculturalism or political anti-racism, towards a 'critical multiculturalism' concerned with holistic forms of citizenship (May 1999).

The 2001 disturbances in Oldham, Burnley and Bradford were a turning point in government approaches to 'race relations'. Following these a new policy concept, 'community cohesion', was deployed. The report of the government enquiry (Cantle 2001) paid scant attention to the actual events, suggesting they were a symptom of much deeper malaise concerning ethnic relations. Local authorities were instructed to measure the impact of community cohesion; all schools now have a duty to promote cohesion. The London bombings of July 2005 and the subsequent policy concern with 'preventing violent extremism' have re-emphasized this agenda.

The central premise of community cohesion is that ethnic segregation is a reality in many areas leading to 'parallel lives' (Ritchie 2001), little contact between ethnic groups and a lack of shared values and understandings. Such segregation is seen as causing ethnic tension and distrust, the solution being a greater focus on bringing people together around common issues, identities and values. Implicit within community cohesion is a critique of anti-racist policies since the late 1980s, which are seen as being unduly focused on difference and with the concerns of specific ethnic groups, rather than on common problems. These policies did not cause segregation, and were necessary in the 1980s, but more recently have had the unintended consequence of exacerbating ethnic segregation (Cantle 2005). It is suggested that anti-racism has been more concerned with 'equality' for specific ethnic groups than with relations between groups or the overall common good.

Thomas (2006) has shown that 'meaningful direct contact' between young people of different ethnic backgrounds is central to this policy agenda. Such interventions focus on shared, common identities and enable cooperation in safe spaces that allow 'rooting and shifting' (Yuval-Davis 1997), the re-thinking of cultural understandings and identities without one's own identity being threatened. This type of activity supports 'contact theory', the belief that to break down ethnic divides and prejudices, action needs to be based on groups rather than individuals and to take place over a period of time (Hewstone et al. 2007). Such activity develops 'bridging social capital' (Putnam 2000) between strong, segregated monocultural communities, suggesting that individuals and communities take some responsibility to foster integration that government cannot create on its own (Giddens 1998).

Criticisms of community cohesion

A key criticism of integration approaches is that placing the responsibility for overcoming segregation on communities and individuals implicitly blames them for segregation (Kundnani 2002). This has been fuelled by the emphasis of some politicians on the agency of Asian communities, with pronouncements on increased use of English, trans-continental marriages and Islamist political activity. There is much less concern with White 'flight' or self-segregation, and support for the far-right British National Party (BNP) (Alexander 2004) or the English Defence League (EDL), which can suggest community cohesion is a return to the failed 1960s policy of 'assimilation'; the idea that all ethnic minority communities should give up their distinct cultures and integrate. Arguably, the practice of community cohesion suggests this is not the case. The Cantle Report (2001) acknowledged the reality of diversity, and the need to continue developing race equality measures, such as Equality Impact Assessments. Thomas (2006) argues this approach to integration works with the reality of difference and rather than being the 'death of multiculturalism' (Kundnani 2002), is a rejection of one type of multiculturalism/anti-racism, with an emphasis on a new 'critical multiculturalism' (May 1999). This recognizes ethnic difference but rejects essentialized and fixed notions, highlighting other forms of identity. Community cohesion is arguably concerned with divisions of class, income, community and 'territory' as well as ethnicity, seeing these as relevant to the realities of segregated and 'tense' communities. Community cohesion's focus on integration and common identity was part of wider attempts by New Labour to create de-centred and inter-sectional identities, 'cooler' or multiple identities, rather than 'hot' ethnic identities that lead to tension (McGhee 2005).

Anti-sexism

Women's representation in public life and employment has improved dramatically since the 1975 Sex Discrimination Act. Consequently there has been a tendency to assume that gender discrimination has been eradicated or, if it still exists, people may claim 'the pendulum has swung the other way', pointing to the underachievement of boys in GCSEs and under-representation of male teachers. However, there is still a gender pay gap, women are not fairly represented in the judiciary or in Parliament, and are under-represented in top level management. Anti-sexist practice moves beyond quantitative demands for political and financial sex equality and looks instead at the qualitative aspects of how we live our lives and how our gender enhances or detracts from the potential richness of experience. For education, the major issues in anti-sexist practice are how to enable a fulfilling work–life balance and how to ensure gender does not force girls/boys and women/men into stereotyped subjects and careers.

Organizations like the UK Resource Centre for Women in Science, Engineering and Technology aim to improve the recruitment of women in associated spheres of employment. They recommend that, in order to attract more women into construction, advertisements and course design should be more focused on women. The same may well apply in areas of male recruitment into health and social care. Ensuring an anti-sexist environment is particularly necessary for learners recruited to occupational areas not traditionally associated with their gender. From the beginning of a course, sexist or gender-stereotyped language should be identified as unacceptable with the teacher ensuring it is dealt with appropriately. When, at the outset, the teacher has negotiated rules of acceptable language with the whole class, students will often take on the responsibility of identifying gender-stereotyped words and suggest alternatives.

Students should be able to encounter learning materials showing images of people of diverse appearance, both male and female. Posters presenting diverse images are available from organizations such as the Equality and Human Rights Commission. Where possible language used in learning materials should be gender neutral. Advice on language use is available from the Equality Challenge Unit (www.ecu.ac.uk). To avoid creating a culture where only one gender feels comfortable, teachers may need to modify their interaction with students. A male construction lecturer may slip into a familiar way of talking to apprentices and say, 'Right then lads . . .' excluding female apprentices. Similarly a female hairdressing lecturer should avoid chatting about 'a girls' night out' as this may exclude male students.

Gendered assumptions about learners' social and family lives should be avoided. For example, we should not assume that a woman will need time off for family responsibilities and a man will not. Positive support and encouragement is the most important factor in retaining women and men in non-traditional subjects. Learners are encouraged if teachers create a cooperative learning environment rather than a competitive milieu. By working on cooperative tasks, students in a mixed-sex environment are more likely to take the risk of revealing what they do not know.

Learning or assessment tasks should aim to draw on contexts familiar to both sexes. For example, an engineering task might involve designing and building a baby buggy or a bicycle rather than a model racing car. No subject, not even science or mathematics, can claim to be completely value free and objective. Part of the teacher's role is to ensure that values and feelings are discussed with respect. For example, when learning about motor vehicle maintenance it might become relevant to discuss the social and environmental implications of choosing one type of vehicle rather than another. A value-based approach to scientific subjects can make these more attractive to some learners.

Lesbian, gay, bisexual and transgender issues

Hunt and Jensen (2006) found homophobic bullying, involving verbal and physical abuse, was prevalent and largely unchallenged in schools and in some cases even condoned by teachers and support staff. They found that 65 per cent of lesbian and gay pupils had experienced bullying and that many teachers failed to respond to homophobic language. Homophobic language does not just consist of intentional abuse, but includes 'off-hand' comments that go unnoticed and unaddressed by teachers. For example, the phrase 'that's so gay' is used negatively to indicate that something is useless. Such language is so pervasive that many think it is 'natural' and do not recognize that it is abusive and can reflect institutional heterosexism and the presumption of its normality. The consequence of institutional heterosexism is that lesbian, gay, bisexual and transgender (LGBT) people may feel excluded and not fulfil their learning potential. In their study Hunt and Jensen commented that school work was affected by homophobic bullying and half of those bullied said they had missed school as a result.

For some LGBTs sexual orientation may be central to their educational experience. Vicars (2007: 21) suggests:

> Cultural homophobia . . . refers to social standards and norms which dictate that being heterosexual is better than being lesbian, gay or bisexual . . . Often heterosexuals do not realise that these standards exist while lesbian, gay and bisexual people are acutely aware of them. This can result in lesbians, gays and bisexuals feeling like outsiders in society.

In some workplaces LGBTs are expected to keep their sexual orientation and family life secret, whereas in others they may be forcibly 'outed' irrespective of their wishes. The Equality Act (Sexual Orientation) Regulations 2007 do not undermine an individual's right to privacy – staff or students have the right not to discuss their sexual orientation and not to have it discussed by others. Some workplaces may profess a commitment to equality policies, but there is still a prevalent culture of heteronormativity, whereby partners are assumed to be of the opposite sex. This can be seen in the way family photographs are displayed, trips and social events advertised and time off from work or study is structured to allow for domestic responsibilities. Consequently LGBTs may feel unable to talk naturally about family life or participate fully in the social milieu of college.

Harassment of LGBTs can take many forms from unintentional to intentional exclusion, and if unchallenged, may result in verbal insults and physical abuse. This could include comments overheard in canteens or corridors, graffiti scrawled on walls and posters, or physically pushing people out of a group of learners in the classroom. The teacher needs be alert to harassment and abusive language, and needs to be familiar with relevant policies in their institution so that their response can be appropriate. Learners' behaviour towards each other and how they respect each others' identity are matters for all teachers and learning support staff.

Mental health

According to the Mental Health Foundation (MHF), one in four people will experience some mental health disorder in the course of a year (MHF 2009).

Teachers may approach the topic of mental health in three ways:

1 dealing with students' mental health conditions and their effects on teaching and learning;
2 maintaining and promoting students' mental health and not causing undue stress or exacerbating difficulties while teaching;
3 maintaining their own mental health by striking a work-life balance, promoting well-being and taking active steps to avoid stress.

Learners may present with recognizable, diagnosed and disclosed conditions. Some learners will not yet have been diagnosed and others will develop conditions during their studies. Learners should not be coerced into disclosure and the stigma of mental illness needs to be considered. Teachers involved with prison education should be aware that 90 per cent of prisoners have a recognized mental health condition. Other providers may have contracts to work with mental health and voluntary groups to deliver provision for learners with specific difficulties.

What can practitioners do?

1 Learners with existing conditions:
  • Research conditions and strategies.
  • Talk to experienced colleagues.
  • Attend awareness training.
  • Keep up to date with official reports and other specialist publications.
  • Expect the unexpected, but not the worst.
  • Consider classroom organization and management issues.

2   Promoting mental health and well-being:
   - Allow space for active listening and opportunities for one-to-one interaction to detect issues and refer to appropriate support.
   - In class, build in anti-stress activities such as relaxation techniques.
   - Be aware of referral procedures and when and how to make these within the institution and community.

3   Promoting teachers' own mental health:
   - Find ways to relax and maintain a healthy work-life balance.
   - Use de-stressing techniques as listed above.
   - Be aware of triggers to negative feelings and adopt effective coping strategies.
   - For all the above seek professional support.
   - Discuss issues with a line manager, equality and diversity representative or union official.

Equal opportunity in practice

Educational institutions collect information about disadvantaged groups represented among staff and students in accordance with legislation and to enable forward planning to redress under-representation. For the teacher, this should not just be 'box-ticking'. Cowan (2006: 8) suggests: 'Monitoring for the sake of it is generally unsuccessful. Before sexual orientation monitoring is introduced, it is important that employers identify why they want to ask about sexual orientation, what they want to find out and what they will do with the information'. Questions about disability, ethnicity, sexual orientation and religion are particularly sensitive and are significantly under-reported, because some see these as a personal matter and not relevant to education.

Inclusivity and differentiation

Inclusive teaching means recognizing and meeting the learning needs of all students. Ideally inclusivity should involve the whole class working and learning together in which there are no 'outsiders' – easier to say than do, as most social groups develop insiders and outsiders over time. Teachers have to perform a difficult balancing act ensuring learners are made to feel their needs are recognized, while making sure differences are not highlighted by constant reference. For example, it would not be helpful to ask a male care student, 'As the only man in the room, what is your opinion on fatherhood?' or to say to a learner with dyslexia, 'I have prepared this handout on coloured paper especially for you'. It would be more appropriate to allow the male student to decide his contribution in whatever role he identifies with. Similarly, it would be more inclusive to allow the dyslexic student the opportunity to select materials in the appropriate format from a display of handouts.

Providing the option to select handouts from a range of different formats and media is also an opportunity to become familiar with particular learning needs and preferences. Many disabled students wish to avoid unwanted attention and public 'fuss' around them reinforces their perceived difference and contributes to social isolation.

When planning lessons teachers should consider how to differentiate teaching and provide learning facilities according to the needs and characteristics of learners. Listed below are possible indicators of inclusivity and differentiation in learning situations.

- Does the teacher draw on the individual experience of all group members?
- Does the teacher direct questions to and seek responses from a range of different learners?
- Does the teacher encourage harmonious relationships between different groups of learners?
- Does the teacher challenge the use of inappropriate language by learners?
- Are learners encouraged to work with others from different backgrounds through group work?
- Are all learners actively engaged in the lesson?
- Do learners show that they expect to be treated differently but with equal respect?
- Is the language used in learning materials and by the teacher appropriate?
- Is the learning support equipment used sensitively and appropriately?
- Is the assistance of learning support workers e.g. signers, amanuensis, bilingual support workers, etc., used appropriately?

Equality and diversity in teaching

All educators are expected to embed equality and diversity in teaching. This may be easier in some subjects than others. Social scientists may feel that these concepts are integral to their discipline. Similarly, artists have a tradition of drawing on other cultures and different life experiences as source material. This may be more challenging in other subjects. How is diversity embedded into teaching a task like changing a gear box or calculating percentages? A teacher concerned with spreading awareness and respect for diversity needs to consider where their subject interfaces with human beings. For example, the teacher of motor vehicle mechanics might discuss clutch pedal adjustments and adaptations and their suitability for drivers with disabilities. Mathematicians could ask learners to calculate percentages of male and female apprentices who chose care courses compared with construction. The contribution of different cultures to the development of academic disciplines can also be discussed. For example, different cultures have given us different number and calculations conventions, including Arabic numerals, Pythagorean triangles and the division of the hour into 60 minutes.

In judging whether an educator is promoting equality, diversity and inclusion we need to consider the values and culture of the learners and the teacher, the physical environment and the learning materials. Some indicators are given below:

1   Culture and values:
    - Are learners aware of their rights and responsibilities?
    - Are the assessment methods valid and varied?
    - Is individual progress in learning identified and celebrated?

2   Physical environment:
    ● Do the displays and images used give an impression of an organization that values diversity?
    ● Are the accommodation and facilities suitable for disabled learners?
3   Learning materials:
    ● Do learning materials avoid stereotyping and reflect the diversity of learners?
    ● Do learning materials reflect the cultural diversity of British society?
    ● Are other cultures considered and used as examples in learning?

Social class

Thus far we have made passing reference to class. However, class relations are fundamental to the way in which we make sense of educational processes, being closely linked to outcomes and destinations. The Youth Cohort Studies have consistently illustrated the close relationship between socio-economic status and educational performance:

> Young people from lower socio-economic classes tended to have lower levels of academic attainment at age 16 compared to the higher socio-economic classes. This gap extends to the age of 17 as those who had not achieved Level 2 at 16 from the lower socio-economic classes were less likely to have gone on to achieve it at 17 than young people from the Higher and Lower Professional socio-economic classes.
>
> (DCSF 2009: 25)

This relationship is similarly found in the connection between parents' level of qualification and those of their children, which on occasion is used as a substitute for class: 'The variations by parental qualifications are similar in size to those by parental occupation. Over four fifths of young people with a parent who had a degree and two thirds of those with a parent whose highest qualification was an A level attained five good GCSEs.' (DCSF 2008: np).

Often in policy reports class is glossed in relation to background or, indeed, disadvantage. It is, as with many of the terms we have used in this chapter, contested and therefore carries different meanings. For the purpose of this section we relate class to culture, life chances and socio-economic position. Different classes have differential access to cultural, social and economic assets. In addition other aspects of diversity are also intimately articulated to class. We are not simply 'classed' but are at one and the same time gendered, raced, aged and so on. This idea is captured by the notion of intersectionality which suggests that these different aspects are interrelated and that any attempt to prioritize one over the other is less than helpful. However, in some circumstances class may for example be lived through the prism of race, or perhaps gender and vice versa.

The notion of class points towards the importance of the social structure of society and the manner in which class inequalities are reproduced systemically over time. This is one of the reasons why educational institutions have difficulty in addressing these issues. For example, the politics of widening participation is contra-dictory. It offers access to HE to those who have historically been excluded, yet HEIs have undergone significant change. HE is a heterogeneous and differentiated sector, with HE provision being offered by FE colleges and private providers as well as new and elite universities. This provision has differing consequences for class reproduc-tion. A key insight of class based analyses is that education cannot of itself transform society. Some forty years ago Basil Bernstein stated that 'education cannot compen-sate for society' and this holds true today. The point being that if we are concerned about class and seek to interrupt those processes that lead to its reproduction, a broader politics is required that extends beyond education to wider society. It is also salutary for us to consider the way in which members of the professional middle class are both complicit in and benefit from these processes. The point is that the notion of class and the manner in which it articulates to other aspects of inequality raises a number of thorny issues. It is easy enough to consider those inequalities that are thought to derive from prejudice, after all none of us likes to think of ourselves as prejudiced or discriminatory. However, when these are related to class and the systemic reproduction of inequality a more challenging and difficult politics arises.

Conclusion

This chapter has ranged over important debates considering the ways in which we make sense of equality and diversity. It examined issues of anti-racism, anti-sexism and LGBT as well the salience of faith and religion in educational settings. Throughout there is recognition that many of the terms are contestable and that there is a constant struggle to sustain practices committed to social justice. We need to recognize that educational processes cannot simply be viewed from an institutional position and that they need to be placed within the relational setting in which educa-tion is located, as well as its wider social context.

PART 2
Teaching in the lifelong learning sector

7

Learning and learners

Margaret McLay, Louise Mycroft, Penny Noel, Kevin Orr, Ron Thompson, Jonathan Tummons and Jane Weatherby

In this chapter

- What is learning?
- Classifying types of learning
- Deep, surface and strategic learning
- Factors influencing learning
- Theories of the learning process
- The learning styles debate
- Widening participation
- Adult learners and 'adult learning'
- Learners from other countries
- Students with learning difficulties or disabilities
- 'Academically more able learners'
- Learners aged 14–16
- Young people not in education, employment or training

What is learning?

The Professional Standards for Teachers and Trainers in Education and Training – England (ETF 2014: 2) assume that teachers are 'dual professionals' expert in their subject and in teaching and learning. However, 'learning' is not easy to define: what is meant by learning will depend on how the process of education is viewed, and vice versa. Rather than being straightforward, the concept of learning requires elucidation. This chapter begins by introducing some ways of looking at learning, with the aim of highlighting a number of issues to be taken up later.

One approach is to begin with specific examples. Learning the names of the bones in the human body, learning to swim, and learning to judge the quality of a poem all seem to be appropriate uses of the word 'learning' yet they are diverse in nature. Ramsden (1992: 26) cites research on adult students' conceptions of learning, which distinguished five 'common-sense' categories:

1   learning as the acquisition of knowledge;

2   learning as memorizing;

3   learning as the acquisition of skills;

4   learning as making sense or meaning;

5   learning as interpreting and understanding reality in a different way.

These differing views of learning are also encountered in the academic literature, and broadly correspond to conceiving knowledge as either individualized or communal. In an influential paper, Sfard (1998) distinguishes between two pervasive metaphors for learning: *acquisition* of knowledge as a commodity, something which can quite straightforwardly be passed from one person to another; and *participation* in the construction of knowledge, a viewpoint which emphasizes knowing as an activity rather than a state. A similar distinction can be made between learning as a *product* (what is its outcome?) and learning as a *process* (how it occurs and sustains itself over time). Table 7.1 shows some comparisons between the acquisition and participation metaphors.

Conceiving learning as a product often involves focusing on the behaviour of an individual thought to have learned something. For example, if a student has learned to play a musical scale on the piano, they might sit down and play that scale. An observer could then *infer*, from the student's behaviour, that learning had taken place. Alternatively, someone who had learned what causes earthquakes might be expected to have the ability to explain how earthquakes are caused, and to answer questions about this. Once again, observable behaviour leads to the conclusion that learning has taken place.

Robert Gagné (1977: 3) defined learning as 'a change in human disposition or capability, which persists over a period of time, and which is not simply ascribable to the process of growth'. All learning relates in some way to change. However, not all

Table 7.1 Comparisons between metaphors of learning

Acquisition metaphor		Participation metaphor
Individual enrichment	**Goal of learning**	Community building
Acquisition of something	**Nature of learning**	Becoming a participant
Recipient (consumer), (re-) constructor	**Student**	Peripheral participant, apprentice
Provider, facilitator, mediator	**Teacher**	Expert participant, preserver of practice/discourse
Property, possession, commodity (individual, public)	**Knowledge/concept**	Aspect of practice/discourse/ activity
Having, possessing	**Knowing**	Belonging, participating, communicating

Source: Adapted from Sfard (1998: 7)

change can be ascribed to learning – for example, physical growth can change our capacity for certain activities. Interestingly, Gagné does not ask for a change in behaviour as such, but of 'disposition' or 'capability' – that is, of the potential for behaviour. You may learn to swim but never be observed swimming; nevertheless, if challenged, you would be able to do so!

In contrast to the product model of learning, David Kolb emphasizes the nature of learning as a continuing process and a characteristic of the human ability to understand and shape the environment: 'Learning is a holistic process of adaptation to the world . . . learning is *the* major process of human adaptation' (Kolb 1984: 31–2, original emphasis). Influenced by the pragmatist philosophy of John Dewey (see Chapter 13), Kolb argues that learning evolves in response to our development as individuals and to changing circumstances. Learning outcomes indicate only what we *knew* at a particular time in the past, not what we know and can do now: 'Learning is best conceived as a process, not in terms of outcomes . . . learning is an emergent process whose outcomes represent only historical record, not knowledge of the future' (Kolb 1984: 26). Related to this idea of learning as an adaptive process is the idea of learning as knowledge construction and of actively making sense or meaning from experience; this view is known as *constructivism.*

The process of learning may also be thought of as a *social practice.* In their study of learning in FE, James and Biesta (2007) draw on a *cultural theory of learning,* 'a theory which conceives of learning not as something which happens in the heads, minds or brains of students, but sees it as something that happens in and "through" social practices' (p. 21). Building on the ideas of the influential French sociologist Pierre Bourdieu and the work of Lave and Wenger (1991; see Chapter 5), James and Biesta argue that the cultural context of learning is not merely a backdrop to the educational experiences of learners; rather, learning must be understood as a cultural practice in its own right. Referring to Table 7.1, we can see that constructivist and socio-cultural views of learning share features of the participation metaphor. However, as Sfard (1998: 7) points out, although the social and constructive dimensions of learning are important in the participation metaphor, they are not necessarily absent from theories based on the acquisition metaphor. The two metaphors are pictures of what learning is, rather than of how it happens.

James and Biesta (2007: 23) define a learning culture as 'the social practices through which people learn' and note that learning is not merely 'done' but is 'done with others' in a community which influences, and is influenced by, its individual members. This leads to the idea of 'learning as becoming' (Colley et al. 2003), in which the self is transformed by a particular learning culture, developing socially approved ways of thinking, feeling and behaving. As Lave and Wenger (1991: 53) observe, 'learning involves the construction of identities', so that knowledge, social membership and identity are inextricably linked.

It should now be clear that there is no single answer to the question 'What is learning?' Saljö (2009: 203) draws attention to increasing conceptual complexity as the field of learning theory has expanded over many decades:

> Behaviours and cognitive processes no longer suffice as basic constructs for providing a coherent and interesting conceptualization of learning; there are

many other issues that have to be considered such as time, situatedness, and reciprocity between individuals and cultural practices. Also, in the literature it is no longer just individuals who learn and remember but also collectives such as organizations, societies and systems of people and artefacts.

However, the different and often conflicting perspectives can be seen as complementary, raising different questions as well as answering the same question in different ways, and providing insights suited to differing contexts and purposes of education and training.

Classifying types of learning

There are different types of learning outcome and different learning processes. The nature of the learning process may relate to the type of outcome involved, although learning outcomes do not always capture what is of value in learning. Indeed, *how* something is learned can sometimes be more important than *what* is learned. Furthermore, individuals can learn in various ways at various times. Each of these observations is important in its own way, and will be pursued further below. First, however, different types of learning outcome will be considered in more detail.

Gagné (1977: 27) identifies five major categories of learning outcome: intellectual skills, verbal information, cognitive strategies, motor skills and attitudes. This highlights the fact that attitudes can be learned as well as knowledge or skills. Gagné also draws attention to hierarchical structures in learning: for example, within the category of intellectual skills he identifies four levels: discriminations, concepts, rules and problem solving, each of which draws on those below it in the hierarchy.

Bloom (1956) developed a detailed classification of learning outcomes in his *Taxonomy of Educational Objectives*. This taxonomy is used extensively in planning for student learning, particularly when the teacher or trainer writes behavioural objectives (see Chapter 9). Bloom's taxonomy classifies learning outcomes depending on the type of learning they represent, using three *domains*: cognitive, affective and psychomotor. As with Gagné, each domain contains a hierarchy of levels, beginning with the simplest and moving towards more complex and challenging types of learning.

Cognitive learning comprises the acquisition and use of knowledge and is demonstrated by knowledge recall and intellectual skills: comprehending information, organizing ideas, analysing and synthesizing data, applying knowledge, choosing among alternatives in problem solving, and evaluating ideas or actions. This domain predominates in academic courses. Bloom identified six levels within the cognitive domain, from simple recall or recognition of facts, through increasingly more complex and abstract cognitive behaviours. Examples of verbs representing intellectual activity on each level are listed in Box 7.1.

Affective learning relates to emotions, attitudes, and values: for example, enjoying, respecting and supporting. The affective domain is important in planning learning which involves working with people; its structure is shown in Box 7.2. *Psychomotor learning* (Box 7.3) involves a range of physical skills and requires atributes such as coordination, dexterity, grace and balance. Its applications cover subjects such as art and dance as well as vocational areas like motor vehicle engineering.

Box 7.1 Levels of learning in the cognitive domain

Knowledge: recognizing and recalling information. Appropriate verbs would be: arrange, define, label, list, name, recall, state.

Comprehension: interpreting, translating or summarizing given information, principles and concepts. *Appropriate verbs*: classify, describe, discuss, explain, identify, locate, recognize, restate, select, translate.

Application: using information, principles and concepts in a context different to the original learning context. *Verbs*: apply, choose, demonstrate, dramatize, illustrate, interpret, practise, schedule, solve, use.

Analysis: separating a whole into parts and making clear their functions and the relationships between them. *Verbs*: analyse, calculate, compare, contrast, differentiate, distinguish, examine.

Synthesis: combining elements to create something different from the original. *Verbs*: arrange, compose, construct, create, design, develop, manage, organize, plan, prepare, propose.

Evaluation: making decisions and judgements based on stated criteria. *Verbs*: appraise, argue, assess, choose, compare, defend, estimate, support, evaluate.

Source: Gronlund (1970)

Box 7.2 Levels of learning in the affective domain

Receiving: showing awareness and attention, for example by listening.

Responding: meeting expectations by responding to stimulus, for example by commenting sympathetically on something said.

Valuing: behaving consistently with stated single beliefs, values and attitudes.

Organizing: behaving consistently with a given system of values and beliefs.

Characterizing: behaving consistently with an internalized value or belief system.

Source: Gronlund (1970)

Ausubel (1963) drew attention to the tendency for Bloom's taxonomy to be used mechanistically emphasizing the lower cognitive levels because they are straightforward to measure. However, it can be invaluable to the teacher when designing programmes of study, framing learning objectives and planning for assessment.

Box 7.3 Levels of learning in the psychomotor domain

Imitation: observes a skill and tries to repeat it.

Manipulation: performs a skill according to instruction rather than observation.

Precision: accurately and independently reproduces a skill.

Articulation: combines one or more skills in sequence with harmony and consistency.

Naturalization: completes one or more skills with ease and becomes 'automatic'.

Source: Gronlund (1970)

The distinction between the cognitive and psychomotor domain can be related to the difference between *knowing that* and *knowing how*. The philosopher Gilbert Ryle (1949: 58) expressed this distinction as follows:

> Learning how or improving an ability is not like learning that or acquiring information. Truths can be imparted, procedures can only be inculcated, and while inculcation is a gradual process, imparting is relatively sudden. It makes sense to ask at what moment someone became apprised of a truth, but not to ask at what moment someone acquired a skill.

For a surgeon, extensive medical knowledge is necessary, but far from sufficient: 'excellence at surgery is not the same thing as knowledge of medical science; nor is it a simple product of it. The surgeon must indeed have learned . . . a great number of truths; but . . . must also have learned by practice a great number of aptitudes' (Ryle 1949: 48–9).

A particular characteristic of learning in the psychomotor domain is that it can be difficult to express 'knowing how' in language or any other symbolic form. The knowledge is *tacit* rather than explicit (Polanyi 1983) and is not understood in terms of formal procedures or codes. Someone may know how to give an injection but may not be able to explain how they do it. Although in some cases, this may be due to incomplete understanding, it may also be a feature of the knowledge itself rather than of how an individual knows it. Tacit knowledge may only be transmissible by means of observation or by the learner becoming immersed in the social practices of a particular organizational culture. In this way, tacit knowledge is acquired by becoming part of a community of practice (Wenger 1998; see Chapter 5).

Deep, surface and strategic learning

Students have varied attitudes to learning. One student may be committed to learning for its own sake, and be passionate about understanding a particular field; another may want to do a minimum of work. Such tendencies are often classified in terms of *deep* and *surface* learning (Marton and Säljö 1976).

Deep learning is associated with a commitment to learning in which the student wishes to acquire extensive knowledge and understanding that is relational as well as factual – that is, based on principles and relationships. The deep learner is likely to ask awkward questions and to want to know why a method works rather than being content with correctly applying it.

Surface learning, as its name implies, is the opposite of deep learning and is characterized by an avoidance of reasoning, explanations or underlying principles. 'Just tell me what I need to know' is an attitude associated with surface learning, which might also be narrow and instrumental (that is, directed towards a specific and immediate goal).

Strategic learning is perhaps the most commonly observed approach from students, and is closely associated with assessment regimes and learning cultures. Students may be largely concerned with obtaining a qualification, or perhaps simply with staying on a course for financial reasons. Such students may be strongly influenced by what is required of them, particularly by the surrounding learning culture. If learning for its own sake, and a commitment to higher level learning outcomes, are not reflected in assessment requirements or in the learning culture, students may simply adopt a surface approach. When immersed in a different, more demanding culture, they may well be able to adapt, taking on the characteristics of deep learning because this is required of them.

Factors influencing learning

A number of factors can be responsible for how quickly and effectively an individual learns, or even whether they learn at all. Some are transient, relating to the individual or the immediate learning environment; for example, the learner's physical state, the perceived relevance of a topic or their response to learning activities. Other short-term factors may include the timing and length of a learning session, or peer group behaviour. Many of these factors may be under the control of the teacher; however, more permanent influences on learning may have greater impact and be more difficult to address. These include confidence and self-esteem, motivation and cognitive development. A learner may have deep-rooted beliefs about learning and their own relationship with education. Peer group pressure and the expectations of teachers, parents or employers are also important. Furthermore, structural issues of race, gender, disability and class have a considerable impact on learning. These wider social factors are discussed in more detail later in this chapter and in Chapters 3 and 6; this section concentrates on individual differences.

Motivation is a key factor in learning, both in its own right and as an underlying element in other factors. For example, the reason *why* peer group pressure influences the learning of an individual can be attributed to more general elements in the motivation of their behaviour. Abraham Maslow (1908–1970) developed an influential theory of motivation which can be useful in understanding the interrelationships between some of the factors noted above – it is illustrated in Figure 7.1. According to Maslow, a hierarchy of needs underlies the motivation for human behaviour. Belonging, and

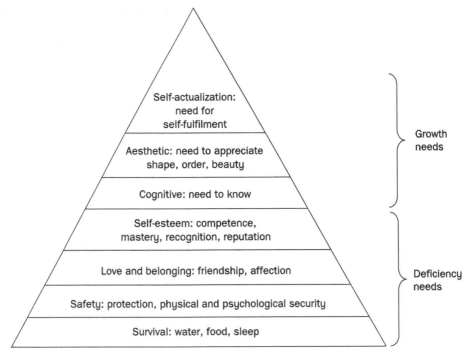

Figure 7.1 Maslow's hierarchy of human needs
Sources: Maslow (1970); Child (2004)

psychological safety, are important elements of this model, so that learning behaviours which mark a student as 'standing out from the crowd' or which could expose them to embarrassment, might be expected to be avoided. In a similar way, several points noted above as factors influencing learning (for example, self-esteem, classroom environment and peer pressure) can be related to aspects of motivation in Maslow's hierarchy.

It is useful to distinguish between *intrinsic* and *extrinsic* motivation – that is, what comes from within (such as a desire to learn or find job satisfaction) as opposed to motivation from outside (for example, receiving praise, being admonished or financial reward). Child (2004: 192) cites evidence that praise has a more beneficial long-term effect than being admonished. Intrinsic motivation is more likely to result when students attribute their achievement to internal factors under their control, such as the amount of effort they make, or when they believe they have *agency* in reaching desired goals (achievements are not determined by luck). Conversely, students may deliberately not stretch themselves so that they may attribute failure to lack of effort rather than ability (Seifert 2004). Extrinsic motivation can be effective; however, an overemphasis on extrinsic rewards may lead to a reduction in intrinsic motivation.

Reinforcement is 'rewarding' learned behaviour with desirable outcomes (positive reinforcement) or removing undesired outcomes (called negative reinforcement by Skinner, although some authors refer to negative reinforcement to indicate punishment). Reinforcement is related to behaviourist models of learning: successful learning is rewarded with something desirable and is therefore more likely to occur again. Equally, unsuccessful learning associated with undesirable outcomes (failure or rejection, for example) can lead to behaviour that prevents learning – it damages confidence, for example. Adult learners often show signs of this when returning to education.

Expectation is a very important influence on learning, whether on the part of a teacher, parents, peers or the student themselves; expectations of success or failure are very often borne out. The 'halo effect' is well known and should put teachers on their guard against 'labelling' groups or individuals. These points are often linked with issues of equality and diversity: where certain groups are labelled as less likely to succeed, they may be given less challenging work, taught less rigorously and given restricted opportunities.

Learning style theories have been influential since the early 1990s, and have more recently taken hold as a way of ensuring that the individual needs of learners are addressed. These theories propose that, although people learn differently, their preferred ways of learning tend to fall into identifiable categories. There are numerous schemes for classifying learning styles, and many educational institutions use them as a diagnostic tool. It is claimed that tutors need to be aware of the learning styles of their students, and alert to possible preferences and weaknesses, in order to provide appropriate learning activities. However, learning styles have come to be seen as problematic; the debates surrounding them are discussed in more detail later in this chapter.

Theories of the learning process

Theoretical discussion of education dates back at least as far as the Greek philosopher Plato (429–347 BCE). Both the word 'education' (from the Latin *educare*, meaning to bring up or draw out) and the word 'pedagogy' (from the Greek word for education but now used to mean the theory of educating), have ancient roots. However, the systematic investigation of how learning occurs in individuals is relatively recent, developing from the general considerations of philosophers such as John Dewey but also from a tradition of empirical research into learning. Within this tradition, the work of the Russian physiologist Ivan Pavlov (1849–1936) on conditioned reflexes, in the early years of the twentieth century, can be seen as originating behaviourism – one of the main theories of individual learning. The following section gives a sketch of this important area.

Behaviourism

Behaviourism attempts to approach learning scientifically, with an accumulation of knowledge based on repeatable and verifiable experiments. Pavlov's well-known experiments on dogs are an early example of this approach, in which he demonstrated that an initial *unconditioned response* – in this case, salivation when presented with food – could be transformed into a *conditioned response* by repeatedly accompanying the food with a characteristic sound. The original unconditioned stimulus (the food)

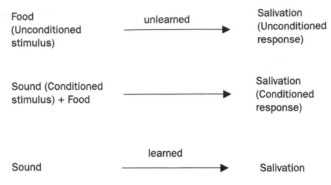

Figure 7.2 Pavlov's conditioning experiment

eventually was not needed to produce salivation; instead, the dogs salivated on hearing the sound (conditioned stimulus). See Figure 7.2 for a description of this process of *classical conditioning*.

Whether this experiment is relevant to the study of learning is debatable; Carr (2003: 88) discusses the limitations of conditioning as a model of learning, an obvious one being that what has been developed is more akin to a reflex than to the voluntary, conscious behaviour we would normally associate with learning. This criticism is partly addressed by the work of E.L. Thorndike (1874–1949) (using cats this time) on what later became known as *operant conditioning*. In Thorndike's experiments, animals 'learned', through a process of trial and error, to escape from a cage – being rewarded with food, as well as freedom. In this case, there seems at least to be an element of purposeful behaviour, directed towards intelligible goals.

Thorndike deduced two principles of learning: the 'law of exercise', which emphasizes the importance of frequent repetition, and the 'law of effect', which introduced the concept of reinforcement discussed above. According to the law of effect, rewarding success increases the effectiveness of learning. In these findings, a fundamental concept of behaviourism appears: the idea of a stimulus-response (S–R) link. In Pavlov's experiment, the link is direct and essentially constitutes a conditioned reflex action; however, in Thorndike's model, the link is indirect and mediated by the organism (S–O–R), the role of reinforcement and goal-directed learning indicating an element of purposive behaviour on the part of the learner.

Experimenting with dogs and cats is all very well, but does any of this relate to humans? Another well-known experiment, conducted by J.B. Watson (1878–1958), shows that conditioning can apply to humans – the infamous case of 'Little Albert'. In this experiment (Watson and Rayner 1920), Watson presented a child of 11 months, Albert B., with a variety of small animals and objects. On each occasion, the researchers frightened Albert by, for example, striking a metal bar with a hammer. Not surprisingly, Albert was soon conditioned to be afraid of the objects themselves. Clearly, then, conditioning does work with humans – an important finding, but perhaps less significant than the illustration this case gives of the need to apply ethical standards to research.

Another key figure in behaviourism is B.F. Skinner (1904–1990), who developed Thorndike's ideas into a sophisticated theory of operant conditioning. Skinner believed that almost anything could be taught by conditioning, and famously taught pigeons to play table-tennis by breaking down the game into a sequence of actions, reinforcing each one separately whenever the pigeons displayed an approximation to the particular action. More generally, Skinner saw this process as representing how learning could be induced – analysing a task into behavioural components and then systematically reinforcing each component in its proper sequence. The later development of *programmed learning* owes a lot to Skinner, and even today a great deal of training follows the principles laid down in operant conditioning.

Skinner distinguished between respondent and operant types of behaviour. The first type is essentially a predictable reflex, such as drawing one's hand away from a flame, whereas the second is a spontaneous act of the individual and may have no obvious cause. Operant behaviour may therefore be directed to a goal not obvious to an observer, something desired or valued by the individual. Skinner argued that operant behaviour can be created or modified by controlled stimuli associated with appropriate reinforcement. A reinforced behaviour will be progressively selected in preference to other behaviours.

Although behaviourism has been hugely influential, it should be clear that it has severe limitations, both conceptual and moral. Its explicitly scientific approach means that behaviourism consciously limits itself to observable, repeatable facets of human behaviour. It thus diminishes the richness of learning and makes it difficult to transfer findings to the complex situations encountered in education and training. All but the most controlled and prescribed situations will therefore be imperfectly represented by behaviourist approaches. In particular, although the agency of an individual is recognized in terms of instrumental learning and motivation, there is no account of how an individual makes sense of their experience – a key element of later theories. Nor is there recognition of the social aspect of learning. Arguably, behaviourism is also morally deficient in that human beings are treated as little more than mechanical systems; the treatment of Albert B. showing what this approach can lead to.

For an interesting discussion of the philosophical limitations of behaviourism, see Carr (2003: 90–3). He notes that behaviourism cannot account for the ways in which people grasp the *sense* or *meaning* of knowledge and social practices. Although learning may involve causal processes such as the establishment of S–R bonds, it cannot be reducible to *only* these processes. For example, a pigeon could be taught to press a red disc to obtain food, in preference to discs of other colours. Does the pigeon *know* that the disc is red? And what would it *mean* to say, 'The pigeon knows that the disc is red'?

Nevertheless, it would be a mistake to dismiss behaviourism. The concept of reinforcement, when interpreted in the human terms of praise, satisfaction and a sense of achievement, indicates the importance of the benefits (material and intellectual) of learning. The potential of classical conditioning for creating undesired learning, such as Albert's fear of animals, also suggests possible explanations for the fear and anxiety often reported by adult learners returning to education following difficult experiences at school. Furthermore, the emphasis on careful analysis of a task or topic to be learned and the systematic reinforcement of each aspect is clearly important in building up an understanding of how to plan learning.

Cognitivism

Cognitive psychology attempts to remedy the shortcomings of behaviourism by accounting for learning 'in terms of the active construction and imposition of principles or rules on experience' (Carr 2003: 94). Its roots lie in the work of the early twentieth-century Gestalt psychologists (Gestalt is a German word meaning 'shape'), who investigated the nature of perception and the ways in which people construct meaning from sensory impressions. Their aim was to discover general laws determining the way objects are perceived; however, unlike behaviourists who break down learning into discrete components, Gestalt psychologists wanted their principles to account for the 'breakthrough' moment in which we perceive something as a whole. Many of the examples used in Gestalt psychology have become familiar: for example, the drawing of a duck that, perceived differently, suddenly emerges as a drawing of a rabbit. In such cases, we experience sudden discontinuities in the way we perceive; we do not learn to see them differently through a sequence of S–R bonds – or at least it does not *feel* that we do.

Cognitivism is concerned with structure: both the intrinsic structure of knowledge and the structures 'within our heads'. For the cognitivist, going beyond mere information requires that we organize and re-organize facts, concepts and principles in cognitive structures. Ideas are related to other ideas, and individual facts acquire meaning by being subsumed into broader, principled structures. A key figure in cognitivism is Jerome Bruner (1915–), who describes how his interest was stimulated by reflecting on the *activity* of cognition. 'Knowing, it soon became clear, was not just passively receiving and associating stimuli from the world and then responding in conformity with rewards or "reinforcements" from outside ... much of *learning* was guided by how you thought about what you were encountering' (Bruner 2006: 1).

Bruner originated the term *spiral curriculum*, meaning a way of organizing the curriculum so that fundamental concepts are introduced at an early stage of a course in a simplified way, and then revisited to bring out their full complexity. For Bruner, this is not merely a matter of teaching technique; it is bound up with the hypothesis that 'any subject can be taught effectively in some intellectually honest form to any child at any stage of development' (Bruner 2006: 47). It follows that anything not worth teaching in a developed form to adults is not worth teaching to younger or less experienced students; 'a curriculum ought to be built around the great issues, principles and values' of a society (Bruner 2006: 56). Hence, the spiral curriculum approach is a way of maintaining these central issues in the foreground of education while recognizing the cognitive structures used by a learner (see Box 7.4).

Bruner is particularly associated with *discovery learning*. He argues that 'Mastery of the fundamental ideas of a field involves not only the grasping of general principles, but also the development of an attitude towards learning and inquiry ... toward the possibility of solving problems on one's own' (Bruner 2006: 41). Developing this attitude, Bruner says, cannot be done by 'mere presentation'; learners must participate in the excitement of discovery. By contrast, David Ausubel is critical of discovery learning and regards *expository* or *reception* learning as wilfully under-rated by some

---

Box 7.4 Some key themes of cognitivism

1　Bodies of knowledge, like the sciences, cohere by dint of ideational structures that serve to organize and give meaning to their empirical details.
2　Understanding any particular body of knowledge requires grasping the underlying intellectual structure that renders its empirical details comprehensible.
3　Such structures vary from the highly intuitive and informal to the deductive-mathematical . . .
4　In the course of coming to understand any particular body of knowledge, we tend naturally to begin with an initial intuitive grasp and progress with its help to a more formalized and verifiable form of understanding.
5　Indeed, the course of human mental growth itself typically progresses from an earlier intuitive stage to a later, more formalized and explicit form of verifiable reasoning . . .
6　It follows then that any body of knowledge, whatever the subject, can be taught to anybody at any age in some initially intuitive form that does it justice.

Source: Bruner (2006: 2–3)

---

authors, resulting in students being 'coerced into mimicking the externally conspicuous but inherently trivial aspects of scientific method' in order to 'rediscover or exemplify principles which the teacher could have presented verbally and demonstrated visually in a matter of minutes' (Ausubel 1963: 141).

Ausubel emphasizes the idea of meaningful learning, in which new material is related to existing knowledge, and advocates the use of *advance organizers* in presenting new content. As their name implies, these help the learner to fit new knowledge into their cognitive structures and aid the development of new structures. Advance organizers should indicate how existing relevant concepts are either basically similar, or essentially different, to the new ideas and information being presented. However, an advance organizer is not quite the same thing as a summary or overview of what is to be learned, but a way of making sense of it. Thus an advance organizer for a lesson on the storage and display of cakes might use the general principle that cakes go stale because of drying out, and also indicate similarities and differences to the principles for storing biscuits learned previously. This will help integrate the specific knowledge gained within a broader conceptual scheme.

Constructivist theories of learning

The only justification for our concepts and system of concepts is that they serve to represent the complex of our experiences; beyond this they have no legitimacy.

(Einstein 1922: 2)

Constructivist learning theories start from a constructivist *epistemology*: a theory of knowledge in opposition to objectivism. Objectivism sees truths as correct and unambiguous representations of an external reality, whereas constructivism regards knowledge as actively constructed by individuals or cultures seeking to make sense of their experiential worlds (von Glaserfeld 1995). According to constructivism, truth and meaning are not inherent in objects, but inferred from our sense experience in complex and interdependent ways. Constructivism is therefore related to the idealist views of philosophers such as George Berkeley (1685–1753), who argued that we cannot know that things exist external to the mind, for *as objects*, rather than bundles of sense impressions, they are known only through the mind. Notwithstanding the force of these arguments, constructivism must deal with the problem of intersubjectivity: that is, how do we account for the fact that, even though our individual 'knowledges' may be subjective, when we speak of objects and their properties we at least appear to be speaking of the same things? For example, if you have a headache this is a subjective experience, in that there is no way for others to know what sense impressions you are having. Nevertheless, if you say 'I have a headache', we can participate in what Wittgenstein (1953) called a *language game*, involving shared meanings and uses of the word 'headache'. For this reason, constructivism has acquired a social dimension, in which intersubjectivity is achieved through participation in communities of practice (Wenger 1998). Constructivist epistemology uses the concept of viability – the power of our concepts, knowledge and theories to help us explain and control the world – rather than seeking a foundation for absolute truth.

These reflections help us to identify three versions of constructivism: the psychological, the social and the radical. *Psychological* constructivism is an account of how individuals construct meaning and, through social interaction, come to persuade others that their concepts and theories are viable – or come to be persuaded that they are mistaken. Through these processes, formal knowledge is produced in a community of equals. In *social* constructivism, the nature of social interaction and its effect on knowledge construction is more closely interrogated. Thus power, ideology, economic and cultural resources, and other aspects of human society enter into the process of knowledge construction, influencing what counts as formal knowledge and introducing gradations of status in what we know. Finally, *radical* constructivism rejects the possibility of intersubjective knowledge, regarding knowledge of all kinds as constructed by the individual and inevitably reflecting the perspective of the knower. According to this view, there are no external criteria for judging knowledge, and one person's knowledge claims are as good as those of anyone else.

Constructivist learning theory draws on all these strands, including a variety of sources from philosophy, psychology and sociology, such as the philosophical pragmatism of William James and John Dewey, the theory of cognitive development proposed by Jean Piaget, and the socio-historical perspective associated with Lev Vygotsky. The participation metaphor of learning is prominent, with learners actively engaging in struggles to integrate new experiences and vistas within existing conceptual structures, modifying old systems of thought or creating new ones in response to change, conflict and contradiction. There are strong links with Bruner's cognitive psychology and the experiential learning theories of David Kolb (discussed below), including central themes such as the learner's cognitive adaptation to new experiences and information.

In Piaget's work, the ability to construct knowledge is seen as a function of cognitive development throughout childhood and adolescence, which is partly a result of physical maturation of the brain. However, he did not regard this development as continuous, occurring through the gradual elaboration of increasingly sophisticated ways of thinking, but as progressing through discrete stages, each one with qualitative differences from the preceding stage (Piaget and Inhelder 1969). For Piaget, learning requires both *readiness* – having reached an appropriate stage of cognitive development – and *adaptation*, in which accumulated experience stimulates the reorganization of learners' understandings. For example, very young children are unable to fully conceptualize quantities such as number and volume: five coins spread out are seen as 'more coins' than five coins closely spaced, and a tall, narrow container is seen as holding more juice than a short, wide one of equal volume. By the age of 7, Piaget thought, most children acquire the ability to *conserve* number and volume correctly.

Piaget's work has been criticized in a number of ways: first, its empirical base is rather thin (Piaget relied a great deal on observations of his own children) and neglects the social context in which children are asked to perform certain tasks; second, the ages at which certain developmental stages are reached has been questioned – in particular, it has been claimed that the stage of formal operations may not appear until late adolescence, if at all. Most fundamentally, theorists such as Bruner and Vygotsky would deny that Piaget's 'stages' are really discrete, proposing instead that there is continuous development at different rates for different individuals. Nevertheless, the notion of readiness has been found useful in other theoretical perspectives – notably in Vygotsky's notion of the *zone of proximal development* (see Figure 7.3).

Lev Vygotsky (1896–1934) is an important figure in twentieth-century psychology, with a range of contributions including work on play and learning disabilities. He is perhaps best known for his emphasis on the inter-relatedness of thought and language: not only do we express thoughts in words, but words frame our thoughts. Language supplies us with concepts as well as signs, and even inner thought achieves a greater sophistication as our grasp of language develops. However, this development of

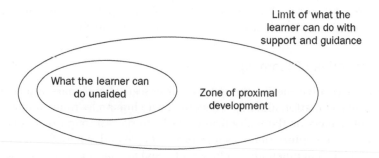

Figure 7.3 Vygotsky's zone of proximal development

thought and language does not take place through solitary introspection: it is fundamentally a result of social interaction.

Other people, through direct intervention and guidance, bring us to understand
and share in the features of a culture. For Vygotsky, there is therefore no firm distinction between what we can and cannot do; development does not precede new cognitive abilities, as in Piaget, but takes place alongside them. The notion of the zone of
proximal development captures this idea, and emphasizes the role of more experienced or knowledgeable people in providing scaffolding (not a term used by Vygotsky,
but currently popular in literature inspired by his work) to help us successfully
complete activities we could not do unaided. This promotes learning and development
so that eventually we are able to perform the task ourselves.

Drawing on Fox (2001) and Boethel and Dimock (2000), Yilmaz (2008: 167)
summarizes the key tenets of constructivist learning theory as follows:

- 'Learning is an active process.
- Learning is an adaptive activity.
- Learning is situated in the context in which it occurs.
- Knowledge is not innate, passively absorbed or invented but constructed by
  the learner.
- All knowledge is personal and idiosyncratic.
- All knowledge is socially constructed.
- Learning is essentially a process of making sense of the world.
- Experience and prior understanding play a role in learning.
- Effective learning requires meaningful, open-ended, challenging problems for
  the learner to solve.'

Although constructivism is currently perhaps the most influential theoretical perspective on learning, it has been criticized for a lack of clarity and for being essentially a
series of metaphors rather than a self-consistent theory. As in cognitivism, construc-
tivists view learning as a process in which the learner builds on existing knowledge,
assimilating new concepts and information in ways that lead to new knowledge structures. However, because they insist that knowledge is not a representation of an
external objective reality, this leads to internal contradictions – for example, the
tension between conceptions of knowledge as being both personal and socially
constructed, or the question: if learning is adaptive, what is it learners adapt to, if not
an external reality? For such reasons, constructivism is perhaps best viewed as a set
of powerful insights rather than a systematic account of learning.

Humanist theories of learning

Whatever their relative merits, the theories discussed above share a *detachment* in
which their subject matter, although concerned with human learning, might as well be
the motion of planets or the multiplication of bacteria. Although this is laudable as
science, it fails to recognize that its subjects are people and can lead to a *technocratic*
approach which is fundamentally undemocratic and alienating. As a student, how you
learn is often regarded as determined by experts, who know best what you need

because they have the theoretical keys to the learning process. Humanist theories of learning contest this viewpoint, drawing on the work of Dewey (1938) as well as on humanist psychology to take a person-centred approach in which true learning comes from within. Particularly associated with the work of Abraham Maslow and Carl Rogers, humanist theories have influenced many developments in education, including student-centred learning and the andragogy of Malcolm Knowles (Knowles et al. 2005).

Humanistic psychologists claimed that behaviourist and cognitivist approaches excluded from psychology much of what makes us human. They aimed to emphasize the notion of 'self' and to cultivate the development of human potential. This view-point is associated with Maslow's concept of self-actualization and connects learning with individual desires. Rogers and Freiburg (1994: 35) state the humanist position eloquently:

> I want to talk about learning, but not the lifeless, sterile, futile, quickly forgotten stuff that is crammed into the mind of the helpless individual . . . I am talking about *learning* – insatiable curiosity that drives the adolescent mind to absorb everything he can see or hear or read about a topic that has inner meaning. I am talking about the student who says 'I am discovering, drawing in from the outside, and making what I discover a real part of me.'

Maslow's work in particular is based on assumptions of human-centredness, personal autonomy, the idea of human dignity and a sense of personal responsibility. These assumptions have found their way into mainstream practice in lifelong learning, particularly through the precepts of andragogy but also within pedagogical principles concerned with younger learners, such as the idea that students should 'take responsibility for their own learning'. Rogers emphasizes the importance of personal relationships between teachers and learners and advocates the creation of a climate based on empathy, trust and respect. Furthermore, he rejects the idea of learning as based on pre-determined outcomes, instead encouraging teachers to facilitate broader experiential and largely self-directed learning.

Critics of humanistic psychology have argued that its assumptions are unjustified, leading to a romanticized view of the possibilities for self-actualization (Pearson and Podeschi 1999). In particular, the validity of assuming personal autonomy is questioned, on the basis of the critiques of individualism discussed in Chapter 3 in the context of structure and agency. Some of these criticisms are especially pertinent to the current discourse of individual responsibility in lifelong learning: 'Those who fail to reach the heights described by Maslow may feel that they are personally to blame for their discontent . . . The individualization of success and failure can also result in blaming those who suffer from social injustice for the hardships they face' (Shaw and Colimore 1988: 60).

Experiential and reflective learning

Experiential learning is much more than the observation that all learning comes from experience. An experiential approach to learning is implicit in humanistic theories; Rogers often equates person-centred or humanistic classrooms with the practice of experiential learning. In fact, experiential learning is a complex integration of theory and practice, based on a view of learning as essentially democratic and inclusive. It is based on an 'education of equals' rather than on 'education from above' (Gregory 2002: 95) and involves personal commitment, interaction with other people and a willingness to engage emotions and feelings (Boud et al. 1993: 1). Some of the central tenets and assumptions of experiential learning are shown in Box 7.5.

Experiential learning aims to involve the whole person in an encounter with learning; the experience is of immersion in knowledge, action and practice. Heron (1989: 13) states that 'Experiential knowledge is knowledge gained through action and practice. . . . It is manifest through the process of being there, face-to-face, with the person, at the event, in the experience.'

However, experience must be transformed for learning to occur. Indeed, Kolb (1984: 38) defines learning as 'the process whereby knowledge is created through the transformation of experience'. Building on the work of Dewey (1933), Kolb developed

---

Box 7.5 Characteristics of experiential learning

Learning is best conceived as a process, not in terms of outcomes.

Learning is a continuous process grounded in experience.

The process of learning requires the resolution of conflicts between dialectically opposed modes of adaptation to the world: for example, between concrete experience and abstract concepts or between observation and action.

Learning is an holistic process of adaptation to the world.

Learning involves transactions between the person and the environment . . . books, teacher and classroom cannot substitute for the wider environment of the 'real world'.

Learning is the process of creating knowledge by the transaction between objective, accumulated human cultural experience and the subjective life experiences of the individual person.

Source: (Kolb 1984: 25–38)

The whole person, both in feeling and in cognitive aspects, is part of the learning event.

Self-initiated involvement is essential for significant learning.

Learning is pervasive – it affects the behaviour, attitudes and even personality of the learner.

The learner's evaluation of a learning event is with reference to the learner – the element of meaning to the learner is built into the experience.

Source: Rogers and Freiberg (1994: 36)

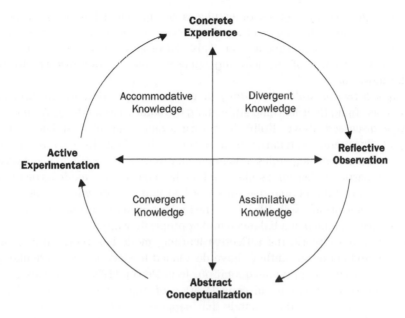

Figure 7.4 Kolb's experiential learning cycle
Source: Kolb (1984: 42)

a well-known model of how this transformation takes place in an *experiential learning cycle* (see Figure 7.4).

According to this model, experience is first *grasped* and then *transformed* into strategies that guide actions. Experience may be grasped through its immediate impact or be mediated by concepts and theories. The transformation of experience may take place through internal reflection or by actively experimenting and manipulating the environment. The process of experiential learning therefore consists of a four-stage cycle involving four learning modes – concrete experience, reflective observation, abstract conceptualization and active experimentation. Kolb (1984: 41) pairs these modes as opposites, concrete experience being 'dialectically opposed' to abstract conceptualization and active experimentation to reflective observation.

In Figure 7.4, the four modes of Kolb's 'cycle' are shown, together with the four types of knowledge arising from these modes. For example, *assimilative* knowledge results from grasping experience by means of abstract concepts and transforming the experience so grasped by reflective observation. On the other hand, *accommodative* knowledge derives from apprehending the immediate qualities of experience, which is then transformed into knowledge by the results of active experimentation.

Kolb's model is not necessarily a sequential cycle; it may also be regarded as a model of different preferences for grasping experience and transforming it into knowledge. This leads to the idea of a *learning style*, in which Kolb was a pioneer. He regards learning styles as originating in our preferences for certain types of experience: 'Through their choices of experience, people program themselves to grasp reality through varying degrees of emphasis on apprehension or comprehension' (Kolb 1984: 64). Similarly, they program themselves to transform their grasp of reality through reflection or experimentation. This self-programming, according to Kolb, determines which parts of the learning cycle receive the greatest emphasis in a particular individual.

Using a *learning styles inventory*, a person's orientation to learning can be assessed, classifying their learning style along the same lines as the different types of knowledge discussed above. Kolb's inventory assigns one of four learning styles: convergent, divergent, assimilative or accommodative (Kolb 1984: 77–8). In view of current debates on learning styles, it is important to note that Kolb does not advocate 'catering for' particular learning styles – in fact, he regards each mode as being incomplete: 'more powerful and adaptive forms of learning emerge when these strategies are used in combination' (Kolb 1984: 65). The highest level of learning occurs when all four modes are combined in a balanced and appropriate way.

Following Kolb's work, the reflective learning mode has received a great deal of attention, and numerous authors have developed models of this particular aspect of the learning cycle. In a famous quotation, John Dewey (1933: 6) defines reflection as, 'Active, persistent and careful consideration of any belief or supposed form of knowledge in the light of the grounds that support it, and the further conclusions towards which it tends'. More recently, Boud et al. (1985: 19) define reflection as 'a generic term for those intellectual and affective activities in which individuals engage to explore their experiences in order to lead to new understandings and appreciations'. They propose a model of reflection in which experience (the left-hand circle in Figure 7.5) is transformed into learning outcomes (the right-hand circle) by means of a three-stage process.

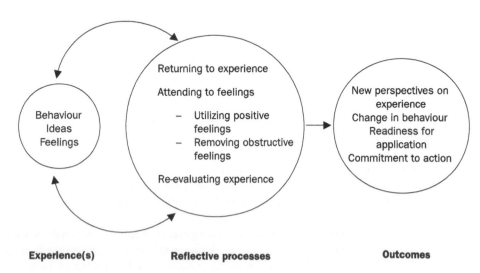

Figure 7.5 Three-stage model of reflective processes and their role in reflective learning
Source: Boud et al. (1985: 36)

The first stage, *returning to experience*, is the description of relevant events. Boud et al. (1985: 27) regard this descriptive activity as crucial in re-presenting events to the mind and recommend that judgements should be avoided at this stage; the aim is to provide data for reflection, not to jump to conclusions. However, feelings and judgements made at the time should be noted as an important part of the data. In the second stage, *attending to feelings*, past and present emotional responses are evaluated either as aids or barriers to learning. Being able to recognize the role of feelings is essential, otherwise entrenched perspectives may prove difficult to surmount due to affective rather than cognitive barriers, for example, if new ideas conflict with cherished values or beliefs.

These two stages establish the foundations for *re-evaluating experience*. In this third stage, new data are related to what is already known. An important element of this stage is validation and appropriation – reconciling the new ideas and feelings with one's own identity and integrating them into new cognitive and affective structures.

The learning styles debate

Learning style theory has been widely promoted as a strategy for supporting learning, with organizations such as Ofsted advocating its use (O'Toole and Meyer 2006: 17). It is argued that learners may be disadvantaged if teachers do not take their preferred ways of learning into account. Although this has an intuitive appeal, notions of 'learning style' are problematic. The term itself is variously defined and used interchangeably with other expressions such as *thinking style, cognitive style* and *learning orientation*. Cassidy (2004: 420) draws attention to the 'variety of definitions, theoretical positions, models, interpretations and measures of the construct'. However, Nixon et al. (2007: 40) describe all learning style models as built around three principles:

> The first principle claims that an individual's behaviour demonstrates a pattern of preferences or habitual ways of acting. That is, the learner's behaviour will follow certain predictable patterns if confronted with a given set of stimuli. Second, these patterns of preferences can be identified and then organized into a classificatory scheme . . . Finally, it is claimed that reliable and insightful diagnostic tools can be devised to link learners to particular preferences.

Teachers are faced with a bewildering array of models. Coffield et al. (2004: 2) note that 'In many ways, the use of different inventories of learning styles has acquired an unexamined life of its own, where the notion of learning styles itself and the various means to measure it are accepted without question.' One popular model involves the identification of *learning modalities* based on the use of a visual, auditory, kinaesthetic (VAK) learning style analysis, in which individuals are said to have a preference for learning through a specific perceptual channel. Teachers are advised to match curricular activities to the needs of students who have been identified as visual, auditory, kinaesthetic or multi-modal learners (for example, see Duckett and Tatarkowsky 2005).

The VAK model has been subject to challenge, and its supposed benefits are disputed. For example, Klein (2003: 48) argues that curricular activities cannot be categorized by modality because 'many and perhaps most kinds of knowledge appear to involve representations of more than one modality'. For example, consider the suggestion that one sign of a kinaesthetic learner might be that they enjoy making things and using their hands (Duckett and Tatarkowsky 2005: 14). This involves over-simplifying the process of 'making something'; for most people, making something also involves the use of visual information – and much else besides.

Coffield et al. (2004) draw attention to the beliefs upon which specific learning style models are built. A number of approaches involve the assumption that learning styles are fixed, inherited traits, although some models stress the influence of contextual, personal and environmental factors. The view that learning style is innate carries the risk of students being labelled – sometimes literally – by means of badges identifying their learning style. Hargreaves (2005: 11) suggests that the uncritical use of learning styles is reminiscent of the 'now largely abandoned notions of fixed and inherited intelligence'. Learning style instruments may be specific to culture, gender or age and can lead to the incorrect assessment of learners from different backgrounds. If a diagnostic tool fails to take account of language variation, responses may be misinterpreted.

In spite of the deficiencies of learning style theory, there are benefits to a critical awareness of learning styles: 'instead of talking about different types of learner we recommend discussing different approaches to learning . . . different orientations to learning . . . different models of learning . . . and different emotions associated with learning' (Coffield 2005: 6). This requires teachers who are 'knowledgeable . . . about learning itself'. In particular, Coffield et al. (2004: 36–9) identify two specific advantages of introducing learners to the idea of learning style: first, it encourages them to engage in *metacognition* – considering their own approaches to learning and knowing; second, it can provide a language for talking about learning. Although at present the evidence is conflicting, the deliberate mismatching as well as matching of learning activities to individual learning styles may enable learners to develop a more rounded and balanced approach to their learning (Coffield et al. 2004: 40–1). Much research remains to be carried out, but the issues should be considered with care before applying labels to learners.

Widening participation

This section, and those that follow, consider a number of specific groups of learners who face particular challenges and opportunities, including adults, learners from other countries, students with disabilities or learning difficulties, and 'gifted' learners. These sections should be read in conjunction with Chapter 6, which discusses broader issues of equality and diversity such as class, race and gender.

The Kennedy Report (1997) highlighted the role of *widening participation*, which explicitly seeks to promote a more diverse social profile of learners. Kennedy described how colleges could tackle social and economic inequality through drawing a wider community into education; a commitment to social justice by means of education throughout life, or *lifelong learning*, was coupled with enhancing Britain's economic competitiveness by improving workforce skills. Improving literacy and numeracy became a key element of widening participation strategies, including the *Skills for Life* agenda developed through numerous policy documents such as *Success for All* (DfES 2002b).

Economic competitiveness and social inclusion motivate today's policy as 'twin pillars of lifelong learning' (Hyland and Merrill 2003: 30). New Labour funded FE more generously than previous governments, but it also directed the sector more closely than before, focusing on tightly defined skills. Widening participation went hand in hand with a narrowing of the curriculum, which became more vocational and increasingly fragmented. The Coalition Government which formed following the election in 2010 argued that de-regulation of FE, with more autonomy for individual institutions, would make the sector more responsive. However, an environment of significant funding reductions called into question whether widening participation would remain more than a rhetorical target.

One of the most significant and ambitious of New Labour's widening participation targets was for 50 per cent of 18–30-year-olds to experience HE by 2010. Part-time students accessing HE in an FE context, especially through foundation degrees, were to provide much of the intended increase. Following publication of the Browne Review of higher education (Browne 2010; instituted by the Labour Government in 2009 but reporting to the then recently-elected Coalition Government in October 2010), FE colleges are (in policy statements, at least) intended to be part of a more fluid, competitive HE market. This market is supposed to offset the effects of increased tuition fees, leading to a situation in which the highest fees are charged by the most prestigious institutions – arguably, those which confer the greatest earning power on their graduates – whilst other institutions offer a lower-cost alternative, often to less geographically mobile students. Funding for increased participation at lower levels of education has also been provided for marginal groups such as those who are not in education, employment or training. Prior to 2010, young people aged 16–18 in full-time education could receive the means-tested Education Maintenance Allowance (EMA). Following the first round of public expenditure reductions implemented by the Coalition Government, EMA was replaced by a system of allowances targeted at those deemed most in need. For a discussion of Labour and Coalition policies on education, particularly those concerning issues of social justice, see Avis (2011).

The overall impact of widening participation has been to increase the numbers in education and training. Much of this has been in part-time courses, often at lower levels, which have a key skills or 'employability' element. The development of 14–19 education has brought in new learners, as has the extension of 'college higher education'. The growth has been rapid, and the nature and content of courses has changed. Nevertheless, developments associated with widening participation can be considered as evolutionary and not a radical break from the history of FE.

Adult learners and 'adult learning'

Changing social circumstances have led to a varied population of adult students in education or training. The aspirations and experiences of adult learners are diverse. Some may want a qualification relevant to their work; some are taking their first steps back into education after a long break; some hope to gain a degree. Many adult learners have had less than positive experiences of education in the past. Each arrives with attitudes to learning which shape their aims and expectations; very often, these attitudes are based on constructing education as difficult and hard to access. Adult learning, therefore, is partly concerned to introduce new ideas about what it means to be a student, about the nature of knowledge, the value of experience and the trans-formative potential of education. This may entail changing the learner's perspective from a view of education as a potentially dispiriting experience to something which is associated with success:

> So, what if we adopted a different perspective, one that placed learning in the context of our lived experience of the world? What if we assumed that learning is as much a part of our human nature as eating or sleeping, that it is both life sustaining and inevitable, and that – given a chance – we are quite good at it?
>
> (Wenger 1998: 3)

Theories of adult learning

Many concepts, theories and models currently inform adult learning. However, a number of common themes or assumptions – often associated with the term *andragogy* – can be identified (Knowles et al. 2005; Morgan-Klein and Osborne 2007; Osborne et al. 2007):

1   *Adults can learn how to learn*: tutors can facilitate this process in order to make learning more effective and meaningful.
2   *Adult learning is self-directed*: that is, adults are or have the potential to be autonomous learners.
3   *Adult learning is purposeful*: adults choose to learn for reasons to do with their lives outside the classroom or workshop.
4   *Drawing on experience is a fundamental property of adult learning*: life or family or work are all valid contexts from which to draw in an experiential learning process.
5   *Adults reflect on their experiences and learn from them*: reflective learning as an individualized form of learning can be facilitated by a tutor.

The assumptions and commitments of andragogy can be seen as reflecting more mainstream concerns with inclusive learning, or discourses of 'learning to learn' and 'employability', all of which are relevant to younger learners. It would be difficult to argue that children do not wish to relate learning to their lives, learn from reflecting on their experiences, and so on. Research about the ways in which young people learn how to play computer games suggests that their learning is self directed and involves learning how to learn (Gee 2003, 2004). However, the legal, social and financial independence of most adults are factors in marking out the assumptions of andragogy as applying with greater intensity to adults.

Practices of adult learning

The ways in which mature students are accommodated are often directly influenced by andragogy. For example, the motivation of mature students is often assumed not to be a significant issue, compared with the motivation of 16-year-old students. At the same time there is a longer standing philosophical and political approach to adult education and training that still has an impact, and which has been influential in forming attitudes around the social implications of adult learning (A. Rogers 2002; J. Rogers 2007; Wallis 1996). Common themes are:

1   Problem-based learning and teaching activities are well-suited to mature students.
2   Learning and teaching strategies should help build the confidence of mature students if they have been away from formal education and training.
3   The biographies of mature students can have a considerable impact on their learning.
4   Mature students return to learning for all sorts of reasons that might not be directly concerned with the subject or topic being taught.
5   Barriers to participation by mature students may be bound up in the practicalities of their lives: childcare; transport; reconciling work with study.

As noted earlier, the assumptions of andragogy are not always treated critically, and the issue of motivation is not necessarily different between adults and younger students. The rise of 'welfare to work' policies such as New Deal has brought large numbers of adults back into learning who are there more or less by compulsion, further questioning the assumptions of andragogy, so that new approaches to both theory and practice in adult learning may be needed.

Many adult educators would acknowledge that instrumental motivations are often responsible for a return to learning, but seek to subvert the notion of workforce development as purely functional education for a series of 'economic units'. Thus students wishing to gain qualifications in sectors such as childcare and community development, where a competence-based approach dominates, may also be encouraged to adopt a more reflexive standpoint. Adult education practice can embody a 'third discourse' which synthesizes instrumental and transformative education (Moore 1999: 132).

Learners from other countries

According to the 2011 census, approximately 7.5 million residents in England and Wales are foreign-born, an increase of 3 million since 2001; the majority were based in London and the South-East. The most frequently reported country of origin was India; however, the numbers of European migrants are increasing, with Poland and Germany appearing in the top six alongside Ireland, Pakistan and Bangladesh (BBC 2012). Many migrant learners engage in Skills for Life provision, particularly ESOL. Although numbers have been declining in recent years, in 2010–11 over 160,000 learners participated in ESOL classes (Data Service 2012). However, most ESOL learners are from UK-born minority ethnic groups (LSC 2007a: 14), so the number of participants is an inaccurate measure of migrants' involvement in ESOL provision. Nevertheless, the LSC (2007a: 13) estimated that 15 per cent of ESOL learners were asylum seekers. Moreover, the expansion of the European Union (EU) has attracted many learners from Eastern Europe.

The skill levels of migrants differ widely: for example, 33 per cent of African migrants and 31 per cent of Chinese migrants are graduates. Sachdev and Harries (2006: 39) conclude that the majority of migrants from the European accession states are highly qualified but lack sufficient English language ability to access employment opportunities commensurate with their qualifications.

The European Council for Refugees and Exiles (ECRE) asserts that 'Education is the key to integration' (ECRE 1999: 5). In England and Wales, NIACE (2006) specifically recommends that ESOL teachers should be involved in providing general advice and guidance to new migrants, particularly relating to employment – partly in recognition that many ESOL teachers already act unofficially in this role.

International students are important participants in UK HE, despite well-publicized changes to visa regulations and the resulting obligations on HE institutions to monitor international students. In 2010–11, there were over 428,000 students from other countries in UK HE, and in London 26 per cent of students were from overseas (UKCISA 2013). Non-EU students account for 60 per cent of all international HE students in the UK, with China and India represented most strongly but with sizeable contingents from other Asian countries, Africa, North America and the Middle East. In order to prepare prospective students for academic study in the UK, many universities now offer summer schools and other induction courses which articulate with their degree programmes. English for Academic Purposes (EAP), which specifically addresses the needs of HE students, is an increasingly important area of ESOL provision.

Students with learning difficulties or disabilities

Social attitudes towards people with disabilities are changing, underpinned by government initiatives and legislation. Excluding disabled students from mainstream educational opportunities is no longer acceptable. The notion of inclusive learning, introduced earlier, is a major step forward in this respect and highlights the ability of institutions to respond to learner needs rather than locating the difficulty or deficit with the learner. Disability legislation is based on this viewpoint and emphasizes the responsibility of education providers to anticipate and adjust to individual requirements; in particular, discrimination against students with disabilities in post-compulsory education is illegal.

According to this legislation, known most recently as the Equality Act 2010, educational institutions must not discriminate against a student or potential student in relation to activities such as admissions, teaching provision, recreational facilities and awards. Institutions have a duty to make *reasonable adjustments* for a student with a disability. These considerations are important in course planning, as potential students are not obliged to disclose a disability and may therefore only have support needs identified once on course.

Teachers' practice can be adjusted in a number of ways to support students with disabilities. For example, a partially sighted student could use a computer with a magnified screen display, or may benefit from access to printed materials with larger font sizes or a magnifying reading lamp. A student unable to create written documents due to restricted mobility could be provided with a computer with speech recognition software, while room layouts may need to be altered for a learner who uses a wheelchair. Some disabilities are 'unseen' and may not be obvious to the tutor or other students. For example, a student with a mental health difficulty may need additional tutorial support because they find it difficult to take part fully in a whole class setting. In other situations, the teacher may need to accommodate support workers – for example, a hearing impaired student may be working with a British Sign Language (BSL) interpreter.

'Academically more able learners'

The provision of enhanced support for students with learning difficulties is largely uncontroversial. Support for students with exceptional ability, on the other hand, is much more contentious and is inextricably linked with questions of equality. As Purdy (2007: 314) notes, 'Deciding how to educate so-called "exceptional" students is both a moral and an educational question.' She contrasts the argument that children who are not challenged may become bored and rebellious, ultimately to the detriment of society as a whole, with the democratic requirement of a common education for all children.

Programmes for academically more able learners are often associated with one of two basic models: enrichment or acceleration. The enrichment approach maintains normal progression through the curriculum but attempts to provide greater depth and breadth, while acceleration allows learners to progress more quickly. Both of these models have advantages and disadvantages, and evidence for and against them is not conclusive.

Whatever model for 'gifted and talented' provision is adopted, a crucial question is whether reliable and valid means of selecting students can ever be produced. This is particularly important given the possibility of gender, race, class and income influencing selection to gifted and talented programmes. Purdy (2007: 318) uses this as part of a moral argument for the acceleration model, which arguably can be accessible to anyone at any time dependent on performance, but whether any form of provision can be separated from injustice in selection is unlikely.

The New Labour Government's (1997–2010) Gifted and Talented programme had most impact in the compulsory sector, where every school was required to have a strategy to 'stretch' the top 10 per cent of achievers in any subject (DfES 2005b). However, the programme extended into post-compulsory education and related to widening participation by aiming to improve attainment, aspirations and motivation as well as the support available for gifted and talented students aged 14–19 (DfES 2004b: 24). In Spring 2012, the term 'gifted and talented' was replaced by 'academically more able', an expression possibly less value laden but also narrower and more focused on curricular achievement. Nevertheless, the idea that the most able require special treatment and motivation remains.

The Gifted and Talented programme created a new variety of special need attracting substantial attention and resources, and illustrated the controversial general questions discussed above. It could be seen as an opportunity for the most able students in state education to compete with those in the independent sector for places in elite universities. However, some question whether the most successful learners really require extra help and funding, which arguably could be better directed towards students who are struggling. Tomlinson (2008: 60) states that the focus on gifted learners in England is 'reminiscent of nineteenth-century debates over gradations of mental retardation' and 'predominantly benefits white middle and upper class students'. As such, special provision for academically more able learners may not fit easily with the egalitarian ideals of much of the FE sector.

Learners aged 14–16

The number of students aged 14–16 in English FE colleges grew considerably throughout the first decade of the twenty-first century, in parallel with an increasing focus on vocational education for younger learners. Although specific initiatives such as the 14–19 diplomas were often short lived, the idea that school is not always the best place for young people to learn, even below the age of 16, has proved attractive to policymakers, practitioners and young people themselves. For the New Labour government, attracting younger students onto vocationally-based courses in FE colleges derived from two central policies: widening participation in education and enhancing the vocational skills of the workforce. Above all, the government wished to reduce the number of young people 'not in education, employment or training' (or NEET). Providing younger students with non-academic courses earlier was part of that strategy. More recently, the idea that some young people are 'turned off' by mainstream schooling, or unsuited to it, has retained its hold. In spite of the doubts cast on some vocational qualifications by the Wolf Report (Wolf 2011), it is likely that FE colleges and work-based learning providers will be seen as alternative places of education for certain young people. Whether this can be done without stigmatizing those involved and reinforcing notions of FE as for 'other people's children' is another question.

Initiatives such as the Technical Baccalaureate are intended to avoid the low status of vocational courses in Britain, and to attract a broad range of younger students. However, Stanton and Fletcher (2006: 3) demonstrate a link between lower social class, poor academic attainment and attendance at colleges within this age group. Moreover, Harkin (2006: 323) found that the initial suggestion to attend a college course often came from school teachers. He described this as 'a process of benevolent herding', with schools directing their most challenging students towards FE colleges.

Nonetheless, Attwood et al. (2003), Harkin (2006) and Davies and Biesta (2007) have all found that the 14–16-year-olds who went to colleges enjoyed it, often because they appreciated greater independence as well as the attitudes of college teachers. However, colleges differed in their management of school-age students, with some integrating them fully and others organizing discrete provision. In an attempt to bring consistency to these disparate practices, more stringent regulations were implemented from September 2013, and colleges enrolling 14–15-year-old learners now to meet a number of requirements, including provision of dedicated accommodation for younger learners. Whilst young students are generally thought to respond well to the more adult environment of a college, and to benefit from access to a broad range of facilities, their presence raises obvious questions about safeguarding and complete integration would be impractical.

Perhaps more problematic is the question of suitable pedagogies for younger learners, and the interaction between school and college. Hall and Raffo (2004) argue that re-engaging young people through vocational education is a complex and multifaceted process, and pupils may respond to it in different ways. They found that learning in workplace and training provider contexts often contrasted strongly with experiences in school. For this reason, learning was often not transferable between contexts and there was evidence that negative attitudes to school could be reinforced by participation in work-related learning programmes. Great care is needed in designing vocational programmes for younger learners, and the attitudes and expectations of teachers can be as important as those of young people themselves. In particular, stereotypes of young learners being 'naughty' or disaffected should be examined critically. Studies of existing good practice in colleges highlight a number of successful teaching and learning strategies, including the following successful practices identified by McCrone et al. (2007: 33–5):

- 'An appropriate and transparent selection of young people onto courses.
- Close liaison with schools.
- Ensuring that 14–16 year olds were taught by lecturers who were committed to and enjoyed teaching them, and who were enthusiastic and positive towards the young people.
- Consideration of the college context, in terms of available facilities and the characteristics of the local community, in determining the type of provision.
- The provision of [pastoral] support for the young people.
- Academic support in the classroom either for specific pupils or more general assistance for lectures.
- A college-wide and holistic approach to the inclusion of this new age group.
- Training for lecturers in teaching and managing a younger age group . . . lecturers with experience of teaching 14–16 year olds said that it was important, for example, to set very clear expectations and objectives, to break tasks down into smaller chunks, to rotate activities, to set out clear ground rules for discipline and to always be on time for lectures.'

Young people not in education, employment or training

In the 1950s and 1960s, leaving education at an early age and with few or no qualifications was not seen as problematic. Relatively few young people stayed on after the compulsory school-leaving age of 15, and fewer still entered HE. Buoyant youth labour markets, and full employment more generally, ameliorated social inequalities in educational achievement. Although sociologists like Paul Willis (1977) explained the stuctural processes that determined that working-class children got working-class jobs, reasonably secure employment on a living wage was a realistic possibility.

Following the 1973 oil crisis, de-industrialization began to change this picture fundamentally. Adult workers displaced from traditional industries provided stiff competition for young people lacking qualifications and experience. The growth of work experience programmes such as the Youth Training Scheme (YTS), and increasing numbers of young people staying in mainstream education beyond the minimum leaving age (raised to 16 in 1974), to some extent offset this situation. However, as more and more young people have gained ever higher levels of education, those who – for various reasons – do not participate in post-compulsory education, and particularly those with no qualifications at all, are increasingly differentiated from their peers. International research over a period of twenty years has demonstrated that young people not in education, employment or training (in the UK this is often abbreviated to NEET) are likely to suffer permanent 'scarring' – not only in employment prospects but also in health and other social indicators (for an extensive discussion of research on NEET young people, see Simmons and Thompson 2011).

Although recent political and media discourse has presented being NEET (and, more generally, being long-term unemployed) as something of a 'lifestyle choice' (Shildrick et al. 2012: 219), it is important to recognize that being outside education and employment is related to poverty and disadvantage in childhood. It is also important to understand that NEET, as a negative definition – constructing a category of young people according to what they are not, rather than what they are – encompasses a diverse set of circumstances, experiences and aspirations. Interventions which treat NEET young people as a homogeneous group, rather than targeting specific individual needs, are therefore likely to be unsuccessful.

A particularly common set of assumptions relating to NEET young people concerns appropriate pedagogies for re-engaging young people who have failed in (or been failed by) the school system. These young people have, so the argument runs, little taste or aptitude for academic learning and require a more practical, 'hands-on' approach which avoids reading, writing and lengthy periods of concentration. Used carefully, this type of approach – which at its best involves embedding knowledge and skills within interesting and challenging contexts – can be successful and aid progression. However, whilst many NEET young people have difficulty with literacy, numeracy and maintaining regular routines of study, pedagogies which effectively exclude young people from powerful knowledge are ultimately self-defeating and offer little more than a short-term 'fix'. Such an approach also neglects the significant proportion of NEET young people who have been academically successful in the past, and have become NEET for various reasons unconnected with the curriculum. As with other groups of learners, provision needs to be responsive to individual needs and avoid stereotypical classifications.

8

The curriculum in the lifelong learning sector

Roy Fisher, Amanda Fulford, Bernard McNicholas and Ron Thompson

---

In this chapter

- What is the curriculum?
- Curriculum theory and models
- Curriculum design and development
- Creativity and the curriculum
- Vocationalism and parity of esteem
- 14–19 education and training
- Apprenticeshlps and higher apprenticeships
- College higher education
- Literacy, numeracy and ESOL: some background
- *Skills for Life* (and after)

What is the curriculum?

'Curriculum' can be defined in many ways, reflecting the complexity of an idea which encompasses meanings ranging from the specification of a programme of study, to the educational outcome of conflict between ideologies. Some introductions begin by explaining the etymology (origins) of the word – in Latin: 'curriculum' means a course, (although originally a racecourse rather than a course of study). In a seminal text first published in 1975, Lawrence Stenhouse (1981: 4) offered the formulation that 'A curriculum is an attempt to communicate the essential principles and features of an educational proposal in such a form that it is open to critical scrutiny and capable of effective translation into practice.'

Stenhouse takes *intent* as an essential element; a broader conception might contain unplanned elements which form part of the educational experience. This would incorporate factors arising from what is referred to as the 'hidden curriculum'. In essence, 'hidden curriculum' refers to the consequences of factors, outside formal teaching, which shape the educational experience. Institutions where learning takes place transmit attitudes, values and ways of being – some of these are intended, some not. While some definitions of the hidden curriculum refer to it as 'unintended' and, generally, imply that it is negative, this is not necessarily the case. The hidden curriculum might be both intended and positive, or benign, in its consequences.

Within educational systems broad frameworks have emerged in an attempt to impose coherence and equivalence. This has been a particular need in Britain, which has seen piecemeal development and reforms, especially in the vocational curriculum. The current National Qualifications Framework (NQF) and the Qualifications and Credit Framework (QCF) for England, Wales and Northern Ireland, and the Framework for Higher Education Qualifications (FHEQ) are outlined in Figure 8.1. The QAA's (2008) FHEQ provides qualification level descriptors for HE in England, Wales and Northern Ireland – a separate framework is published for Scotland. The European Qualifications Framework (EQF) compares the level of qualifications across Europe. Some commentators have seen trends of improving results in the UK as indicative of falling standards. Ofqual (2012a) intends to strengthen GCSEs and GCE A Levels through end-of-course assessments and a focus on international bench-marking. Ofqual is also committed to review Functional Skills and the QCF in relation to vocational qualifications, as well as to improving the regulation of ESOL.

Curriculum theory and models

The curriculum is a social product and a social practice. Curriculum Studies is a broad field informed by philosophy (particularly epistemology – the theory of knowledge), sociology, social policy, politics and psychology. There are also important questions relating to the practicalities of curriculum planning and design. This chapter intro-duces some fundamental theoretical concepts; it will be selective in its exploration of associated debates. The interest in curriculum history points to a recognition of the significance of the curriculum in analysis of education. Goodson (1994: 40–1), writing specifically about schools, stated that curriculum history is important because it provides insight into the way in which:

> courses of study have constituted a mechanism to designate and differentiate students. It also offers a way to analyse the complex relations between school and society because it shows how schools both reflect and refract society's definitions of culturally valuable knowledge . . . curriculum history . . . enables us to examine the roles that professions – like education – play in the social construction of knowledge.

The social history of curriculum subjects demonstrates how teachers have been encouraged to define knowledge in particular ways in return for status and resources.

Curriculum theory and the associated curriculum models must be placed in the context of educational ideologies. Kelly (2009) provides an account of curriculum theory. Flinders and Thornton (2004) present a collection of source papers from the early years of curriculum thinking.

The traditional curriculum associated with the elite universities and academic 'school' subjects is generally regarded as having knowledge at its core. Golby

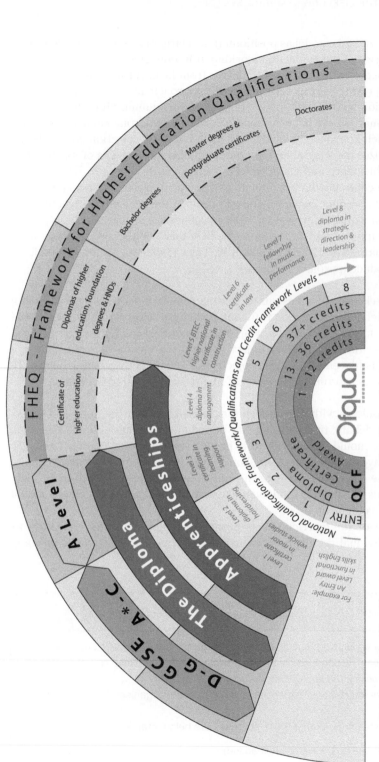

Figure 8.1 The National Qualification Framework/The Qualification and Credit Framework/The Framework for Higher Education Qualifications

Source: Ofqual (2012b)

(1989: 36) characterized this model as positioning the learner as 'a postulant to be initiated into the mysteries of the subject by working at it alongside a "master"'. Modern variants of this conception have tended to derive from Liberal-Humanist approaches to knowledge. Kelly (2009: 56) has referred to this approach as one of 'curriculum as content and education as transmission'. This kind of curriculum, taken to extremes, would be not much more than a list of knowledge to be passed from teacher to student. Questions as to which knowledge exactly, and the basis of its selection, are problematic and Kelly criticizes the 'curriculum as content' model on the basis of its tendency to be culturally exclusionary and uninformed by pedagogy.

Kelly (2009: 67) contrasts the 'curriculum as content' approach with a conception of the 'curriculum as product', which manifests itself in the pervasive 'objectives' or 'outcomes' model of curriculum design. With its genesis in American behavioural psychology (see Chapters 7 and 9), the key figures in this technocratic tradition were John Franklin Bobbitt (1876–1956) and Ralph W. Tyler (1902–94). Golby (1989: 30–1) summarized the product approach as follows:

> The idea that decisions about designs for learning can be achieved by recourse to a means-end model of human action is fundamental here. If we are clear about what we wish to teach, and the reasons why, curriculum decisions are to be reached through the specification of clear objectives and the choice of technically apt methods for the achievement of those objectives. Clear objectives entail the specification of outcomes in terms of the learners' abilities at the end of the course . . .

Golby identified problems with this conception. It assumes that the aims and objectives will not be for debate; that learning can be reduced to behavioural statements; that the teacher will mould the learner to a 'predetermined shape' (Golby 1989: 32); and that the objectives of a curriculum should hold primacy over content. Despite these difficulties, the objectives model of the curriculum has been immensely influential. Box 8.1 indicates Tyler's four fundamental questions, which he considered should guide curriculum development.

The conception of the 'curriculum as process' (Kelly 2009), and education as concerned with individual development rather than the needs of employer or state,

---

Box 8.1 Tyler's (1949) four fundamental questions for curriculum development

1   What educational purposes should the school seek to attain? *[aims and objectives]*
2   What educational experiences can be provided that are likely to attain these purposes? *[choosing the appropriate learning experiences]*
3   How can these educational experiences be effectively organised? *[organising the learning]*
4   How can we determine whether these purposes are being attained? *[evaluation]*

Source: Stenhouse (1981: 3, italicized text added)

might be a way to counteract some of the tendencies discussed above in relation to the 'curriculum as product' model. 'Curriculum as process' rests on the assumption that a teacher must focus on the process of learning rather than the outcome. In effect, the art of the teacher is to take the position not of an expert, but to be 'cast in the role of a learner' (Stenhouse 1981: 94). From this vantage point the teacher exercises judgement regarding how to enable learning, becoming a resource for stimulated learners. The model is nonlinear, resting on a 'specification of content rather than by pre-specifying outcomes in terms of objectives' (Taylor and Richards 1979: 72). It demands of the teacher a careful consideration of learning activities. If the curriculum as product model is concerned with ends, the process model is concerned with means, and inevitably leads to the 'student-centred learning' associated with educational progressivism.

All curricula are the outcome of historical circumstances. Current educational practice is substantially a product of social and cultural developments within a time of economic progress and administrative rationalization in Europe. This period, widely referred to as *modernity*, stemmed from the rise of capitalism and the productive power unleashed by the Industrial Revolution, and from the intellectual force of the eighteenth-century Enlightenment. The resulting philosophy, of material and social progress based on science and technology as opposed to a static society based on tradition and authority, is known as *modernism* and pervades official thinking on education. Contemporary educational practice is situated within a social context containing critiques of modernism, in which the term 'postmodern' has enjoyed currency. The literature on *postmodernism* is considerable. Essentially, postmodernism questions the primacy of scientific and other established forms of knowledge as a source of truth and progress, and elucidates the power and ideology associated with apparently neutral academic enquiry. This calls into question many of the established values concerning the knowledge and culture to be expressed and transmitted in a curriculum. What and how we teach are no longer purely technical issues concerned with selection of content and teaching method; for many, the curriculum is an expression of dominant ideologies within society in such a way that we are barely conscious that they *are* ideologies.

The remainder of this section discusses a range of analyses. Beginning with a survey of older standpoints, and in particular the distinction between 'traditional' and 'progressive' conceptions of the curriculum, we move to outline some of the ideas of postmodern writers, in particular Michel Foucault (1926–1984) and Jean-François Lyotard (1924–1998).

Given the centrality of educational processes within the civil life of society, and also in the sphere of the *personal*, there is a sense in which all social theory relates to Curriculum Studies. Morrison and Ridley (1989) identified five prevalent 'schools of thought' or 'clusters of educational ideologies' relating to the curriculum. Unfortunately, these do not always have the same description or 'label', but the ways in which they are generally described are as follows:

1   *Progressivism*: places emphasis on the individual child; also referred to as child-centredness or Romanticism.

2   *Academicism*: places emphasis on high status knowledge for elites; also referred to as Classical Humanism, Traditionalism or Conservatism.

3   *Liberalism*: focuses on making high status knowledge accessible to all; sometimes referred to as Liberal Humanism.

4   *Instrumentalism*: aimed at improving existing societal and economic relations. This is sometimes referred to as Revisionism or Economic Renewal.

5   *Democratic*: focuses on changing societal and economic relations; also known as Reconstructivism or Democratic Socialism.

Each of the above has its own view of the theory/nature of knowledge; learning and the role of learners; teaching and the teacher's role; and implications for resources and the organization of learning situations and the method of assessment to be utilized. For the sake of brevity, we shall focus here on differences between the broadly 'traditional' and the 'liberal/progressive' philosophies of education. Some of the dimensions (or oppositions) of traditional and progressive values have been summarized by Carr (1995) and are shown in Table 8.1.

Carr (1995) pointed out that the 'traditional' and 'liberal-progressive' educational philosophies are not 'ahistorical', and there are areas of overlap. The vocational curriculum (meaning related to preparation for employment) in England embodies most of the characteristics associated with the liberal progressive model. Knowledge of the philosophical underpinning implicit in Table 8.1 can be useful in making

Table 8.1 Dimensions of traditional and liberal-progressive education

	Traditional	*Liberal-progressive*
Political perspective	Conservative	Liberal/communitarian
View of society	Elitist	Egalitarian
Guiding educational slogan	'Academic excellence'	'Learning from experience'
Canonical texts	Plato's *Republic*	Rousseau's *Emile*
Types of schools	Grammar/selective	Community
Classroom organization	Rigid grouping on ability	Flexible grouping on needs
Curriculum content	Subject centred; rigid subject differentiation	Student centred: weak subject differentiation
Curriculum knowledge	Objective	Subjective
Teacher's role	Expert, transmitting cultural heritage	Facilitator of personal learning
Teaching methods	Formal instruction	'Discovery' methods
Assessment procedures	Traditional examinations testing knowledge	Informal evaluations of qualitative developments in understanding

Source: Adapted from Carr (1995: 55)

practical decisions about the kind of pedagogy to be employed – where there is choice – or in reflecting on the kind of pedagogy that is being employed where there is no choice.

The work of Michel Foucault is primarily associated with the concepts of discipline and power, and the idea of educational processes as being concerned with the construction of an obedient or governable 'subject' (that is, person). In *Discipline and Punish: The Birth of the Prison* Foucault (1991) charts how the eighteenth century saw a transition from public execution to penal retention as a technique of social control. Within this period a number of technologies associated with the control of individuals were developed. At the level of the human body, as opposed to the intellect, a requirement for control was that of physical enclosure within space and over time. By the division of buildings educational spaces took on some characteristics of the factory. These designs facilitated supervision, hierarchy and reward. Donald (1992) identified the English monitorial schools of the early nineteenth century as illustrating the kind of architecture which Foucault described as permitting this kind of control.

Foucault referred to Jeremy Bentham's penitentiary design, the *Panopticon* (a central watch-tower from which an observer could oversee a circle of tiered cells) as ideal for surveillance. A prisoner could be observed 'round the clock' but would be unaware whether or not observation was taking place at a given time; control would thereby become 'internalized' within the mind of the individual. Many recently designed college buildings, with large overlooked atrium spaces, incorporate similar features. Another important factor in imposing control was the timetable. Time was planned, organized and controlled in increasing detail and within the curriculum this was manifested in organizing learning into lessons and terms. Foucault (1991: 178) explains that

> the workshop, the school, the army were subject to the whole micro-penalty of time (latenesses, absences, interruptions of tasks), of activity (inattention, negligence, lack of zeal), of behaviour (impoliteness, disobedience), of speech (idle chatter, insolence), of the body ('incorrect' attitudes, irregular features, lack of cleanliness), of sexuality (impurity, indecency).

Deviance from the norm was, in a sense, pathologized and as a consequence of this the systems through which people pass function as processes of normalization. Over time this required the exercise of observation and judgement, and the creation of norms and averages, of passes and fails. The means were various forms of testing and examination through which the student is allocated a grade, determining whether or not they progress.

Lyotard (1984) has been credited with bringing the term 'postmodernism' into general circulation; certainly his work *The Postmodern Condition: A Report on Knowledge* has been massively influential. Lyotard defines the postmodern as 'incredulity towards metanarratives' (1984: xxiv), pointing to a crisis of the status of knowledge and to a perceived end of 'universalist' or overarching systems of thought (such as Marxism). Science has been the privileged discourse of the modern era and, as a consequence of this primacy, has dominated education and the associated pedagogic and research methodologies. The claim that science is the key to progress enables the State to control education in the name of freedom and progress. It works against the fragmentation of ideas and towards the one big truth which will 'explain'. The twin imperatives of progress and the seeking after truth constitute the two metanarratives upon which the modern university has rested. The current displacement of the role and social authority of universities may be taken as evidence of the end of the modernist vision.

Lyotard argues that the primacy of concepts such as truth and falsehood in relation to knowledge has been replaced by issues of efficiency and inefficiency. He describes this new focus as 'performativity'. Knowledge becomes a commodity. That which does not fit is disqualified and the curriculum becomes a repository of 'official knowledge'. The performance of 'competence' and the positioning of education as a service to business become orthodoxies of policy. A curriculum based on the performance of competencies and the development of skills, delivered through resource centres by facilitators of 'student-centred learning', would represent the culmination of processes that have been at work in the transition of learning institutions. A factor in these changes has been funding pressures arising from mass participation in both FE and HE.

Curriculum design and development

Involvement in curriculum design and development may range from the creation of learning materials by an individual teacher for a particular class, to working collaboratively to design, plan and implement a major course to be delivered through a national network. Many teachers and trainers have opportunities to become engaged in curriculum design and development activities – often without consciously regarding themselves as 'curriculum developers'. Not all participants will be involved in every stage of the process. A formal curriculum development initiative would normally contain the following elements.

Rationale

This would outline the reasons for the course. These might concern the learning needs of the students and/or the needs of society, employers or a specific organization. For example, a tenants' association might identify a need for provision dealing with housing legislation; a teacher might identify a learner's need for a programme designed to support difficulties in working with number; a bank might identify its need to ensure employees were able to use new technology. A training needs analysis might identify broad departmental needs. A course rationale explains why the particular approaches to learning, assessment and evaluation had been adopted.

Aims and objectives

Depending on the philosophy of the author/team, a curriculum would normally incorporate aims and broad and/or specific learning objectives. The current dominance of the product (or objectives/outcomes) curriculum model means that detailed learning objectives are often expected.

Content

This will normally be a description of the topics to be covered. A critical factor is to ensure that content is designed to address the reasons identified for developing the curriculum.

Teaching and learning methods

A curriculum encapsulates the teaching and learning methods used. Questions to consider include: is the course to be delivered at a regular time? Will there be open, distance, blended or e-learning? Will the course employ lectures, group work or other techniques? Will the course be held in a classroom, a laboratory, in the workplace, or elsewhere? Will the course utilize specific learning materials? Crucially, what are the learners' needs?

Assessment strategy

Assessment (see Chapter 11) is an integral part of a curriculum. An outline of the curriculum should clearly identify the assessment methods used. These should be designed to check that learning outcomes/objectives specified have been met and that content has been covered. What is to be the balance of formative, ipsative and summative assessment? The form of assessment should be appropriate for the students and for the subject.

Resources

What are the staffing, learning technologies, equipment, material and other needs of the programme? A further important question to consider is the environmental impact of the course – how does the course design fit with a commitment to sustainability? Recent years have seen an increased recognition of the importance not only of making ecologically sensible decisions in relation to the use of resources, but also of raising consciousness of sustainability issues within the content of the curriculum (see Jones et al. 2010; Clarke 2012).

Evaluation

Curriculum planners need to consider how they can best determine whether or not the curriculum is successful – that is, how to evaluate the curriculum (see Chapter 18). The curriculum will normally include, for example, mechanisms for gathering evidence from students, teachers and employers about its effectiveness. 'Performance indicators' are sets of criteria against which to measure the curriculum – for example, whether it has recruited to target, levels of student satisfaction, assessment results and so on.

Creativity and the curriculum

Tension between traditional, liberal-progressive and instrumental views of the curriculum are evident in the place of 'creativity' in education. This is made more complex by the curricular and pedagogic implications of the new vocationalism that emerged in the 1980s, and the growth of performativity.

For many, creativity is associated with progressive, learner-centred approaches which contest a curriculum increasingly seen as narrow and dull. As Cullingford (2007: 133) notes, this viewpoint emphasizes 'open-mindedness, exploration, the celebration of difference and originality . . . an automatic opposition to the language of targets, to instrumental skills, the measurement of outcomes and the dogmas of accountability'. Set against this, government policy has portrayed creativity as simply one more in a set of economically valuable skills. For example, *Opportunity for All: Skills for the New Economy* (DfEE, 2000a: 3) claimed that 'Economic performance depends increasingly on talent and creativity.' 'Enterprise' has constituted a similar if more overtly economic 'watchword' in curriculum discourse.

This instrumental view has led to a change in the place of creativity in officially-sanctioned curricula. As writers such as Kolb, Bruner and Rogers discussed its place in education, creativity came to be associated with progressive and learner-centred approaches. At the time this was viewed positively, but concerns over 'progressive' education in the 1970s prompted then Labour Prime Minister James Callaghan's 'Great Debate', and a more general Conservative reaction in the 1980s. Jones (2003: 165–6) notes that Conservatism 'defined itself against progressive education, and regarded "creativity" as a term which disguised educators' lack of commitment to raising standards and to passing on established values'.

During the 1990s the decline of manufacturing industry and claims of a burgeoning 'knowledge economy' caused the pendulum to swing again, positioning workers in the arts and knowledge industries as the ideal employees of the twenty-first century. Creative, flexible and re-trainable, they would be relatively immune to the vicissitudes of the labour market. The 1990s saw the rhetoric of creativity re-fashioned to meet the demands of neo-liberal values associated with innovation and entrepreneurship; as Jones (2003: 166) puts it, this new discourse 'synthesized and transvalued elements from the past, rehabilitating creativity under the sign of capital'.

Buckingham and Jones (2001) identifed a 'cultural turn' in New Labour policy following its election in 1997. Creative and cultural education was indeed rehabilitated, and seen not only as a way of preparing school-leavers for the knowledge economy but also as a vehicle for promoting 'a new mode of social cohesion, no longer so dependent on tradition and authority' (Buckingham and Jones 2001: 5); expressed more popularly, this was the notion of 'Cool Britannia'. This 'cultural turn' was associated with a number of official publications on creativity in education, of which perhaps the most influential was the report *All Our Futures*, produced by the National Advisory Committee on Creative and Cultural Education (NACCCE 1999). The report took a *universalist* approach, distancing itself from elitist conceptions of creativity; in its view, *all* learners and *all* teachers are capable of creativity. This implies redefining creativity to some extent, removing criteria of high absolute value and originality and replacing them with more prosaic, everyday virtues.

According to *All Our Futures*, creativity 'First . . . always involves thinking or behaving imaginatively. Second, overall this imaginative activity is purposeful: that is, it is directed to achieving an objective. Third, these processes must generate something original. Fourth, the outcome must be of value in relation to the objective' (NACCCE 1999: 4). Although this is not an unreasonable definition of various forms of educational activity, it is perhaps not what comes to mind when we think of creativity in an absolute sense. The NACCCE definition seems to channel creativity into safe byroads. As the film critic Pauline Kael (1970) suggested: 'we encourage creativity among the mediocre, but real bursting creativity appals us. We put it down as undisciplined, as somehow "too much." ' In this respect, Jeffrey and Craft (2001) offer a helpful distinction by dividing creativity into 'low' or 'little c' creativity: an everyday, 'means-ends' form of creativity, associated with mainstream educational goals; and 'high' or 'big C' creativity, which is paradigm-breaking and encountered much more rarely.

All Our Futures defined creative teaching as: 'Using imaginative approaches to make learning more interesting and effective' (NACCCE 1999: 89). Curriculum approaches which actively engage students in learning can be identified in these terms, although the prescribed curricula which currently prevail in England mean that creative teaching cannot necessarily be equated with a 'curriculum as process' viewpoint. Further discussion and examples of creative teaching may be found in Eastwood et al. (2009) and Harvey and Harvey (2013). However, this type of creativity corresponds more to Craft's 'little c', and is arguably less concerned with developing creative learners than with helping them fit more comfortably into prescriptive curricula driven by the performative cultures that currently dominate the LLS (Simmons and Thompson 2008).

Vocationalism and parity of esteem

The term 'vocationalism' is generally used in relation to the curriculum movement associated with work-related learning – it can be used approvingly, pejoratively or as a neutral technical term. Successive reforms of the vocational curriculum have failed to gain the recognition accorded to the 'gold standards' of the General Certificate in Secondary Education (GCSE) and the GCE Advanced Level (GCE A). The Diploma courses, available from September 2008, are the latest such initiative, following a succession of 'new' vocational awards that began in the late 1970s (see Fisher 2004). It was considered something of an achievement for the proponents of vocational education when in 2012 many Edexcel and Business and Technology Education Council (BTEC) awards featured in a DfE list of non-GCSE qualifications which would be incorporated in 14–16 performance tables from 2015 (DfE 2012b). In April 2013 the DfE announced a new Technical Baccalaureate (or 'TechBacc') to operate from September 2014. This would be in the form a 'performance measure' for those aged 16 to 19 and would mark achievement in the following three areas:

- a high-quality Level 3 vocational qualification;
- a Level 3 'core maths' qualification, including AS level maths;
- an 'extended project'.

Vocational qualifications (VQs) must meet the national occupational standards (NOS), set by Sector Skills Councils, for a particular sector/work place. Following the Apprenticeship, Skills, Children and Learning Act 2009 they are regulated by Ofqual in England and Northern Ireland. Vocationally-related qualifications (VRQs) are less prescribed in content and aim to provide progression within FE/HE as well as to work.

High culture in England has held an antipathy, manifest in the elite public schools and universities, towards the vocational. Beyond this, the implications of new modes of production, information technologies, and the associated new industries for the vocational curriculum have not been fully articulated. That vocational courses have exhibited characteristics associated with progressivism has been a problem in relation to parity of esteem. GCE A Levels fit received notions of what might constitute the preparatory stage of an education leading to the production of some form of 'intellectual', but that term is not one which can be used with conviction in relation to the aspirations of vocational curricula.

In 1923 in Italy, Mussolini was implementing educational reforms that attacked the traditional 'instruction' of the old curriculum, arguing for 'active education'. This was opposed by the leading Marxist Antonio Gramsci. Writing during the 1920s, Gramsci (1971: 40) argued that,

> Schools of the vocational type ... are beginning to predominate ... The most paradoxical aspect of it all is that this new type of school appears to be advocated as being democratic, while in fact it is destined not merely to perpetuate social differences but to crystallise them ... The labourer can become a skilled worker, for instance, the peasant a surveyor or petty agronomist. But democracy, by definition, cannot mean merely that an unskilled worker can become skilled. It must mean that every 'citizen' can 'govern' ...

Gramsci was expressing fears similar to those which would exercise liberal and radical educationalists in Britain during the 1980s and 1990s as attempts were made to promote vocationalism. The idea that education at all levels should align itself more closely with the needs of business became known as the 'new vocationalism'. The argument that education should concern itself with equipping young people and adults with economically valuable skills has a strong hold on public opinion. In a society which places different values on different knowledge and skills, to acquire a particular set of skills to the exclusion of others is to be allocated a particular position in society.

Gramsci (1971: 41) was also critical of the 'active learning' approach which was associated with vocationalism: 'It is noticeable that the new pedagogy has concentrated its fire on "dogmatism" in the field of instruction and the learning of concrete facts'. More recently, Avis (1995: 63) identifies the creation of a framework within which 'teachers become transmogrified into facilitators of the learning process, [and] professional and disciplinary knowledge becomes marginalised. The emphasis in these new teaching relations is on the student "learning how to learn". Studies which chart and analyse vocational provision are vital to the formulation of a *theory* of these forms of curricula.'

Lyotard (1984: 4) identified 'a thorough exteriorization of knowledge with respect to the "knower" at whatever point he or she may occupy in the knowledge process'. The vocational curriculum in England presents such a point. The relegation of knowledge in the face of skill has clashed with the goal of parity of esteem. The vocational curriculum occupies a difficult place in the field of educational classification and hierarchies. Official positions speak reassuringly of its equivalence to courses such as GCSE and GCE A Level, and its acceptability for entry to university or professional training. Alongside these official positions are the personal beliefs of various 'gatekeepers'. The Edge Foundation, an independent educational charity, actively works to change attitudes and to raise the status of vocational learning (Edge Foundation 2012).

The vocational curriculum is regarded as necessary and worthwhile, yet it is circumscribed by its instrumental nature. It is the individual recognition of limits which is part of what it means to be rendered governable, and that is still the prime need for effective vocational deployment. Foucault (1991: 194) suggests that power 'produces reality; it produces domains of objects and rituals of truth'. A curriculum may well be seen as an instrument, or a machine, which is situated within domains and power structures, which is filled with rituals, and which manufactures *kinds* of truth. The evidence of the vocational curriculum experience, however, is that while it may empower by enhancing life chances, and by developing knowledge and skills, it *can* also repress and it *can* be exclusionary in its consequences for some people. Different curricula are not the same and some, in Orwellian terms, are more equal than others.

14–19 education and training

The *14–19 Education and Skills White Paper* (DfES 2005a), which emerged from the Working Group on 14–19 Reform chaired by Sir Mike Tomlinson, proposed an ambitious ten year plan and transition for 14–19 education and training. The concept of a 14–19 continuum was proposed by the Manpower Services Commission (MSC) in the early 1980s. It was supported by a group known as the 'Conservative Modernisers' (Chitty 2004) with proposals highlighting the ideological struggle that had been raging in England since James Callaghan's speech at Ruskin College in 1976 (Callaghan 1976). The so-called 'Great Debate' surrounding education can be viewed as signalling a change in the way education policy would be formed and administered. More recent developments in the 14–19 arena still reflect debates which originated in the 1970s.

Chitty (2004) highlighted the increased political focus on education following the Great Debate by comparing the volume of legislation before 1976 and after, identifying 30 Education Acts between 1979 and 2000 as opposed to only three between 1944 and 1976. The prevailing ideology has been a 'utilitarian' view that places education at the forefront of attempts to 'deliver the skills and knowledge essential . . . for an economy seeking a strong position in a globalised political world' (Lumby and Foskett 2007: 87).

As Stasz and Wright (2007: 157) suggest, 'Forming a picture of policy for 14–19 education in the United Kingdom is a bit like the proverbial blind man confronted by an elephant. It is possible to understand specific parts, but the size, shape and sheer complexity of the elephant remains obscure.' This complexity was understandable given the fragmented nature of policy initiatives and the entrenched academic-vocational divide based on selection at 16+ along institutional, curriculum and assessment lines. The 14–19 curriculum reforms being implemented at the turn of the first decade of the twenty-first century sat alongside other fundamental changes. These included the introduction of the QCF and the raising of the age of compulsory education or training to 18 by 2015.

The role of education as a function of the economy was highlighted with the twinning of the White Papers *14–19 Education and Skills* (DfES 2005a) and *Skills: Getting on in Business, Getting on at Work* (DfES 2005c). Proposals included strengthening of the GCSEs and GCE A Levels, an expansion of apprenticeships and the introduction of a new Diploma route. These three routes would be offered at Levels 1, 2 and 3 with the apprentice route being mostly offered at 16+. There would also be the introduction of a new Foundation Tier at Levels 1 and 2, which would allow achievements at these levels to be recognized. Existing key skills were to be replaced by 'functional skills' in English, Maths and ICT which would be embedded in all three routes. The 'specialized' Diplomas were the defining element to the 14–19 curriculum proposals, whereas the existing traditional and apprenticeships routes were to be modified in an attempt to create a coherent and cohesive offer allowing movement between routes.

The new Diplomas were originally to be offered across 14 lines of learning, subsequently increased to 17 with the inclusion of academic Diplomas, to be phased in over a period of four years from September 2008. Achievements were to be recognized at all three levels: Foundation (Level 1), Higher (Level 2) and Advanced (Level 3). Each Diploma line was to consist of three components: principal learning, generic learning and additional and specialist learning. There would also be a compulsory element of experiential learning with a minimum of ten days work experience incorporated within the generic learning at all levels (QCA 2008).

The plan to introduce academic diplomas was abandoned by the Coalition Government when it came to power in 2010. Also in 2010 the 'English Baccalaureate' (EBacc) was introduced as a performance measure recognizing grade C or above in English, mathematics, history or geography, the sciences and a language. It should be stressed that the EBacc is not currently a qualification. In September 2012, however, the Coalition Government announced plans to end competition between awarding bodies in relation to the EBacc subjects with the intention that from 2015 a single awarding body should be responsible for new English Baccalaureate Certificates (EBCs). In February 2013 this plan was abandoned. The 'TechBacc' (see above) was announced the following April.

The dizzying pace of educational policy development precludes a comprehensive summary here, but see Gillard (2011) for a clear longitudinal account.

Apprenticeships and higher apprenticeships

The idea of the apprentice as a 'time served' craftsmen (they were usually male) trained over several years to a high standard is deeply fixed in the national psyche. The National Apprenticeship Service (NAS) was created in April 2009. As in the last century, apprentices normally work and earn a wage whilst receiving 'day-release' off the job training either with a local college or a training organization. In England modern apprenticeships are open to all aged over 16 years and normally last between one and four years. Intermediate (Level 2), Advanced (Level 3) and Higher (Level 4) apprenticeships are available. Over 440,000 people started on an apprenticeship in 2010–11 (BIS 2011a). In 2011 the Coalition Government's *Plan for Growth* (HM Treasury/BIS 2011) announced a planned expansion of Higher Apprenticeships. All apprenticeships include a competencies qualification; a technical knowledge qualification; a module on employee rights and responsibilities; and a module covering personal learning and thinking skills. Apprentices also complete Functional Skills (mathematics and English) qualifications or a GCSE with enhanced content (mathematics and English).

College higher education

The existence of higher education in FE colleges (formerly referred to as 'HE in FE' but now know as 'college higher education') is far from new. Many FE colleges have established traditions and expertise in the delivery of HE. It is generally recognized that around 10 per cent of HE study takes place in FE institutions. Approximately 180,000 HE students in FE study for HNCs, HNDs, foundation degrees, degrees, higher apprenticeships and professional awards (BIS 2011b). Much of this provision has, historically, taken place through franchising. Woodrow (1993: 207) defined franchising, as 'the delivery of the whole or parts of a course in an institution other than the centre in which it is developed and validated'. The White Paper *Students at the Heart of the System* (BIS 2011b) spoke of an HE system which would be more responsive to choice and provide an improved student experience whilst promoting social mobility. Part of this would be achieved by changes to student number controls and the processes relating to institutions, including FE colleges and 'alternative providers', being able to achieve taught degree-awarding powers. It now seems likely that college HE will expand and become more widely acknowledged as an important part of the FE college 'curriculum offer', as well as a properly respected route to higher level qualifications.

Literacy, numeracy and ESOL: some background

The words 'literacy' and 'numeracy' are no longer the preserve of the classroom, the inspectorate report, or of the latest policy briefing – they have now become part of everyday discourse. This derives from increased media attention on the attainment of school leavers and on methods of teaching young children how to read, as well as concerns about low levels of literacy and numeracy within a workforce facing intense global competition. Initiatives such as family literacy programmes, where children learn alongside parents or carers in educational or community settings with the support of specialist staff, have increased adults' and young people's skills. In addition, they have improved adults' understanding of the requirements of literacy and numeracy curricula in schools and related pedagogical approaches.

Despite growing awareness of issues surrounding literacy and numeracy in the general population, there is debate over the nature of what, if any, difference exists between literacy and the curricular subject of English, and similarly between numeracy and the subject of mathematics (Green 2006; Medway 2005). While it might be argued that literacy and numeracy are concerned with the practical application of skills and knowledge for everyday tasks and effective participation in civic life and the workplace, perceived distinctions are often not clear either in research or in policy. In the latter case, for example, the titles of specialist teaching qualifications for post-16 literacy and numeracy have referred to 'English' and 'mathematics', reflecting policy shifts and uncertainties over the nature and status of adult basic skills. .

Such difficulties are less pronounced when considering courses for learners whose first language is not English. In this area, though the terminology is no less complex, the distinctions are clearer. The terms English as a Second Language (E2L) and English as an Additional Language (EAL) generally refer to provision for school children studying in British education and accessing the National Curriculum who have varying levels of English, and who may be receiving additional support and teaching to develop their spoken and written English language skills. This is distinct from English as a Foreign Language (EFL) provision that typically refers to courses for visitors to Britain, many being young people on short intensive programmes who wish to develop their English language skills. English for Speakers of Other Languages ESOL is provision mainly, though not exclusively, delivered to adults studying in adult and community or FE settings to develop their skills in spoken and written English and reading for a wide variety of purposes. These might include gaining a qualification or passing the 'Life in the UK' test and becoming a British citizen. ESOL qualifications are offered at the same levels of the NQF as the related national literacy (and numeracy) awards, namely entry Levels 1 to 3 and Levels 1 and 2.

Literacy, numeracy and ESOL, though distinct curricular areas, share a number of important features: established methods and tools for initial and diagnostic assessment of skills; subject standards; curricula; and a national system of assessment. This provision is essential given that not only are the skills learned required for effective participation in a wide variety of social contexts, but they are also the means of access to all other curriculum subjects. Notwithstanding this, seeing these subjects primarily in terms of skill acquisition – a predominantly government driven policy viewpoint – continues to be problematic (Pahl and Rowsell 2005; Papen 2005).

Criticism from practitioners in the field tends to focus on the narrow curriculum and the methods of testing, which can lead to teaching directed solely towards passing national tests in order to reach achievement targets and secure funding. Research highlights the performative culture that pervades much literacy, numeracy and ESOL provision (Pahl and Rowsell 2005; Papen 2005). In challenging this performative focus and in proposing a social theory of literacy, a framework for thinking that came to be known as the 'New Literacy Studies' (Barton et al. 2000) has been developed, turning attention to the relationship between, particularly, literacy and wider social practices:

> The traditional view of literacy as the ability to read and write rips literacy out of its sociocultural contexts and treats it as an asocial skill with little or nothing to do with human relationships. It cloaks literacy's connections to power, to social

identity and to ideologies, often in the service of privileging certain types of literacies in certain types of people.

(Gee 1996: 46)

Skills for Life (and after)

In March 1999 an influential report was published (DfEE 1999), dealing with the literacy, language and numeracy skills of Britain's adults. Commonly known as the 'Moser Report' (after Sir Claus Moser who chaired the working party), this found that one in five adults was not functionally literate, that is, they did not have the literacy skills of the average 11-year-old. In terms of the number of adults with the very lowest level of literacy skills, only two developed countries were then ranked worse than Britain. A higher number still of adults had serious difficulties with numeracy and operated at the lowest level.

The Moser Report did not consider definitions of 'literacy' or 'numeracy', matters regularly discussed in other studies. The still under-researched notion of what was meant by, for example, being literate or numerate was similarly not examined by the Working Party. The emphasis of the opening sections of the Report was on the results of skills assessments devised by organizations including the Centre for Longitudinal Studies (CLS) and the Organisation for Economic Co-operation and Development (OECD), and on analysis of results from the International Adult Literacy Survey (IALS). In response to what could have been considered alarming statistics on the low levels of literacy, language and numeracy skills, the Report proposed a ten element national strategy for adult basic skills. This covered all aspects of provision including planning, delivery and assessment for post-16 literacy, language and numeracy. New achievement targets were set; the statement of an entitlement to learn was compiled; proposals for a new curriculum and system of qualifications were planned; and an overhaul of specialist teacher training and related qualifications was recommended.

The New Labour Government's response to Moser, in the form of a national strategy for adult basic skills, was far reaching and its title, *Skills for Life* (DfEE 2001), is now suggestive of a whole range of teaching and learning in adult basic skills. These skills are defined as literacy and ESOL (reading, writing, speaking and listening), numeracy (the basic mathematical skills of number; measures, shapes and space, and handling data) and most recently, information technology. One of the initial responses to the Moser Report was the writing of sets of standards for the respective skills at Levels one and two of the NQF, and, below these, at entry Levels 1, 2 and 3 (QCA 2000). Following on from these, specialist curricula were devised which drew heavily on units for the key skills of communication and application of number as devised by the QCA, on international curricula, but also on the frameworks for teaching literacy and numeracy as elaborated in the National Literacy and Numeracy Strategies in the schools' sector.

The terminology surrounding *Skills for Life* has, in recent years, seen a number of different acronyms emerge including ALLaN (Adult Literacy, Language and Numeracy), LLN (Literacy, Language and Numeracy), as well as the more dated term, 'basic skills'. The idea of functional skills draws together the notion of the provision itself with considerations of delivery, resourcing and assessment. The White Paper

Skills: Getting on in Business, Getting on at Work (DfES 2005c) was the impetus for the idea of 'functional skills', which were subsequently described as 'practical skills in English, mathematics and information and communication technology (ICT) that allow individuals to work confidently, effectively and independently in life' (QCA 2007).

The adult Foundation Learning Curriculum (FLC) relates to provision at Entry Level and Level 1. It 'includes (but is not limited to) the units and qualifications at these levels within the Qualifications and Credit Framework (QCF) ... *Personalised learning programmes* will be developed for learners following this curriculum that will support progression to appropriate destinations or other agreed outcomes' (2010 SFA: 2, original italics). Aimed at learners aged 18 or over, except for those aged 19–24 with a learning difficulty assessment, the adult FLC shares its aims with those of the FLC for young people (aged 14–19), that is, to support engagement, participation and achievement; bring coherence to programmes; ensure a minimum level of skills which provide a foundation for progression; and to support programmes which meet individual needs as well as the wider goals of social mobility and inclusion.

In *New Challenges, New Chances*, BIS (2011a: 10–11) recognized that since 2003 there had been a substantial improvement in literacy at Level 2 and above, but reported no improvement in lower level literacy and that numeracy skills had shown a slight decline. It was stated that 'despite considerable efforts over the last 10 years to improve the basic skills of adults, our new national survey shows that 24% of adults (8.1 million people) lack functional numeracy skills and 15% (5.1 million people) lack functional literacy skills. This is unacceptable.' BIS undertook to promote a national Maths campaign which would seek to 'engage champions', including employers. Ofsted would focus more strongly on teaching English and maths skills. There would be a focus on assessing the English and maths needs of job seekers and of offenders. An interesting dimension was a resolve on the part of the Coalition Government to re-establish the terms 'English' and 'maths' for adults.

Though the move to functional skills might be suggestive of a significant change in this curriculum area, the standards to be covered and skills in literacy, numeracy and ICT that learners are required to demonstrate, and indeed the overall purpose of these elements of the curriculum, seem little changed from that articulated by the report of Moser's Working Party. Moser's vision for literacy and numeracy had been one of an 'ability to read, write and speak in English, and to use Mathematics at a level necessary to function at work and in society in general' (DfEE 1999: foreword). This may seem modest enough but it remains a necessary aspiration.

9

Practical teaching

Liz Dixon, Josie Harvey, David Powell, Ron Thompson and Sarah Williamson

---

In this chapter

- Planning learning sessions
- Aims and objectives
- Learning activities
- Using questions to promote learning
- Learning resources
- Whiteboards
- Differentiation
- Lesson plans and schemes of work
- Modelling good practice
- Teaching groups of learners
- Managing learner behaviour
- Tutorials and pastoral support

Planning learning sessions

Planning a learning session involves making decisions about content and learning objectives; learning activities and resources; support for individual learners; how to deal with skills issues; and how learning will be assessed. In making these decisions, the teacher should draw on the theoretical perspectives discussed in Chapter 7 and also take into account specific factors such as those shown in Figure 9.1. Learning sessions will normally follow a structure consisting of an introduction, followed by development of the main learning themes and, finally, a conclusion. Although such a format may seem obvious, it is worth discussing this structure in more detail.

Introduction: This phase should be fairly short; however, it is important because it provides an opportunity to cover basic issues such as registers, health and safety, and returning assessed work. Learning from a previous session is often revisited (a 'recap' or recapitulation of key elements, perhaps involving some form of assessment such as a quiz). The teacher will introduce the session, often displaying the learning objectives

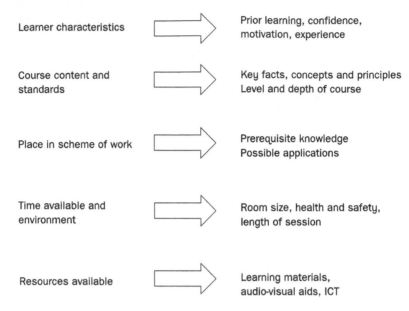

Figure 9.1 Factors influencing decisions in lesson planning

and providing an overview of the lesson content, why it is important and how it relates to previous learning. An advance organizer may be used. The introduction may also include a short but stimulating 'starter' activity intended to get learners 'in the right frame of mind'.

Development: In this phase the main content is developed through a series of learning activities. It will occupy the majority of the lesson time. It is important to ensure that all learners are involved and that the teacher is in a position to assess progress. How many activities are included in this phase will depend on the time available and the characteristics of the learners. As Child (2004: 50, 159) points out, attention span is limited and the position of information within a session can affect its retention.

Conclusion: In the final phase of the lesson the main ideas are reviewed and related to the aims and objectives stated in the introduction. There will normally be a recap of the learning achieved and some evaluation of the learning processes. In some situations, learners will need to reflect formally on what they have learned and record their reflections in an individual learning plan or record of achievement – if this is the case, sufficient time should be allowed. The conclusion will often look ahead to the next session and cover issues such as 'homework'.

Transitions between learning activities

The development phase will normally include more than one learning activity. This makes the issue of *transitions* between activities important – each one will need to be concluded effectively and the next introduced. As well as practical considerations

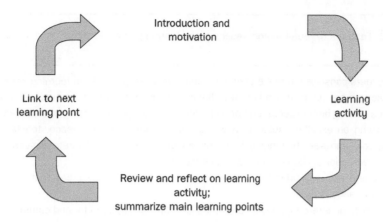

Introduction and
motivation

Learning
activity

Link to next
learning point

Review and reflect on learning
activity;
summarize main learning points

Figure 9.2 Cyclic structure for the development phase of a learning session

such as collection and distribution of learning materials or equipment, learners need to understand 'where they are' and 'where they are heading'. The basic structure outlined above therefore becomes embedded in miniature within the development phase. It is helpful to think of this phase in terms of a reflective learning cycle as in Figure 9.2, so that learners are able to reflect and make links between activities.

Although evaluations of quality in teaching and learning are to some extent subjective and even ideological, it can be helpful when planning to consider relevant inspection frameworks. For many teachers in the sector, external judgements of their teaching will be made according to the *Common Inspection Framework* for post-16 education and training. Guidance (not to be used as a checklist) on what constitutes 'outstanding' teaching and learning within this framework is shown in Box 9.1.

Aims and objectives

In almost any teaching session, learning of some form takes place. However, the learning might not be intended, or even desirable. How can the teacher judge whether to be satisfied? One possibility is to state in advance the intended learning outcomes and then to assess the extent to which they have been achieved. This section deals with the formulation of learning outcomes by means of behavioural objectives, drawing on the discussion in Chapter 7 of behaviourist theories of learning and Bloom's taxonomy of learning.

Behavioural objectives have a number of advantages. For example, they help in the process of lesson planning by requiring the teacher to make explicit the nature of the intended learning outcomes and the relevant subject content. They are important for lesson evaluation. Learning objectives are a useful tool for ensuring the validity of assessment.

An *aim* is a general statement of aspiration, usually associated with a course or subject as a whole. For example, 'the aim of humanities teaching is to forward under-standing, discrimination and judgement in the human field'. Aims often focus on

Box 9.1 Features of 'outstanding' teaching and learning selected from post-16 inspection criteria

- Learners consistently make very good and sustained progress in learning sessions.
- Teachers are adept at working with learners from different backgrounds. They have consistently high expectations of all learners in a range of learning environments.
- Drawing on excellent subject knowledge and/or industry experience, teachers plan astutely and set challenging tasks based on systematic, accurate assessment of learners' prior skills, knowledge and understanding.
- Teachers use well-judged and often imaginative teaching strategies that match individual needs accurately.
- Teachers generate high levels of enthusiasm for participation in, and commitment to, learning.
- Teaching and learning develop high levels of resilience, confidence and independence in learners when they tackle challenging activities.
- Teachers check learners' understanding effectively throughout learning sessions.
- Time is used effectively and every opportunity is taken to develop crucial skills, including learners being able to use their literacy and numeracy skills on other courses and at work.
- Appropriate and regular coursework contributes very well to learners' progress.
- High quality learning materials and resources including information and communication technology are used by staff and learners during and between learning sessions.
- Marking and constructive feedback from staff are frequent and of a consistent quality, leading to high levels of engagement and interest.
- Teachers and other staff enthuse and motivate learners to participate in a wide range of learning activities.
- Equality and diversity are integrated fully into the learning experience. Staff manage learners' behaviour skilfully; they show great awareness of equality and diversity in teaching sessions.
- Advice, guidance and support motivate learners to secure the best possible opportunities for success in their learning and progression.

Source: Ofsted (2012b: 49–50)

teacher behaviour, such as providing certain types of learning experience; for example, 'the aim of this customer care unit is to provide trainees with simulated experience of dealing with abusive clients'.

A *general objective* is a broad statement of what the learner is expected to achieve as a result of the learning session. A *specific objective* is a precise and verifiable statement of expected learner behaviour or potential. For an individual learning session, there would normally be a single general objective and a small number of specific objectives (typically four or five).

Since a general objective is meant to be a broad statement of the overall learning outcome from a unit of study, some care is needed to achieve the right level of generality. For example, consider the three statements below (adapted from Gronlund 1970: 10):

1   Writes clear, effective English.
2   Applies correct punctuation to sentences.
3   Uses the full stop to terminate sentences.

The first would normally be too general for a single lesson, although it could be adapted for an extended period of learning. The third is probably too specific for use as a general objective for a complete learning session. The second is probably the most appropriate, although factors relating to the course content and the learners would need to be taken into account.

When writing behavioural objectives, the key words are verbs describing intended learner behaviour or potential. Gronlund (1970: 10) suggests that, for general objectives, appropriate verbs describing learning in the cognitive domain would include: applies, comprehends, knows, understands, uses. For example, 'understands the principle of the lever' would be an appropriate general objective for an engineering lesson.

As its name implies, a specific objective is meant to be more particular than a general objective, and to be directly verifiable. Specific objectives are written using verbs describing observable learner behaviour. They are now often referred to as SMART objectives. This acronym is derived from the words Specific, Measurable, Achievable, Realistic and Time-related; although 'achievable' and 'realistic' may seem to overlap, the distinction usually made is between being achievable in principle and realistically achievable given the available resources and conditions.

A specific objective consists of up to three parts. It begins with an indication of the behaviour that will provide evidence that the learner has met the objective, for example 'defines correctly the terms "profit" and "interest"'. Often, the objective consists *only* of this indication. However, in the interests of clarity, it can be helpful to describe the conditions under which this behaviour is to be demonstrated (for example, 'making use of reference books' or 'without the use of a calculator'). In addition, the objective may include criteria for an acceptable level of performance (for example, 'state correctly at least three of the following points . . .' or 'within a tolerance of ten per cent'). Some complete examples are given in Box 9.2.

Identifying appropriate learning objectives is not easy. In broad terms, the objectives approach asks the teacher to interpret the question 'What do learners need to *know*?' in terms of the question 'What should learners be able to *do* as a result?' Bloom's taxonomy can be helpful, by encouraging the teacher to take into account the appropriate domain of learning and the level within this domain. For example, within the cognitive domain, relatively simple learning outcomes relating to knowledge, comprehension and application may be reflected in objectives that use verbs such as 'states' or 'calculates'. However, uncritically adopting these simple verbs may overlook opportunities for higher level learning involving analysis, synthesis and evaluation, or underestimate the learning that is taking place.

Box 9.2 Examples of general and specific behavioural objectives

General objective: Apply Pythagoras' Theorem to plane right-angled triangles.
Specific objectives:

1   State Pythagoras' Theorem with reference to a given diagram.
2   Use Pythagoras to calculate, correct to three significant figures, the length of the hypotenuse of a right-angled triangle given the other two sides.
3   Use Pythagoras to calculate, correct to three significant figures, a side of a right-angled triangle given the hypotenuse and one other side.

General objective: Understand the role of a receptionist in a beauty salon.
Specific objectives:

1   State four of the main responsibilities of a beauty salon receptionist.
2   Explain why it is important for the reception desk to be staffed whenever the salon is open, giving at least three reasons.
3   Identify situations where the receptionist must pass enquiries to a qualified beauty therapist.

This highlights a broader issue relating to the use of behavioural objectives: do they actually diminish our view of learning by reducing it to observable behaviour? We saw in Chapter 7 that Kolb regards learning as a dynamic process which is difficult to capture in terms of learning outcomes. Rogers and Freiberg (1994: 188) give an example of learning expressed as an outcome and as an experiential process:

- The students will list five contributions of ancient Egypt to modern world societies.
- Class members will design, plan and go on a field trip to the ancient Egyptian collection at a museum.

The process-driven approach provides a broader learning experience and does not predetermine the learning that will take place. Although we might reply that his process example is perfectly consistent with achieving the learning outcome, and other outcomes could be constructed to reflect a broader view of learning about Egypt, Rogers is concerned that the outcomes approach contains an inherent tendency to reduce expectations and limit learning.

Learning activities

The range of learning activities can seem bewildering. Although a number of studies of the effectiveness of different learning methods have been carried out, they need to be used with care, bearing in mind the observation of Hodkinson and James (2003:

401), that learning in FE appears to be strongly culture and context dependent: 'what works, or is deemed good practice in one learning site may not work or be good practice in another'. Studies of teaching effectiveness may also suffer from bias according to the model of effectiveness they use; for example, many studies are based on a process-product paradigm in which there is an assumed direct causal relationship between effective teaching and the successful acquisition of knowledge and skills, rather than a relationship mediated by broader individual and sociocultural factors (Muijs and Reynolds 2011: 1).

Hattie (2009) provides a careful synthesis of over 800 'meta-analyses' which consider the impact on learner achievement of a range of educational interventions. In a meta-analysis, the outcomes of an intervention over a number of research studies are reduced to a common measure, known as 'effect size'; the effectiveness of the intervention can then be compared with other interventions, and with the influence of factors such as home background and individual learner characteristics. A positive effect size of 0.5 is equivalent to an increase of one grade in achievement at GCSE level (Black et al. 2003: 9). Hattie (2009: 17) argues that an effect size of 0.4 constitutes a 'hinge point'; below that level, the benefits of an intervention may not justify the effort involved.

Table 9.1 shows the effect sizes of some teaching methods in common use, together with information on the number of studies included in the meta-analysis and the degree of variability between studies (high variability would suggest considerable sensitivity to context). Note the impact of direct instruction (*not* didactic instruction!) on learning and the effectiveness of learners teaching others. Table 9.2 shows, for comparison, the effect sizes of some other factors influencing achievement.

Selecting learning activities can be made easier by distinguishing between teacher-centred and learner-centred activities. This distinction is based on who is the main focus of the activity, particularly in terms of the balance of control and decision

Table 9.1 Effect sizes of selected teaching/learning methods

Method	Effect size	Variability	Number of studies
Formative feedback	0.73	Medium	1,287
Direct instruction	0.59	High	304
Worked examples	0.57	Medium	62
Peer tutoring	0.55	High	767
Small-group learning	0.48	Not given	78
Questioning	0.46	Medium	211
Computer-based instruction	0.37	Medium	4,875
Simulations	0.33	High	361
Audio-visual methods	0.22	Medium	259
Team teaching	0.19	Medium	136
Web-based learning	0.18	High	45
Mentoring	0.15	Medium	74

Source: Adapted from Hattie (2009)

Table 9.2 Effect sizes of factors not related to teaching method

Factor	Effect size	Variability	Number of studies
Own estimate of achievement	1.44	Low	209
Teacher–student relationships	0.72	Low	229
Prior achievement	0.67	High	3,607
Socio-economic status	0.57	Low	499
Peer influences	0.53	Not given	12
Parental involvement	0.51	High	716
Motivation	0.48	Medium	327
Quality of teaching	0.44	Medium	141
Teacher expectations	0.43	High	674
Class size	0.21	Not given	96
Gender (Males–Females)	0.12	Low	2,926

Source: Adapted from Hattie (2009)

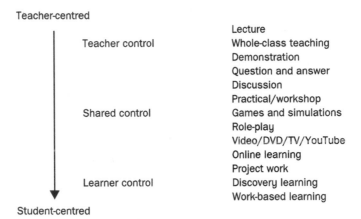

Figure 9.3 Minton's Matrix of Control
Source: Adapted from Minton (1991: 112)

making. It has been expressed by Minton (1991) as a matrix of control for various learning activities, as shown in Figure 9.3.

Learning activities directed by the teacher, and in which the teacher is considerably more active than the learners, lie near the teacher-centred extreme of this matrix. The teacher may feel 'safe' with these activities, as they are able to determine what happens next. Teacher-centred activities are predictable and may be valuable in situations where new material is to be covered. However, the learners will be relatively passive. It may be difficult to ensure that all are involved and focused. On the other hand, the teacher may feel that learner-centred activities, in which learners work individually or in groups, at their own pace and generating their own ideas, are 'risky'. They may result in learners heading in unexpected directions or in important learning being missed out. Nevertheless, only by giving learners the opportunity to express their ideas and solve problems can their true level of understanding be explored and enhanced. Carl Rogers encourages the teacher to take on the role of facilitator, creating a community of learners: 'I see the facilitation of learning as the function that may hold constructive, tentative, changing *process* answers to some of the deepest perplexities that beset humankind' (Rogers and Freiberg 1994: 153, original emphasis).

Using questions to promote learning

Dialectic, or the method of seeking knowledge by means of question and answer, has a distinguished history, dating back to Socrates (c 470–399 BCE) – in fact, it is often referred to as the 'Socratic method'. Asking questions of learners provides a simple and immediate way of monitoring progress and understanding; it can be used to develop understanding and promote reasoning. Skill and patience is required.

Oral questioning provides a way of turning a teacher-centred activity, such as whole-class teaching or a demonstration, into something interactive and challenging. It allows the teacher to draw on knowledge and experience that learners bring, to seek opinions and contradictory views, or to collaboratively explore a problem. In addition, it encourages students to contribute ideas. However, anyone who has asked a question and then waited in deafening silence for an answer will know that there are pitfalls and disadvantages. Apart from varied levels of involvement from different group members and the anxiety caused by being 'put on the spot', there are problems related to the structure of the questions themselves. What *kind* of knowledge do they develop and assess? How can teachers know whether a correct answer is a valid indicator of knowledge?

The simplest technique is to ask an *overhead* question. The question is asked of the whole class, and an answer taken from anyone who responds. While being a relatively non-threatening approach, it has the disadvantage that some students may dominate, misleading the teacher as to the level of understanding and excluding others. One solution to this problem is to ask the question of a specific learner – a *nominated* question. However, this can be quite stressful for students and is often avoided by teachers. Another strategy is to pose the question and ask students to discuss it in pairs; after a few minutes ideas are compared and discussed. This can be particularly helpful if the question is open ended, with many possible answers. Nominated questions can also be useful when asking students to talk about their experiences, as clearly they will know the answer – reducing, although not eliminating, pressure.

A variation on nominated questions is *redirection*. The teacher asks a question with a number of possible answers, nominates a student to answer, then a second student and possibly a third. Other students are invited to comment on and evaluate the answers, followed by evaluation from the teacher. The teacher may also employ *reflected* questions: when Student A asks the teacher a question – for example, 'What does the word "numerator" mean?' the teacher passes on this question to Student B, who then has the opportunity to explain the concept to the class. The teacher may also simply pass the question back to Student A – a *reversed* question – but if this is done frequently some students find this frustrating.

One consideration when using nominated questions is that naming the student before asking the question can be a signal to other students to 'switch off'. To counteract this tendency, the teacher may give time for all students to think about the question before asking a particular student to answer it.

Using question and answer in the classroom requires confidence and patience. A common failing is to give too little time for students to think – five seconds of silence can seem a long time, and can tempt an intervention too early. Re-phrasing the question can help if contributions do not flow, but another common failing needs to be avoided – asking 'leading questions'. A question such as, 'Can understanding play types help childcare staff to identify limitations in a play environment?' may get a correct response, but does not indicate understanding as the answer has been effectively 'fed' to the student. A further weakness of this example is that it gives no scope for the student to express ideas – it is a *closed* question.

Closed questions have a yes/no answer or a limited set of answers; for example, 'What are the main constituents of air?' They are useful for checking factual knowledge, but will give little indication of deeper understanding. By contrast, *open* questions have no predetermined answers and provide scope for different explanations, interpretations or opinions. A question such as, 'How may the concept of play types help childcare staff to plan activities with young children?' will have a number of different answers, all equally valid, and each one will require some understanding of the concept under discussion and its application. Closed questions may be thought of in terms of a behaviourist approach (see Chapter 7), their advantage being that they are straightforward to ask and can be specific in nature. This allows frequent reinforcement, for example by praising correct answers, and enables the discrete behaviours characteristic of this approach to learning to be developed. However, closed questions will tend to emphasize lower cognitive levels in Bloom's taxonomy, rather than higher level cognitive behaviours such as evaluation and synthesis.

Open questions, on the other hand, ask students to relate learning to their experience, to make connections between different areas and to imaginatively explore the implications of what they are learning. It is not difficult to translate closed questions into open ones – for example, simply by inserting the word 'why'. A question such as, 'What is the capital city of the United States?', which asks for a trivial item of general knowledge, transforms into, 'Why did Washington become the capital city of the US?', a much more challenging exploration of historical, political and geographical factors. Questions based on imagining the consequences of certain states of affairs – 'What if?' questions – are also useful in terms of a cognitivist approach to learning. Thus, a closed question such as, 'Name the principal arteries supplying the heart with blood and state their functions' would become, 'What would happen if one of the arteries supplying the heart became blocked?'

Socratic questioning in its original form is bound up with the possibility of a priori knowledge – that is, knowledge which is independent of experience. In Plato's dialogue *Meno*, Socrates is challenged with what has become known as the *learning paradox*: 'And how will you enquire, Socrates, into that which you do not know? . . . And if you find what you want, how will you ever know that this is the thing which you did not know?' (Plato, *Meno*, translated by Benjamin Jowett). Socrates replies that 'all enquiry and all learning is but recollection'; that is, the nature of the human mind is such that all knowledge is already present, embedded within it. He proceeds to demonstrate this by calling for an uneducated slave and, through careful questioning, brings the slave to construct a geometrical proposition. Although to a modern reader the questioning technique Socrates uses is a shameless example of leading a witness, the idea that new knowledge and understanding may be achieved through a carefully constructed logical sequence of questions, each one of which may reasonably be answered by the learner, has proven popular. The technique works best when the leap from what is known to what is to be learned is not too great, and when the knowledge to be gained is analytic in nature – that is, it follows logically from definitions and/or existing knowledge. Even the best Socratic questioner might find difficulty in teaching French to someone who knows only English!

A model of Socratic questioning can be found in Paul and Elder (2006); this model classifies critical thinking according to:

- components of thinking, such as goals, problems, concepts, assumptions, information and inferences: Why are you writing this? Who is your audience? Is there an alternative conclusion? What is the main idea you are using? Can you explain it?

- the quality of reasoning, including clarity, precision, accuracy, relevance, depth and breadth: Could you give me an example or an illustration of your point? How could we check that to see if it is true? Could you explain the connection between what you are saying and the issue we are working on?

- the values associated with thinking, such as viewpoints and perspectives, implications and consequences, significance and fairness: Is there another point of view we should consider? If we do this, what is likely to happen as a result? Is this the most important factor to consider?

Encouraging learners to ask questions

When students know how to ask their own questions, they take greater ownership of their learning, deepen comprehension, and make new connections and discoveries on their own. However, this skill is rarely, if ever, deliberately taught to students from kindergarten through high school.

(Rothstein and Santana 2011: 1)

Perhaps one of the greatest joys for a teacher is when a student asks a question which shows real interest and engagement. In some cases, this happens spontaneously and independent of anything the teacher might do; more often it will be the result of careful planning and shows that the teacher has been able to create an environment which promotes a community of enquiry rather than simply a place where knowledge is transmitted. As Rothstein and Santana point out, it is still not common for students to be taught to ask questions yet, as with any other aspect of learning, students benefit from support and structure.

Box 9.3 Prompts for learners to formulate their own questions

Produce your questions
- Ask as many questions as you can
- Do not stop to discuss, judge, or answer the questions
- Write down every question exactly as it is stated
- Change any statements into questions

Improve your questions
- Categorize the questions as closed or open
- Name the advantages and disadvantages of each type of question
- Change questions from one type to another

Prioritize your questions
- Choose your three most important questions
- Why did you choose these three as the most important?

Next steps
- How are you going to use your questions?

Source: Adapted from Rothstein and Santana (2011).

In addition to providing an opportunity to clear up specific points, student questions provide the teacher with valuable information on attitudes to learning, level of conceptual development, and possible misconceptions. Chin and Brown (2002) found differences between the types of questions asked by learners with a deep or surface orientation to learning, and a greater propensity for problem-solving activities to stimulate what they called the 'wonderment' questions associated with deep learning. From the learner's point of view, asking questions is a particular form of elaboration on what is being learned (King 1992), in common with other learning strategies such as explaining in one's own words or teaching one's peers, and therefore facilitates deeper forms of learning.

Rather than wait for learners to ask questions spontaneously, question-forming can be planned into a lesson structure, with students working individually or in small groups to identify key questions. A possible structure for this kind of activity might include the prompts shown in Box 9.3.

Learning resources

Learning resources range from equipment, models and real objects for use by the teacher, to materials designed to be used by the learner, either in the learning session or independently. Well designed resources can engage learners and add variety. They aid conceptualization and offer communication through different channels – for example, visual resources help learners to 'see' and understand more clearly. Learning resources can be analysed from theoretical perspectives, including behaviourist, cognitivist, humanist and social learning theories. For example, do resources:

- help structure information, develop concepts or provide 'advance organizers' (Cognitivist)?

- focus attention, provide practice and feedback or enhance reinforcement (Behaviourist)?

- support learners in identifying and achieving their own goals, promoting intrinsic motivation (Humanist)?

- provide enhanced opportunities to learn from tutors or other students, and to create a community of practice (Social learning)?

There is an ever-increasing range of multimedia tools available for use as learning resources (discussed in Chapter 10). This section reviews other teaching and learning resources.

Whiteboards

The ability to use a whiteboard effectively is essential. Advance preparation of the whiteboard, with a welcome message and general notices and reminders, is an effective way to instantly personalize a room for learners. 'Setting up' in advance also allows legibility and spelling to be checked. Writing lesson objectives on the board provides a visual focus at the start of a lesson. It can also help learners who arrive late.

The size of lettering is important – writing a few words and checking for legibility from all parts of the room is important. Generally, lower case text is easier to read than capitals. Visual separation, or emphasis of different points through colour, can be helpful. Content should be visually organized, using bullet points, boxes, sub-headings and other indicators. 'Talking to the whiteboard' while writing is a common error, and as well as making the teacher inaudible, results in the teacher having their back to the learners. As a matter of courtesy to colleagues, the whiteboard should be left clean at the end of the session.

Handouts

Giving a handout to learners does not guarantee that learning will take place. Handouts which require learners to engage with them in some way are likely to be the most effective. Incomplete (or 'gapped') handouts have spaces for learners to complete – for example, diagrams to be labelled or space for notes, comments and answers to questions.

Layout and design are important. Large blocks of text can be off-putting; leaving 'white space' allows room for learners to annotate a handout. Overuse of upper-case letters is best avoided, as the shapes of words in lower case are an aid to reading. Teachers often develop a consistent style for all materials produced for a particular group, possibly with a heading or logo, rather than new designs for every session.

Illustrations and clipart can break up text and make handouts look more interesting and attractive. However, some learners may feel patronized by excessive use of certain types of illustration.

Coloured paper, rather than colour printing, can be a relatively inexpensive way to introduce colour. Pastel tones may also be helpful to learners with literacy difficulties, while a bright colour can be used to highlight the importance of a certain handout. Learners can be asked to read handouts in advance and to make summary points for discussion in class. This helps learners with literacy difficulties who may find it hard to read quickly. Using 'committed space' can be helpful and guide responses to tasks and activities; for example, a handout may ask learners to 'list five reasons in the space below'.

Learning materials may be tested for readability, for example by using the FOG index. In this method, a sample of 100 words of text is taken. The number of complete sentences in this 100 word sample is counted, together with the number of words contained in the complete sentences. From this information, the average sentence length, L, can be calculated. The next step is to count the number of words, N, of three or more syllables in the 100 word sample. Finally, the FOG index is calculated using the formula

$$\text{FOG Index} = 0.4 \times (L + N)$$

For example, suppose the 100 word sample of text contained five complete sentences containing a total of 86 words. Then $L = 86 \div 5 = 17.2$; if the sample also contained six words of three or more syllables, then $N = 6$ and

$$\text{FOG Index} = 0.4 \times (17.2 + 6) = 9.3$$

correct to one decimal place. For comparison, newspapers such as the *Guardian* have FOG indexes of around 12–14; text aimed at most learners should normally fall into the range 6–10, although this would vary depending on the level of the course. The FOG index is designed to correspond to US school grades; to convert a FOG index to an approximate reading age, add five to the value of the index.

Data projectors, presentation software and electronic whiteboards

Using presentation software, such as Prezi or Microsoft PowerPoint, with a data projector has become a popular method of communicating. However, a long series of slides presented to a passive audience should be avoided. The inclusion of photographs, other images and diagrams as well as sound and video clips can be effective, adding a multi-sensory dimension.

The most effective slides are clear, bold and simple. Key words and short phrases are preferable as space is limited. A useful guideline is to limit text to six to eight lines, with six to eight words in each line. A square central area on the slide should be used, as the top and bottom can be distorted when projected.

The size of text is important. At least 18–20 points will be necessary. Handouts in various forms can be produced from presentation slides, but care must be taken over readability as the resulting text may be too small. On each slide, points can be revealed one at a time, or all together. Excessive use of special effects can be distracting or irritating.

Colour schemes need to be carefully considered as contrasts which are easily readable on a PC screen may be illegible when projected. Two or three colours on a slide are enough for most purposes and rainbow effects or colours similar in tone should be avoided. It is tempting to include a plethora of animations, transitions, word art and sound effects. However, these can be irritating and detract from the points made. The teacher should have a printed copy of the slides to refer to, so that reading from the screen is avoided and eye contact with learners is maintained.

Electronic whiteboards are now commonplace. These boards allow handwritten text to be captured and include a variety of software tools to enable the teacher to increase the interactivity of presentations and other whole-class activities. With an electronic whiteboard, presentation slides can be annotated on screen and the resulting modifications saved.

Flipcharts

Flipcharts are portable and can be as effective as more sophisticated equipment. They are useful in community settings and their lack of formality or technology can be helpful. Individual flipchart sheets can be torn off a pad and used for group activities, then pinned up for presentation, feedback and reference.

As in the case of whiteboard pens, visibility of colours must be checked. Strong, dark colours are effective; orange and yellow will not show up clearly on a white ground. Flipcharts can be prepared in advance with key points in sequenced pages and also saved for further use, while sticky notes can be used to 'book mark' pages on a flip chart pad. Faint pencil lines can be ruled onto sheets to provide guide lines and aid neatness.

Audio-visual resources

Audio-visual resources such as DVDs and sound recordings can be used to enhance and support learning. For example, they can 'set the scene', shock, stimulate discussion, give a wider perspective and demonstrate a particular technique or expertise. Digital technology now enables a wide range of material to be searched and used effectively in a classroom. For example, YouTube offers a wealth of short film material, and some television channels offer 'replay' facilities online.

The teacher should ensure that learners remain engaged and active as they view or listen to the resource. For example, an incomplete handout can be used, learners can be asked to note down specific examples or points, or a film stopped at intervals for discussion. DVDs should be viewed in advance so that the teacher can become familiar with content. Starting points for DVDs and audio tapes need to be set up so that time is not wasted looking for them in a lesson. The teacher should, of course, always check *in advance* that they know how to use the audio-visual equipment.

Differentiation

For many years, education in England has been attempting to come to terms with changing social and economic circumstances. These changes have been reflected in curricula, but also in the recognition that individual learners must be supported in achieving their potential. The influential Warnock Report (Warnock 1978: 5) set out the key idea of differentiation for all learners: 'The purpose of education for all children is the same; the goals are the same. But the help that individual children need in progressing towards them will be different.' Differentiation is therefore about the ability of institutions and teachers to respond to the varying needs of individual learners, to help them achieve appropriate outcomes.

> Differentiation is not a single event, it is a process. This process involves recognising the variety of individual needs within a class, planning to meet those needs, providing appropriate delivery, and evaluating the effectiveness of the activities in order to maximise the achievements of individual learners.
>
> (NCET 1993: 21)

Maker (1982) has developed a model of curriculum differentiation for teaching gifted students, which can be applied to work with other learners. She suggests that the curriculum should be differentiated in four ways, in terms of modifications to the *learning environment*; the *content* of learning; learning *processes*; and learning *products*. Differentiation may therefore take a variety of forms, each one adapted to particular circumstances.

Differentiation may occur by *task*, either by different learners undertaking different tasks or with all learners undertaking a single task which has been graduated in difficulty. Extension material may be provided for the more able or experienced learners. In a graduated task, not all learners will be able to achieve all parts, but the task must be structured so that every learner can successfully complete a significant part of it. Differentiation may also take place by *outcome*; learners all undertake the same task, responding to it in different ways and achieving at their own level.

Creative writing provides an example of differentiation by outcome, as different learners could respond to the same title or stimulus material, but produce markedly different compositions. Differentiation by outcome may also be achieved by varying the nature of learning and assessment tasks – for example, by giving learners a choice of forms in which to present their work. Thus an assignment could be presented using posters or web pages rather than by a conventional written report; different presentation methods could also be used for different assignments. See Jones (2006) for further discussion of differentiation.

In differentiation by *support*, learners with different needs are given different forms or levels of support. This may be informal and within the context of the teacher's normal activity, such as individual help given during learning activities. More formally, group work may be planned so that stronger learners are paired with those less able – an example of peer support – or additional help may be provided in the form of tailored resources or support from a colleague. Writing frames can be helpful in some situations by providing key words or phrases to act as 'scaffolding' for learners undertaking an assignment. Effective writing frames will structure the content of learners' work by providing prompts to ensure that all key areas are covered, but may also be used to help learners achieve higher cognitive levels. One way of doing this is for the writing frame to explicitly direct learners to discuss evidence for their views and strengths or weaknesses in theories that they use.

For some learners, *additional time* may allow them to successfully complete a learning activity. Differentiation may also be achieved through the *feedback* provided following assessment – in this case, the feedback relates to the individual starting points and goals of the learner, giving advice on how to get from one to the other. This approach to differentiation is associated with the idea of *assessment for learning*, which is discussed in detail in Chapter 11.

Lesson plans and schemes of work

Lesson plans

There are many ways of recording the plan for a learning session. Teachers may be free to devise their own approaches but often institutions will adopt a standard format to be used by all teachers. Wherever possible, lesson plans should be adapted to the nature of the teaching and learning taking place, as an approach suitable for formal classes in an academic subject may be inappropriate for an engineering workshop or training carried out in a hospital ward.

The most common format for lesson plans is a cover sheet containing brief details about the course and learners, together with one or more pages in the form of a grid setting out the structure of the session (see Figures 9.4 and 9.5 for an example of this format). The cover sheet may state the time and location of the session and should outline strategies for assessment and differentiation, unless these are indicated elsewhere in the plan. The grid pages usually give rough timings for key phases in the session and have headings such as content, learner activity, teacher activity, assessment and resources. Columns for learner and teacher activity are sometimes merged to avoid repetition, but it can be useful to keep them separate as scanning up and down the learner activities can indicate whether a lesson involves the learners appropriately.

The scheme of work

A lesson plan should not stand alone; it should form part of a coherent sequence of learning expressed in a scheme of work. The use of schemes of work allows individual learning sessions to be placed in a wider context and related to the overall aims and content of a unit of learning. Knowledge, understanding and skills can be shown building up systematically over a period of time, and the role of language, literacy, numeracy and ICT in a course of study can be made clear.

A scheme of work will normally cover an extended period of learning, particularly for groups meeting once or twice a week throughout an academic year. However, the concept can also be applied to more intensive courses, such as a one-week

Class/Group: Level 2 Certificate for the Children and Young People's Workforce	**Room:** PF1/09 **Tutor name:** Angela Johnson

Topic or reference to scheme of work: Providing a safe and effective childcare environment	**Day:** Tue **Date:** 2 Nov 2014 **Time:** 10.15–12.15

No. on Register: 13 **No. in attendance:** 12 (11F, 1M)	**Module/Unit:** 048

General aims	Understand key principles and procedures involved in providing a safe childcare environment which promotes learning and positive behaviour.
Specific learning outcomes for the session:	• Know how to prepare and maintain a safe and healthy childcare environment • Be able to follow procedures for accidents, emergencies and illness • Explain procedures and methods that safeguard children from abuse • Suggest ways of encouraging children's positive behaviour
Anticipated inclusive learning issues and differentiation strategies for the lesson	Variety of student placements can be used to relate learning to individual experiences; however some learners have limited practical experience as yet. The lone male student in the group can feel isolated at times. I will adapt approach to individual needs through discussion, one-to-one support, and mixing experienced/less experienced learners in group work.

Assessment planned for during session, including key skills:
Observation of student practical activity, question and answer, discussion of paragraphs written by individual students. Drawing activity will allow practice and observation of numeracy skills. Group discussion enables development of communication skills. Written paragraph develops literacy skills.

Figure 9.4 Sample cover sheet of a lesson plan for a childcare class

Time	Topic	Teacher Activity	Learner Activity	Resources
11.15	Introduction	Welcome learners, take register. Brief recap of previous session. Introduce unit: it is about keeping children safe during day to day activities	Take part in Q/A.	Aims and objectives on whiteboard.
11.20	Responses to accidents, emergencies and illness	Explain key principles and procedures, using Q/A to involve learners and encourage them to contribute from own knowledge and experience.	Take part in Q/A; share placement experiences.	Whiteboard; teacher's notes.
11.30	Practical activity: produce diagram showing placement of safety equipment	Ask learners to draw layout of their placement setting, label rooms, add furniture. Example on whiteboard using Q/A.	Take part in Q/A; make initial drawings and share with others.	Workbooks, sharp pencils, rulers.
11.45	Practical activity continued	Ask learners to add furniture, play/learning equipment and safety equipment.	Complete drawings and discuss safety hazards and reasons for position of safety equipment with others in group.	Workbooks, sharp pencils, rulers.
12.00	Write a paragraph about how the rooms are organized	Explain activity.	Write paragraph, including discussion of safety factors. Refer to p. 31 in textbook.	Course textbooks.
12.10	Conclude first part of session	Review key points; check understanding of first objective by Q/A. Thank learners for contribution and link to next part of session.	Take part in Q/A.	

Figure 9.5 Extract from a lesson plan for a childcare class

Date	Content	Learning Activities	Resources	Embedding Language, Literacy, Numeracy and ICT	Formative Assessment
Term One					
30 Sep	Introductions. Role of the teacher.	Group work Presentations	Role of teacher handouts Flipchart paper	Developing communication skills	By trainee presentation/ discussion
07 Oct	Factors influencing learning. Learning styles.	Tutor input; Group discussion Completion of Learning Style Inventory (LSI)	Factors handouts Powerpoint; LSI	Statistics analysing LSI	LSI; Q&A Presentations on group work
14 Oct	Theories of the learning process	Tutor input; Group discussion Posters on learning theories	Powerpoint; YouTube video; Theory handouts	Using YouTube for educational purposes	Q&A Poster presentations
21 Oct	Planning learning sessions and schemes of work	Tutor input Small group work Differentiation case studies	Powerpoint Example lesson plans Trainees' own plans	Giving constructive feedback to peers	Q&A Own lesson plans
28 Oct	Library induction on e-resources	Librarian input Hands-on practice Group work; game	Research activity handout	Use of online journals; Referencing	Completion of activities
04 Nov	Teaching and learning methods and materials	Group discussion Tutor input	Materials for game; Powerpoint; Handout on effectiveness of teaching methods	Percentages, effect sizes for teaching methods	Q&A; reflection on issues raised by game

Figure 9.6 Extract from a scheme of work for a Certificate in Education class

residential induction for newly-appointed trade union workers. Whatever the time period, the scheme of work will show the sequence of learning sessions, together with brief details of the general objective for each session, key learning activities and resources, and the schedule of assessment to be used. A sample scheme of work is shown in Figure 9.6.

There are several ways of deciding on a learning sequence for the scheme of work. In subject areas where there is a hierarchical organization of knowledge – with more advanced concepts and principles building on simpler ones – it is necessary to pay careful attention to the precedence of particular topics, so that concepts and methods are available when needed. The sequence may therefore be constructed from an analysis of prerequisite knowledge at each stage. However, even in a highly structured subject area, a purely logical development may not always be the best pedagogic approach. These considerations lead to the contrast between a *depth-first* approach, in which a particular topic is explored in detail before moving on to the next one, and a *breadth-first* approach in which a topic is taken only as far as is needed to be used in other topics. The breadth-first approach allows a broad survey of a subject or occupational area to be established at a relatively early stage, thus encouraging holistic learning. The topics can then be revisited in more depth later on, achieving the spiral curriculum approach advocated by Bruner (see Chapter 7).

Rather than use a topic-based approach, in some cases it may be better to adopt a thematic structure for the scheme of work. For example, 'climate change' is a theme that could draw together different topics in a science course, integrating otherwise abstract ideas and showing how they may be applied.

Modelling good practice

Research on teacher education programmes (Wood and Geddis 1999; Loughran and Berry 2005; Lunenberg et al. 2007; White 2011) suggests that modelling can be a highly effective teaching method when used by skilled practitioners to discuss, interrogate and theorize their practice. Lunenberg et al. (2007) identified four forms of modelling and evaluated the effectiveness of each. The first form is implicit modelling involving demonstration of a method or skill without explanation. Research suggests that this form of modelling is widely used, but that its impact on learners' practice is often limited (Lunenberg et al. 2007). Implicit modelling requires learners to interpret correctly the teacher's behaviour, and this might be difficult when 'companion meanings' (Wood and Geddis 1999: 108) exist within the modelling. The second form is known as explicit modelling and involves the teacher commentating on, explaining and debating the methods they are modelling. The third form of modelling combines explicit modelling with the concept of 'bridging' (Petty 2009: 298), which requires the teacher to ask learners to consider how the teaching method might be applied to their own practice. The fourth form is where the teacher uses explicit modelling and 'unpacks' their practice to discuss aspects of theory that lie behind the method they have modelled, what Lunenberg et al. (2007: 592) call 'connecting exemplary behaviour with theory'. The most effective and transformative form of modelling in terms of influencing learners' practice is when the teacher is able to discuss their explicit modelling of a method, explore the theories behind their practice and then enable individual students to see how what they have learned might be adopted and adapted for their own practice.

Teaching groups of learners

In lifelong learning, groups can take many forms, ranging from a class meeting several times a week in a college to work-based learning groups attending for a specific training event. Different types of group may need different approaches, appropriate to varying circumstances and learner characteristics. Many teachers emphasize the importance of high expectations from the very beginning of their work with a learning group, advocating the model of the *confident professional* (LSDA 2007: 20) who expects, and is generally rewarded with, good social behaviour.

Tuckman and Jensen (1977), in their classic model of group development, suggest that all groups move sequentially through five different stages: *forming, storming, norming, performing* and *adjourning*. More recently, a seven-stage model for learning groups has been proposed by Johnson and Johnson (2006: 28). According to their model, group development begins with three initial stages: *defining and structuring procedures, conforming to procedures and getting acquainted* and *recognizing mutuality and building trust*. These early stages, when a group comes together for the first few times, are a period of uncertainty and group members are often heavily dependent upon the tutor. Learners need to be welcomed and may need clear direction on aims, expectations and procedures.

Teachers need to establish rules and boundaries, rights and responsibilities, and routines and protocols with the group (Vizard 2007), and to then *habituate* what they establish (Rogers 2004). Negotiating ground rules with learners allows both teachers and learners to have a shared understanding. Through activities which encourage cooperation and socialization, the teacher can help learners get to know each other and can create a supportive, inclusive atmosphere in tune with Maslow's hierarchy of needs.

Rebelling and differentiating, the fourth stage of this model, can be compared to the *storming* period of Tuckman and Jensen. This phase may be short, or conversely one from which some groups find it difficult to progress. There may be conflict, disagreements and challenges or resistance to procedures. This may be exhibited openly or through passive behaviour such as minimal effort or withdrawal from collaborative learning. Johnson and Johnson see this as a natural part of the development process, a move towards independence, which should be dealt with in an open and accepting way. They recommend smoothing, reasoning and mediating while recognizing learner autonomy and individuality. It is important to repair and rebuild relationships following intervention, to prevent the erosion of relationships and damage to self-esteem (Rogers 2004).

Committing to goals, procedures and other members and *functioning maturely and productively* are the next stages of Johnson and Johnsons' model. In a similar way to the *norming and performing* phases of Tuckman and Jensen, norms are established and cohesion and commitment increased, and the group works effectively and productively. Learners become intrinsically motivated to provide support and assistance to each other and regard the group as *their* group, not the tutor's. Positive relationships exist between the learners themselves and with the teacher.

For groups that have matured into cohesive, effective units where strong friendships and emotional bonds have been formed, the final phase of *terminating* (Johnson and Johnson 2006) or *adjourning* (Tuckman and Jensen 1977) can be accompanied with some sadness. The teacher needs to recognize this and provide closure for the group in some way. Review and evaluation exercises, acknowledgement and celebration of success and achievement and opportunities to 'say goodbye' can all be valuable at this stage.

Attention to group management and the building of positive relationships between all learners can play an important part in promoting effective learning. In any group there is a complex play of relationships, which may result in an 'emotional swirl' (Jacques and Salmon (2007:11). This should not be underestimated by the tutor and indeed it needs to be proactively managed to develop and maintain a positive group culture.

Managing learner behaviour

The Elton Report stated that 'teachers' group management skills are probably the single most important factor in achieving good standards of classroom behaviour' (DES 1989, 70). Ofsted (2005[b]) emphasises as important a somewhat broader range of [institutional] factors, such as leadership, training, consistency and monitoring of behaviour via information systems.

(Hart 2010: 353)

Different age groups may present different forms of behaviour and although where problems occur they tend to be associated with younger learners, some adults can also be difficult and demanding. Behaviour which may be regarded as 'challenging' includes the following:

- behaviour that disrupts routine teaching to an extent that challenges the teacher's resources and concentration of other learners; this may not be violent, offensive or dangerous, simply disruptive
- behaviour that is offensive or violent, interfering with routine activity
- offending behaviour, including offending in the criminal sense, which bullies or ridicules fellow learners and creates an intimidating environment
- extreme passivity or non-engagement in learning
- intermittent patterns of attendance.

(LSDA 2007: 2)

As a starting point, it is essential to analyse the causes of disruption. Jacques and Salmon (2007) suggest that many incidents are a consequence of a lack of structure in sessions. Transitions between activities should not leave gaps which learners can exploit to pursue their own agenda. Providing learners with appropriate tasks will also reduce opportunities for disruption. Overtly challenging behaviour can indicate disengagement from learning; it can also be a signal that learners are not placed on the most appropriate programme, or that the level of learning is inappropriate. Some learners may seek attention through misbehaviour. For some young people, 'egos are much more insecure and fragile than in fully fledged adults' (Blum 2001: 7). As a result of such factors, learners may respond to certain situations with overt resistance, avoidance, 'herd' behaviour or inertia.

Hart (2010: 356–9) discusses four conceptualizations of classroom behaviour and associated class management strategies: behaviourist, psychodynamic, systemic and humanist. Behavioural approaches aim to increase desired behaviours through positive reinforcement, and to decrease undesirable behaviour using strategies such as ignoring unwanted behaviour or using 'time out'. Although popular and often effective, these approaches have been criticized for reducing intrinsic motivation, diminishing learner autonomy and replacing the development of social skills with arbitrary systems of rewards. Psychodynamic approaches emphasize the importance of secure and trusting relationships, as well as emotional containment and expression. Effective teachers are seen as providing consistent, positive expectations and as disposed towards nurturing; however, caring and nurturing models are very intensive of staff resources and may also reduce learner autonomy. Systemic approaches focus on the social interactions framing problematic behaviour, emphasizing the social environment and social cognitions and/or skills. According to this type of view, behavioural problems result from complex interactions between the individual, school, family, community and wider society. Teachers and students should therefore be supported by the institution in collaborating to solve problems connected with learner behaviour. An effective learning environment is identified as the priority for intervention when behavioural problems occur. Humanistic strategies are characterized by the idea that students' motivation, and consequently their behaviour, flows from underlying psychological needs – essentially, those found in Maslow's hierarchy. Like psychodynamic approaches, humanistic behaviour management emphasizes teacher-student relationships and the creation of a safe and positive learning environment, but attempts to strengthen learner autonomy by building in choice and individual responsibility.

These different conceptualizations of behaviour management underpin a range of specific strategies that have been found helpful. Hart (2010: 335–6) refers to Little and Akin–Little's (2008) identification of the importance of:

- establishing firm and fair ground rules;
- reinforcing appropriate behaviour;
- responding to undesired behaviour;
- creating and maintaining positive relationships with students;
- having high expectations about behaviour and achievement;
- establishing procedures for responding to persistent behavioural difficulties;
- a good learning environment – displays celebrating students' work, clean and bright classrooms, good acoustics, having sufficient space to store equipment and having dedicated spaces for special equipment or activities.

Gibbs (1995) suggests three practical strategies for meeting the challenges of group management:

1   *Don't start from here.* This refers to problems which may arise because action was not taken earlier. For example, ground rules may not have been established, or initial assessment may have been ineffective.

2   *Use structures.* Both content and methods need to be structured effectively; planning and preparation are important. In addition, prior consideration of classroom organization will promote the smooth running of a lesson, including protocols for different types of work which take account of health and safety (Vizard 2007: 25).

3   *Make leadership interventions.* These are the things which teachers say and do, for example to redirect groups or defuse certain situations. Larger groups may need more emphatic intervention. Problems in groups can become part of a group culture which, if not dealt with promptly, can be very hard to change. Cliques may form and teachers need to discourage them.

First impressions with a group are important, to 'make a significant initial impact on students and to get initial interactions right' (Vizard 2007: 22). Although approaches may vary, parameters of acceptable behaviour need to be established as outlined above. Rules and routines should identify unacceptable behaviours, for example, using mobile phones; racist, sexist or other inappropriate language; and unexplained lateness. It is useful to note the difference between an authoritarian approach with imposed rules and a democratic one in which boundaries are established by both teachers and learners. Leadbeater (2005) cautions that some learners with challenging behaviour may not be able to articulate their expectations, as immediate concerns may dominate their thinking. Such learners may express anger or discontent loudly as a way of being 'heard'. However, the underlying message and cause should also be heeded, and help provided to examine and change behaviour. Vizard (2007) notes that students are often told not to behave in a certain way but are not given the skills and strategies necessary to manage their feelings and behaviour in a more positive manner.

To prevent unwanted behaviour, teachers should appreciate the importance of non-verbal communication and body language. Being aware of 'psychological geography' (Vizard 2007) and frequently moving around the classroom in a confident manner are characteristics of an effective teacher – although care should be taken not to over-control students who might otherwise settle down to work if their attention-seeking behaviour is not rewarded. Eye contact can indicate awareness of individual learners. Overtly scanning the class, using a sweeping, 'lighthouse' effect to include all learners in the field of vision, can also be effective.

It is helpful to identify in advance learner behaviour that may cause concern and to research and practise strategies. Vizard (2007: 139) suggests preparing a 'script' for response to particular types of behaviour, as 'the choice of words we use and how we say them influence the management of behaviour'. He emphasizes the need to remain assertive, giving clear instructions and avoiding emotional

Table 9.3 Positive and negative approaches to motivating learners

Positive teacher behaviours	Negative teacher behaviours
Motivates with praise and trust	Motivates with fear for the present or future
Rewards students to motivate them	Indifferent to learners' achievements
Focuses on the goals and expectations of learners	Focuses on own goals
Manages own behaviour effectively	Loses self-control
Builds learners' self-esteem	Undermines learners' self-esteem
Shows empathy with learners	Behaves insensitively towards learners

Source: Adapted from Wallace (2002b)

language, pleading or apologetic delivery. Cowley (2003) suggests that teachers will benefit from knowing exactly what they want and expect from learners (although the title of her book indicates that teacher expectations can be negative), and from maintaining a psychological distance to retain feelings of control and prevent emotional reactions. In some situations, a 'blocking' and 'broken record' technique can be helpful. 'Blocking' involves ignoring a comment made by a student while repeating a redirecting statement like a 'broken record'. Reprimands should be in private, as this removes the audience which some learners may seek, and sanctions should be applied consistently.

Learners should be aware of the consequences and sanctions embedded in institutional policies on disruptive behaviour. Allowing time for learners to conform and comply with instructions can be helpful and will give both parties some 'time out'. Direct confrontations should be avoided wherever possible as they may cause an already difficult situation to escalate. When dealing with challenging behaviour, it is advisable to avoid making personal comments and to criticize the behaviour, not the person. Wallace (2002b) draws attention to positive and negative styles used by teachers to motivate and control challenging students (see Table 9.3). In particular, teachers should model good behaviour, reinforce positive behaviour in students through praise, and maintain standards of respect and politeness towards students.

Tutorials and pastoral support

In the LLS, tutorials focus on the academic and pastoral requirements of learners, as well as promoting retention, attendance and punctuality. In many cases, personal tutors will also teach their students in subject classes, generating further insight into their academic progress and pastoral needs but also blurring the boundaries between roles and possibly compromising the tutorial relationship. Tutors need to develop and demonstrate a wide range of qualities and skills to manage tutorials; being a supportive and empathic listener is important, but on occasion poor behaviour or attendance may have to be challenged.

The amount of time devoted to tutorial activity varies; for full-time students, one hour per week is common but part-time students may have significantly less. To ensure consistent tutorial support, many institutions use a common scheme of work for all groups of students. This will begin with an induction period, followed by other tutorials focusing on pastoral and academic support. Induction may be the first opportunity for students to bond with each other. Often, they are anxious about starting the course, making new friends and coping with the transition from school, college or a previous job. In HE the student may be living away from home for the first time. Icebreaker activities can be used to develop peer bonding and support, which in turn, will help to improve retention and attendance. Often, team-building events away from the college environment are organized.

Induction is also the best time to establish ground rules about conduct, attendance and punctuality, and completion of work. Treasure hunts and quizzes can be used to introduce and consolidate information about the institution and course requirements. Induction will also provide an opportunity to inform students about enrichment activities, and the use of facilities such as library, IT and learning support. At this stage, students may also be given diagnostic assessments to identify learning support needs.

Pastoral support throughout the course will be one of the key roles of the personal tutor. Activities may focus on issues such as developing research skills, revision techniques and time management, along with careers tutorials dealing with CV writing and educational or job applications. Pastoral support will also include one-to-one supervision, requiring the tutor to establish a supportive and trusting relationship with their students. However, knowing where the tutorial role ends and specialists need to be involved is important. Unless a personal tutor is sure of their competence, it is best to refer complex issues to an appropriate support service, or involve more senior colleagues. Martinez and Munday (1998) identify the importance of supporting inexperienced tutors through staff development and sharing good practice within a course team.

Personal tutors will often be the first point of contact for students, and may offer the help and advice needed to prevent an unhappy student from dropping out. Designated times for individual tutorials will help to manage the demands on tutors, especially with large tutorial groups. Some tutors use a virtual learning environment to supplement tutorials, especially with part-time students, although students still favour face-to-face contact (Sweeney et al. 2004). Students may be encouraged to develop links within the tutorial group through social networking sites such as Facebook and Twitter.

Monitoring retention, attendance and punctuality are important tutorial roles and diligence in following up attendance or punctuality issues is essential. Students who attend irregularly soon get behind and are highly likely to fail or leave the course. In HE monitoring attendance is not so straightforward, as students are often living away from home and are expected to be more responsible for their actions. However, it is still important to track poor attendance as this could be the result of underlying personal problems; for the mature student, it could be the effect of combining the course with the demands of family life. Records should be kept of any calls or meetings, as these may be needed if the student is suspended or withdrawn from the course.

In some courses, an individual learning plan is a formal part of tutorial support and is used to set targets and identify learning needs. Individual learning plans are initiated early in the course, and then regularly reviewed and updated to monitor progress; in some courses, they are updated weekly or even after each learning session. When reviewing an individual learning plan, discussion should include progress since the last review and learning support needs, as well as attendance and the balance between study and social life.

10

Learning and teaching with technology

Liz Bennett, Steve Burton, Alison Iredale,
Cheryl Reynolds and Andrew Youde

In this chapter

- The value of learning with technology
- Developing teachers' e-learning practices
- Concepts of learning with technology
- Technologies for learning
- Teacher-led or student-initiated?
- Designing for learning with technology
- The potential of digital tools for social, moral and personal harm
- Conclusion

The central concern of this chapter is the impact of recent technologies upon educational practices. That today's students are not the same as yesterday's is evident from how they communicate with one another, create and maintain friendships, consume information, access services and engage in study. Technology, frequently conceived as merely a set of tools for creating discrete, re-usable learning objects or lessons, is now increasingly thought of and treated as a medium within and through which we communicate; the interactions that occur there being the very stuff of the learning process. Marshall McLuhan's notion that 'the medium is the message' argues that mode of communication rather than broadcast content is the most significant characteristic of new media (McLuhan 2001). In this sense, it matters less what students say online and more that they are invited to participate in an online world. What does entering this medium do to them, to their relationships and identities? What social forces operate in this milieu and what shaping effect do they have on students' ideas and on education as a whole? If the medium is the message, the message is discursive, interactive, engaging, visible and mobile. Students are as likely to shape what they find on the Internet as they are to absorb it, to re-purpose information tools to their own ends and to find ways of exploiting technology that subvert its original intentions.

In this context, developing an enquiring approach to the educational use of technology is the teacher's greatest asset. Some teachers believe that they are 'hopeless with IT'. This idea arises from a misconception; that technological competence is all about skills. It is rather a disposition and an attitude; a willingness to experiment and to try new approaches and an acceptance that technology can provide challenges or disappointment as well as wonderful answers to educational problems. Tenacity, resilience and imagination are the key characteristics of teachers who use technology well. Coupled with these characteristics, an awareness of its effect on people can help us to exploit technology in ways that improve or extend learning and make it more accessible and socially just. Critical reflection upon the impact of technology on the learning process is valuable as it puts the emphasis in the right place: on the learner rather than the computer. In this chapter we explore and categorize a number of technologies in terms of their educational potential. We then illuminate some of this potential through four case studies. The case studies are intended as examples to reflect upon rather than ideal scenarios, with an invitation to critique their impact and to consider the drawbacks as well as the benefits of technology.

The value of learning with technology

There are many reported benefits of using technology to support learning. The *Technology Strategy* (Becta 2008) suggests that building technology into the curriculum improves engagement, retention and progression, accelerates learning and promotes more efficient teaching. In particular, effective use of ICT can enable greater learner choice within the curriculum, lead to improved assessment and facilitate more learner-directed teaching. Learners can be more involved in target-setting and teachers are better able to provide individualized feedback.

E-learning may provide the opportunity for learners to revisit and absorb key concepts in their own time and at their own pace, in a personalized way linked to their individual learning preferences and preparedness. Other evidence for the value of e-learning comes from the Joint Information Systems Committee (JISC), a government-funded body whose role is to promote learning technologies. Their work identifies six key benefits:

- Connectivity – access to information is available on a global scale.
- Flexibility – learning can take place at any time, in any place, and allows students to reflect and to revisit material.
- Interactivity – assessment of learning can be immediate and autonomous.
- Collaboration – the use of discussion tools can support collaborative learning beyond the classroom.
- Extended opportunities – additional e-content can reinforce and extend classroom-based learning.
- Motivation – multimedia resources can make learning fun.

(JISC 2004: 7)

Another JISC-funded study examined the impact and possible benefits of using e-learning in 16 universities. Tutors in the same subject area at different institutions drew up case studies describing and analysing the use of e-learning. They also considered the potential benefits of e-learning, grouping them under six main headings:

- Cost-saving and resource efficiency.
- Recruitment and retention.
- Employability skills.
- Achievement.
- Widening participation.
- Support for students with learning difficulties or disabilities.

(JISC Infonet 2008: 14–26)

Other potential benefits included enhanced reputation, invigoration of teaching, changes to institutional policy and supplementing or reinforcing face-to-face learning. The project report provides a succinct statement of the potential of e-learning:

> The most fundamental point ... is that the appropriate use of technology is leading to significant improvements in learning and teaching across the sector and that this is translating into improved satisfaction, retention and achievement. e-Learning is facilitating the expansion of the sector [and] is allowing broadly the same numbers of staff to educate a larger and more diverse student body.
>
> (JISC Infonet 2008: 33)

However, other studies find insufficient evidence to make unequivocal statements about the impact of technology on learning (Twining et al. 2006; Condie and Munro 2007). These studies conclude that many factors impact on the success or otherwise of learning with technology. The context in which learning takes place and support within the organization are at least as important as the nature of the technology and ways that it is used.

Developing teachers' e-learning practices

It has been argued that teachers hold the key to unlocking the potential of technology in the curriculum. Rebbeck and Ecclesfield (2008:1) report that *e-maturity*, that is, 'the extent to which organisations ... use technology effectively to support learning, teaching and other business processes', is dependent on the skills of teachers. Similarly, Masterman and Vogel (2007: 60), in their study of how teachers approach VLE tools, conclude that 'the process of design for learning has as much to do with the dispositions and preferences of individual practitioners, their subject domains and the community pressures on them as with the availability and affordances of the tools used'. Thus an understanding of one's own attitudes to learning technologies is a key component to their successful use in the classroom.

Dispositions towards the adoption of technology vary considerably, and the following (somewhat light-hearted) typology may be helpful:

- The 'expert' knows a lot about learning technology but may lack experience of teaching. Their knowledge may not be embedded in an understanding of classroom subtleties.

- The 'enthusiast' has a positive approach to new technologies, but may lack critical awareness.

- The 'Luddite' has an inherent resistance to change. This may provide a critical test of new ideas; however, the Luddite may resist change out of hand, whatever the evidence in its favour.

It is interesting to note that, although the popular image of the Luddite is of perverse resistance to progress, the eminent historian E.P. Thompson saw Luddism as a transitional conflict, partly looking backwards to old customs and traditions, but also looking forward to 'a democratic community, in which industrial growth should be regulated according to ethical priorities and the pursuit of profit be subordinated to human needs' (Thompson 1980: 603). This view resonates with current debates on the impact of 'digital Taylorism' on contemporary professional practices (Brown et al. 2011).

A further type of response, perhaps with a more balanced and positive perspective, is the 'digital practitioner' or 'agile adopter' – the practitioner who is well grounded in existing practice but willing to experiment with new technologies and share them with colleagues. The notion of being alive to experimentation is echoed by Bennett (2012) who found it to be a critical and defining feature of teachers who are adopting web-based tools and who see their potential to support students' learning as a reason to overcome some of the risks implicit in changing pedagogical practices.

Online and blended learning tutoring skills

A full discussion of the skills, dispositions and practices needed for effective online tutoring is beyond the scope of this chapter. However, there are some critical differences that tutors teaching in an online environment need to consider. Writing on theory and practice in distance education, Holmberg (1989: 163) states that 'learning is encouraged by frequent communication with fellow humans interested in study'. The feeling of belonging – to a course or institution – is just as important as discussions about the subject being studied. Wenger (1998) explains that learning is derived from participation in a community of practitioners, the shared practice being central to the community and helping to form relationships and develop identities. Moore's (1980) notion of *transactional distance* refers to the connectedness a student feels to the course and tutor. Even students working online can still feel part of a community if such a relationship has developed. The strategies discussed in this chapter will help to foster transactional presence and facilitate the development of communities of practice among students.

The importance of the tutor in facilitating a successful online and blended learning experience cannot be overestimated. Smith (2004: 37) notes that in distance learning, 'Quality is influenced by the usefulness of feedback students receive on assignments, the availability and accessibility of lecturers, and the promptness with which lecturers respond to and reply to students'. She emphasizes the importance of responding to questions with enthusiasm and the lecturer's ability to meet individual needs. An online tutor must be able to foster group identity, develop collaboration and link theory to personal experiences and practice (Creanor 2002; Salmon 2003). All the skills that lecturers in traditional classroom environments possess are essential; however, an online tutor generally does not have the benefit of non-verbal feedback (body language and facial expression, for example). Therefore, knowledge of pedagogical principles and empathetic consideration of the learning environment are also valuable.

Concepts of learning with technology

A range of concepts and terminology has emerged to describe the application of technology to learning (see Box 10.1). This is a developing field where concepts are being refined and adapted. In this chapter, we define e-learning as 'any learning that uses ICT'. This definition includes learning that takes place in the classroom and learning at a distance. However, the distinction between face-to-face and distance learning is being blurred by technology. Traditionally, distance learning involved studying alone (perhaps occasionally attending a tutorial) whereas classroom-based learning involved working with others but at a pace dictated by the teacher. Nowadays, distance learning students may be working on a web-based group project or communicating with other students and tutors online. Even within a classroom setting, students may be working at their own pace – for example, using a laptop computer to

---

Box 10.1 Definitions of terms relating to learning with technology

Learning technologies (LT) Technologies used to support and potentially enhance learning.

Technology supported learning The use of technology to support the learning process. This term places emphasis on the learning process which technology is trying to facilitate.

Technology enhanced learning The use of technology to improve the student's experience of the learning process. The term places emphasis on the benefits that can arise from use of technology.

Distributed learning This term focuses on remote delivery of learning or learning materials although it may incorporate some face-to-face elements as well.

Flexible learning Used often in conjunction with distributed learning; for example flexible distributed learning (FDL). Flexible distance learning means that some aspects of a course are delivered remotely.

Distance learning A term used when *all* the mandatory aspects of a learning programme are delivered remotely.

Blended learning This term is most commonly used to reflect systematic combination of delivery models that includes both face-to-face and online learning.

access learning materials or to search the web for ideas and resources. This blurring of the boundaries between classroom-based and distance learning is part of the transformative potential of technology (BECTA 2008; HEFCE 2005).

Thompson (2007: 52) argues that the term 'e-learning' is problematic because it limits our ability to conceptualize the subject. Clearly, learning is multifaceted, involving a delicate interplay between a range of factors – including national policies, institutional policies and practices, students' characteristics, teachers' skills and curriculum requirements. The use of the term e-learning creates a mystique, suggesting a new and different process. This chapter analyses the factors affecting the success of e-learning and suggests that learning with technology depends on getting the balance of these factors right – taking into account the particular context in which learning is taking place.

Technologies for learning

This section introduces some of the learning technologies currently available. There is an inherent danger when focusing on e-learning that attention moves from the learning process to the technologies themselves. Care is needed to focus on *how technology can be used* to enhance learning. Excessive attention to the tools gives them a status that distracts from the principles underpinning their use, and may promote the tool for its own sake rather than adding something useful and meaningful for the learner. Such an approach is referred to as *technological determinism*, whereby technology is viewed as having a 'natural trajectory': inherent properties and uses that make certain things occur. In contrast to this view is the notion of technology as social construction, in which technology is part of the social world and developments in its use need to be seen as inextricably linked to other social phenomena (Van Lieshout et al. 2001). These perspectives affect how the lecturer thinks about technology, the possibilities it offers and how they may be integrated within teaching and learning. Simply using tools will not inevitably deliver their pedagogical benefits; we need to shape their use.

Table 10.1 outlines some of the web-based tools available for teaching and learning, indicating the *affordance* of each tool – that is, the role for which it is most obviously suited. However, the notion of affordance is problematic – is it a property of the tool or of the way it is used? An affordance is really a socially constructed property, and as a tool is used in new and imaginative ways, its affordances can change. With this proviso, Table 10.1 provides a way to conceptualize some commonly encountered tools. The term Web 2.0 is often used to denote these tools and services; available online, often free to use, they allow participation and collaboration and may potentially be used on massive scales. The Centre for Learning and Performance Technologies produces an annually updated list of popular technological tools and is an excellent source of information about their possibilities (http://c4lpt.co.uk/).

Table 10.2 provides another way to conceptualize e-learning tools by considering the type of interaction they afford. The table categorizes the tools according to the numbers of people involved in their use: for example, one-to-one may involve a single tutor being in contact with a student. The tools are also grouped by whether they operate synchronously or asynchronously. A *synchronous* activity requires users to be involved all at the same time, whereas an *asynchronous* activity does not. This

Table 10.1 Web-based tools available for teaching and learning

Tool and explanation	Possible affordances
Asynchronous, text-based communication Users can post, read and respond to messages without being online at the same time (for example, discussion forums or message boards)	Group work; learning through discussion of course topics
Wiki A website which can be edited by users	Production of a shared resource e.g. a collaborative project
Blog An online diary where users can post entries in date order	Reflective diary
Podcast An audio or enhanced audio file that is syndicated, i.e. automatically sent to a user's computer	Delivery of lecture material; learning offsite e.g. field work
Screencast A video captured from what is happening on the computer screen with audio voice over	Delivery of lecture material
Voice over Internet Protocol (VoIP) Internet-based phone technology such as Skype	Tool for mutual support and for voice-based communication
Chat or instant messaging	Texting over the Internet by means of networks such as MSN
Webinar tools Enables events such as lecturers, seminars to be held online, for example Elluminate, Adobe Connect	Online lecturers, tutorials; collaboration on a project
Repository A storage area for digital files that enables sharing of resources	Finding teaching and learning resources
Multimedia sharing services For example YouTube, Flickr, Slideshare	Accessing resources generated by others, sharing resources widely
Social networking sites Facebook, Ning, Yammer, Twitter.	Connecting with a group of dispersed people
Web collaboration tools E.g. book marking	Identifying and sharing web resources
File sharing tools e.g. dropbox, scribd, Google docs	Facilitating group work
Massively multiplayer virtual world (MMVW) An online 3D environment populated by 'avatars' – representations of human or animal form; examples include Second Life	Modelling real world scenarios, for example, marketing, fashion shows; online role-play

important distinction clearly derives from the affordances of a tool: synchronous tools facilitate an immediate response whereas an asynchronous activity does not require the same commitment in terms of students and staff being available at the same time. In addition, the nature of the interactions is significantly different because of the temporal separation involved in asynchronous activities.

Table 10.2 Collaborative tools available for learning

Type of interaction	Asynchronous	Synchronous
One-to-one, for student support or tutorials	Email; blog	Telephone; VoIP; chat
One-to-many, for teacher-led activities or group learning	Email; blog; discussion forum; podcast; Screencast	Chat; webinars; VoIP; MMVW
Many-to-many, for collaborative projects or sharing resources	Wiki; repository	MMVW; webinars; VoIP

Table 10.3 Mapping technologies against approaches to teaching and learning

Theoretical approach	Pedagogic approaches	Examples of technologies
Constructivist	Problem-based learning	Using scenarios taken from real world practice identified using the web
Constructivist	Resource-based learning	Using resources located on the web
Social constructivist	Contributing student model (see below)	Wiki, discussion boards, email groups
Humanistic and constructivist	Reflective learning	Blog
Social constructivist	Community of practice	Discussion board, blog, wiki, chat, virtual world
Social constructivist	Collaborative learning	Discussion board, blog, wiki
Didactic	Content led learning	VLE content area, webinar

Finally, Table 10.3 matches some pedagogical approaches to some of the technological tools introduced above. The mapping is indicative, as it is possible to apply the tools in different ways. Indeed, this chapter argues that the success of a particular learning activity depends on a number of factors rather than the particular tool being used.

Teacher-led or student-initiated?

It is important to understand the notion of social shaping of technology in order to critically explore technology and its potential in the classroom. The way that technological tools are shaped by existing cultural norms is particularly evident in the design and implementation of the institutional virtual learning environment (VLE). The VLE combines many of technologies outlined in Table 10.1 into a single web-based package and is the face of online learning in most FE and HE institutions. VLEs tend to be shaped by institutional practices – for example, structured around course modules and thereby separating learning into compartments. This is sometimes described as a *silo* approach to learning design. However, the advantages of a VLE lie in the possibility of integration with other institutional systems such as student records. It will also acquire familiarity and support amongst staff and students. Yet because of its ubiquitous nature within the institution, the VLE has become synonymous with e-learning in many people's minds. Its frequent use as an institutional repository for lecture notes and PowerPoint slides often limits our conception of what might be possible with e-learning (Weller 2007).

An alternative way of envisaging learning with technology is embodied in the terms Personal Learning Network (PLN) or Personal Learning Environment (PLE). These terms recognize that students make use of a range of learning tools corresponding to personal needs and preferences. The tools and devices offered by a PLE are highly personalized and fluid, changing as new tools and services emerge and as learners acquire devices and develop skills. They may include mobile phones and social networking sites such as Facebook or Twitter, alongside those found in the institutional VLE.

The notion of *digital learning literacies* has been used to articulate the range of skills, practices and attributes that students might need, both in current and future study and in their working lives. It is easy to assume that students have a level of familiarity with technology, especially those that have grown up with a culture that is pervaded by gadgets. In the early 2000s the terms 'digital natives' and 'net genners' took hold to characterize the skills and dispositions of these young people (Oblinger and Oblinger 2005; Prensky 2001). However a more critical exploration has identified that actually these generalizations hide many differences between learners and their attitudes and skills when using technology in their learning (Luckin et al. 2009). Nicholas et al. (2008) concluded that learners' ICT skills are less advanced than some educators and learners think. Beetham (2009) noted that some aspects of learners' practices are at odds with academic practices – contrasting the ease of embedding a YouTube video into a Facebook page with the conventions of academic referencing. Similarly, Selwyn (2009) found that skills connected with knowledge building and sharing are generally developed through academic studies and are not normally part of students' online practices.

Understanding and planning for digital learning literacies using a holistic and institution-wide approach ensures that educators are developing students' skills and attributes without making assumptions about the digital skills and practices of learners. However, whilst there have been some initiatives that support institutions to address digital literacy within an institution-wide framework (such as JISC's Digital Literacies programme http://www.jisc.ac.uk/developingdigitalliteracies), this work is under-developed in many institutions (Bennett 2012).

Digital literacies have been represented as including five aspects (see Figure 10.1). They include the traditional skills of information literacy but go beyond this to include other dimensions such as understanding how writing for a particular audience or searching for information are different in the connected, digital world. The centre of the diagram indicates that, at the most fundamental level, students need to be able to access networks, devices and software. Given this functional access, students can apply their skills to a range of practices. For example, they may need to find

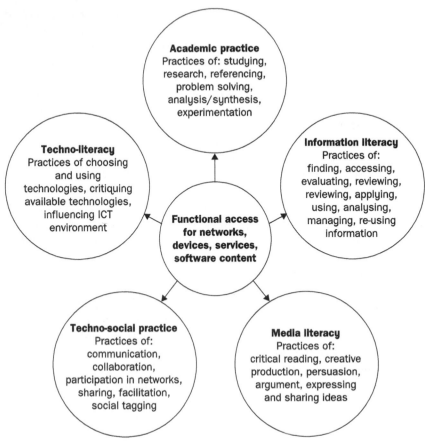

Figure 10.1 Digital literacy anatomized
Source: JISC (2011)

and evaluate literature (information literacy), but they may also need to choose appropriate media and create artifacts in new formats (media practice).

Designing for learning with technology

Earlier in this chapter we explored the idea of technological determinism, in which technology is assumed to have innate properties. A technological determinist approach might assume that adopting a particular tool will deliver inherent benefits. Alternatively, conceiving technology as socially shaped leads to thinking more deeply about the complexities and range of factors that influence how technology works (or not). When designing with technology, teachers need to consider, not only the tools and their possible affordances (see Table 10.1), but also the particular context.

Whilst the view that pedagogy should always lead technology in learning design is dominant, several studies have challenged this. They argue that teachers need knowledge of both the technological tool and its potential use in learning contexts (Bennett 2012; Vogel 2010). Thus an effective way to start designing using technology is to gain, through experimentation, familiarity with a tool and how it can be used. Another effective approach is to experience being taught using the technology through participating in courses which use a high component of technology enhanced learning features.

There are several prominent theoretical frameworks to support teachers in learning design for learning which are worthy of further explanation – for example, Salmon's five-stage framework (2003) and Laurillard's Conversational Framework

---

Box 10.2 Case study: flipped classroom

Flipping the classroom involves using time outside the classroom for individual activities associated with reading and assimilating new knowledge. This provides more time in class for engagement with other students and with the teacher. Thus traditional homework activities, where students apply knowledge, may be carried out *in* the classroom, whereas taking in information occurs *outside* the class.

This approach requires students to be self-disciplined and to apply themselves to the tasks set for out-of-classroom time. This in itself is an important independent learning skill. In addition, Strayer (2012) found that students exposed to the flipped classroom approach had a deeper approach to their learning and were more willing to participate in class and to explain topics to others. Strayer (2012) also found that students developed a deeper understanding of their own learning process.

Technologies

Screencasting software (e.g. Jing, Camtasia) can be created by turning a lecture into a video format which can then be uploaded to the VLE.
or
VLE can be used to provide notes in wordprocessed format that students can read.
or
Online books or online journals can be linked to within the VLE.

Barriers

Strayer (2012) found that the adoption of an inverted or flipped approach was not straightforward. Whereas students taught in the traditional format valued its familiarity and pattern, those who experienced the new approach found it unsettling. Students in the flipped classroom perceived face-to-face time as lacking direction compared to the traditional classroom, which was seen as more stable and predictable. In addition, the flipped classroom requires students to be self-disciplined and to make time for out-of-class activities.

(2002). However, in this chapter we adopt a more practical perspective and present some examples of technology-enhanced learning drawn from our professional practice. The examples are not provided as a blueprint for success or a guide to 'good practice', but to stimulate thinking about how technology might be used to promote students' learning.

Box 10.3 Case study: contributing student model

Collis and Moonen (2006), drawing on other models of active, authentic and meaningful learning, articulate a *contributing student model* – a pedagogical approach that makes use of some of the affordances of technology to provide a place where student-created artifacts can be collected and shared.

Suitable artefacts include:

- identifying resources and posting these;
- working together on the design of an artifact such as a web site or poster or podcast;
- developing a piece of course material;
- reviewing a book;
- commenting on a set text;
- creating a shared course glossary;
- drawing on wider experiences related to the course content.

Technologies

Document sharing facilities such as those provided by DropBox or Google Docs could be used during the production of the resource. The choice of tool for drawing together contributions is complex. Blogs, wikis and discussion boards all have some similar affordances, being asynchronous tools which allow students to work at a time that suits them and can support group work.

In selecting one tool over another the teacher will need to evaluate the tools available and how they are supported within their institution. For instance, the VLE may have a very cumbersome discussion board but a blog tool which is easier to navigate; students might already be familiar with using one tool and this would make its uptake more straightforward.

Barriers

This approach needs to be adapted to student needs and the tools they are familiar with. Students need to be adequately prepared for this approach with clear and achievable guidance on what is to be contributed.

If group work is used, it can be challenging to ensure that everyone contributes. However, technologies such as a wiki page, which store the history of the page's development, may motivate participation.

Box 10.4 Case study: supporting learners through email

Email can foster learner motivation, promote dialogue and underpin effective support. The high level of immediacy of email (Wheeler 2007) – although it affords quick responses which can be motivating for students (Smyth et al. 2012) – requires careful management by tutors. This case study illustrates how email can be used, outlining its benefits to students and some considerations for tutors who use email with students. The case study focuses on adults studying part time; however, its themes are also pertinent for full-time students.

It is sometimes difficult to know when a student is struggling and, perhaps, becoming disengaged from a course. Course teams may therefore monitor email and telephone communications throughout the academic year. This process requires:

- an email folder for each student in which every exchange is stored;
- a telephone log recording the date and a brief summary of any conversation.

During a review the course team noticed that a particular student had no email or phone contact during the last month. In the student's email folder, the last communication indicated they were moving house but were keen to maintain their studies. This enabled tutors to contact the student to enquire about their studies and the house move. Such personal communication was only possible because of the saved emails, with the learner quickly re-engaging with the course. These methods of monitoring are more important with large group sizes, where it is harder for tutors to know learners individually.

Email can motivate learners if used effectively. However, care must be taken to ensure the intended message is correctly conveyed. Zimmer and Alexander's (1996) 'netiquette' is pertinent here, relating to the attributes needed to conduct effective and socially acceptable online communication. It is difficult to express, and therefore interpret, emotions in text-based media and comments intended to be humorous can appear sarcastic or insulting. Correct punctuation, such as appropriate exclamation marks, can help students' understanding, as can 'emoticons' – graphic icons intended to convey particular feelings. Messages, if carefully considered and written, can facilitate the development of interpersonal relationships between tutors and learners and offer space where care, empathy and learning can mutually coexist (Doherty and Mayer 2003). Furthermore, as students and tutors can take time over composing messages, they are usually better informed and more clearly expressed than face-to-face discussions.

For tutors making substantial use of email, time management becomes important and different work patterns need to be developed. Responding to each message when it arrives can have an adverse effect on tutor efficiency and they may also experience pressure from learners for quick responses and more individual attention (MacDonald and McAteer 2003). It is sensible to use filters and rule features to direct incoming messages into particular folders, setting time aside to deal with each.

Box 10.5 Case study: social networking

The context for this case study is a module where social networking was used as the primary platform for delivery and assessment. It was delivered to a group of mature students studying on a part-time, blended learning, two-year MSc in Multimedia and e-learning at a UK university. The module was delivered over 12 weeks, with face-to-face day schools at the beginning and the halfway point. Strategies adopted might therefore transfer well to similar, mature age cohorts following blended learning courses, but are also applicable as adjuncts to more traditional face-to-face delivery and for all types and level of learner where technology is not a barrier. The platform was a private one. It was selected in response to the difficulties educators typically experience in engaging learners in lively and productive communities of practice within traditional VLEs. Alternative solutions that use advertisement-rich, global sites like FaceBook compel learners to enter an environment in which not all feel happy or safe or in which some who feel confident may leave themselves exposed to censure through unguarded exchanges. Learners who were either nervous or too blasé were therefore able develop strategies for managing their online identity in a safe environment.

The site was created within Yammer©, a Microsoft product allowing users to 'collaborate securely across departments, geographies, content and business applications' (Yammer 2013). On signing up for an account using an institutional email, individuals are automatically added to that institution's private network. Discrete 'external' networks can then be created. An external network of this kind, with its social affordances within a separate, private group, can support individual cohorts of students without the 'noise' associated with more public platforms. The main affordances of the site included facilities to share updates, attach documents and images, link to websites, embed video, reply to or 'like' posts, create a poll or an event, tag posts with key words, collaboratively edit webpages and collaboratively annotate documents. These affordances provided an engaging, student-centred, fast-paced and fluid set of interactions. The key drawbacks perceived by students lay in the anxiety that some felt about not being able to keep track of everything that was happening. However, this aspect was also reported as underpinning the flexible, democratic, fun, stimulating and supportive nature of the experience.

The potential of digital tools for social, moral and personal harm

As we have argued in this chapter, technology has the potential to motivate learners, to make learning more interactive, to make the classroom more flexible and the learning more personal. For these reasons, it can be seen as an essential resource at any level of the education system. However it can also provide access to content of a more insidious nature. Concerns relating to online safety have, in some circumstances, instigated moral panic and associated attempts to control and limit the uses of digital communication by young people. An awareness of the issues surrounding online safety is important for teachers and this section provides an overview of potential types of dangerous and inappropriate use of digital tools and suggests how lecturers might develop a considered response to these challenges.

Burton (2013) suggests that such content can be classified into four areas:

1   inappropriate content and/or behaviour;
2   cyberbullying;
3   mutual online sexual activity;
4   stranger activity.

Inappropriate content or behaviours refers to the variety of morally, culturally or legally inappropriate content available online, such as pornography, hate sites, or pro-suicide sites. Cyber-bullying involves youth-to-youth harassment via text message, email or messaging services, and is a phenomenon that has entered the lexicon since the early 2000s. It is thought that between 17 and 21 per cent of 14–16-year-olds have suffered incidents of cyber-bullying, and for around one in ten (in the same age group) the bullying is persistent (Cross et al. 2009). Mutual online sexual activity primarily involves 'sexting', or sending sexual content via technology. Stranger activity, or grooming, is by far the least common of the four dangers but represents the most serious threat to young and vulnerable people. The potential for grooming activities is significant: US research reveals that over a quarter of youngsters admit to sending personal information to unknown people online, and that one in twenty children admit to talking about sex with unknown people online (Wolak et al. 2010).

Educators have a duty of care towards young people, vulnerable people and children, yet the area of e-safety or online safeguarding is still considered by many to fall within the domain of technical staff (Becta 2006). However, in a government-funded report (DCSF 2008), Tanya Byron recommends that e-safety education and digital literacy development should continue throughout life, that parents should be supported in understanding the issues and risks associated with young people's use of digital technologies and that educational establishments have policies and procedures on e-safety.

For the practitioner, e-safety translates into a number of responsibilities and challenges. The main responsibility is to be aware of the possible dangers and to promote safe use with learners. Familiarity with the four categories outlined above, and appreciating which learners are likely to be more susceptible to such threats, will enable educators to use technology to help ensure that it has a positive outcome.

Conclusion

This chapter has provided an overview of key technologies and theories in relation to using technology within teaching and learning wholly online, in blended learning and in classroom based teaching practices. It has provided practical guidance on how these tools might be effectively used to support learning and teaching practices.

The main argument in the chapter is that there are many reported benefits from using technology within teaching. To access these, teachers need to approach practice with a critical yet interested disposition, open to the benefits that might accrue and willing to explore and experiment. Of course, danger and risk are associated with adopting new pedagogical practices, yet if we are committed to preparing students for living and working in a technology-rich environment, we must ensure that our practices develop this understanding. The report of the Further Education Learning Technology Action Group (FELTAG 2014) underlined that the LLS may well have a digital future, highlighting the need to fully exploit the potential of learning technologies and recommending that all publically funded programmes should have a 10 per cent wholly online component by 2015–16, with incentives for this to reach 50 per cent by 2017–18. These recommendations received both a welcome and strong encouragement from BIS (2014)

11

Assessment

*Ros Ollin, Ron Thompson and
Jonathan Tummons*

In this chapter

- The nature and purpose of assessment
- Assessment tasks
- Planning and designing assessment
- Summative, formative and ipsative assessment
- Providing feedback
- Norm-referenced and criterion-referenced assessment
- Validity and reliability
- Example: a test on food hygiene
- Recognizing and accrediting prior learning
- Moderation and standardization
- Double marking

The nature and purpose of assessment

Assessment often appears so embedded in our experience of education that we hardly question its role. However, the importance of assessment lies beyond recognizing the attainments of learners. Interpretations of assessment – what it is, how it is done and what it means – are bound up in broader assumptions about learning and teaching that may have profound individual, institutional and social consequences. Underlying the diversity of assessment processes is a variety of functions, both educational and social, including the following.

Supporting and accrediting student progress and achievement

This is the most obvious reason for assessment, and often the only one made explicit. We may wish to know whether learning outcomes have been achieved, or if the student is of the standard required for a certain grade. Sometimes, it is important to know how a student has performed in relation to their peers. Questions of this type are best answered at or near the end of a course, and require what is known as *summative* assessment. Alternatively, determining a student's development needs during a course or giving feedback designed to help students learn requires *formative* assessment. Unlike summative assessment, which would almost always be carried out formally using examinations or coursework, formative assessments can be informal as well as formal, and may be undertaken during learning sessions.

Evaluation of the teacher or institution

Assessment may be used to provide information about a course, a teacher or the institution for the purpose of evaluation. The teacher may ask whether the learning objectives are appropriate – are they too easy or too difficult? Are the teaching methods effective? Such questions could aid reflection, or possibly inform the *appraisal* of the teacher by the institution. Assessment may also provide information relating to the *accountability* of the institution to outside organizations (such as funding or inspection bodies – see Chapter 18). Is the curriculum suitable? Is the institution providing value for money?

Motivating students

Assessment, particularly in the form of external examinations, provides motivation and assists in setting goals. Formal assessment within a curriculum area signals to students that it is taken seriously by teachers and awarding bodies. The 'strategic learners' described in Chapter 7 may be reluctant to embrace a particular topic or skill unless they see that it will impact on their success.

Social regulation

Assessment plays a subtle and complex role in the social structure of the UK, regulating entry to occupations or levels of education through specific entry requirements. The frequent press debates concerning academic standards attest to widespread interest in the social implications of assessment. Success in public examinations is closely linked with social advantage and disadvantage. Although there are reasons for this not connected with the ways in which learning is assessed, it is at the point of assessment that such inequalities become visible.

Assessment tasks

There are numerous types of assessment task in use, for example:

- written tests of various forms, including essay questions, multiple choice tests and short answer tests;
- practical assessments and simulations;
- project work;
- oral assessment;
- observation of natural performance;
- evidence-based or 'portfolio' assessment;
- online and computer-based assessment.

Box 11.1 Examples of selection-type questions

Multiple choice:

In a 3-pin electric plug, the *earth* wire is coloured:	stem
(a) Brown	distractor
(b) Blue	distractor
(c) Green and yellow	key (correct answer)
(d) Red and black	distractor

Alternative choice:

If litmus paper turns from red to blue in a solution, the solution is
(a)   acid
(b)   alkaline

A variation of multiple choice using combinations of statements:
Which of the following statements is true?
(I)   A force is required to change the position of a particle
(II)   A force is required to change the speed of a particle
(III) A force is required to change the direction of motion of a particle

(a)   Statement (II) only   (b) Statements (I) and (II) only
(c)   Statements (I) and (III) only   (d) Statements (II) and (III) only.

These may be used for summative, or may contribute to formative, assessment. Whatever task is used, assessment involves taking a *sample of learner behaviour* and making *inferences about their learning* from this. The degree of trust that can be placed on assessment outcomes will depend on a number of factors relating to the sampling process and the interpretation of the resulting behaviour. This should be kept in mind when examining the features of each form of assessment.

Most of the examples above are *supply-type* assessments; that is, they ask the student to provide some form of response to a stimulus. Both the stimulus (for example a question, an assignment brief or a mathematical problem) and the response (for example, an essay, a calculation or a diagram) may be written or oral. However, *selection-type* assessments are often used and have the great advantage of being straightforward to mark. In a selection-type question, the candidate must select an answer from a number of alternatives. For example, in a *multiple choice* question it is usual to offer four possible answers, of which only one is correct. Box 11.1 gives some examples of selection-type questions.

Planning and designing assessment

The assessment process may be thought of as having the stages illustrated in Figure 11.1: planning for assessment; collecting the evidence; making judgements; giving feedback; and recording achievement. Each of these stages is important, and a range of

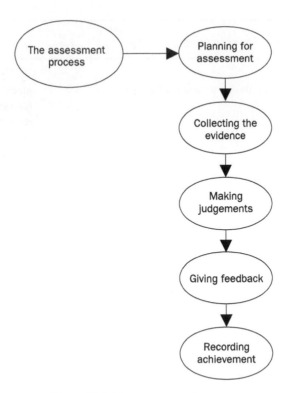

Figure 11.1 The assessment process

knowledge and skills is required to implement them effectively. The planning stage is particularly important, and includes making decisions or assumptions about what constitutes achievement and planning an *assessment strategy* to measure this. The detailed design of assessment tasks can then be undertaken, including the preparation of marking schemes or other specifications for applying the assessment criteria to the selected tasks.

A teacher's degree of control in planning assessment will depend on the nature of the courses they teach. For external awards, such as GCSE, many of the decisions will be made at national level. On the other hand, teachers involved in courses tailor-made to suit local needs are likely to have much more responsibility for design.

Assessment planning must integrate with the curriculum philosophy and design. The assessment strategy chosen must be consistent with the course aims, and with the model of achievement being used: for example, in a vocational course practical and interpersonal skills may be of higher importance than theoretical knowledge; it would therefore be inconsistent to design assessments which ignored these, or gave them an insufficient weighting. It follows that assessment, and curriculum design more generally, depends crucially on value judgements: 'What we choose to assess and how shows quite starkly what we value . . . effective assessment depends upon having a view of what it is that we are trying to do in a programme and hence of what we ought to assess' (Knight 1995: 13).

Once we have decided on what constitutes achievement it is essential to ensure that it can be measured, selecting methods of assessment which can give information on student achievement. We must not emphasize certain attributes simply because they are more straightforward to assess than other, more important, areas of learning. In other words, the assessment strategy must 'make what is important measurable, rather than . . . making what is measurable important' (SEC 1985: para. 2). It is often argued that the assessment strategy should allow candidates to show what they know and can do: in other words, it should allow for differentiation so that all can succeed at an appropriate level.

Examples of models of achievement and associated assessment strategies will now be considered.

Example 1: GCSE English

GCSE English is based on the National Curriculum for schools in England and Wales, and with other GCSE subjects must meet subject criteria specified by Ofqual. Four areas of achievement are recognized, for which Ofqual provide assessment objectives with prescribed weightings: Speaking and Listening (20 per cent), Study of Spoken Language (10 per cent), Studying Written Language (35 per cent), and Writing (35 per cent) (Ofqual 2011: 6–7). Although aspects of this model of achievement may seem obvious, it is interesting to note the value judgement implied by the inclusion of Speaking and Listening. Some earlier qualifications in English (such as GCE 'O' level) were essentially academic tests, based entirely on written examinations. The inclusion of Speaking and Listening as an attainment target gives a clear message that these skills *are* valued. At the same time, the subject criteria illustrate the shifts in the nature of learning and assessment as the political climate changes; earlier versions of the GCSE subject criteria had three areas of achievement: Speaking and Listening, Reading and Writing. The movement to the *study of* spoken and written language reflects an increasing emphasis, associated with the policies of the Coalition Government, on a return to traditional academic models.

Once an area such as Speaking and Listening is included in a model of achievement, there has to be a way of assessing it. Thus, the assessment strategy devised for GCSE English must correspond to the areas of achievement just identified. This moves us away from sole reliance on written work, and suggests that some form of continuous assessment or 'coursework' should be an element of assessment – although again, the balance between coursework and terminal examination, as well as the degree of teacher control over the assessment of coursework, has been contentious. In particular, Speaking and Listening can most effectively be assessed through coursework. Detailed decisions on the weighting of these elements and the nature of the assessment tasks are then made in relation to the assessment objectives of the course. In the current subject criteria for English Language, 40 per cent of the marks are for external assessment, with the remaining 60 per cent for coursework, or 'controlled assessment' as it is now referred to.

Example 2: Assessment of NVQs

NVQs are competence based awards introduced in 1994 as a system for accrediting workplace skills and identifying where a person's work-related skills and knowledge need updating (Ollin and Tucker 2012). In 2010, NVQs were brought within the QCF, a government framework for regulating vocational qualifications in England, Wales and Northern Ireland. Within this framework, vocational qualifications have acquired new titles (Awards, Certificates and Diplomas) and have arguably become more knowledge based (Ofqual 2012a); however, the original NVQ model of achievement retains interest for any discussion of assessment. This model was based on a *functional analysis* of a given occupational area, related to National Occupational Standards. Different levels of achievement were identified, corresponding to different levels of complexity in the job role: NVQ level 1, level 2, etc. For a given occupation at a given level, the ability to do the job was specified in terms of *elements of competence* and these elements were supplemented by criteria for success (*performance criteria*) and a *range* of situations in which successful performance must be demonstrated. As in the previous example, having defined achievement, it was necessary to think about how this achievement could be measured. Controversially, the major source of evidence of achievement for NVQs was taken to be actual job-related performance, so an assessor would observe candidates performing their job role. However, the requirement for a range of situations could require additional *supplementary* evidence to be used, for example oral questioning or even written tests. This also allowed *underpinning knowledge* to be assessed where appropriate. Figure 11.2 illustrates this 'classical' NVQ assessment strategy.

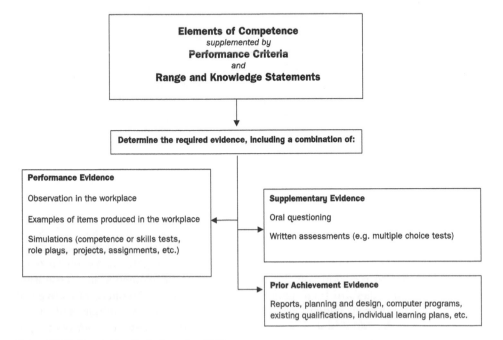

Figure 11.2 Assessment strategy for NVQs

For any type of assessment, once the broad assessment strategy is decided, detailed planning and design of assessment tasks can take place. For many teachers working on externally assessed courses, mock examinations and formative assessments provide an opportunity to be involved in planning and design even though the external assessment is determined by others. Box 11.2 gives an overview of guidelines for the design of written assessment tasks; similar considerations can be applied to other forms of assessment.

Box 11.2 Design of written assessment tasks: some guidelines

A Specifying the task

The following questions should be asked:

- What learning is being tested? It is usually better to test a small number of objectives, one or two at a time, unless there is a specific reason for assessing a larger number of objectives.
- What *types* of objective are involved in terms of Bloom's Taxonomy? Questions will vary according to the level and type of learning involved. Often, the wording of the objective will suggest the required question (State . . ., Explain . . .).
- Does the question have an answer? A mathematical problem may have no solution; an ambiguous question may have several alternatives. A badly written question may have an (unintended) one-word answer ('yes').
- Have you given all necessary information? Unless there is a data sheet, you may need to give formulae, values of constants, etc.
- Is the language appropriate? The reading level of the question should be checked, and stereotypical images avoided.
- Is the time allocation reasonable? If graphs have to be drawn or essays written, you need to check that you have allowed enough time.

B Designing a marking scheme

- Make sure you supply a detailed worked answer, including acceptable alternative answers.
- Allocate marks in detail, trying for decisions like 'one mark or none', rather than 'how many marks out of five'.
- Ensure that the marks reflect the nature of the objective. Pure recall would normally deserve fewer marks than understanding.
- Check that similar tasks in the same or other questions are given similar marks.
- Consider whether to award marks for presentation. If you decide to do this, make it clear in the assessment task.
- Consider how to award marks to time-consuming but straightforward tasks such as graph plotting or drawing diagrams.

Summative, formative and ipsative assessment

Three distinct types of assessment can be identified according to the stage at which they occur and the purposes for which they are used. These types – summative, formative and ipsative – are not necessarily discrete: there is often an overlap or blurring of distinctions. Nonetheless, the typology provides a framework for analysing assessment processes.

Summative assessment

Summative assessment is used to determine whether students have acquired the skills, knowledge, behaviour or understanding that the course of study provides. It gives an overall picture of performance within a complete unit of learning. Summative assessment is always a formal process, and is normally carried out at or near the end of a course or module.

Summative assessment normally leads to the award of qualifications: grades, diplomas and certificates. For some students, a qualification will lead to changes in employment. For others, it may be needed for educational progression. Employers rely on qualifications and records of achievement to ascertain the skills and abilities of their employees. Summative assessment can therefore be described as *high stakes* assessment (Knight and Yorke 2003). However, summative assessment can also be formative. Particularly in a modular curriculum, summative assessment can provide 'feed forward' in anticipation of the next summative assessment to be attempted.

Formative assessment

Formative assessment is assessment for learning – it takes place during a course or programme of study, as an integral part of learning. Formative feedback (also known as 'feed forward'), contributes to the learning process by providing guidance to students on how to bridge the gap between current performance and desired achievement.

Any assessment activity has the potential to be formative. The kinds of activities that might be employed are similarly varied: case studies, quizzes, presentations, multiple choice tests, practical tasks and simulations. Students may be involved in their own assessment: for example, a short answer written test may be followed by peer marking and feedback. Formative assessment activities may also be a spontaneous, small scale or even unconscious part of the teacher's repertoire: for example, asking oral questions or observing student posture and body language to gauge understanding and motivation. From this perspective, it is clear that many learning and teaching strategies have an aspect of formative assessment. It is the systematic employment of these activities within a classroom or workshop that provides the key characteristics of formative assessment:

- assessing learning with the intention of making future learning more effective;
- providing information to teachers on how students are progressing;

- providing feedback to students concerning their progress;
- diagnosing students' needs or barriers to learning.

Formative assessment is sometimes confused with continuous assessment and these terms need to be distinguished. In its correct sense, continuous assessment is a form of summative assessment that accrues over time: for example, through the gradual completion of a portfolio. Formative assessment may well take place throughout a programme of study, but it is not continuous assessment.

Ipsative assessment

This is a process in which students' own starting points are identified and targets set against which future progress can be assessed. The student can then reflect on their learning goals independently. The ipsative assessment process will often be formally recorded, generally on paper, although web-based e-portfolios are widespread (see Chapter 10). Learners' goals may be stated or negotiated within a learning contract, and progress and achievement recorded by means of learning logs or similar. Where ipsative assessment is a formal part of a course, learners will often be supported – or constrained – by writing frames or other 'scaffolding' such as checklists and self-assessment pro formas.

The use of ipsative assessment is now strongly embedded, with the increasing penetration of discourses concerning 'key skills', 'learning how to learn' and the 'self-regulated learner'. Records of achievement and individual learning plans (ILP) are commonplace, while in HE personal development plans (PDP) are widely used. These documents are updated by the student throughout a course and may be a part of formal course assessment; students are encouraged to use them as a means of directing their learning.

Providing feedback

Providing feedback to students is a crucial part of formative assessment. Unlike summative assessment, which relates to assessment *of* learning, feedback relates to 'assessment *for* learning', assessment which helps the learning process (Black and Wiliam 1998; Torrance and Pryor 1998). The skills of giving and receiving clear, constructive, developmental feedback are integral to good teaching.

Feedback should motivate the learner and help to develop the ability to self-assess in the future – in other words, it teaches the learner what should be considered important and how improvement can be measured. This conception of feedback is associated with the notion of *self-regulated learning*, defined by Pintrich and Zusho (2002: 64) as 'an active constructive process whereby learners set goals for their learning and monitor, regulate and control their cognition, motivation and behaviour, guided and constrained by their goals and the contextual features of the environment'. In this definition, the reference to contextual features recognizes that self-regulated learning may operate within an environment where specific goals, such as the completion of assignments, are determined by teachers or external agencies; nevertheless, self-regulated learners will not be passive recipients of assessment tasks but will reinterpret them in the light of their goals.

In an influential paper, Sadler (1989) gives three conditions which must be fulfilled if students are to benefit from feedback on assessment. First, they need to understand what constitutes good performance in the task, so assessment criteria must have been clearly explained beforehand and revisited in the feedback. Second, the feedback must help the student to understand how their current performance compares with good performance; and finally, the feedback must help the student understand how to close the gap between current and good performance. According to Sadler (1989: 119), this implies that students need to acquire some of the same evaluative skills as their teacher, thus emphasizing the importance of developing self-assessment skills as an integral part of learning.

Black and Wiliam (1998) draw on Sadler's work in developing their analysis of research and practice in formative assessment, making three fundamental arguments:

- Improving formative assessment can improve learning.
- There is room for improvement in formative assessment.
- There is research evidence on *how* to improve formative assessment.

These arguments were supported by a review of research; furthermore, many of the studies cited 'show that improved formative assessment helps the (so-called) low attainers more than the rest, and so reduces the spread of attainment while also raising it overall' (Black and Wiliam 1998: 3). Although some have questioned the soundness of the evidence base (for example, Bennett 2011), and the specific terminology 'assessment for learning' has been appropriated as a 'brand name' to legitimate a diverse range of assessment approaches (Black 2006, cited in McDowell et al. 2011), the idea of formative assessment as an integral part of teaching and learning has become something of an orthodoxy. A widely used definition of assessment for learning is that of the Assessment Reform Group (ARG): 'Assessment for Learning is the process of seeking and interpreting evidence for use by learners and their teachers to decide where the learners are in their learning, where they need to go and how best to get there' (ARG 2002: 2–3). Following from this definition, assessment for learning should:

- be part of effective planning of teaching and learning;
- focus on how students learn;
- be recognized as central to classroom practice;
- be regarded as a key professional skill for teachers;
- be sensitive and constructive because any assessment has an emotional impact;
- take account of the importance of learner motivation;
- promote commitment to learning goals and a shared understanding of the criteria by which they are assessed;
- provide learners with constructive guidance about how to improve;

- develop learners' capacity for self-assessment so they can become reflective and self-managing;

- recognize the full range of achievements for all learners. (adapted from ARG 2002: 2–3)

Weeden et al. (2000) report on research into students' experiences and expectations of feedback, involving 200 learners aged between 8 and 19 years. As might be expected, older students had experienced a wide range of types of feedback. Students of all ages felt that positive comments boosted their confidence and reported using feedback to improve their performance. However, although simple comments, ticks, smiley faces and evaluations such as 'good work' were welcomed as signifying approval, they did not help students to 'bridge the gap' between present performance and future goals. Teachers and students preferred prompt oral feedback and discussion and felt this improved performance.

Constructive criticism was found to be useful when it helped students understand what the task required and engaged them in thinking about their current performance and how to improve. Conversely, critical comments that damaged self-esteem were unhelpful and demotivating. It is interesting to note that *criticism of effort* was found to be demoralizing and tended to be ignored or treated with hostility, especially if the student's perception of the effort made was at variance with the teacher's. Older students expressed concerns that teachers' comments were sometimes inaccurate or unfair. 'The comment says – Not thinking about it enough – But I did!'

Black et al. (2003: 43) discuss research on comment-only marking. This research showed that, of three feedback schemes – marks only, comments only, and a combination of marks and comments – the *most* effective feedback was comment only. This may be due to a number of factors, but students presented with both marks and comments tend to focus on the mark at the expense of the more detailed comments. However, the evidence on comment-only marking is not conclusive (see Smith and Gorard 2005; Swaffield 2011).

Research into how adult learners respond to feedback (Young 2000) supports many of the findings discussed above, particularly the need for positive feedback. Young relates attitudes to feedback to self-esteem, noting that for students with lower self-esteem feedback was taken personally and could damage confidence. She argues that, in order to 'customize' feedback to the needs of learners, it is essential to ascertain what their needs are in terms of the type of feedback that will be most helpful at a particular stage in the course, and that these needs will relate to their self-esteem as learners.

Feedback should be given as soon as possible after the assessment, and give a clear indication of the standard achieved. It should also be precise and detailed, giving specific examples and guidance on how to improve. Highlighting good aspects of the student's work as well as detailing what can be improved will help them to understand explicitly what is required. Black and Wiliam (1998: 6) recommend that 'Feedback . . . should be about the particular qualities of [the learner's] work, with advice on what he or she can do to improve, and should avoid comparisons with other [learners]'. As with good teaching, feedback needs to be customized to the individual learner's personality and preferred way of learning and be expressed so that the student understands and accepts points made.

Nicol and Macfarlane-Dick (2006: 207) identify seven principles of good practice in feedback, based on their effectiveness in strengthening students' capacity to self-regulate their performance. These principles are:

1   Clarify what good performance is (goals, criteria, expected standards)

2   Facilitate the development of self-assessment (reflection) in learning

3   Provide high-quality information to students about their learning

4   Encourage teacher and peer dialogue around learning

5   Encourage positive motivational beliefs and self-esteem

6   Provide opportunities to close the gap between current and desired performance

7   Provide information to teachers that can be used to help shape their teaching.

Giving oral feedback to a student may benefit from additional strategies. These include giving the student first say, so they can demonstrate their own appraisal of their performance; giving praise before criticism in a 'sandwich' approach which ends on a positive note; and focusing on just two or three key areas so the student is not overwhelmed with information. The student also needs to be given time to think and respond – oral feedback should be a dialogue. The teacher needs to listen to how feedback is received and allow the student to ask questions and express their view.

Norm-referenced and criterion-referenced assessment

How do we know whether someone has 'done well' in an assessment? It might appear that this question has a simple answer: I've done well in my test if I obtained a high mark, or if I've demonstrated that I have achieved certain learning outcomes, or I have performed a practical operation (such as changing a wheel) successfully. However, a score of 80 per cent in a test could be the lowest. Is this a good performance? In order to think clearly about such matters the concepts of norm- and criterion-referencing are helpful.

A *norm-referenced* assessment is one which contains no absolute criterion of competence; it is intended to rank students rather than to measure their achievement against a fixed scale. The test may tell us that student A lies in the top 15 per cent of the students assessed, but not whether that student has reached any definite level of attainment. Indeed, the level of attainment of the top 15 per cent (or of any other group) could vary from occasion to occasion. Obviously, the test must be a fair one, taken from the syllabus as taught and containing questions at an appropriate level. But there is no need for the entire syllabus to be covered in the test, or for the test to have the same degree of difficulty every year.

A *criterion-referenced* assessment is one which measures the achievement of a student against specific criteria of competence. In this type of test, the standing of a student in relation to their peers is irrelevant. What matters is that they meet the prescribed criteria for award of a pass or an individual grade. A criterion-referenced test looks for mastery of skills, rather than superiority over one's peers. An example of this type of assessment is the practical driving test.

These two methods are often described as if they were mutually exclusive; however, it is easy to see that they can never be wholly separated. For example, a norm-referenced test will always test *something*, at a level determined by some criteria, so that a high or low ranking will always be meaningful in terms of absolute attainment. Furthermore, if the test population remains approximately the same from year to year, a certain ranking will always correspond to very similar levels of competence. Although traditional exams such as GCE A Level are often described as being norm referenced, the examining bodies go to great lengths to establish assessment objectives and criteria to ensure that a particular grade one year implies a similar level of performance as the same grade another year. At the other extreme, a criterion-referenced test needs to have realistic criteria which are within the grasp of at least some of the target population, so that the distribution of levels of competence within the population and the length of training required will help to determine criteria. We should therefore think of the *emphasis* of a test as being to one extreme or the other, rather than thinking in terms of absolutes.

Closely related to the idea of criterion-referenced tests is that of assessment based on *competence*. In this approach, a particular occupation is analysed in order to say what makes a competent practitioner at various levels. Such an analysis results in 'elements of competence' which can form the basis for units of study and ultimately of assessment, which is typically carried out in the workplace and based on the candidate's performance in job-related activities (Ollin and Tucker 2012). In order to achieve a competence-based award, a candidate must reach a satisfactory standard in all elements of competence associated with the award. In the UK the competence based approach has been particularly associated with NVQs.

Validity and reliability

An assessment is effectively a measuring instrument, and to give useful information it must be both *valid* and *reliable*. Validity is about *getting the right assessment* – that is, matching assessment tasks and judgements to what has been learned. Reliability is about *getting the assessment right*, in terms of ensuring a consistent approach to the assessment tasks and the process of making judgements and giving feedback.

Validity

A valid assessment covers the course content and is appropriate to the subject or vocational area. An assessment may be invalid if, for example, there is an inconsistency between the importance of a topic and its weighting in the assessment; there are problems which are too easy or too difficult; the questions are not relevant to the assessment objectives; range statements are inappropriate; and so on. Formative assessment involving syllabus content not yet covered would also be invalid.

Clearly, a test must be reliable if it is to be valid, but a reliable test is not *necessarily* valid – think of a set of scales which consistently indicates a weight which is two kilograms out. The aim, of course, is to provide assessments which are both reliable and valid, and a number of possibilities exist to achieve this. For example, we might use commercially available tests, which are thoroughly trialled and often come with statistical measures of their reliability and validity. However, many teachers are required to design their own assessments (and this would obviously be the case for formative assessments such as homework or class tests), and need to be aware of certain elementary steps which must be taken to achieve a reliable and valid test. For example, how can teachers check the validity of a test once it has been constructed or build in validity to a test as they write it?

Some general conditions will always be necessary if assessment is to be valid. These are *sufficiency* – the assessment tasks generate enough evidence to demonstrate that the learning objectives have been achieved; *currency* – the candidate's present level of attainment is being assessed; and *authenticity* – the performance being assessed is the candidate's own. In addition, various approaches to checking validity are used. They involve asking the following:

- Does the test accurately predict future performance in the subject (*predictive validity*)?
- Does the test provide a similar picture to other, independent measures of performance carried out at the same time, for example success at work (*concurrent validity*)?
- Does the test cover the objectives of teaching in proportion to the importance allocated to them (*content validity*)?
- Does the test capture the essence of what it is trying to assess (*construct validity*)? For example, do personality tests or learning style inventories measure something identifiable as 'personality' or 'learning style' respectively?

All four of these approaches could be useful in checking validity retrospectively. However, only content and (in a more limited way) construct validity is of much help in test design. As a simple initial test, *face* validity may be helpful before going any further – does the assessment *look* valid, or does it have some obviously invalid features?

Table of specifications

This is an aid to test design which attempts to increase content validity by making explicit the objectives to be tested and the weighting to be attached to them. These decisions are presented in a two-way table with *content* on one axis and *process* on the other. Here 'process' refers to the type of objective involved (for example, recall of knowledge, comprehension, application, etc.) and is usually related to levels in Bloom's Taxonomy.

Example: a test on food hygiene

Suppose a teacher wishes to assess a unit on food hygiene, with the following broad headings:

1 Food safety hazards

2 Food handling

3 Principles of safe food storage

4 Premises, equipment and cleaning

Inspection of the learning objectives would reveal how they relate to Bloom's Taxonomy. In this example, there would probably be categories such as recall of knowledge, comprehension and application. The teacher must decide what *weightings*, as a percentage of the total test mark, to give to each topic and to each type of objective. In general, the weightings would reflect the importance of each topic and the nature of the objectives.

To see how this would work, suppose that the test is to be marked out of 100, and that 20 per cent of the teaching time, and therefore 20 marks, is allocated to food safety hazards. Suppose that inspection of the learning objectives for this topic indicates that just over one-third of the objectives ask for recall, the remainder being equally divided between comprehension and application. The teacher might choose to allocate marks as eight for recall, six for comprehension and six for application. The same idea would then be applied to the other topic areas.

An example of a completed table of specifications is shown in Table 11.1. This would provide a statement of intent, which would help in designing the test. For example, the table shows that 16 per cent of the marks should be for recall of knowledge of premises, equipment and cleaning, and the test items and marking scheme should reflect this.

Validity can also be achieved by a number of further strategies (Tummons 2011), for example: wording, explaining or defining the assessment tasks correctly, to prevent students performing activities that do not match the course objectives; setting assessments that include all relevant areas of the course and taking care not to include something that was not part of the course; and finding ways to ensure authentic assessment.

Reliability

In a system where assessment takes place on a national basis across hundreds of sites employing thousands of tutors, the need to prevent local or personal factors affecting assessment practice is self-evident. Reliability relates to consistency in a

Table 11.1 Table of specifications for a unit on food hygiene

	Recall	Comprehension	Application	Total
Food safety hazards	8	6	6	20
Food handling	12	9	9	30
Principles of safe food storage	4	3	3	10
Premises, equipment and cleaning	16	12	12	40
Total	40	30	30	100

number of ways: markers or examiners will agree on the mark or grade to be awarded to a given piece of work; there will be consistency between the students' work and the markers' or examiners' grades; students' grades or marks will not depend on where or when they were assessed; the language used in the assessment process is clear, unambiguous and inclusive; the environment in which the assessment is carried out will not affect the process; and students or candidates will not have been given preferential access to knowledge about the assessment. Achieving reliability depends on consistency throughout the assessment environment.

Plagiarism

As we have seen, a key aspect of valid assessment is authenticity – the work being assessed is the candidate's own. The academic offence known as plagiarism – the intentional use, without acknowledgement, of another person's work – is therefore a serious threat to validity. The problem of plagiarism is a complex one for assessors and covers a range of possible levels of academic misconduct. At one extreme, deliberate copying of another person's work, or even 'ghost writing' – which may involve downloading essays from commercial websites – are regarded as extremely serious offences by examining bodies. On the other hand, instances of apparent plagiarism often arise with no intent to deceive and result from underdeveloped academic skills. Some students, however, are tempted by the opportunities arising from the internet (and elsewhere) and seek unfair advantage. It is important to be aware of institutional policies on plagiarism, and of how to effectively utilize systems such as the plagiarism detection software known as Turnitin. This software analyses work against a database containing published material and work submitted by other students, providing an 'originality' report based on the matches that it finds with similar work. A significant level of matching may indicate (possibly accidental) plagiarism. However, there is a need to exercise judgement when interpreting the report – plagiarism may not have been committed as all sources are correctly referenced. Nevertheless, over-dependence on direct quotations from sources would normally be regarded as reducing the quality of the student's work, and feedback would need to be given in relation to this.

Recognizing and accrediting prior learning

Current policy in the LLS emphasizes the importance of recognizing what individuals have learned through previous experiences. This is reflected in teaching strategies that build on learners' existing knowledge and skills, and in formal accreditation systems which acknowledge prior learning or experience, and, as a result, provide exemption from part of a qualification. Whilst recognition of prior learning (RPA) refers broadly to a range of processes that can be used to acknowledge the learning that students have already acheived, the term 'accreditation of prior learning' (APL) is often used to describe a formal process in which course credits are awarded in recognition of previous learning. Accreditation of prior learning achievement (APLA) is used where the learner has relevant prior *certificated* learning. Accreditation of prior experiential learning (APEL) is used where the learner has relevant previous *experience* which has not been formally accredited.

Processes for APL

Balancing ease of recognition and transfer for students against maintaining standards can produce tensions within APL and the rigour of APL procedures can vary. However, certain features are expected as good practice. Challis (1993: 1) states that

> The fundamental principle underpinning APEL is that learning is worthy and capable of gaining recognition and credit, regardless of the time, place and context in which it has been achieved. It thus represents a move to accept that learning is not dependent upon any particular formal setting, and to acknowledge it as being of value in its own right.

The candidate must take responsibility for providing and organizing the evidence, although the amount of advice and support available will vary. In the case of APLA, the candidate must produce proof of formal certification and for APEL appropriate evidence of previous experience. Sometimes a claim may be based on a mixture of APLA and APEL.

Depending on the context, the claim will be assessed by an APL assessor or the course tutor. The evidence will be considered against the outcomes or criteria in specific modules or units in the qualification (although in some contexts a broader approach that the evidence generally 'fits' is possible). The APL process will be documented so that internal and external moderators are able to confirm its reliability and validity. Box 11.3 shows useful questions that APL assessors should ask when considering a claim. These conditions must be satisfied to justify the award of APL since an individual who gains exemption through APL will achieve the same award as those completing the entire course. It is important that standards are not compromised by exempting a student from certain modules.

Box 11.3 Useful questions when considering accreditation of prior learning

- Is the evidence valid? Does it match the learning outcomes of the modules the candidate wishes to gain exemption from?
- Is it reliable? Will two different tutors agree that the evidence meets module requirements?
- Is it sufficient? Is there enough evidence to cover all aspects of the modules for which exemption is claimed?
- Is it authentic? Is the evidence the property of the candidate?
- Is the evidence current? The evidence needs to be up-to-date, normally less than five years old.

(see Tummons 2011: 16–17)

Moderation and standardization

Judgements about students should depend as little as possible on who assessed the student or the particular setting in which the assessment was undertaken. However, the most reliable methods of assessment are often those with least validity and vice versa. Procedures are needed to maintain standards without compromising the validity of the assessment or its ability to engage students.

Moderation and standardization procedures are designed to increase the reliability of assessment through opening up assessors' judgements to scrutiny. Assessment of students' work or performance can be subject to kinds of bias, particularly if the assessor is inexperienced. The assessor may favour particular students, prefer a particular way of approaching a task, or misjudge the required standards. Bias can be *moderated* through comparison with other people's judgements about the same work.

Different contexts and qualifications moderate student work or performance in a variety of ways. Local and informal procedures may be sufficient, but national qualifications are usually subject to formal processes of internal and external moderation. Moderation conducted internally within an organization aims to ensure that assessors have a common understanding of course requirements; external moderation ensures that these understandings are comparable to those in other organizations. The terms used to describe these processes vary. For example, 'verification', using internal and external verifiers, is often used instead of 'moderation', especially in relation to vocational qualifications. In FE, external verifiers will be appointed by the awarding body. In contrast, universities appoint their own external examiners.

External examinations

Written examination papers for qualifications such as GCSE are sent directly to be marked by assessors appointed by the awarding body. Assessors will have been trained through marking cross-moderated samples of work and their assessments will also be subject to moderation by the awarding body.

Double marking

For internally assessed written assignments, 'double marking' is sometimes used. Each piece of work is marked twice, with the second marker often assessing 'blind' without seeing the initial assessment. Marks are then compared and adjusted if necessary following discussion between the markers. Double marking is particularly useful when a student is on the pass/fail borderline or is being considered for a high grade.

Practical work or performance

The most valid forms of vocational assessment may involve practical tasks or observing performance 'on the job'; these are likely to be the major forms of assessment in WBL. If these assessments contribute to a qualification, then they need to be moderated, even if the nature of the assessment makes it difficult, for example, when observation in the workplace is involved.

When practical work leads to a product, the items produced can be moderated in a similar way to written work. For example, in a workshop containing sections of wall built by NVQ bricklaying candidates, an internal verifier can moderate the assessor comments against each candidate's work. When observation of performance is involved, moderation may entail an internal verifier observing at the same time as an assessor and then comparing their judgements.

Moderation and standardization have an important role in ensuring academic standards are uniform across institutional, geographical and curriculum boundaries. They provide valuable opportunities for professional development, allowing teachers to 'test out' their judgements against those of their peers, providing exposure to alternative interpretations and values. This will inform not just summative assessment practice, but also the ability to provide constructive formative feedback and to enhance the quality of 'assessment for learning'.

12

Subject specialist pedagogy
Steve Burton, Roy Fisher and David Lord

In this chapter

- Subject specialist pedagogy in lifelong learning
- The subject specialist dimension
- Some wider considerations

This chapter introduces debates surrounding subject specialist pedagogy in the LLS (for an extended account, see Fisher and Webb 2006). It offers advice on how to maintain and enhance subject specialist knowledge and pedagogic skills. The unprecedented level of policy interest in teacher education for the LLS that arose during the years of the New Labour Government (1997–2010), and which continued under the Coalition Government which followed it, has frequently highlighted 'subject specialist pedagogy' as a key issue.

Subject specialist pedagogy in lifelong learning

Healey and Jenkins (2001: 3) situate disciplinary communities centrally within educational development, suggesting that the 'view that teaching is generic reduces it to the technical matter of performance . . . unconnected to the disciplinary community at the heart of being an academic'. They argue that 'different clusters of academic disciplines and their respective degree programmes have distinctive norms and values; and academics in different disciplinary clusters show wide difference in their teaching practices' (pp. 3–4).

What constitutes a bounded 'subject' or academic discipline is always in flux. Over time elements of knowledge emerge, coalesce and dissipate. Alchemy, for example, has ancient roots but its influence in the West waned as modern sciences developed. Psychology is a relatively young field having emerged in the second half of the nineteenth century, and it has relatively porous boundaries with physiology and, through the 'sub-discipline' of social psychology, with sociology. The subjects (or disciplines) of politics, psychology and sociology can be 'packaged' along with anthropology and economics as components of the 'social sciences' as a field. These kinds of mutable disciplinary relationships are also found in the natural sciences and the humanities.

Goodson (2003: 9) suggests that 'scholars working in disciplinary modes normally develop their first allegiance to their home discipline'. In her discussion of the move towards integration of academic and vocational education in American High Schools, Warren Little (1992: 4) referred to the presence of a 'legacy of subject specialism', comprising 'intellectual orientation, social relations, emotional satisfactions, and formal organization', viewing this as a barrier. These legacies are at work in twenty-first century education though they have been eroded by new currents in knowledge production and consumption. Schools and HEIs still largely structure the curriculum in 'subjects' but this is less so in FE, and is not the case in the wider LLS. The idea of 'subject specialist pedagogy' remains a powerful one, but it contradicts strong intellectual and epistemological trends. Browne (2005: 3) suggests that:

> Academic curricula are being strengthened and enriched through the enlightened realization that no discipline is an island unto itself. Instead, each is a part of the curriculum mainland, to which it feeds important nutrients and from which it draws life-giving nourishment in the form of intellectual commerce and trade . . . Interdisciplinary study is a breaking down of what Marjorie Garber in *Academic Instincts* (2003) called 'Disciplinary Libido'.

Changing conceptions of knowledge, derived from postmodernism and associated ideas, have incorporated notions of interdisciplinarity. Lyotard's (1984) pronouncement of 'the end of metanarratives' and the rise of performativity (see Chapter 8) has altered the ways of organizing knowledge on which the force of the concept of subject specialist pedagogy rests. In other words, the idea of subject specialist pedagogy cannot be taken for granted even if it has continued to hold policymakers and some regulatory and inspection bodies in its grip.

In March 2003 the DfES (2003a: 1) issued its consultation document *Subject Specialism* which discussed 'how professionalism in subject specialism might be more effectively supported and developed through the school workforce'. It was argued that, 'It is a combination of deep subject knowledge and a range of appropriate teaching and learning techniques which make for the most powerful interactions between teachers and pupils' (p. 2). The (now abolished) GTC's response appeared the following June (GTC 2003: 1) and indicated that their own research on teachers had shown 'love of their subject' to be 'the first reason for them wanting to teach'. The GTC, however, also pointed to 'a danger in separating it [subject specialist pedagogy] from other aspects of teacher pedagogy'.

Thornton (1998: 38), discussing subject specialism in primary education, saw the concept partially emerging as a response to supposed progressivism within that sector. She cited Ball's (1995) argument that the Education Reform Act of 1988 established the National Curriculum as a mechanism designed to 'deconstruct the comprehensive modernist curriculum' putting in its place 'a political but depoliticized, authoritative curriculum of tradition'. This perception of subject specialist pedagogy as a reactionary response to progressivism is one that has interesting parallels.

An Ofsted (2003: 23) survey of FETT reported that:

[U]nlike ITT for secondary school teachers, most courses for FE teachers are not designed to provide subject-specific or vocation-specific training, although some have done so in the past. It is assumed that trainees will already have the necessary specialist skills, or that they will receive specialist training within the college faculties or departments in which they work. While this may be true in some cases, many new FE teachers do not receive this specialist input.

The report stated that, 'many trainees who are not employed by the college in which they are doing their training receive no specialist mentoring' (Ofsted 2003: 24). A major finding was that '[t]he content of the courses rarely includes the development of subject specific pedagogy to equip new teachers with the specific knowledge and skills necessary for teaching their specialist subject or vocational area' (p. 3).

One of eight recommendations was that HEIs and awarding bodies should 'give substantially more attention to developing trainees' expertise in teaching their subject' (p. 4). The DfES (2003b: 7) response to Ofsted's report included under the heading 'Our starting point' the assertion that '[t]eachers in our sector need two sets of skills – to be expert in their subject, and to be trained to teach it'. A specific way to address the Ofsted recommendations, DfES claimed, would be through 'The introduction of formalised subject specific mentoring as part of the workplace development of trainee teachers' which 'will ensure that all trainees have access to subject pedagogy' (p. 8). Recognizing some practical difficulties DfES (2003b: 23) acknowledged:

> It will not always be possible for the trainee to be assigned to a mentor teaching the same subject. The wide variety of subjects taught in the learning and skills sector means that in some colleges and providers, more specialist subjects may have only one teacher. In such cases, the trainee should be paired with a teacher of a related subject ... Trainees will also be able to access support materials online.

The DfES (2004a: 5) issued its plans for the reform of ITT for the LLS in the document *Equipping Our Teachers for the Future*, stating that teachers in the sector would be 'trained and qualified in':

- the skills and subjects they teach at the levels appropriate to their teaching, which may be level 1 or degree level; and
- the skills of teaching their subject in the workshop, laboratory or classroom.

This thinking would be reflected in the LLUK (2007a: 8) professional standards (see Chapter 2), within which 'Domain C' was devoted to specialist learning and teaching. According to these standards teachers in the LLS need to demonstrate a commitment to:

- understanding and keeping up to date with current knowledge in respect of own specialist area;
- enthusing and motivating learners in own specialist area;

- fulfilling the statutory responsibilities associated with own specialist area of teaching;
- developing good practice in teaching own specialist area.

The 2007 standards also related directly to subject specialism in Domain F 'Access and progression' where there was a requirement for commitment to 'Maintaining own professional knowledge in order to provide information on opportunities for progression in own specialist area' (LLUK 2007a: 14).

The new Professional Standards issued by the Education and Training Foundation (2014: 3) in May 2014 called for the development of 'deep and critically informed knowledge and understanding' in relation to a need to 'Maintain and update knowledge of your subject and/or vocational area'.

It was clear from *Equipping Our Teachers for the Future* (DfES 2004a) that mentoring was seen as the route to subject specialist pedagogic skills and there was the affirmation that 'an essential aim of the training is that teachers should have the skills of teaching in their own specialist or curriculum area' (p. 8). The importance of teachers knowing their subject is a principle that few would dispute though there is a difference between subject knowledge and subject pedagogy. Whether or not there are distinct subject specialist pedagogies, and whether these should be an organizational/structural factor in teacher training for the LLS is not so clear. It is easy to detect in both Government and Ofsted thinking an understanding of curriculum issues strongly informed by practice in secondary schools.

Issues of subject specialist pedagogy have both epistemological and cultural dimensions. Crawley (2005) suggested that a review of an FE college prospectus would identify up to 200 subject specialisms. The wider LLS is awash with 'subject specialisms' (bearing only a passing relationship to traditional academic disciplines). The LLS and FE colleges are populated by vocational curricula. These have a tendency to 'atomize' in relation to workplace roles, while incorporating remnants of the academic disciplines from which they are derived. Within FE a 'specialist' in business studies is likely to be expected to teach a range of subjects. A typical Business Studies Diploma, for instance, might incorporate (versions of) English, mathematics and newer disciplines such as economics and alongside contemporary curricula constructions such as IT, and other new 'bundles of knowledge and skills' that attract a wide range of descriptors (for example 'managing people'). These newer 'subjects' are inter- and trans-disciplinary.

The Business Education Council (BEC), and its successor the Business and Technology Education Council (BTEC), transformed pedagogic practice in FE between 1979 and 1985 (see Fisher 2004). Lecturers were challenged to work cooperatively and to break away from traditional lecturing. Advice about delivery of the curriculum was reinforced by the monitoring of assignments and programmes. During the 1980s this, together with vocational progressivism, practically eliminated 'old school' subject specialist teaching in business related FE. Subjects such as economics became integrated and shifted away from their academic origins. The (then) new style of student centred curriculum introduced by BEC/BTEC had a major impetus in changing the role of the FE lecturer from something approaching that of an instructor to that of a facilitator. FE practitioners today do not generally conceive themselves as 'subject specialists' in the sense of working within defined academic disciplines.

The everyday experience of teaching within FE and its associated culture has seen a move away from practices that could be characterized as an 'insular model' of working, towards a 'connective model'. Lucas (1995) argued for the creation of a teacher training provision for FE which would serve the needs of the concept of the 'connective specialist'. The development of such teacher training programmes would be predicated on 'an alternative model based on a new relationship between theory and practice . . . articulating a view of the skills needed for the future' (p. 13). Lucas recognized that merely adding the concept of reflection to that of competence would not be enough because the skills required for the needs of the future could not be derived from an examination of current practice. Dimensions for the training needs of the 'lecturer of the future' identified in related and contemporaneous work by Young et al. (1995) were:

> *Curriculum knowledge*: 'Lecturers . . . will still be subject specialists' [in our view this was mistaken] but this will be based on 'an understanding of how her/his subject relates to other forms of subject specialism'. (p. 32)

> *Learner-centred pedagogic knowledge*: 'Lecturers will need . . . to be experts in the management of learning and in how to enable their students to become managers of their own learning.' (p. 33)

> *Inter-professional knowledge*: 'lecturers will depend more and more on other professionals . . . lecturers will need to know about these different sources of expertise and how students can access them.' (p. 33)

> *Organizational knowledge*: In a situation where they will increasingly be working in teams with very diverse memberships lecturers will need to 'develop teamwork and collaborative skills . . . they will also need negotiating skills'. (p. 33)

> *Connective knowledge*: Lecturers will 'need to be able to help students connect their past, present and future learning as well as have enough knowledge of work-places to be able to support a student's workplace learning'. (p. 33)

The above model still has much to commend it as a framework.

The subject specialist dimension

A House of Commons Education Committee report (2012: 19) stated that 'no sensible person would suggest that having a good degree automatically makes you a good teacher. Strong subject knowledge is necessary but not sufficient'. In its 2011–12 annual report on learning and skills Ofsted (2012a: 7) adjudged that only 56 per cent of providers inspected 'were good or outstanding for teaching or learning . . . Key features of the weaker sessions remain the teacher/trainers' lack of updated expertise in the specialist vocational and subject areas'. In an echo of its survey (Ofsted 2003) of almost a decade earlier in relation to initial teacher education for FE, Ofsted's 2011–12 report stated that,

> Often, the training and feedback that participants on these courses receive do not focus sufficiently on how well they apply their specialist knowledge and skills to their teaching to develop learners' skills and understanding. In the best provision, teachers take modules related to their area of specialism . . .
>
> (Ofsted 2012a: 28)

A major evaluation of FE teachers' qualifications (BIS 2012d: 58) found 'limited evidence . . . that teachers have up to date vocational subject knowledge'. Teachers have a duty to keep up to date with developments in their field as new subject knowledge emerges. It is clear that the idea of subject specialist pedagogy, whatever the strength of its conceptual basis, is still a powerful concept. As thinking about teaching and learning develops teachers need to be aware of the new pedagogic techniques which have relevance to their field. At the practical level, teachers benefit from proactive involvement with the various 'communities of practice' (Lave and Wenger 1991) which relate to their work since a fundamental element of learning arises from social practice. The following are ways in which these requirements can be addressed.

Engagement with colleagues (and self)

It can be easy to take immediate colleagues for granted, yet most workplaces contain diverse expertise from which to learn. This can be through designated mentors or coaches; through formal peer review and appraisal processes; or simply by making a concerted effort to learn from colleagues. All teachers are, whether consciously or not, in effect 'modelling' their own notions of what constitutes teaching. Taking advantage of this, of course, includes observing, reflecting on and learning from poor practice as well as good. It is also important, through reflection (see Chapter 13), for a teacher to critically consider their own practices.

Engagement with scholarship and research

Scholarly activity and research, both in relation to subject fields and learning/pedagogy, are central to teacher professionalism. Keeping up to date with the published literature is an obvious requirement. The direct conduct of and/or participation in research projects provides a way to actively create new knowledge and practices. Small but valuable action research projects can often be incorporated into the supposedly 'routine' work of teaching.

Subject associations

There is a vast range of academic and vocational subject associations: examples include the Historical Association (HA), the Council for Hospitality Management

Education (CHME), the Association of Law Teachers (ALT), and the Association of Painting Craft Teachers (APCT). These and similar organizations frequently provide learning resources, journals and opportunities to meet others to share ideas and discuss issues of mutual interest.

Teaching/professional bodies

The Education and Training Foundation, and the Higher Education Academy are both bodies which, in their particular ways, support and promote teacher professionalism (including pedagogy).

Networks

Beyond the formal subject and professional associations there are many electronic networks, discussion groups and blogs that provide fora in which to debate subject knowledge and teaching. These networks/e-communities are often international, presenting opportunities to access ideas and resources from across the globe.

Conferences

Formal conferences have the advantage of enabling practitioners to meet and engage in structured discussion as well as, importantly, affording opportunities to informally speak 'in person' with peers.

Continuous professional development

Many colleges and training organizations mount CPD programmes, or belong to associations through which CPD can be accessed. Finding the time to attend CPD, or to access online CPD, is crucial to maintaining the currency of knowledge and skills as well as building a professional profile (see Chapter 19).

Some wider considerations

There is a trend towards the disintegration of disciplines and an intensified fluidity of knowledge that suggests that inter-disciplinarity is a sensible approach to research and to much teaching at HE level. In many cases, this applies in FE. The atomization of the FE curriculum reflects the reality of vocational application, and the 'super-complexity' of the LLS makes the concept of subject specialism and the associated primacy of workplace mentoring difficult to implement. There is sometimes an absence of specific expertise and frequently of dedicated funding to release that expertise.

The density, compactness and 'contrary directions' of the ITE curriculum for the LLS, creaking under the weight of imperatives to address literacy, numeracy and ESOL, have created the need for more 'space' than is available. It is difficult to address core educational issues in a way that is appropriately critical. In one sense the key question is, 'What constitutes legitimate knowledge in this context?' Moreover, we are conscious that new technologies and mechanisms such as mentoring, appraisal, research activity and engagement with CPD may be open to utilization by management for monitoring, performance review and, in Foucauldian language, surveillance.

Lyotard (1984: 4) referred to a trend towards 'a thorough exteriorization of knowledge'. We hope that the positive potential of new technology (see Fisher and Fisher 2007) may work against this by enabling practitioners to engage directly and freely in the critical resolution of everyday problems. This engagement, we anticipate, will be in the context of an ethos that asks 'why?' as well as 'how?'. One that moves beyond the technique of subject specialist pedagogy to embrace deeper issues surrounding contemporary and future professional practice.

13

Reflective practice

Barbara Reynolds and Martin Suter

In this chapter

- What is reflection?
- The process of reflective practice
- Levels of reflection
- Theories of reflective practice
- Criticisms of reflective practice

What is reflection?

> Active, persistent and careful consideration of any belief or supposed form of knowledge in the light of the grounds that support it and the further conclusions to which it tends constitutes reflective thought.
>
> (Dewey 1933: 9)

The quotation above is from *How We Think*, a seminal work by the philosopher and educational theorist John Dewey, considered by many to be the most important influence on notions of reflective practice. It encapsulates Dewey's belief that there are many complex situations in modern society which require choices to be made, and often no clear cut, ready-made answers. Dewey was suspicious of claims to easy solutions, speaking of individuals being 'confused' and 'perplexed' by problems, but proposing that through 'careful consideration' they would find solutions adapted to their particular situation. This position derives from Dewey's philosophical pragmatism, an approach that views knowledge as produced by an adaptive process in which human beings succeed in understanding and manipulating their environment. According to Dewey, knowledge *is* successful practice: we have knowledge in a particular context only when we can overcome the difficulties it sets.

It is easy to see the attraction of reflective practice. Writers on the subject (see Carr 1995) argue that teaching is a complex activity, often contingent, in which it is difficult to be prescriptive. Teachers are often faced with 'perplexities': what is the right thing to do in a particular situation?

What elements of professional practice, then, should receive 'careful consideration'? The use of teaching and learning strategies and resources is an obvious one.

The teacher must consider the most effective strategies, and how to adapt them to different subjects and groups of learners. There are the learners themselves: what are the best ways to manage particular groups and help learners achieve? How does the teacher differentiate to ensure that learning is effective? These complexities of practice are compounded by the rate of curricular change. Of course, help and guidance is available, but often it is up to the individual teacher to 'adapt' that guidance, to make it 'work' in their particular situation. To cope effectively with the contingencies of practice the teacher needs to 'actively' and 'persistently' consider what works. In so doing, what constitutes 'good practice' must receive scrutiny, the teacher being wary of 'ready-made' solutions. Dewey's suspicion of ready-made solutions is reinforced by research indicating that learning in FE appears to be strongly culture and context dependent: 'what works, or is deemed good practice in one learning site may not work or be good practice in another' (Hodkinson and James 2003: 401).

In this chapter we first consider the process of reflective practice. This is followed by a discussion of the levels of reflection in which a teacher might engage, for instance the 'technical' relating to everyday classroom and workshop practice, and 'critical' reflection on the *context*. We then explore three influential 'models' of reflection, and conclude by reviewing criticisms of reflective practice, recognizing that limitations should be acknowledged.

The process of reflective practice

How do we reflect on practice? Figure 13.1 illustrates the basic process of integrating the practice of teaching with reflection on that practice. The process starts with 'practice': a teaching session, or other engagement with learners, after which the

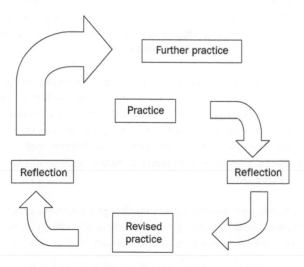

Figure 13.1 Basic model of reflecting on practice

practitioner reflects upon the session. As a result, the teacher may decide to make some changes, perhaps introducing new learning activities and resources. When reflecting on the next session, the teacher considers how effective or otherwise the changes have been. Note that the cycle is not 'closed': if it were, reflective practice would be exactly the 'quick fix' to problems that Dewey rejects. On the contrary, the notion of a teacher as 'reflective practitioner' implies that reflective practice is ongoing – hence the arrow pointing towards 'further practice'. Boxes 13.1 and 13.2 provide examples of an ongoing process of reflection.

In both examples it can be seen that neither of the practitioners was content to continue with situations they had inherited. As a result of reflection, effective solutions were found. Notably in both cases the cycle is not 'closed'; further issues have arisen which call for refection and consideration of ways to ensure a sound learning experience for *all* learners.

Levels of reflection

We turn our attention now from *how* we might reflect on practice to consider what a teacher might reflect *about*. There are two levels of reflective practice that, while not mutually exclusive, can nevertheless be distinguished from one another: (a) technical; and (b) critical-organizational.

Box 13.1 Example of reflection (1)

Chantelle teaches an 'Access to HE' class. The teaching room was laid out with the tables in rows facing the whiteboard at the front. Initially, this posed no problems, but layout difficulties become evident when she attempts to engage the students in group discussion. Students at the front have to turn around awkwardly to see a speaker behind them, while those at the back have difficulty in seeing the speaker. This results in a stilted discussion where some students make no contribution.

On reflection, Chantelle feels she has to make changes to the layout. She considers group discussion to be an important learning activity and resolves to find a way of making it work. Given that she had planned for a mix of 'teacher centred' and 'learner centred' activities, Chantelle decides against laying out the room for subgroups, as some of the students would have difficulty seeing PowerPoint presentations and whiteboard work. She decides instead on a 'U' shaped arrangement of tables to enable a range of teacher and learner centred activities to take place.

In the next session, having made the necessary changes, Chantelle notes more effective interaction among the students during group discussion. She observes, however, that two or three students tend to monopolize the discussion and a few make little or no contribution . . .

Box 13.2 Example of reflection (2)

Peter works for a charity offering training to young people previously not in education, employment or training (NEET). He teaches landscaping skills, with the object of readying learners for employment or to progress to FE.

As part of his training role, Peter is required to ensure trainees build a portfolio demonstrating learning and achievement in literacy and numeracy skills. The trainees demonstrate their literacy skills largely by logging their progress on the course, with appropriate support and guidance from Peter. Building of the numeracy portfolio has tended to be undertaken when the weather is inclement and trainees cannot work outdoors, an arrangement that Peter inherited from the previous tutor. For this purpose, Peter has used worksheets found in the cabin used by the group.

These numeracy sessions are unpopular with trainees, with much grumbling when the worksheets are produced. After one particularly fraught rainy afternoon in the cabin, Peter reflects upon his own experiences as a learner. He recalls his dislike of mathematics at school, only finding 'meaning' in the use of number when he became an apprentice landscape gardener, when tasks such as calculating quantities and areas became part of the job. Peter reflects that much of the numeracy work undertaken by trainees had little relevance for them, perhaps replicating negative school experiences. This leads him to think about ways of integrating numeracy with landscaping projects. He creates worksheets on linear measurement, area and volume on which the trainees can perform the calculations that any landscape gardener would reasonably be expected to. In this way, Peter increases the relevance of numeracy to the trainees, with the bonus that there are fewer behavioural issues.

Reflecting on the integration of numeracy skills with project work, Peter is pleased with the results, but he still has the problem of how to cater for the range of abilities in his group.

Technical

This is the type of reflective practice likely to be undertaken on a regular basis. It is a reflection which acknowledges the complexities and often uncertainties of the learning environment. It is often thought of as a problem-solving approach, addressing issues of teaching and learning as they arise. The 'technical' level deals with the techniques of planning and delivering learning. Thus a teacher reflects upon the use of teaching and learning activities; are they effective in achieving learning outcomes? Do they help stimulate active learning? Are the students motivated by the activities? The teacher may also reflect upon the use of teaching and learning resources: are they 'pitched' at the right level? Are they designed to differentiate learning? Have they been designed to take into account any specific learning need, for example dyslexia? Box 13.3 provides an example.

> **Box 13.3** Example of technical reflection
>
> Aisha teaches a 'human sciences' module on a level 3 social care course. It is evident in the first week that there is a wide spread of attainment in the 'sciences', with some students having gained GCSE Biology at A grade, most having grades D to F and some having no science background. Aisha reasons that if she does not differentiate learning by content, the problems already experienced of some students not being stretched while others struggle to 'keep up', will only increase. As a result of this reflection Aisha decides to design worksheets with tasks ascending in difficulty. This she reasons would help ensure that outcomes are being achieved for all, while providing the necessary challenge for the more able.

Critical-organizational

This level is identified as 'critical' because it may be necessary to question the actions, decisions and opinions of others; 'organizational', because the practitioner is reflecting upon the management and deployment of teaching and learning activities, resources and learner support. Box 13.4 provides an example.

Where teaching and learning activities are concerned, a teacher might reflect upon the methods employed on a particular course, and having done so might consider that they result in learner passivity. The teacher might persuade the course team to employ more methods that promote active learning. Crucially, it is important that they are suggesting activities that have 'worked' for the teacher making the suggestion.

A teacher may reflect upon the teaching and learning resources available. Perhaps there are too few resources, or the resources are not suitable for a certain type of learning. Whereas a teacher reflecting at the technical level might try to find a way of working 'creatively' within such constraints, at the critical-organizational level the teacher is questioning these, and working, where possible, to overcome them. One important resource where there might be constraints is the spaces or environments where learning takes place.

There is a variety of learner issues upon which a teacher has cause to reflect. They might become concerned about the challenging behaviour of a group of learners. Through reflection at the technical level, they may find solutions that work in the learning environment. However, the teacher may reason that challenging behaviour is a more general organizational issue, and having reflected upon the reasons for this, might put forward suggestions for a 'policy' for dealing with it.

Theories of reflective practice

Donald Schön

Schön's (1983, 1987) work has had a great influence on reflective practice. Schön was critical of 'technical rationalism', the idea that there is 'one best way' to undertake

---

Box 13.4 Critical-organizational reflection

Louise works for an NHS trust, training care workers in manual handling skills and 'back awareness'. She had been required to train a group at a home for the elderly. This was somewhat unusual, as training is usually undertaken in a suite of specialist rooms at the Trust buildings. In this instance, however, Louise's manager felt that, given the number of participants involved from one location, it would be more efficient for Louise to deliver the training at the care home, which she duly did. The training session was less than successful. The room allocated was too small, and initially there were not enough chairs. There was not enough room to set up some of her equipment, restricting the efficacy of the training. The training was continually interrupted by participants leaving on work-related errands.

Louise wrote up her reflections on the session. Having done this, she approached her manager, telling her what had happened, and proposing how future training sessions for such groups should be conducted. Louise suggested that ideally all training sessions should be held in the Trust's own training suite. If not, she should be able to assess the suitability of 'off site' facilities, and that an agreement should be reached with the management of the homes that participants should not be disturbed during training sessions. Louise's manager was not prepared to establish the principle that all training should be conducted in the Trust training suite, but agreed that where practicable Louise should be able to assess facilities for their suitability. Also, it would be 'written into' any training agreement with management of the homes that participants should not be disturbed during training.

---

a task, and that this prescription is followed at all times and in all circumstances. Greatly influenced by Dewey, Schön argued that professional practices are complex, contingent and even 'messy', and do not lend themselves to a 'technical-rational' approach.

For Schön, the professional is knowledgeable in a unique way and demonstrates through *reflection in action*, practical or personal knowledge, what he called *knowing in action*. Reflection in action has been described as the teacher 'thinking on his or her feet', being spontaneous, creative and unique. According to Schön, the professional exhibits a kind of 'artistry', building up a 'repertoire' of knowledge and skills. This is built up by the teacher gaining understandings of situations that inform action. When the practitioner experiences 'puzzlement' or 'confusion' in a situation, an 'experiment' is carried out to generate new understanding. A teacher will learn a range of classroom management skills, or an understanding of when learners are finding a topic difficult, by 'experimenting' with different ways of dealing with these situations, and if successful, these will be added to the repertoire. Knowing in action results in what Van Maanen (1995) has called a 'competent performance', where the teacher 'just knows' what to do.

This process of thinking on one's feet can be built upon through *reflection on action*, after the encounter with learners. Reflection on action may involve writing up reflections, or discussing practice with a mentor or colleague. It enables a teacher to 'slow things down' (Schön 1987), to explore what happened and why, allowing the formulation of questions and development of ideas for future practice.

The attractiveness of Schön's ideas is easy to see. First, there is an acknowledgement of the complexities of teaching, and the need to build a repertoire of knowledge and skills to deal with the many and varied situations encountered. What distinguishes this from a 'craft' model of teaching (Larivee 2000) is the expectation there will be an ongoing purposeful *reflection on action*, subjecting the 'tacit knowledge' (Polanyi 1983) of professional practice to careful, sustained thought.

There are, however, several criticisms of Schön's model. First, is it always possible to 'slow things down' sufficiently for reflection to take place in busy teaching situations? Second, is it always wise for a teacher to disclose professional dilemmas and perceived limitations in their own practice? Third, does it take into account sufficiently those factors which are outside the individual teacher's control?

Tripp's critical incidents analysis

Critical incident analysis is a model of reflective practice closely associated with the work of Tripp (1993). He argues we need to explore the incidents that occur in the daily work of teaching which can be used to question a teacher's own practice, enabling them to develop an understanding of the processes of teaching, and crucially, to develop their professional judgement. A critical incident is that which we interpret as a challenge in the professional context. Tripp suggests that when something goes wrong, teachers need to ask what happened and why. It is therefore important that the incidents are framed as *questions* that the teacher asks him- or herself.

The process starts by choosing a critical incident, which is not necessarily dramatic. It might be a commonplace event, but is significant because it might indicate underlying motives, structures and processes (Pollard et al. 2005). For example, a teacher might notice that adult learners are reluctant to give individual presentations to their peers. This reluctance would probably not be surprising, but in this instance the teacher has chosen to deal with it as a critical incident. The teacher gives a careful description of it: who was involved; where it happened; what actually happened; what the teacher's reaction to the incident was.

The next step is to analyse the description, to look for the underlying 'structures', 'motives' and 'processes'. This is where the teacher starts to ask 'why' the incident happened: is the location or context of the incident significant? Is it something to do with the nature of the group of learners? Was it subject related or is the teacher's role significant? The teacher in this example might ask questions about the nature of the presentation; students might be particularly apprehensive if it forms a summative assessment. The background of the students may be considered. Could relatively low levels of prior educational attainment have resulted in a lack of confidence? The topic of the presentation might have been significant. Had the students been struggling with the subject? In considering their own role, the teacher might reflect on the preparation given to learners and whether enough guidance had been given on what was expected.

When the teacher has considered the questions framed on the critical incident, the analysis continues with what can be learned from the episode and ends with what can be done to resolve it. However, before implementing any solution, the teacher may find it beneficial to seek the perspective of a colleague or mentor. Here the teacher shares their interpretation of the incident. In the light of this discussion the teacher may modify their analysis, and the solution to the problem.

Brookfield's 'critical reflection'

Brookfield (1995) argues that teachers' reflection on practice should be a process of 'hunting assumptions', where assumptions are the 'taken for granted' beliefs about the world. He argues that there are three sets of such assumptions:

- *Prescriptive assumptions*: what we think *ought* to happen in a given situation, for example, adult students *ought* to be self-directed learners.
- *Causal assumptions*: if we do x, then y will happen, for example, if a teacher uses games and quizzes, followed by rewards, the motivation of young learners will be improved.
- *Paradigmatic assumptions*: the most difficult assumptions to uncover. They are the structuring assumptions we use to order the world into different categories, for example those operating within a 'conservative' paradigm may categorize learners as 'deserving' or 'undeserving' of their support, while those operating within an 'emancipatory' paradigm draw on categories of 'those with or without power'.

Brookfield suggests that teachers can 'hunt' these assumptions by viewing their practice through four 'critical lenses':

- *Our autobiographies as learners and teachers* Brookfield sees as a prerequisite for the 'working' of the other lenses. Through self reflection a teacher becomes aware of the paradigmatic assumptions that influence their work. When a teacher knows what these are they can begin to test their accuracy.
- *Teachers looking at practice through their students' eyes* For Brookfield, this allows a teacher to check whether the learners are engaging with teaching in the way intended.
- *Colleagues' experiences* Brookfield argues that by inviting colleagues to observe practice and engage in 'critical conversations' the teacher can become aware of aspects of professional practice normally hidden.
- *Theoretical literature* This helps to 'inform' practice. Brookfield argues it provides the teacher with 'multiple perspectives' on familiar situations. For example, reading literature on 'transforming learning cultures' (James and Biesta 2007) might provide insight into the motivations and learning experiences of young learners.

Criticisms of reflective practice

As can be seen in the preceding discussion the debate surrounding reflective practice could be located on two continua. One is concerned with approaches that are essentially technical, contrasted with those adopting an emancipatory orientation. The other continuum ranges from the individualist to the collaborative, which is allied to collective notions of reflective practice. In those instances where emancipatory interests are addressed connections can be made to social justice, as well as with forms of critical pedagogy. On the other hand the more technical approaches can be lodged within the classroom or workshop, being managed by a teacher. There is a connection that could be made between this type of practice and that concerned with continuous improvement and/or effectiveness of pedagogic practices. The point is, even though notions of reflective practice can be set against quasi-scientific models of school improvement, with the former being sensitive to the nuances and specificity of classroom practice (Hammersley 2007), they nevertheless pursue the same ends, that is the enhancement of pedagogic outcomes. It is this that renders such approaches conservative despite their progressive veneer. This is the case unless we associate radicalism with the pursuit of meritocratic conceptions of equal opportunities (see Chapter 6).

Those approaches that adopt an emancipatory framework proffer rather different understandings of society. Such perspectives could draw on a variety of theoretical positions, for example Habermassian theory (Carr and Kemmis 1986; Moon 1999), neo-Marxism (Mclaren 2013), feminism (Luke and Gore 1992), critical race theory (Taylor et al. 2009) among others. This is akin to Brookfield's (1995) paradigmatic assumptions whereby those orientated towards emancipatory practice adopt conflictual models of society, whereas technicist orientations veer towards consensual perspectives that are reformist in character, seeking gradual improvement. Conflictual approaches are more explicitly political with the classroom seen as just one site in the struggle for social justice, one that is linked to wider society. In other words, the pursuit of emancipation necessitates not only the transformation of educational practices but also society.

While reflective practice is widely accepted and some would say ubiquitous (Loughran 2006) throughout education, it is not without critics. There are: first, doubts about the efficacy of the reflective process; second, concern over the extent to which organizational cultures are 'enabling' of reflective practice; third, allied to this, concerns that the wider context in which teachers' practice is located may not be supportive; and fourth, there is scepticism about teachers' commitment to reflective practice.

Some writers (for example Cornford 2002) have argued that there is a lack of empirical evidence on the efficacy of reflective practice. It is claimed that many academics have an 'ideological' commitment to reflective practice; consequently research showing reflective practice to be 'non-significant' remains unpublished. It is argued that this commitment is often to a 'critical' or 'emancipatory' reflective practice which is seen as rather abstract by many teachers (Parker 1997). Such abstractness is claimed to cause other problems. Husu et al. (2008) argue that the rather vague commitment to reflective practice presumes that everyone 'knows' how to reflect, but that some teachers need 'structured' help with the *process* of reflective practice which is not always available. Most writers making these criticisms do not suggest the abandonment of reflective practice. However, it is suggested instead that we should be sceptical about the claims made for it (Cornford 2002), and that there should be more guidance on the process of reflective practice (Husu et al. 2008).

Another criticism is that the importance of the milieu in which reflective practice takes place is overlooked in the literature. Suter (2007) found that the 'culture' within which it is enacted is crucial to its success. He found managerial regimes and levels of peer support to be as important as individual teachers' dispositions. Teachers interviewed for the research commented that their relationship with managers was an important consideration when embarking on reflective practice. Some stated that managers actively encouraged suggestions made as a result of reflection, while others commented these would not be welcomed, and in some instances were actively discouraged. In the same research, it was found that some teachers were working in teams where dialogue, trust and collaboration meant that teachers were comfortable in voicing concerns about their own professional practice, but others felt that this might be seen as a sign of weakness or incompetence. Such a critique can be developed to acknowledge the wider socio-economic context. In much the same way as we can interrogate managerial processes for the affordances they offer for reflective practice, so too can we question the wider structural and policy context in which teachers work. Such an analysis points toward an expansive notion of practice, one that moves beyond a focus on individual practitioners and aligns with a rather more political understanding of education.

Finally, Suter (2007) notes the dangers of reflective practice becoming 'routinized', just one more thing that the teacher is required to do alongside all the other paperwork required to keep up to date. When one considers the workload of teachers in the LLS, it is difficult not to sympathize with the view of some teachers that they do not have the time to reflect deeply on their practice, perhaps making a cursory note of an evaluation on a session plan which may or may not be followed up. This perfunctory approach to reflective practice is an example of 'strategic compliance' (Shain and Gleeson 1999) where teachers comply minimally with what is required by management, creating the space for what they consider to be the 'real' job of teaching. It is ironic that some teachers come to regard as a chore that which is meant to 're-professionalize' them. But we should be attentive to the way in which notions of reflective practice can themselves become technicized and accented towards managerial interests – after all they can be used to keep us all up to the mark and in this sense are inherently contradictory (Avis 1994). Suter did find, however, that strategic compliance is by no means universal, and that some teachers will, with the right support, engage in reflective practice to enhance teaching and learning. If we are to take seriously the emancipatory promise of reflective practice it needs to be lodged within a critical orientation that extends beyond the immediate pedagogic context. Nevertheless, we must not forget the central importance of the pedagogic context as this is the immediate locale of our practice.

14

Coaching and mentoring

*Wayne Bailey, Chris Blamires, Liz Dixon,
Alison Iredale, Denise Robinson and
Judith Schoch*

In this chapter

- What are coaching and mentoring?
- Experiential learning and coaching
- Social and situated theories of learning and coaching
- Getting the best from the coaching relationship
- Mentoring teachers in lifelong learning
- The role of the mentee
- Being observed in the classroom
- Conclusion

> I deeply believe that traditional teaching is an almost completely futile, wasteful,
> overrated function in today's changing world.
>
> Carl Rogers (1983: 137)

What are coaching and mentoring?

Carl Rogers (1902–87) is a major figure in humanist psychology, a leading progenitor
of the counselling movement, as well as a force behind the development of person-
centred therapies. He was also an apostle of student-centred learning, and advocates
of coaching have been drawn to Rogers for theoretical inspiration.

Today's coaches are often to be found working in the corporate world of human
resources, frequently as consultants, and normally on a one-to-one basis. In that
context, those being coached are usually referred to as 'clients' or as 'coachees', and
despite the term 'client' carrying consumerist connotations, it will be used in this
discussion (coachee having an association with transport). A term such as 'trainee'
would certainly be antithetical to the ethos of coaching. Central to the role of a coach
is the facilitation of learning, and a fundamental tenet is that learning is controlled by
the learner.

There are similarities between coaching and mentoring. Part of the role of a mentor is to support development, providing advice and encouragement as well as challenging assumptions. It has been suggested that coaching is more concerned with the acquisition and refinement of 'skills' (Clutterbuck 2005; Jones et al. 2008) or where this is not the case, on specific, more immediate goals. This understanding may have its basis in that 'coaching' is frequently associated with sports, often with a focus on physical skills rather than on 'the total development of the individual' (Jones et al. 2008: 3). Coaching, however, often goes beyond skills development. Arguably, the core of coaching is concerned with the engendering of attitudes and dispositions in order for an individual to be successful *on their own terms*. Not all mentors will adopt a coaching approach in their role, though Jenny Rogers (2007: 179) suggests they will be 'far more powerful' if they do. Coaching has become fashionable, and a number of sub-categories have emerged, including 'life coaching' and 'conflict coaching'. Here we consider coaching more generically.

Parsloe and Leedham (2009) describe the relationship between coaching and mentoring in terms of their positioning on a continuum with four dimensions: developmental focus (from skills to personal development); objectives (from simple and concrete to complex and evolving); duration; and style (from directive to non-directive). This implies that there is no clear-cut divide between the processes of coaching and mentoring, and that in deciding which term to use we should consider the nature, context and aims of the relationship (see Figure 14.1).

Informal coaching is frequently incorporated into everyday learning situations, and in such circumstances the individuals involved are unlikely to attempt to distinguish between activities that may involve a mix of coaching, mentoring, facilitating, and teaching and training. There are, however, particular skills and attributes associated with effective coaching that can make a difference to performance, whether used in the classroom, or with individuals at work.

Within businesses, as is the case with mentoring, it is not unusual for coaching to be carried out by a line manager who is placed to see how a person works. With this

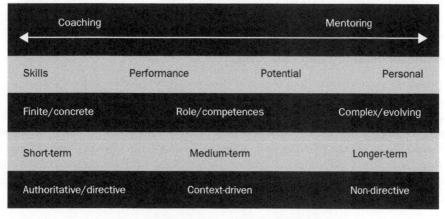

Figure 14.1 The coaching–mentoring continuum
Source: Parsloe and Leedham (2009: 12)

'operational coaching', however, there is the possibility that reflective and transformational dimensions in the process will be neglected in the face of the imperatives of 'getting the job done'. In essence, coaching techniques are employed, but this kind of arrangement would not fit a purist vision of coaching.

Starr (2003), discussing sports coaching, highlights the seeming contradiction of a world class athlete being coached by someone without world class status. Conversely, a world class athlete may lack the attributes required to coach effectively. In most situations coaching is more about intuitive facilitation and inspiration than it is about the transmission of technique. Using the expertise of staff in an organization can effect change in a focused way, relating to performance criteria established from external quality enhancement measures such as the *Framework for Excellence* (Information Authority 2012; LSC 2007b). This performative approach is, however, unlikely to nurture human potential in the way envisaged by Carl Rogers.

Coaching in the LLS, and in particular as part of CPD for teachers, is a relatively recent phenomenon. However, since *Success for All* (DfES 2002a), coaching has enjoyed an increased profile and is entering the mainstream of learning and teaching. For a wide-ranging discussion of coaching in vocational education and training, including the training of teachers, see City and Guilds Centre for Skills Development (2012). In teacher development in the LLS, the coach is usually a qualified teacher and sometimes a close colleague of 'the client'. Here the client ('coachee') is usually identified through appraisal, which may include management assessments of their teaching. In addition to the formally designated position of coach, there are several roles within ITE for the LLS which may require coaching sensibilities. These include teacher/trainer, mentor, learning support worker and academic skills tutor. Another descriptor finding currency is that of 'critical friend', a term which describes an informal role where a colleague seeks to provide a realistic and thought-provoking 'sounding board' to bring clarity to a person's thinking.

Later in this chapter the concept of mentoring will be discussed in more detail. There will be a specific focus on mentoring trainee teachers. Many readers of this book will be trainee teachers who are currently being mentored, and may themselves be mentors in the future.

Experiential learning and coaching

Chapter 7 presented some key learning theories, including experiential learning, a foundational element underpinning the philosophy of coaching. The nature of coaching recognizes that people learn in different ways. John Dewey (1859–1952) argued for experience as an important part of the educational process. Dewey was interested in the nature of reflection, and the non-linear process of learning, paving the way for Kolb's (1984) model of experiential learning. Both the coach and the client need to be aware of this embodiment of learning as a holistic activity, taking into account the experiences of both parties.

An experience is always what it is because of a transaction taking place between an individual and what, at the time, constitutes his environment, whether the latter consists of persons with whom he is talking . . ., the subject talked about . . .; the book he is reading . . .; or the materials of an experiment . . .

(Dewey 1938: 43–4)

Dewey's thinking has much to offer coaching practice, particularly in the areas of observation, reflection and deliberation. Coaching practice uses observation as a key strategy for success, along with listening, questioning and reflection (Starr 2003: 48). The observational process is reciprocal, and the coach must in some sense expose or 'open up' elements of the client's needs, powers and potential trajectories. There is a complex and mutual process of envisioning.

A major method of assessing teachers in relation to the quality of their practice, and the effectiveness of the learning they manage is by observation. In the case of a trainee teacher this is carried out 'on them' primarily by a teacher educator or by their mentor, but they also routinely see their tutor, their mentor and their peers teaching. A qualified teacher might be observed by a college manager. In all these instances feedback provided is generally intended to be supportive and developmental, but, unless carefully managed, power imbalances can mitigate against the potential to enhance performance.

Social and situated theories of learning and coaching

Jameson (2012: 51) explains that 'Coaching can be described as a "learner-focused constructivist experiential approach" . . . [that] recognises students' prior knowledge and aims to build on it, complementing instructional and workplace demonstration'. However, she notes that coaching 'has also been characterised as a socio-cultural and cognitive apprenticeship-like technique that fosters both independence and self-directed learning' (p.51). Both of these perspectives provide a clear imperative for a coach to situate facilitation within a context which is meaningful to the client. For Lave and Wenger (1991) learning is a function of the activity, context and culture in which it occurs. They have suggested a movement from cognitive development to socially situated practice where learning is embedded in activity, and this activity needs to be close to 'real life' in order to be meaningful (see Figure 14.2). There is a distinction, however, between learning and performance, between the potential for competence and actual competence, and this lies at the heart of coaching practice.

Social and situated learning theories view learning as problematic, especially when there is significant time between the learning and the performance. Classrooms are economically viable places of learning, but they are artificial. The knowledge required by a learner can be distilled into a classroom setting, bringing together learners with similar needs, but knowledge into action requires individuals to work together with shared purpose. Wenger (1998: 6) described such a group as a 'community of practice' stating,

[w]e all belong to communities of practice. At home, at work, at school, in our hobbies – we belong to several communities at any given time. And the communities of practice to which we belong change over the course of our lives. In fact, communities of practice are everywhere.

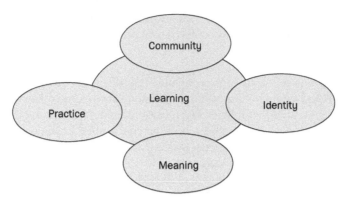

Figure 14.2 Components of a social theory of learning
Source: Wenger (1998: 5)

The (generally) one-to-one nature of the coach/client relationship may place it in tension with social theories of learning. The social environment is crucial in the dynamics of coaching, but some elements of the coach/client nexus rest on exclusion (of others) and on an element of closure to enable the client to develop self-understandings.

Getting the best from the coaching relationship

Coaching has the capacity to identify opportunities for improvement, motivate through targets, facilitate knowledge and skills, and to provide individualized constructive feedback. Carl Rogers (1983) stated his desire to wave an imaginary wand that would cause teachers to forget that they were teachers, to develop 'complete amnesia' for their teaching skills. Instead he wanted to find each teacher 'holding the attitudes and possessed of the skills of a *facilitator of learning* – genuineness, prizing, and empathy' (p.135, original emphasis). Rogers suggested that a teacher would ask, 'How can I make the mug hold still while I fill it from the jug with these facts that the curriculum planners and I regard as valuable?'. In contrast, a facilitator would ask, 'How can I create a psychological climate in which the child [or learner] will feel free to be curious, will feel free to make mistakes, will feel free to learn from the environment, from fellow students, from me, from experience?' (p. 136). There are many advanced skills that a coach should possess in order to support a client and to foster a positive learning relationship; these include the abilities to motivate and to inspire. The coach needs to be an active listener who can question wisely; they need acute observation skills, a reflective disposition and the ability to provide insightful feedback. To be an effective coach is demanding; the role is not suited to all. (The same can be said of the traditional teaching which Carl Rogers abhorred).

Given the underpinning humanistic philosophy and the quasi-therapeutic ethos of coaching, the relationship between the coach and the client is of the utmost importance, and this is based on the qualities of each person and the dynamics of the context (Brockbank 2006). There are, however, boundaries that must be acknowledged. If the coach is also the line manager of the learner then there will inevitably be issues with regard to the sharing of personal or emotionally charged information. Although it is far from unusual for line managers to adopt either coaching or mentoring roles within organizations, this does not create the best context (Clutterbuck 2004; Goldsmith 2008).

The coach and the client need to know their own and each other's responsibilities and boundaries. The frequency of meetings should be agreed, and expectations made explicit; there should be agreement on confidentiality. Most models of coaching involve developing aims and objectives, establishing improvement opportunities, and the identification of changes that are necessary to promote development. Both parties must be motivated and committed to the relationship (Jones et al. 2008), a point also made by Wallace and Gravells (2007) who have usefully summarized the coaching process as set out in Figure 14.3.

There are times when a person knows their goals and how to realize their ambition; at other times they need support in this. Sometimes a coaching arrangement is put in place by management for 'remedial' purposes, though this contradicts the client-centred focus of coaching. Whatever the background to the initiation of coaching, good coaches will take time to propose goals that are achievable, and which are formulated sensitively and collaboratively. Expectations, both personal and organizational, must be clear. If a coach is working with a group, then it is best if similar goals are shared – coaching is not entirely compatible with group scenarios.

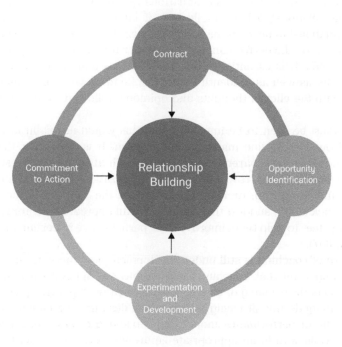

Figure 14.3 The coaching process
Source: Wallace and Gravells (2007: 67)

Clutterbuck (2004) has argued that, 'Coaching is a relatively directive means of helping someone develop competence' (p. 17). LSIS (2009), however, contend that, 'Coaching is non-directive and can be used to help an individual solve their own problems through listening, reflecting and asking questions. Subject Learning Coaches are non-judgemental, critical friends who can help their peers view fresh perspectives; this is what makes it so powerful.'

Although there is not a single model of coaching one that is used widely in England is GROW (variously interpreted but broadly entailing a staged process of 'Goal, Reality, Options, Way Forward'). This provides a structured approach. There is a plethora of coaching models which can be readily accessed via Internet searches; many are essentially commercial products and some will be more suited to a specific context. More important than the particular coaching model is grounding in the key principles of coaching and recognition of personal strengths and limitations. The Employment National Training Organisation (ENTO) has published *National Occupational Standards for Coaching and Mentoring in a Work Environment* (ENTO 2006).

Feedback from a coach should be given promptly. A delay in feedback may mean that the learner will forget or become demotivated. Performance-based feedback is often used in coaching. Effective coaches will consider any performance problems and provide appropriate feedback, guarding against possible defensive reactions. It is important for a coach to describe situations accurately and to both cultivate and give respect – Jenny Rogers (2007) has advised that a coach should not work with a client they cannot respect. In most coaching situations verbal feedback is provided (Jones et al. 2008) – the relationship is normally one of immediate dyadic interactions. The coach/client relationship needs to be based on trust. Where there are criticisms, feedback should focus on the performance of the client rather than on the person (Wallace and Gravells 2007). It is essential to discuss what has gone right, and to stress the client's strengths, as well as to identify what can be improved. Performance debriefs should start with the client's thoughts and opinions, followed by those of the coach (Haidar 2007).

A coach must be seen to be impartial, and this would normally mean that they should stand outside the line management function. It is important that reporting procedures should be transparent and that the coach always remains supportive of the client. According to Sparrow (2008) more organizations are using a combination of coaching and mentoring, or choosing to ignore the subtle differences between them. Clutterbuck (2005) suggest this can be a useful approach. Mentors may need to coach their mentees to help them improve their performance in certain areas (Wallace and Gravells 2007).

The theory of coaching is still under development, and there are many emergent models. It is important that coaching interventions are applied with due sensitivity and recognition of the primacy of the client in the relationship. Principles such as trust and confidentiality do not sit easily with systems designed for management, quality assurance, audit, or performance monitoring. Coaching offers great potential when applied in the right way in an appropriate environment for the benefit of the client. The coach/client relationship is a privileged one in both senses of the word – and it should not be abused.

Mentoring teachers in lifelong learning

Megginson and Clutterbuck (1999: 3) define mentoring as 'Off-line help by one person to another in making significant transitions in knowledge, work and thinking'. In this definition, 'off-line' is taken to mean a relationship outside the organizational hierarchy and without line management authority. Similar definitions are used by Rodd (2006) for mentoring teachers and by Mumford (1995) in his work on managers. The principle used is that, having no managerial responsibility for the *mentee* (the usual term for the person being mentored), the mentor is more able to be impartial. The relationship therefore has greater potential for mutual trust, empathy, cultural sensitivity, critical friendship and openness, without being supervisory and linked to specific management priorities. Mumford captures this argument succinctly when he observes 'a boss is not a mentor to a subordinate' (1995: 4). Mentoring may therefore be seen as a 'protected' relationship with the purpose of developing the mentee from apprenticeship to independence. This relationship will involve learning and experimentation and the development of competencies rather than coverage of specific course content. Ultimately, the effectiveness of mentoring for new or trainee teachers will depend on how successfully the mentoring relationship develops.

A variety of skills and attributes are needed to enable both mentor and trainee to get the best out of their relationship. Clearly, the main objective of mentoring is to support the mentee's development, both in achieving a teaching qualification and in providing a sound basis for CPD. A mentor needs to be friendly and approachable, build rapport with trainees and offer the right blend of challenge and support. The mentor needs to encourage mentees to reflect on their development and, in discussions, to listen actively and ask probing questions. These qualities are discussed in more detail below.

Be friendly and approachable in order to help build rapport

Mentors need to be actively interested in the development of mentees (Carter and Francis 2001) and to have a *mentoring attitude*, which involves the mentor valuing their own learning and that of their mentee in order to assist the mentee's development. A mentoring attitude can be developed by being open minded, responsible and wholehearted in the relationship with mentees. Building rapport is a crucial part of the mentoring process and a 'culture of trust' must be developed (Taylor 2002). It is important that the mentee feels that their mentor cares about their development. The mentor must maintain 'transparency', by having clear and open expectations of the mentor–mentee relationship (Wallace and Gravells 2007). Confidentiality is an important aspect of a trusting relationship, as is being patient and non-judgemental.

Sharing what Egan (2002) calls 'empathic highlights' can also inspire trust. This involves the mentor sharing their understanding of the mentees' key experiences, behaviours and feelings. Egan asserts that they are 'empathic' because they are driven by the mentor's desire to understand their mentee and to communicate this understanding, and that they are 'highlights' because they focus on the key points that the mentee is making. Similarly, mentors need to share their own experiences and critical incidents with mentees; this can in turn help the mentor and mentee trust one another.

Listen actively and question appropriately

Mentors can engage in *active listening* by maintaining regular eye contact and giving full attention to the mentee. Active listening helps to ensure that the mentor is open to all information and is free to follow, rather than to lead, the mentee (Wallace and Gravells 2007). Questioning skills are also important. The use of open, probing questions enables issues to be considered in detail and to be fully explored. Similarly, questions that connect ideas or events can also promote new understandings, helping mentees to explore the cause of an incident as well as its effects (Wallace and Gravells 2007). Conversely, the excessive use of closed questions and leading questions that invite particular answers can be detrimental to the mentee's development.

Encourage reflection

Reflective practice models currently dominate teacher education and it is therefore important that a trainee teacher's understanding of critical reflection is developed by the mentor. Mentoring is not only about personal support; it should also provide professional development by challenging mentees' ideas and beliefs (Le Cornu 2005). Mentors should encourage mentees to take a critical stance towards their practice, which in turn encourages them to evaluate their teaching through reflection (Halai 2006). Boud et al. (1985) discuss the role of a facilitator in assisting the process of reflection, particularly in describing events as objectively as possible and in being aware of affective barriers to learning (see Chapter 7). In contrast to Egan (see above), they note that 'It is vital that facilitators offer no interpretations or analyses of their own' and that 'The single most important contribution facilitators can make is to give free and undivided attention to the learner' (p. 37).

Offer the right amount of challenge and support

There is abundant evidence that challenge is an appropriate mentoring strategy. Butcher (2003: 38) explains that 'challenge is seen as a discourse in which a mentor can guide, advise and question their student teachers in a collaborative context'. Challenge needs to be specific and focused and must involve a mentor setting tasks which could introduce conflicting ideas or even involve the mentee questioning their own assumptions (McNally and Martin 1998). Yet, if mentees are to be challenged then appropriate support mechanisms are needed. According to Butcher (2002: 198) challenge should be used 'in the context of a supportive and trusting training relationship'. This in turn fosters an atmosphere of empathy and trust. If challenge is used inappropriately, this can lead to the mentee leaving teaching altogether (Stanulis and Russell 2000). There is also evidence to suggest that effective mentoring requires challenge and support that encompasses appropriate mechanisms for feedback (Stanulis and Russell 2000; Butcher 2002).

McNally and Martin (1998) propose a model of mentoring that involves both challenge and support. They discuss three types of mentors:

- The *laissez-faire* mentor sees their role as nurture and support, but offers little or no challenge to trainees.

- The *imperial mentor* has strong views and is interventionist, but offers little support to the trainee as the needs of the novice teacher are not seen as important.

- The *collaborative mentor* combines challenge and support, empowering trainees to engage in critical reflection as they develop.

Having a collaborative mentor brings clear benefits to trainee teachers; however, the balance between challenge and support is crucial (Butcher 2002; Stanulis and Russell 2000). Too much challenge without support may lead to the mentee withdrawing or retreating due to lack of trust. In contrast, support without challenge does nothing more than confirm the status quo without developing the mentee; support combined with challenge is more likely to enable mentees to grow. Experienced in-service trainees may both require and expect more challenge from the outset of the mentoring relationship, although this cannot be assumed in advance. On the other hand, novice trainees (whether pre-service or in-service) may require more support than challenge in the first instance, a balance to be reviewed as the mentee develops. The model shown in Figure 14.4 gives a useful indication of how the varying combination of support and challenge impacts on the novice trainee.

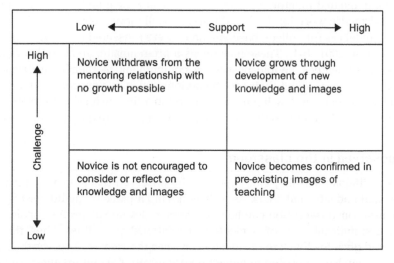

Figure 14.4 Support and challenge in mentoring novice trainees
Source: Elliott and Calderhead (1993)

The role of the mentee

The skills acquisition model of Dreyfus and Dreyfus (1980) can be applied to inexperienced trainee teachers. It identifies the following stages: novice; advanced beginner; competent; proficient; and expert. According to this model, the novice trainee may have a rigid adherence to taught rules or plans and limited situational perception. Novices may hesitate in undertaking reflection in and on action. The role of the mentor is to draw out deeper understanding from the mentee enabling them to view situations holistically rather than in terms of individual aspects. The mentor needs to encourage reflective practice so as to aid mentees in their decision making.

The role of the mentee is closely related to the approach or model of mentoring that is adopted (consciously or unconsciously) by the mentor, as well as the previous teaching experience of the mentee. As noted earlier, models of mentoring tend to incorporate some aspect of reflective practice; the role of the mentor within this approach is one of supporting a professional colleague on a mutual basis of development and for experienced mentees this may well be appropriate. However, due to the changing profile of in-service teacher training, new entrants will be unlikely to have substantial teaching experience and this model may become less appropriate, at least in the initial stages of trainee development.

Various approaches may be useful with less experienced mentees. Furlong and Maynard (1993) suggested that a flexible framework which reflects the growing knowledge and skill of the mentee is preferable. A novice mentee can initially be introduced to professional culture as well as skills-based development. With growing experience, they may be offered more responsibility and move away from peripheral participation to one closer to the centre of the professional community (Hankey 2004). Using communities of practice to analyse mentees' experiences with their mentors, Maynard (2000) suggests that mentees need to 'manage' their mentor as well as their own learning and that mentors can strongly influence the quality of their experience. This is confirmed in work by Hankey (2004) and Cullimore (2006).

Some guidelines for college-based mentees were presented in *Mentoring Towards Excellence* (LSC 2001: 154). These include, as a pre-requisite, an attitude of openness to the process. Mentees 'should possess: a commitment to their own development; honesty and openness about their own behaviour; a positive approach to the value of feedback; [and] time and willingness to develop relationships with their mentor'. Further protocols for mentees drawn from this document are given in Figure 14.5.

Being observed in the classroom

Teachers in lifelong learning can expect to be observed teaching by colleagues on both a formal and informal basis. As well as having a place in quality assurance processes, classroom observation can help teachers to develop as professionals, and will often be a significant part of a mentoring relationship – either when the mentor observes and gives feedback to the mentee, or when the mentee observes their mentor. Observation can have a profound impact on organizational culture and may lead to a more open climate, greater trust between colleagues and the development of strong

Protocols for mentees
Mentoring may be defined as a means of developing individuals to their potential. Mentoring can be used in different ways at different stages in an individual's career. Whatever the reason for using a mentor, as the mentee, you should possess the following:

- Commitment to your own development
- Honesty and openness about your own behaviour
- A positive approach to the value of feedback
- Time and willingness to develop a relationship with your mentor
- Willingness to listen and clarify your understanding
- Willingness to learn about the organization and about possible new ways of working
- The ability to accept the support and encouragement offered by the mentor and to consider advice in the spirit it is offered
- Willingness to challenge your own assumptions
- Willingness to consider options suggested by the mentor which you had not previously considered
- Willingness to review and reflect on your own behaviour and performance
- The wish to take responsibility for your own personal development
- Acknowledgement to share in the decision-making process to ensure the maximum outcomes from the mentor relationships.

Figure 14.5 Protocols for mentees
Source: LSC (2001: 155)

professional relationships (Marriott 2001). However, some teachers may feel threatened by observation of their practice, and may view the process with apprehension. This section considers a number of contexts in which teaching observations take place, highlighting their positive aspects while acknowledging that the experience of being observed may not be unproblematic.

Observation in initial teacher education

Teaching observations have always been an important part of ITE and are an essential element of the professional development of teachers. Observations contribute to the assessment process in ITE and provide trainees with feedback on their progress and development. In order to achieve a teaching qualification, the trainee will be required to demonstrate that they have achieved an appropriate standard based on a series of observations during the course. Where possible, trainees should themselves observe other teachers in order to learn from their practice; this will also help to broaden the trainee's experience, particularly if the teacher observed works in a different context to the trainee.

Although the nature of observations for ITE is generally developmental and supportive, they contribute to summative as well as formative assessment and decisions have to be made as to whether or not the trainee has reached the standard required. For trainees in lifelong learning, these decisions will be based on the teaching standards discussed in Chapter 2. However, awarding institutions need to align their assessment criteria with current inspection frameworks and it is therefore likely that trainees will be assessed against *how well they achieve the teaching standards*. Certainly these are referred to by Ofsted in their specification of grading criteria for assessing trainees in the course of ITE inspections (Ofsted 2014: 30–1). Because trainees are developing towards qualified teacher status, these criteria differ from those used in inspecting college provision other than ITT.

Conduct of initial teacher education observations

Within the present system of ITE, observations will normally be carried out by either a course tutor or the trainee's mentor. In the case of in-service trainees, practical teaching experience is gained through employment as a teacher and the timing of observations will depend on the trainee's pattern of work. For this reason, in-service observations are normally arranged by negotiation between the trainee and the observer. Pre-service trainees, whose practical teaching is based on a placement in an appropriate organization, may have less control over the scheduling of observations. In particular, pre-service trainees may be teaching classes normally taught by their mentor, who could observe at any time – at least in principle. Nevertheless, pre-service trainees will normally have some say in when they are observed. Although it may be tempting for a trainee to 'steer' observers towards lessons in which they are confident, it can be more beneficial to be observed in a more challenging situation which gives greater scope for developmental feedback (Cosh 1999).

Observers need to be able to make sense of the learning session and the trainee should provide them with copies of planning documents (lesson plan and scheme of work) as well as learning resources and assessment materials relating to the lesson. Some courses require trainees to provide a written rationale for the lesson. This would include information such as the background and context for the session, a brief profile of the learners in the group, known learning support needs, an outline of the overall approach (including strategies for assessment and differentiation) and any specific areas on which the trainee might wish to have feedback.

The observer may stay for the whole or part of a session. In either case it is important that the trainee receives both verbal and written feedback following the observation; verbal feedback provides the opportunity for dialogue and clarification, while written feedback provides a more detailed and permanent record for the person observed. In many ways, the process and content of feedback will relate to the principles of mentoring discussed above, although of course the feedback on an observation can be highly specific and deal with immediate practical issues while they are still fresh in the mind. However, observers need to go beyond procedural details, encouraging the trainee to reflect upon the issues arising and identify some specific areas for further development. It is possible that having received their feedback, the trainee or teacher who was observed will not agree with the comments and judgements of the observer. Nevertheless, the feedback can still provide a catalyst for further reflection on the issues raised.

Peer observations

Peer observations take place between colleagues, either as an informal means of developing their own practice or as a formal part of quality assurance systems. Mentoring relationships will normally involve an element of peer observation, possibly including reciprocal observations between mentor and mentee. Peer observation may be useful to individuals or groups of colleagues who are keen to explore and experiment with new ideas or problematic areas of practice. A fresh viewpoint in a supportive environment may stimulate insight, discussion and collaboration among colleagues. However, if feedback is overwhelmingly confirmatory it may become merely an exercise in mutual congratulation (Cosh 1999). As with mentoring relationships, an appropriate balance of challenge and support is necessary if peer observation is to be effective as a developmental tool.

Peer observation may be used for the purpose of appraisal, and this can sometimes be detrimental to teacher confidence and to a supportive teaching environment (Cosh 1999). As noted earlier, many authors regard an 'off-line' relationship (Megginson and Clutterbuck 1999: 3) as the most productive in building a mentoring climate based on mutual trust. Similar considerations suggest that peer observations may work best when they are outside a line-management relationship or quality assurance system.

The focus of peer observations may be chosen by the observer or the person observed. In the first model, standard pro formas provide a framework to direct the observation towards certain predetermined issues. This may be helpful to inexperienced observers and may serve institutional agendas, but can be restrictive. By contrast, an observed-led model allows the person being observed to set the agenda and to highlight, prior to the observation, certain key issues on which they would like the observer to give feedback. A strongly developmental focus is therefore possible, although considerable experience may be needed if the required balance of challenge and support is to be achieved.

Conclusion

It should be clear from this chapter that the quality of relationships is crucial to the effectiveness of both coaching and mentoring. Achieving the right balance of support and challenge, and accepting that both parties can learn from the process, will allow these activities to be constructive experiences in professional development. Teaching and learning are becoming much more open and collaborative, with a broader range of people being welcomed into classrooms and professional discussions. Mentoring and coaching have the potential to be valuable elements in creating and maintaining the new communities of practice arising from this process.

PART 3

Working in the lifelong learning sector

15

Getting to know the organization

James Avis, Julie Dalton, Liz Dixon, Ann Jennings, Kevin Orr and Jonathan Tummons

In this chapter

- Your first visit
- Structures and hierarchies
- Informal networks
- Managerialism and performativity
- The staffroom

This chapter has two interrelated tasks. The first is to provide advice to pre-service trainees preparing for a college placement. To reflect this, some sections are written in the second person, addressed to 'you' (as the trainee). Second, the chapter aims to provide a framework for understanding college relations.

Your first visit

'Be prepared for anything' is useful guidance when attending a placement college for the first time. Some colleges may interview you before offering a placement, others will assume you are suitable because you have been selected for your ITE course. In this case you may be introduced to staff and shown where you will be working.

Prepare for the visit as you would for a job interview. Study the college website, which should contain maps, lists of courses and news items. Most give information on policies and procedures, and many offer a virtual tour. The Internet can provide a wealth of information, including Ofsted reports.

If possible, go to the college before the formal visit. How far is it from the bus or train station? If driving, be aware that college car parks are often reserved for staff and 'VIP' visitors. If you visit on a 'normal' college day you will be able to assess the character and ethos of the college.

Many colleges have some form of dress code for staff. Appearance is important, and first impressions count (see Ofsted 2014: 32 in relation to the need for trainees to 'adhere' to 'appropriate professional dress'). It is advisable to dress modestly and smartly. Many organizations do not allow jeans to be worn and consider visible tattoos or body piercing inappropriate. Staff are often regarded as role models for students, with the same expectation applying to trainee teachers. As a guest you should attempt to 'fit in'.

Prepare documentation for the visit so that you can easily find what you need. The staff you are meeting may have seen your CV, but do not assume this. Have your contact details and times of placement ready to give to staff you will be working with. It is advisable to take several copies as you may be working in more than one section. Take your ITE course enrolment card with you as proof of identity, as well as any course documents needed by college staff. Some college Human Resource departments may request evidence of your Disclosure and Barring Service (DBS) check. Be equipped to take notes. As in a job interview, be prepared to 'sell' yourself. Other trainees may be seeking placements at the college so you may have competition.

Be early rather than late, but not too early. Busy college staff may not appreciate someone arriving half an hour early. Report to reception unless you have been told otherwise and be ready to explain clearly who you are, why you are there and who you are meeting. Turn off your mobile telephone. You will probably be asked to complete the visitors' book, giving your name and the name of the person you are to see, the name of your university or college, and time of arrival. You may be given a visitor identity badge. You will probably be asked to wait for the member of staff to collect you. If waiting in the reception area, take the opportunity to browse the college leaflets and information sheets often situated there.

If nervous take a few deep breaths. Look cheerful, smile, appear enthusiastic and confident. You have something to offer the college. As you are led to the staff room or office, note the location: rooms and corridors may be numbered or colour coded. Establish where facilities such as toilets and drinks machines are located.

The rest of the visit very much depends on who you are meeting. It may be someone with cross-college responsibility for teaching placements. Alternatively, it may be your mentor or another member of staff from your vocational/discipline area. Before the visit, consider questions you need to ask; you will probably think of further questions during the visit. Remain polite and courteous. Discuss what is required but do not be over familiar.

You might want to show that you have learned about the college and its courses. You may have read the latest Ofsted report. If this was favourable, you might comment; if not, it may be better not to. Note how people address one another. It is usual nowadays for first names to be used, but in some colleges and vocational areas more formal terms of address may be used. Remain professional and discreet at all times.

Structures and hierarchies

The organizational structures of a college or other provider are often prominent. The organizational charts indicate lines of responsibility and communication between different areas, departments or directorates. The procedures and paperwork that accompany the work of the teacher are grounded in the structures and hierarchies of the organization. Evaluation reports, line management meetings, appraisals and other procedures follow the formal structures of the organization.

Informal networks

As a new member of staff or trainee on placement, spend time getting to know the organization. As well as formal procedures, it is also important to develop a realistic awareness of timescales and possible delays in these systems so that you can plan work in good time. For example, printing services may have a heavy workload and large-volume photocopying may not be possible on a same-day basis. Circumventing such procedures, which is often possible in large organizations, may help in the short term but will not make you popular with colleagues or the college hierarchy.

Whatever the ethics, staff will often find ways to do what is expected but these do not necessarily coincide with formal organizational practices and procedures. Such *inventive resourcefulness* is a characteristic of any community of practice and is part of the *shared repertoire* (Tummons 2008).

As a way of understanding the FE workplace inventive resourcefulness can be seen as an aspect of work-based learning. From this point of view, there is no theoretical distinction between learning how to complete a requisition form correctly and learning how to acquire the requisitioned article by other means. Both are part of the workplace, but only one is officially sanctioned by established policies and procedures.

Becoming part of informal networks is not straightforward. They will look and behave differently across different colleges, and even within the same college will vary between different staffrooms and departments. A workplace mentor can serve as a useful conduit on such occasions. Taking time to make introductions and ask questions can also be helpful. Generally, it is through participation, trial and error and experience that inventive resourcefulness is learned and developed. Informal networks of practice, participation and activity are ways to learn about the organization.

Managerialism and performativity

Prior to the Further and Higher Education Act of 1992 FE colleges were controlled by local authorities. However, in the years immediately following incorporation, more strident forms of managerialism developed (Randle and Brady 1997). These were frequently set within a form of bullying masculinity (Kerfoot and Whitehead 1998). During this period there were significant numbers of redundancies, with many early retirements.

Partly as a reaction to the rigours of incorporation and with the retirement of many male senior staff, the climate of management has moderated and a less 'masculine' culture exists. There has been an increase in the number of women principals. However, despite these changes colleges remain set within a performative context. That is to say, a context in which activity is focused upon measurable outcomes with an emphasis upon meeting targets. Targets may relate to year-on-year improvement in student performance, scores in satisfaction surveys, efficiency gains, and so on. Targets for individual teachers and the degree to which previous targets have been met may be discussed in appraisals.

There is a real question about the way in which we conceptualize waged labour within FE. The move towards managerialism undermined previous forms of control, breaking away from the rhetoric of professionalism and collegiality. It also accented the division between managers and teachers as well as highlighting potential antagonisms surrounding professional autonomy and the intensification of labour. Not everyone would accept this analysis. Some writers argue that FE teachers occupy contradictory positions involving both teaching and elements of managerial responsibility (Simkins and Lumby 2002). Others suggest that there is a possibility of progressive alliances that cross over hierarchical divisions. Gleeson and Shain (1999) described the different orientations held by those working in the sector, including unwilling, willing and strategic compliance. Unwilling compliers are those most likely to take redundancy or early retirement, willing compliers accept managerialism, whereas strategic compliers adopt a pragmatic stance. For Gleeson and Shain, these orientations are not tied to particular institutional positions and could just as easily be inhabited by senior management. Strategic compliers seek to wrest progressive possibilities from the conditions in which they find themselves. The difficulty with this particular orientation is that such a stance could easily be appropriated by a particular form of managerialism, becoming a veneer for managerial control.

Edwards (1980) outlined various ways through which managerial control is enacted. These range from the patriarchal to those based upon what we now call managerialism. Forms of management that celebrate the creativity and contribution of the labour force may be as much about control as the more authoritarian types. The strategy developed by management will be in part shaped by the institutional context as well as power relations. Neither should we forget the impact of the orientation of a particular principal, who may wish to accent a specific aspect of management. For while performativity and target setting are currently ubiquitous, the way in which they are accented varies, with some institutions seeking to mitigate their effects while others seemingly relish the rigours involved. Finally, we should remember that different managerial regimes may well co-exist within a particular college, whereby particular sections or departments mediate approaches in ways that afford staff more or less autonomy.

The staffroom

Although teachers spend a great deal of time in classrooms, the staffroom is important in their professional lives. The staffroom is typically where teachers have a physical base and spend varying amounts of time during their working day, engaged in a range of activities both social and work related. The staffroom is arguably a taken-for-granted space, and as such, perhaps mistakenly, is afforded little significance when trainees are prepared for their teaching practice or when considering trainees' learning on placement.

The highly distinctive nature of individual staffrooms make general observations difficult. Each staffroom is likely to have its particular culture; the complexity of these cultures may be influenced by such factors as the personalities who populate the space, the curriculum areas or shared specialisms of the staff, and its physical size, layout and decorative style. Biott and Easen (1994: 71) note the significance of context and suggest that teachers work in interwoven social structures created partly by themselves, partly by management, and by organizational arrangements and processes. The staffroom may be defined by its own characteristics, explicit and implicit rules and boundaries, and could be said to represent a microcosm of social and professional life. It may offer clues as to the history, culture and practices of the institution as a whole and may also reflect social and political concerns of the time.

A staffroom is both a private and public space and the balance and interplay of these may indicate the culture and values associated with it. On approaching a staffroom it is interesting to note the detail of access and what this signifies about the staffroom itself and the institution as a whole. Is there open access to the room? Do individuals knock on entering? What clues do signs give – 'Staff Only', 'Please knock before entering'? Are students and visitors welcomed into the staffroom space? The culture and values of any particular staffroom may be highly idiosyncratic and may mirror or diametrically oppose the culture and values of the institution as a whole.

Allocation of space and working areas may be clearly defined and territorial, where each member of staff has a demarcated space that may double as a place of work and recreation. Personalized spaces may speak volumes about those who occupy the area. On the other hand the space may be much less clearly defined with shared areas designated for 'hot-desking'. This is arguably a telling reflection of working practices in a sector whose responses are typically short term, rapid and reactive and where the emphasis lies on product as opposed to process. It may also reflect the transient, temporary and unstable nature of employment for many staff on short-term or part-time hourly paid contracts.

We might also consider the nature of the conversations and exchanges which take place in staffrooms. What proportion of time is devoted to conversations about teaching and learning? This may be highly significant for a trainee teacher who may be expecting and looking for opportunities to speak with their mentor and colleagues about teaching, learning and wider educational issues.

It is interesting to reflect on the individual and shared characteristics and culture of the teachers who populate the staffroom. Is it a noticeably gendered space, and if so, what are its defining characteristics? Is there a higher proportion of male or female staff? Is this linked in any way to the curriculum area? Is it an orderly, tidy space or is it chaotic? Is the staffroom personalized by artefacts such as photographs, notices or personal belongings or is it a neutral place devoid of any defining characteristic? Within any institution, a staffroom is likely to be populated by different groups and individuals who may be constituted according to shared curriculum areas or subject disciplines. They may include teachers and support staff employed under different types of contracts and with different conditions of service. Indeed, a trainee teacher may find difficulty in distinguishing the myriad individuals using the staffroom. Yeomans (1986) noted that teachers' interactions were frequent, if sometimes fleeting, and that their personal and professional concerns were rarely kept separate, claiming also that flat hierarchies meant that those with leadership and management roles were (at that time) not easily distinguished.

Does this staffroom culture suggest a place where, irrespective of numbers, layout or proximity, teachers operate in isolation or is there an indication of working together with notions of collegiality? What is the impact of that culture on the trainee teacher who may be a newcomer or is in the process of 'becoming' a teacher? The staffroom may be a place where new and developing teachers seek to access guidance and support from experienced staff and colleagues. However, 'Individuals or cohorts of individuals will experience different kinds of affordances, depending on their affiliation, associations, gender, language skills, employment status and standing in the workplace' (Billett 2004: 116). These differentiations may be apparent within the confines of the staffroom and may help to explain the extent to which individuals or groups are included or choose to involve themselves in workplace activities. While some trainee teachers may have only limited formal contact with permanent staff in a staffroom, it is likely that they will be influenced by them and learn from them in an informal, *ad hoc* manner. This is likely to be brought into sharp focus in the staffroom environment where teachers learn and respond to the implicit and explicit values, practices and hierarchies which pertain to that place. Other aspects of identity such as gender, race, age and sexual orientation may also play a part in determining how individuals are perceived by others and feel themselves to 'fit in'. Each staffroom will contain a unique culture characterized by the teachers who inhabit that space. For any trainee or new teacher, the staffroom can be a rich source of reflection and is likely to offer insights into the wider aspect of a teacher's life beyond the confines of the classroom.

16

Health, safety and well-being

Julie Dalton, Roy Fisher and David Neve

In this chapter

- Risk
- Legal responsibilities
- Health and safety in the workplace
- Who is responsible for risk assessments?
- Bullying and harassment
- The Disclosure and Barring Service
- Security
- From *Every Child Matters* to *Help Children Achieve More*

Risk

According to Ulrich Beck (1992), processes of modernization have generated unprecedented levels of risk. These arise from new technologies, increased mobility, the environmental consequences of economic activity and other features of globalization. Educational establishments can be seen as places brimming with the potential for harm – both physical and psychological. Furedi (1997) critiques what he sees as a disabling tendency for Western society to become absorbed by concerns for safety and the anticipation of threat; this climate can stifle thinking, limit creativity and bind people in bureaucracy. Ecclestone and Hayes (2009) argue that there is a damaging tendency for teachers to regard students as vulnerable. Concerns with issues such as stress, bullying and harassment have led to a plethora of policies and committees that can feed (and feed on) a discourse of caution, perpetuating 'victimhood'. Places of learning, like other workplaces, do harbour dangers – especially in vocational training areas. There *are* responsibilities, and these need to be taken seriously.

Legal responsibilities

We will not provide an exposition on the law in relation to teaching in the LLS, not least because information and case law are subject to rapid change. JISC (2003: 1) provides guidance on terminology, explaining that:

Duty of care is the obligation to exercise a level of care towards an individual, as is reasonable in all the circumstances, to avoid injury to that individual or his or her property.

Duty of care is therefore based upon the relationship of the parties, the negligent act or omission and the reasonable foreseeability of loss to that individual.

A negligent act is an unintentional but careless act which results in loss. Only a negligent act will be regarded as having breached a duty of care. Liability for breach of a duty of care very much depends on the public policy at the time the case is heard.

In the FE and HE system duties of care will govern relations with a wide variety of groups including, but not limited to, employees, students and even visitors.

Any individual facing a work-related legal issue should seek current legal advice (normally available via trade unions for members).

Health and safety in the workplace

Employers have legal duties relating to workplace safety, the operation of day-to-day activities, and the way that equipment or substances are handled and stored. Under the terms of the Health and Safety at Work Act 1974 employees also have responsibilities, reflecting the fact that good safety practice stems from working collaboratively. Within educational institutions governors play an important role in establishing health and safety policy at the institutional level, and the governing body will have the main role in management and responsibility for health and safety, together with the allocation of funds to ensure safe working and that health practices are compliant.

The Health and Safety Executive (HSE) enforces health and safety law. The HSE has legal powers backed up by the criminal courts, and through its inspectors can issue improvement notices or prohibition orders. It is worth emphasizing that any breaches of Health and Safety law under the 1974 Act are likely to result in a criminal offence being committed and action being taken. Employers and employees are often subject to legal action in this form.

The HSE education website (http://www.hse.gov.uk/services/education/index. htm) is a useful source of guidance. Employer responsibilities include:

- provide all necessary information, instruction, training and supervision to enable individuals to be safe
- provide and maintain a safe place of work with safe entry and exit
- provide and maintain a working environment that is safe and without risk to health
- provide and maintain systems of work that are safe
- arrange for the safe use, handling, storage and transport of articles and substances
- assess risks in the workplace.

Employees' duties are as follows:

- to take reasonable care of the health and safety of themselves and of others who may be affected by what they do or forget to do
- to cooperate with the employer on health and safety matters
- not to misuse any equipment that is provided for safety purposes (for example, fire extinguishers or safety goggles)
- to follow instructions from the employer on health and safety matters and attend relevant health and safety training
- to report hazards and defects observed in the workplace.

HSE (2011a) provides a useful downloadable health and safety for classrooms check-list. The HSE also hosts safety and health forums for FE and HE.

Employees should refer to the health and safety policy which employers are legally required to provide. Further information on the responsibilities of employers is avail-able on the UCU website. For advice and guidance related to vocational areas it would be wise to check the appropriate Sector Skills Councils.

Risk assessment

> Some of the 'elfandsafety' stories are just myths . . . But our research shows that behind many of the stories, there is at least a grain of truth . . . Of course the untold story is that many organizations manage risks sensibly, responsibly and proportionately.
>
>   Bill Callaghan, Chair of the Health and Safety Commission (HSE 2006a)

An effective risk assessment is key in the management of risks. The National Union of Teachers (NUT 2003: 1) published guidance defining risk assessment as

> an important tool in ensuring health and safety at work. It means, simply, that employers set out to identify hazards to health and safety, evaluate the risk of harm resulting from those hazards and take appropriate action to protect employees and others.

In the LLS, teachers in areas such as hairdressing or construction will have experi-ence of industry-based risk assessment. As teachers or trainers, health and safety will be a central part of course content as well as classroom practice. In some NVQs this will entail assessing trainees in safe working practices and risk assessment. More generally, in any educational setting risks posed by the environment must be consid-ered, together with any specific risks presented by learning activities. Practical work-shops are potentially hazardous. Computer workshops and field trips or study visits also present varying degrees of risk. Teachers must undertake appropriate risk assessment.

Some likely risk assessment categories are summarized here:

- *General risks*: (management of the Health and Safety at Work Regulations)
- *Exposure to substances which may cause damage to health*: (Control of Asbestos at Work Regulations; Control of Lead at Work Regulations)
- *Computers and workstations*: (Health and Safety [Display Screen Equipment] Regulations)
- *Hazardous lifting or carrying*: (Manual Handling Operations Regulations)
- *Noisy environments which could cause damage to hearing*: (Control of Noise at Work Regulations)
- *Fire Safety*: (Regulatory Reform [Fire Safety] Order)

Teachers need to carry out risk assessments regularly in relation to their working areas. Risk assessments do the following:

- provide an assessment and evaluation of risks which might occur as a result of training and educational activities and document corrective and or preventative action;
- demonstrate performance standards for the control of risks;
- help organizations reduce risks to the lowest level, providing a safe system of work;
- enable trainers and teachers to model what trainees will need to do in the workplace.

Who is responsible for risk assessments?

The employer has legal responsibility for risk assessment. In the LLS this will normally mean the governing body of the organization. The NUT recognize that in practice the risk assessment process will need to be delegated to someone who manages the process, and someone who carries out risk assessments. The extent to which teachers should be involved in risk assessment will depend on two things: first, their conditions of service, professional duties and any management responsibility which they have for health and safety matters; and, second, whether they are competent to take part in the process on the employer's behalf.

Risk assessments can be (and often are) completed on a single page and need not be complicated. HSE (2011a: 2) advocate a five stage plan.

1 Identify the hazards.
2 Decide who might be harmed and how.
3 Evaluate the risks and decide on precaution.
4 Record your findings and implement them.
5 Review your assessment and update if necessary.

HSE (2011b) provides a health and safety checklist for classrooms.

Bullying and harassment

There are a number of broad categories of bullying and harassment that may concern teachers. These can be summarized as:

- learner to learner
- teacher to learner
- learner to teacher
- management to employee.

Websites may prove useful in exploring aspects of bullying and harassment and, in particular, in the context of online communications including social networking media. Bullying Matters (2009) refers to bullying in the workplace as follows:

> Workplace bullying makes people's working lives a misery and can have devastating effects on an individual's health, family and career . . . Bullying impacts on staff turnover, health, morale, production and performance and can result in costly lawsuits as well as damaged reputation and public confidence.

Harassment may refer to a spectrum of offensive actions and behaviours that are experienced as threatening or disturbing, and beyond those sanctioned by society. Sexual harassment refers to persistent and unwanted sexual advances. In general terms, harassment involves behaviour that is unwanted, unwarranted and likely to cause detriment and stress. It can take the form of physical, verbal and emotional abuse, gestures and the written word. Cyber forms of harassment and bullying are now common through email, text messages and web-based social networking.

In effectively managed working environments there should be written policies on harassment and bullying – and allegations should be documented. There should be a programme of staff development related to the policies and procedures. For further information see the following relevant websites:

- **ACAS** at http://www.acas.org.uk
- **Government advice** at http://www.education.gov.uk
- **TUC** at http://www.tuc.org.uk

Trade unions normally provide guidance and representation for their members.

The Disclosure and Barring Service

The Disclosure and Barring Service (DBS) was established in 2012 to carry out functions of the former Independent Safeguarding Authority (ISA) and Criminal Records Bureau (CRB). The DBS assists employers to 'make safer recruitment decisions and prevent unsuitable people from working with vulnerable groups, including children, through its criminal record checking and barring functions' (DBS 2013). The barring service provides caseworkers who consider referrals about those who have harmed or pose a risk to children or vulnerable persons. They decide whether they should be placed on the children's or adult's barred lists. The checking side of DBS enables employers to 'access the criminal record history of people working, or seeking to work in certain positions, especially those that involve working with children or adults in specific situations' (DBS 2013). Employers of teachers and trainers, and those recruiting to teacher training courses, must take care to ensure that inappropriate persons are not able to work with vulnerable groups.

Security

Theft

The theft of personal items and institutional equipment is commonplace, with institutions combating this by issuing identity cards to staff and learners, and by installing security systems and CCTV. The opportunity to steal valuable items has increased with the use of mobile phones, tablet pcs and laptops. Simple steps can be taken to avoid thefts. Valuable items should not be left in an unlocked teaching area or office. Items should be security marked or locked down wherever possible, and should not be displayed unnecessarily.

Computer security and online safety

Harmful programs spread between unprotected computers, especially when connected through networks. In the best practice users will have up-to-date anti-virus software. Because the risks are high most educational institutions will provide specialist advice and guidance to users. Policies on the use of computer facilities should be read carefully, as there will normally be restrictions on what can be accessed and these restrictions may affect teaching activities.

Many learners and teachers do not take sensible precautions in relation to the security of computer files. It is wise to ensure that files stored on computer hard drives are 'backed up' at regular intervals by writing them to CD, DVD or similar secondary storage systems. Some social software provides users with a free account and storage space for files. These files can be made public, for sharing across a community, or locked for personal use. The servers used for these services are themselves backed up, duplicated or triplicated, and therefore a secure environment is created.

Networks in universities and colleges are often targets for mass emailings and malicious requests. It is important to exercise caution when suspect mail appears. It is not uncommon for hoax email messages to warn of viruses that do not exist. Other hoax messages often spread, and advice should be sought from the institution's computing services staff. Personal computers are best protected with an anti-virus package, which will automatically update itself as new threats appear.

Besides technical security there are crucial issues concerning online (or cyber) safety and young people (see Chapter 10). These relate to the responsible use of social networking sites and of the internet more widely. Issues include the avoidance of threatening behaviours, bullying and harassment as well as abusive, racist, sexist, pornographic or other offensive content and images. It is important that young people are made aware of the need for strong passwords; that they should not disclose private information over the internet; that they should check their security settings; and that they should not post inappropriate or illegal content. The UK Council for Child Internet Safety (UKCCIS) works to keep children and young people safe online. (UKCCIS sponsors research and publishes advice at http://www.education.gov.uk/ukccis.)

From *Every Child Matters* to *Help Children Achieve More*

Staying safe, being healthy and making a positive contribution are part of The Children's Act 2004 and are outcomes inspected by Ofsted. In 2003 New Labour's *Every Child Matters* (ECM) (DfES 2003c: 13) had outlined a new approach to the well-being of children and young people up to the age of 19, identifying the need 'to ensure we properly protect children at risk of neglect and harm within a framework of universal services which aims to prevent negative outcomes and support every child to develop their full potential'.

The focus of ECM was on enabling young people to meet five key outcomes:

- *being healthy*: enjoying good physical and mental health and living a healthy lifestyle

- *staying safe*: being protected from harm and neglect and growing up able to look after themselves

- *enjoying and achieving*: getting the most out of life and developing broad skills for adulthood

- *making a positive contribution*: to the community and to society and not engaging in anti-social or offending behaviour

- *economic well-being*: overcoming socio-economic disadvantages to achieve their full potential in life.

(DfES 2003c: 7)

The Education Act 2002 required local authorities and the governing bodies of schools and FE institutions to 'carry out their functions with a view to safeguarding and promoting the welfare of children' (HM Government 2003: 76). This came into force on 1 April 2004.

It was thought that the aims of ECM were unlikely to meet with criticism from any reasonable source but the initiative and policy were critiqued. Hoyle (2008: 10) argued that:

Central to the *Every Child Matters* way of thinking is a re-enforcement and perpetuation of a focus on visible 'symptoms' in the lives of children, young people and families. A shallow focus obviates any critical dialogue about the structural inequalities in contemporary England from which such 'symptoms' can emerge.

Hoyle further criticized the way in which ECM invaded children's rights to privacy, and what he regarded as a tendency to 'centralization of credit: diffusion of blame' that he saw as inherent within ECM. Following the formation of the Coalition Government in 2010 it quickly became evident that ECM was to be less prominent and some of its proponents feared that it would be 'ditched'.

The Green Paper *Youth Matters* (HM Government 2005) constituted a development of ECM with a view to improving the services supporting young people through enhanced coordination and use of technology. It would seek to engage young people through various initiatives including volunteering. The New Labour Government proposed a targeted programme of reform for youth services (DCSF 2007). Targeted youth support aimed to help vulnerable young people achieve the ECM outcomes. The most important goal for post-compulsory providers was to 'raise young people's aspirations and help them to achieve and feel positive towards learning. This included helping them to be engaged and stay engaged in the wider range of learning opportunities becoming available for 14–19-year-olds' (p. 6). The Green Paper *Raising Expectations: Staying in Education and Training Post-16* (DfES 2007) recognized that 'vulnerable' and 'low achieving' young people were those most likely to leave education at the age of 16. Consequently, it was proposed that young people should be required to remain in education or training until the age of 18 (Simmons 2008).

Issues of 'well-being' emerged as an important element in New Labour social policy. Indeed, there was a convergence of initiatives that, with a focus on multi-agency working, saw aspects of the education, social welfare and health systems intersect. Educational institutions came to constitute a critical site where connections between health and education for young people were expected to mirror government imperatives for 'joined up' thinking. A greater emphasis on social inclusion has meant that young people with special educational needs (SEN) and/or behavioural, emotional or social difficulties (BESD) are likely to be educated in 'mainstream' institutions within the LLS. A growing number of young people have been identified as suffering from mental health and psychological problems. Greater student diversity demands much of teachers, who must adopt differentiated strategies. Teachers are expected to promote learning environments conducive to well-being. At the same time, however, they face unprecedented pressures to raise educational standards. These apparently contradictory drives may be incompatible. Pressures to raise standards are not always reconcilable with the type of 'caring' relationship that promotes well-being.

The policy thrust that came with New Labour may be seen as a positive development which was indicative of a concern to alleviate disadvantage and to facilitate equality of opportunity. Alternatively, it can be regarded as an attempt to mask inherent inequalities through initiatives that, while ostensibly enabling, placed responsibility on individuals to comply with economic imperatives that were unlikely to serve their best interests.

Barker (2011) has outlined the Coalition Government's seemingly uneasy relationship with the ECM initiative. Since 2010 there has been a change in terminology which signalled a process of moving away from ECM. ECM and the five outcomes would now be known as 'Help Children Achieve More'. This signalled a shift from well-being to a focus on 'achievement'. There were also moves to reform 'safeguarding' (renamed as 'child protection'). The Government commissioned Eileen Munro to review child protection in England (Munro 2011). The thrust of Munro's report was to recommend an emphasis on local freedom in decision making. Professionals would be given more 'trust' and there would be better training for social workers, with improved coordination between services. Ofsted would focus more on the experiences of service users.

The early years of the Coalition Government saw the rhetoric of the 'Big Society' combine with a determination to reduce expenditure in a time of economic austerity. It seems, however, that the fundamental rationale behind ECM, that is the recognition that achievement is contingent on well-being, is too much of a self-evident truth to be swept away.

17

Course management and administration
Frances Marsden and Andrew Youde

In this chapter

- Maintaining records
- Managing a course
- Marketing
- Working with administrative staff
- Awarding bodies
- Committee membership
- Conclusion

Some years ago Jackson and Wallis (2006: 251) stated that:

> Post-compulsory education is living through an extended period of unprece-
> dented upheaval and change in a climate of increased public accountability. A
> culture of target setting, action planning and monitoring underpins the allocation
> of public funding . . .

This has not changed. Effective procedures assist the maintenance of accurate course
records and student information systems, enhance quality assurance processes, and
serve the requirements of external funding or inspection bodies. Teachers and administrators have an important inter-professional relationship and academics normally
carry course management responsibilities with an administrative component.

Maintaining records

The priority for a teacher will be their pedagogic work. ITE courses normally incorporate reference to the wider responsibilities of curriculum development and evaluation,
though frequently the administrative role of a teacher is first addressed in the workplace. While the maintenance of records may be experienced as a bureaucratic imposition there is a link between effective administration and a positive learning experience.

Registers of attendance are key records, and it is important that they are accurate
for audit purposes. Each institution will have its attendance monitoring system, often
utilizing electronic ('swipe card') systems with the data automatically downloading to

the Management Information System (MIS). Under UK Border Agency regulations (UKBA 2012) for international students educational organizations must be able to prove that they have weekly contact.

While summative achievement is usually monitored centrally, formative assessment records are normally maintained by individual teachers. It is the responsibility of all teachers to prepare teaching materials, teach students, assess work and monitor student progress. Each of these activities must be evidenced.

Government funded FE is inspected primarily by Ofsted, as are ITT courses, with the QAA reviewing most HE. Following a survey of colleges leading to its report *How Colleges Improve* Ofsted (2012c: 5) stated that

> Good management information was clear, accurate, authentic, available and timely. The improving and high-performing colleges used such information effectively to challenge, motivate and make changes. It gave these colleges confidence, self-belief and knowledge about themselves and their learners, and it was the basis for robust and accurate self-assessment.

Strengths and weaknesses are identified through the self-assessment process utilizing relevant quantitative data and rigorous qualitative analysis.

Managing a course

A course leader's role involves management of the following:

- annual course evaluation
- the curriculum
- the course team.

Annual course evaluation

A course leader is heavily involved in course evaluation. O'Connell (2005: 197) advises that course teams should consider the strengths and weaknesses of the provision, informing the production of an action plan. This process can be rationalized by the use of standard institutional documentation or by the use of forms derived from Ofsted's inspection handbooks or similar. Institutional and national training opportunities will normally keep course teams abreast of changes in inspection frameworks. Advice regarding evaluation grading of the course will often be provided as part of this training, as the allocation of grades frequently forms part of the annual evaluation process which will usually involve a meeting with the senior management team (SMT). This should ideally be a development process where targets are agreed, however, these meetings can be quite judgemental. Many institutions follow Drucker's (1993) 'Management by Objectives' philosophy, and targets will usually be agreed around the following areas:

- attendance
- retention

- progression
- achievement
- measures of value added.

Information from the course annual evaluation process will normally inform an institutional self-evaluation report that will be subsequently reviewed by external inspectors.

Of increasing importance to course leaders is obtaining, evaluating and implementing changes in response to student feedback. As students are increasingly seen as 'customers' they sometimes adopt a consumer mentality in relation to what they may regard as a service they have purchased. Systems should provide a 'voice' for students – theirs is an important means of improving provision. Common methods of obtaining student feedback are through questionnaires, focus groups and staff/student liaison panels, however, informal discussions provide more immediate feedback. A transparent and collegial process for responding to formal feedback is essential. Ofsted (2012b: 4) stated that, 'The overall aim of inspection is to evaluate how efficiently and effectively the education and training provision meets learners' needs.'; how student feedback systems inform self-evaluation documents will inform their judgments.

Curriculum management

Careful management of the curriculum and a team approach to the planning, preparation and delivery of teaching is important. Course leaders should encourage a culture of openness and sharing. Each lecturer will produce schemes of work, lesson plans and resources and these can be stored electronically on shared networks for others to adapt and use. If this planning and preparation is divided equitably, a whole team ethos can be encouraged and duplication saved. O'Connell (2005) outlined the benefits of teamwork in the success of a college, with the sharing of resources and the acknowledgment of good practice being integral; he recommends that ground rules should be established for team behaviour.

Planning of timetables and the allocation of teaching rooms and office accommodation for staff should be equitable. The course leader may find they have to negotiate with senior managers and other course leaders for appropriate rooms.

A department may work with a specific awarding body, with resources tailored to meet their requirements, however, the responsibility to select the most appropriate body and possible optional modules may rest with the course leader. This decision should be made in consultation with the team and the institution's examination officer, who will probably have developed a relationship with each awarding body. An important aspect of a course leader's role is the accurate collation of examination entries, and it is necessary to work closely with the course team to ensure that students are entered correctly. Errors in the process can be expensive for the institution, with late entry fees incurred and stress and uncertainty for students and staff. The examination entry process will normally be driven by the examination officer.

Managing teaching staff

Institutions are seeking to use teaching staff more flexibly. A course leader could adapt human resource management (HRM) practice by undertaking a form of job analysis and matching this to the qualities of the course team to allocate teaching responsibilities (Stredwick 2005). It is unlikely that a course leader will feel they have enough time to fully manage staff and the curriculum. The professionalism of the teaching staff in undertaking their individual responsibilities is crucial, and this is fostered by an open culture where help can be requested. Troman (2003) argued that educational relationships cannot be maintained without a strong bond of trust. Regular course team meetings, appropriately conducted and recorded, will facilitate efficient management while encouraging a team culture.

Chairing meetings requires care to ensure that the agenda is followed, the debate is focused, and participants feel they can contribute. It is not unusual for senior managers to attend course team meetings. This can be intimidating for a new course leader, however, it provides an opportunity to draw on the management expertise and to demonstrate competent running of a course. An administrative colleague may take minutes at team meetings, though in some cases course leaders are expected to minute and disseminate the proceedings.

Course management is complex work as teams increasingly have to integrate full-time, part-time and temporary supply staff. This teamwork is facilitated by developing a system of centrally stored key documents such as teaching resources, schemes of work and lesson plans to enable sharing.

Besides the day-to-day course management outlined above, institutions require formal systems of teacher accountability for quality monitoring and the course leader will be integral to these processes. Appraisals, observations of teaching, peer review of teaching and student feedback mechanisms are methods of ensuring accountability and enabling professional development. Most institutions will have these performance management systems embedded within their quality assurance and enhancement procedures.

Performance management systems and appraisals are an important aspect of educational HRM. Bush and Middlewood (2005: 176) state that performance management systems 'are based on a rational model of goal-setting and reviewing, and have the aim of connecting organisational and individual planning' and, depending on the culture of the organization, these may be carried out in a judgemental or developmental manner. A course leader needs to allocate sufficient time to carry out individual appraisals sensitively within a suitable and private environment. There should be negotiation regarding the time and place.

Like appraisals, teaching observations can be carried out in a developmental or judgemental manner and the process can be stressful. While there will be an institutional system of teacher observations, a course leader should, in line with institutional policies, provide opportunities for peer observation of teaching to support and encourage innovative practice. This can help to alleviate the stress of the formal observation process. The introduction of some team teaching facilitates creativity within a safe and supportive environment, allowing natural mentoring, and it also provides continuity should absences occur.

Marketing

Due to the range of choices available, marketing activities have increased in importance. The growing amount of information within the public domain, such as inspection reports, league tables, and key information sets (KIS) for HE necessitates the consistent promotion of a corporate brand. Competition within the sector with the aim of efficiency gains ensures that marketing will continue to be an important aspect of corporate strategy.

Traditionally, 'above the line' (media based advertising) methods have been adopted, but more recently there has been an increased prominence of 'below the line' (for example direct mail, public relations activities, customer care) relationship marketing. Social media such as Twitter and Facebook provide effective marketing opportunities. A course will commonly be promoted via the institution's website, prospectus and through leaflets, all of which will be produced by marketing personnel with detail provided by course leaders. This will result in accurate course information being promoted within the vision of the marketing strategy. Further marketing communications will usually take the form of open days, 'taster sessions' and presentations to 'feeder institutions', all of which the course leader will be expected to actively engage with.

Institutional websites are used to market courses with online application processes. Course leaders find that a growing number of enquiries are generated by email, and they must be prepared to respond via the same channels. Email communication provides an easy system of storing potential student contact information for future promotions. A potential applicant's first action when researching an institution will often be to search the website, and a course leader should use this opportunity to promote positive aspects of their department.

A total quality management (TQM) philosophy states that everyone within an institution has an important role to play in its quality and image. Fidler and Atton (1999) endorsed this by stressing the importance of a receptionist as a first point of contact being as crucial to marketing as the role of any lecturer. Both academic and administrative staff must ensure that all external contacts are dealt with in a professional and helpful manner. A potential applicant will search elsewhere if dissatisfied with their first contact.

Internal marketing targets stakeholders within the institution, and in the educational context it is relations with students and with all categories of staff that provide the most obvious opportunities. O'Connell (2005: 142) stresses the importance of the quality of internal marketing. Successful internal marketing will entail the course leader developing provision reinforces to students that they are important and that they will benefit from their course. Interesting educational and social events, a supportive VLE, and being treated with respect are all factors that create satisfied students who become ambassadors for the institution, providing a powerful marketing tool. This notion is at the heart of 'relationship marketing' (Harwood et al. 2008).

Meeting recruitment targets is always important in the LLS, and this is a pressure on course leaders. Effective marketing will go a long way to achieving this. The course leader has an important role in marketing, but the most vital aspect of this is managing a course which has high-achieving and happy students.

Working with administrative staff

Teachers, trainers and lecturers work with a wide variety of administrative professionals who are able to guide and support them. A positive relationship with administrative colleagues can alleviate some of the pressures of teaching.

The prominence of self-governance in the LLS has led to an increased professionalization of administrative roles, which has not always been fully appreciated. O'Connell (2005) felt that where problems in relationships between academic and support staff have occurred this has followed teachers ignoring procedures and placing unrealistic demands on support staff. Bush and Middlewood (2005: 38) recommend that effective work between higher level teaching assistants, (this would apply equally to administrative and technical support staff), and lecturers depends on:

- clarity of roles
- recognition of the different but complementary skills each brings to the partnership
- mutual respect
- agreement about what are the common goals
- the opportunity for good communication.

It is important for a teacher or trainer to understand the value of different administrative roles. Fostering an open dialogue will help build mutually beneficial relationships. To develop respect between academic and support staff O'Connell (2005) recommends that teachers should communicate with support staff in a positive manner to encourage improved service; and he recognizes that this is a two-way responsibility.

Many organizations now have a 'business manager' (Bush and Middlewood 2005), who heads a department of support staff including those working in finance (bursars), management information systems, marketing, HRM and student support. To illustrate the increasing professionalization of support staff roles, Donovan (2005) outlines the changing roles of examinations officers, which include the development of their own professional institute and framework for training and development. Degree courses are now available specifically for educational administrators, with many senior administrative managers holding masters level qualifications and above. Institutions have long sought to harmonize the working conditions for all staff (Lumby 2001), with many having adopted a common pay spine.

Awarding bodies

Lecturers in the LLS deliver qualifications from a variety of awarding bodies. Each of these has their own support mechanisms for lecturers.

Of primary importance is for a teacher to gain familiarity with relevant syllabi (or programme and module specifications), and copies of these should be available within academic departments. Syllabi guide the production of schemes of work and lesson plans. Resources are normally freely available to download from the awarding body website. Specimen assessment materials, past examination papers, marking schemes and exemplar student responses are valuable documents together with coursework assessment guidance. Coursework will often come under the scrutiny of an external moderator and it is usual for the course leader to prepare for this event with the teaching team being available to discuss specific issues. All teachers will be involved in preparation for external moderation by ensuring that all coursework is assessed accurately and to deadline, and that a sufficient sample is internally moderated.

Awarding bodies are increasingly proactive in the CPD of teachers, offering training days and conferences. While these events are useful there is often a charge which can quickly consume training budgets and they need to be selected carefully. Feedback from these events should be disseminated. Another opportunity for CPD is undertaking assessment work for an awarding body. Specific training is given for examiners over and above what is offered to teachers, and this can present an opportunity to earn extra money (depending on institutional policies) while enhancing assessment skills.

Committee membership

Committees and working parties allow teachers at all levels to contribute to the decision-making process and take ownership of agreed outcomes (Bush and Middlewood 2005). A new teacher should volunteer to join a group to which they feel their skills will contribute, while those with more experience are likely to be invited to join a wide range of committees during their career. Common examples of committees are:

- equality and diversity
- student welfare and guidance
- teaching and learning
- e-learning
- health and safety
- marketing
- research

Internal committees provide an overview of how the organization operates, together with an understanding of the decision-making process. Working parties are often formed from a committee membership for specific short-term issues with a remit to report back their findings. For example, an e-learning software working party could be formed from the e-learning committee.

Within a committee environment a new academic may feel unable to express their opinion, or may have not fully formed their opinions. New staff should not be afraid to ask questions to clarify the discussion, particularly if institutional terminology is being used. Familiarity with the operation of the committee builds confidence, and contributions will become more frequent. New committee members provide a valuable fresh perspective.

Conclusion

This chapter has provided an overview of aspects of management/administration for teachers in the LLS, and its importance to institutional success. Reference has been made to teachers' responsibilities in meeting funding and inspection body requirements; however, on a day-to-day basis the important routines relate to maintaining records and monitoring student progress. For other administrative tasks a teacher should utilize the appropriate support staff wherever appropriate, and should value their professionalism. A collegial approach underlines that all have an important role to play in the quality of provision and, crucially, the provision of a rewarding student experience. To be successful in undertaking the administrative and course management dimensions of their role a course leader would need to foster a team culture, with a strong ethos of mutual trust. There is a growing educational management literature and a number of education sector specific MBA programmes have been developed, reflecting the need for those aspiring to leadership positions to be able to demonstrate appropriate engagement with a broad range of management theories and practices.

18

Evaluation and quality assurance
Roy Fisher, Alison Iredale, Ros Ollin and Denise Robinson

In this chapter

- The audit culture and professional autonomy
- Evaluating teaching and learning
- Methods of evaluating teaching
- Evaluating the curriculum
- Retention
- Ofsted
- QAA Higher Education Review
- Conclusion

The audit culture and professional autonomy

> It is essential that principals have a firm grasp of modern management techniques so that they have a better knowledge of such matters as performance statistics . . .
>
> (From *The Administration of Technical Colleges*, Charlton et al. 1971: 153)

The idea of running educational institutions on management principles is not new, but the extent to which colleges and universities have been required to adopt systems in which staff must comply with a culture of control, measurement and audit is unprecedented. The consequences of this ideological shift have included the casualization of work, the imposition of inspection regimes, funding mechanisms based on performance indicators, and the introduction of industrially derived quality systems. Educational and academic values have often been sublimated and, even by the mid-1990s, the following sentiment from Crombie et al. (1995: 61) seemed appropriate:

> [W]e need constantly to remind ourselves of the essentially moral and social purpose – not only of education but also of training. Jerome Bruner's three

questions 'What makes people human?' 'How did they become so?', 'How might they be more so?' have sadly become instead 'What makes people wealthy?', 'How do they become so?' and 'How might they be more so?'

Quality *assurance* (QA) systems in education are concerned with safeguarding academic standards through systematic monitoring. The QA process is normally conducted through devices such as validation procedures, annual course evaluation, module surveys, the use of student and employer feedback, and the monitoring of statistics relating to recruitment, retention, progression, achievement, success and destinations. Quality *enhancement* (QE) focuses on the improvement of performance and of learning experiences, and has generally been conceptualized as subordinate to QA. In recent years, however, QE has become more prominent although a universally accepted definition has yet to emerge (HEA 2008).

During the early years following incorporation, effectiveness and quality concerns within FE focused on the newly established structures and procedures associated with governance and management. They have now reached all aspects of the operation of educational institutions, including teaching and learning, and scholarship and research. HE has not been immune, developing a culture of league tables and accountability that threatens to undermine some of the values associated with the idea of a university (Barnett 2013).

It is important that teachers in the LLS are able to conceptualize themselves as professionals. Elliott (1998) connected the working practices of FE lecturers and their sense of the value of their work. This underlines the necessity of recognizing the centrality of teaching and learning in questions of college effectiveness, and the crucial task of ensuring that these are given a higher profile in debates surrounding quality. As conditions of employment have changed the processes of teaching and learning have been altered by stealth, sometimes within a disarming rhetoric of educational progressivism.

Avis (2002: 81–2) argued that

Lying behind managerialism is a set of taken-for-granted assumptions. Management becomes the means by which a society's economic success can be pursued. The goal is unequivocal – the end to be pursued is known [economic success] . . . Management becomes a quasi-technical pursuit to devise the appropriate means to attain the desired end . . . Managerialism through the use of targets, performance indicators and the like sets the terrain on which individuals are to act.

Among the key factors in the identity of a professional is the capacity to make decisions in a relatively independent way. The autonomy of teachers has been eroded both by routine monitoring systems and by external inspection regimes. Rennie (2003) provided an account of the negative impact of Ofsted inspections on the morale of FE staff. It would, however, be wrong to present teachers in the sector as lacking confidence and wholly at the mercy of managers and inspectors, or to imply that processes of evaluation are implicitly negative. Effective and critical evaluation is an important dimension of professional practice.

Evaluating teaching and learning

The terms 'assessment' and 'evaluation' are often confused. Assessment relates to the measurement and testing of performance; evaluation considers the 'value' or worth of what has taken place. The results of assessment generally inform evaluation.

Individuals and organizations operate within value systems and evaluation is not a neutral process. For example, government departments, driven by targets, are likely to place store by statistical indications of qualifications achieved. In this context, evaluation is linked to accountability and 'value for money'. In contrast, community organizations delivering education in disadvantaged areas may place a greater value on learning experiences which promote self-esteem and enjoyment of learning. The community organization may rely on funding from government, and quantitative rather than more subtle qualitative evaluation may be necessary.

Teaching to maximize the achievement of qualifications (often evaluated statistically), and teaching to create a love of the subject/skill can pull in two directions. The organizations in which teachers work are driven by the need to obtain funding, linked to performance judged through inspections. Evaluating teaching and the curriculum takes place within this performative context. The LLUK Standards (LLUK 2007a: 5) asked teachers to evaluate their practice in terms of 'efficiency and effectiveness'. The ETF (2014: 1) professional standards which superseded them aim to 'set out clear expectations of effective practice'. Who defines what is 'efficient' and 'effective'? While it is important to work within government and organizational requirements, teachers need to consider their values and beliefs, and to ensure that evaluation processes give meaningful information for use in developing understanding and skills. If teachers only think 'inside the box', then possibilities for changing ineffective policies or asserting good practice will be limited.

The influence of Ofsted over how teaching and learning are evaluated has increased significantly since the late 1990s. The current *Common Inspection Framework for Further Education and Skills* (CIF; Ofsted 2012d), like its predecessors has its benefits, including a focus on the learner. Organizations in the LLS have often used the CIF as a basis for evaluation. Teachers are required to evaluate, drawing on learner feedback and learning theories. Apart from the development of technical teaching skills, evaluation involves becoming more aware of the promotion of equality, inclusivity and differentiation.

When planning how to evaluate teaching, it might be asked:

- What is the purpose?
- What information is needed?
- Who is this information for?
- What methods will be best?
- What evidence will inform development?

Many teaching evaluations are conducted at the level of the group. For example:

- Have the learning outcomes been achieved?
- Has this session been enjoyable?

- Has everyone felt included?
- Have the students learned what was intended?
- Did students learn anything not anticipated?

Groups are made up of individuals, so a teacher may wish to differentiate evaluation by focusing on particular students, for example: what have I observed about Nasreen today? What has she learned?

Methods of evaluating teaching

Evaluation mainly works on the principle that to be effective there should be a range of perspectives. As with other aspects of teaching, the type of learner needs to be considered. The most useful information gives the teacher an insight into how learners experienced the session and what they learned. Evaluation of this kind uses information from the learners as feedback.

Evaluation of teaching through silent watching and listening

Teachers can gain information about learners' experience by observing and listening. It is important to bear the following in mind:

- Where learners are working independently, or in small groups, avoid unnecessary intervention and observe how each individual approaches the task or relates to others. Body language can provide useful information.
- Listen carefully to a learner's exact words; these can give valuable information about *how* they understand. 'Errors' give insight.

These observations are from the teacher's perspective. Other means involve the learners more directly.

Written evaluations of teaching

Examples include the following:

- *Questionnaires*: 'happy sheets' with smiley/frowning faces; tick boxes with yes/ no answers; rating scales asking for responses to aspects of the session; headings and space for 'open' written comments;
- *'Sticky notes'*: everyone is given a sticky note on which they comment about the session and then post on the wall. This can be extended by asking different people to comment about particular aspects of the session, then displaying the notes under headed sections;
- *'Lucky dip'*: students are given blank sheets of paper and asked to write anonymously the 'best' and 'worst' things about the session. The students fold the sheets and drop them into a container. The container is then passed round and each

student picks out and reads a paper without commenting themselves. Alternatively, the teacher can read out the comments.

Spoken evaluations of teaching

An *individual* example is the verbal 'Round Robin': asking each student in turn to answer the same question, for example, one of the following:

- What is the most important thing you learned today?
- What have you enjoyed most/least today?
- What are you most proud of in what you achieved today?

A *group* example utilizes small group/pair work. Using flip charts to coordinate and present sub-group/pair feedback, or one student reporting back from their sub-group, for example, feedback on:

- things we would have liked more/less of;
- what we would keep the same/what we would have preferred to be done differently;
- tips for the teacher – 'things you can do to motivate us'.

These are some ways to obtain information about teaching. However, it is only when an analysis of results leads to action to improve that evaluation becomes worthwhile.

Evaluating the curriculum

There are many approaches to curriculum evaluation, underpinned by a variety of values. The four examples below illustrate a range of positions that can be adopted in this context:

- Tyler's (1949) objectives model leads to evaluation based on whether objectives have been achieved.
- Scriven's (1967) formative evaluation model emphasizes the developmental aspect of evaluation.
- Eisner's (1985) 'connoisseurship' model is based on the notion of education as artistry. An evaluator takes the role of connoisseur and critic, feeding back what they perceive and helping those involved to view their work from a critically constructive 'expert' perspective.
- Kirkpatrick's (1998) 'four level' model is based on review of:

  1 reactions of learners
  2 actual learning – resulting increase in knowledge/skills
  3 transfer of behaviour – improvement in real life behaviours
  4 results – impact on organization.

Curriculum evaluation is likely to involve formal procedures and organizations operate a variety of systems as part of their quality improvement processes which often derive from Tyler's (1949) objectives model. Curriculum evaluation may be ongoing, or it may occur towards the end of a course and will draw on a range of sources such as:

- assessment results linked to targets for achievement;
- student feedback, often through electronic questionnaires;
- course tutor and course team feedback.

Within a quality improvement cycle this information is fed into the organizational system and is considered at senior level. Areas for improvement are identified and actions are taken, monitored and fed back. At an organizational level, curriculum evaluation will take into account achievement of intended outcomes of the course, and the number of successful student completions.

Ofsted influences institutional approaches to curriculum evaluation, both through the CIF and through an increased focus on organizational self-evaluation. Ofsted (2012c: 6) reported that,

> the most successful colleges show clearly that thorough self-assessment is key to quality improvement. For a college to publish its discerning self-assessment on its own website is a resounding demonstration of accountability and transparency in the use of government funds for education and training. It also serves as a public record of the college's commitment to raising standards and the steps it is taking to offer the best experience for its learners.

Whilst institutional evaluation systems frequently integrate with management information systems and employ performance indicators to measure success for an individual teacher, there could be a different approach. In the evaluation process, the values and philosophy underpinning the aims of the course should be taken into account. In evaluating a course, a teacher might ask: 'What did I *really* want to achieve by the end of the course with this student/group?' Here it is tempting to focus on the stated learning outcomes for the course, which will be couched in terms of knowledge and skills. However, there may be broader and more fundamental aims, such as developing learners' self-esteem and empowerment, the ability to be independent learners or to be caring members of society. Curriculum evaluation against these kinds of values might lead to these questions:

- How have the teaching/learning and assessment methods helped or hindered these aims?
- How has the overall learning environment (social/cultural/environmental) helped or hindered these aims?
- What might be changed to better achieve these broader aims?

Evaluation is used to monitor quality and bring about improvement. However, perceptions of quality may vary according to the nature of the value system underpinning them. The demands of target-driven evaluation can create pressures for teachers who are working to provide rewarding learning experiences. In this situation, it is important that teachers and managers keep a critical eye on how different types of evaluation are used, to ensure that these provide valid and reliable information for improvement.

Retention

The post-incorporation funding methodology ensured that student retention became a major concern in FE. The existence of a 'retention problem' was underlined by various studies undertaken in the 1990s (for example, Martinez and Munday 1998). More nuanced understandings of the retention issue began to emerge (Bloomer and Hodkinson 2000) recognizing that an outcomes-based approach might not best serve either the evaluation of quality or the development needs of young people.

A National Audit Office Report (2007) showed that some HE institutions were failing to retain almost one in five of their full-time students. The associated costs are high for institutions, the economy and, often, for the people who leave before completing their studies. The cultural capital and skills needed for a learner to progress derive, according to Halsey et al. (1997), largely from social class. Bloomer and Hodkinson (2000) have shown that the learner's journey can be haphazard, involving a set of connections with education. The decision to withdraw from a course can sometimes be a positive one for an individual, involving a complex interplay between the costs and benefits of staying or leaving. From the institutional perspective, however, the impact of a student leaving is generally seen as negative with regard to funding and, crucially, performance indicators.

Retention and achievement research has tended to focus on ideas derived from the institutional perspective. Analysis is generally about how well an educational institution keeps learners, and its efficiency in maximizing achievements against a set of benchmarks compared to other institutions. If an institution concentrates attention on achieving benchmarks teachers inevitably focus on enrolment related decisions. Yorke and Longden (2004) highlight the risks of 'taking the safe option' at the point of entry to a course, rather than working to improve the overall quality of the learning experience.

Concepts such as 'retention' (keeping students on the course), 'attrition' (normally the rate of withdrawal on a course), and 'progression' and 'achievement' can have slightly differing sectoral or institutional definitions – it is important to clarify the precise meaning in any specific context. In recent years there has been significant progress in improving retention rates, but there are particular challenges in supporting and retaining learners beyond secondary education. Many learners, whether straight from school or after a break from education, need to develop learning skills alongside managing their time around work and domestic commitments. Good teachers will identify the learning skills needed by students and will develop these integrally within the curriculum. The starting point is analysis of data relating to recruitment, retention, progression and achievement to review existing courses, and to consider whether new provision may be needed. This is often termed 'curriculum mapping'.

Analysis of data can reveal courses which have poorer retention than similar provision. Trends can be analysed, such as early withdrawals and issues for particular groups of learners (such as part-timers or those with specific disabilities). Gender or ethnicity-related factors may be identified. Teachers can use 'live' data, for example, where a course has relatively poor retention early in the academic year the recruitment strategy should be reviewed. Did applicants receive appropriate guidance prior to entry? Did they have the stated entry qualifications and attributes, and were they prepared for the demands of the course? Once learners are enrolled careful monitoring of attendance and performance can pinpoint the effectiveness of initial assessment tools which identify not only levels of literacy and numeracy, but also more affective skills. An understanding of the profile of each learner, and a dialogic analysis of strengths and areas for development, provides a starting point for progress towards the stated goal. Without this it is not possible to be clear about how far an individual learner is able to commit to the demands of the course.

Ofsted

Today's inspection procedures are enforced through the Education and Inspections Act 2007; this saw a merger of various agencies. The newly extended Office for Standards in Education, Children's Services and Skills in England (Ofsted) came into being on 1 April 2007, bringing together the Adult Learning Inspectorate (ALI), the Commission for Social Care Inspection (CSCI), Her Majesty's Inspectorate of Court Administration (HMICA) and the Office of Her Majesty's Chief Inspector of Schools (the former Ofsted). During 2011–12 Ofsted (2012a: 4) 'carried out more than 30,000 inspections across the education, children's services and skills sectors'. This work was undertaken at a cost of £167 million.

A brief history

Prior to 1993 Her Majesty's Inspectors (HMIs), alongside the FE advisers from LEAs, were responsible for the inspection of FE. HMIs date back to 1839 and, even at that point, their work included the observation of teachers (Norton Grubb 1999). The stated purpose was for the monitoring of public funds and for school improvement. HMIs provided advice and were regarded as 'wise practitioners'. Up to 1993 inspections in FE colleges occurred every ten years or so. With the introduction of the National Curriculum in schools, the HMI 'wise-guidance' model was considered no longer appropriate and in 1993 Ofsted was born. Thus began the standardization of procedures and approaches to making judgements, including grading and the publication of reports on individual schools and, later, colleges. The focus for the basis of the judgements was on observing teachers and discussion with staff and students.

The year 1993 brought the FEFC into existence. The main thrust of the inspection arm of the FEFC was to ensure that the newly independent FE colleges maintained standards. The focus of this regime was on teaching together with an emphasis on procedures and systems associated with the new status of FE colleges with responsibility for estates, human resources, finance and administration. The Learning and Skills Act 2000 moved funding from the FEFC to the newly formed LSC (which would close in 2010 to be replaced by the SFA and YPLA) and also removed inspection powers from the FEFC. The Act stated that the LSC was responsible for overseeing quality, standards and the effective use of funding (DfEE 2000: part 1, ch. 1). FE colleges now found themselves responsible to at least three government-directed bodies with some remit for standards: the LSC, Ofsted and ALI.

ALI had been set up under the Learning and Skills Act 2000 to be concerned with the inspection of adult and work-based learning. It was responsible for work-based learning for all aged over 16; provision in FE for people aged 19 and over; Learndirect provision; adult and community learning; training funded by Jobcentre Plus; and education and training in prisons (this 'at the invitation of Her Majesty's Chief Inspector of Prisons'). From 2000 to 2007, that is prior to the formation of the presently constituted Ofsted, Ofsted had responsibility for the joint inspection of FE colleges with ALI.

The stated purpose of inspections

Inspections prior to 1993 had a remit to provide guidance; after this date this system was one of regulation rather than advice. However, Ofsted annual reports and occasional papers do offer examples of good practice, and Ofsted publishes good practice resources identified through inspection. This does not include the kind of direct support that ALI formerly provided. Neither would the Ofsted approach necessarily be regarded as one that incorporated a dispassionate analysis of the data; rather Ofsted have been seen to support government policy (Smith 2000). In the 2007 incorporation of ALI within Ofsted it would be the remit and culture of Ofsted that dominated.

Impact and issues arising from inspections

A number of issues are raised by practitioners in relation to inspection regimes.

- *Stress* As inspection brings judgements on teaching, teachers often experience stress; furthermore, considerable time and effort is put into preparation for inspections (Wallace and Gravells 2007).

- *Balance of power* The relationship of the inspector to both the teacher and the institution is unequal; the inspection process can lead to the closure of an institution.

- *Improvement in qualifications of learners* Research points to little improvement in achievement or, indeed, to a negative effect (Cullingford 1999; Fielding 2001). A study of school results indicated that

> there exists no evidence that the occurrence of an Ofsted visit has beneficial effects on the exam performance outcome of the school following the inspection. Indeed, the results show a small but well-determined *negative* direct effect on exam results: Ofsted inspections seem to affect adversely student performance in the year of the visit
>
> (Rosenthal 2004: 144).

- *Use of statistics and other data* Does the focus on data (for example, retention and achievement) and comparison to national benchmarks tend to shift attention to that which can be measured?

- A *'snapshot' approach to inspections* Do teachers and others give a false impression by simply adapting to the presence of the inspector?

The culture and practices of Ofsted may be regarded as congruent with a government philosophy of control through measurement. The notion of the 'coasting college' has emerged. A 'coasting college' is one that is regarded as not striving to achieve the relevant standards. Ofsted's four-point grading scale (Ofsted 2012b) is now as follows:

- grade 1: outstanding
- grade 2: good
- grade 3: requires improvement
- grade 4: inadequate.

Grade 3 had previously been 'satisfactory', and Ofsted was now clearly signalling that a judgement of satisfactory was no longer going to be considered acceptable.

QAA higher education review

Using peer review, the QAA operates a range of audits. Universities and colleges of HE have been reviewed through an 'institutional audit'. From 2007 until 2012 FE colleges providing HE in England underwent a process of Integrated Quality and Enhancement Review (IQER). For 2012–13 IQER was replaced by QAA's Review of College Higher Education (RCHE) which examined academic standards and the quality of the student experience. From 2013–14 a new 'risk based' process of Higher Education Reviews replaced both the existing HEI review mechanism and the short-lived RCHE.

Conclusion

Some have claimed that professionals do not need to be inspected, but most practitioners accept that inspections are a permanent feature of public service. The inspection system has offered some leeway to institutions that perform well (a 'lighter touch'). Fielding (2001: 695) highlighted 'the conceptual and practical inadequacy of "accountability" as an agent of reciprocal public engagement in a participatory democracy. In its stead a more robust, more open notion of "reciprocal responsibility" is offered as a more fitting means of professional and communal renewal.'

Fielding's work exposes how the accountability regime can impact negatively on trust and openness. Important skills in teaching are qualitative and there are intuitively based dimensions to practice that are not easily observable. The work of inspectors may be taken to represent a quest for greater rigour and a concerted response to

Government imperatives to drive up standards; more pessimistically, it can be seen as an example of a culture in thrall to performativity and audit. It is, however, the committed and critically reflective teacher, not the inspector, that is to be found at the heart of educational evaluation and enhancement.

19

Career planning and continuing professional development

Robin Simmons and Martyn Walker

In this chapter

- The FE context
- Employment and roles in FE colleges
- Job applications
- The interview
- The first post and career progression
- Part-time teaching and agencies
- Creating and maintaining a curriculum vitae
- Staff appraisal and planning CPD
- Trade unions
- Getting promotion
- In transition

This chapter surveys a range of issues related to obtaining a teaching post in the LLS and considers some factors regarding CPD. Employment practices differ markedly from those in schools; indeed, there are diverse approaches within the LLS. Universities and other HEIs have their own approaches and these may differ within subject areas. This chapter deals primarily with posts in FE and is informed by interviews conducted with college HR managers during 2008, as well as by the recent experiences of trainee and serving lecturers (given our focus on FE we shall use the term 'lecturer'). We believe that some general principles can be cautiously applied to job seeking across different parts of the education system. Readers applying to particular institutions should study the specific context and procedures.

The FE context

A post in FE is unlikely to be a lecturer's first experience of employment. Teaching may be a second, or even third, career for the majority of FE lecturers. Entering FE after extensive previous employment is not a new trend: as Ainley and Bailey (1997: 2) stated 'the basic work of the colleges has always been the teaching of theory and practice of the skills used in everyday occupations' and this remains true.

Teaching brings challenges. The education system in England has undergone extensive change since the 1990s and FE has experienced profound effects (Hyland and Merrill 2003). For several decades after the second World War, LAs ran the majority of both school and post-school education in England. Despite the recent increase in schools with academy status, most state funded schools remain under the auspices of LAs. Following the 1992 Further and Higher Education (F and HE) Act, FE, sixth-form and specialist colleges in England were removed from LA control. This process, known as incorporation, ended a period of almost fifty years of municipal responsibility for FE. From 1 April 1993 individual colleges became self-governing and, for the first time, direct employers of their staff.

Nowadays college principals are regarded, perhaps primarily, as business managers or 'chief executives'. In contrast, their role under LEAs tended to be a combination of 'chief academic' and 'senior administrator'. The LEA took the roles of employer, budget maker, estates manager and much else (Fisher 2010; Simmons 2009). The system of national collective bargaining meant that managers were detached from the determination of pay and conditions and their role was mainly administering arrangements negotiated elsewhere.

Despite the traditionally localized nature of FE, national pay bargaining had been established during the 1920s. Following the 1944 Education Act there was the requirement for national pay scales and the creation of the 'Burnham FE Committee' to preside over such issues. The remit of national bargaining grew and in the early 1970s, became enshrined in what was known as the 'Silver Book' agreement for teaching staff. There were limits on the maximum number of teaching hours, teaching sessions, and the continuity of work that could be required. There were also arrangements for additional payment and remission of teaching hours in recognition of non-teaching duties performed (Waitt 1980). Incorporation ended this. Lecturers were forced off the 'Silver Book' onto 'flexible' localized contracts.

The changed circumstances of FE teachers since incorporation, in addition to increased class contact hours, included additional administrative duties and reduced holidays, high levels of control and a culture that often emphasizes 'business' values. In a study of over 3000 staff working across FE, Villeneuve-Smith et al. (2008) found that over 85 per cent believed they were making a valuable social contribution. However, in almost every dimension of their labour, working conditions were challenging, and over 90 per cent regularly worked beyond their contracted hours. A new or aspiring teacher should be aware that workloads are heavy. Teaching in the LLS can be interesting and stimulating, but it is necessary to be hard working, committed and resilient.

Employment and roles in FE colleges

FE provision ranges from vocational to professional programmes as well as traditional academic subjects. The levels span from 'entry' to college HE. In private training and work-based learning contexts there is a vast range of job-specific courses. While most FE lecturers primarily teach their specialism, many teach in other areas that challenge the boundaries of their knowledge. Flexibility and the ability to apply knowledge and skills across subject boundaries are useful attributes.

Applicants looking for their 'ideal' post may have a long wait. While a sociology graduate may obtain a post teaching their subject on GCSE, GCE A level and Access to HE courses they may also teach modules in health and social care and other vocational courses. Similarly, an accountant may secure a post in a business studies department which entails teaching a range of business subjects. This can be stretching, but it will broaden experience, putting the lecturer in a position to take directions not previously considered. Experiencing a range of programmes and seizing some of the unexpected opportunities that arise can be rewarding.

Government policy and the pressure of changing funding regimes contribute to the diversification of FE. For example, in the four colleges consulted to inform this chapter (referred to henceforth as Colleges A, B, C and D respectively), College B had decided to concentrate on vocational subjects rather than GCE A Levels. College C tended to focus on provision at level 2 and below, and had a relatively large proportion of students with special educational needs.

With the fall in numbers of 16–18-year-olds as a result of demographic change and the decline in funding for adult education, College B had decided to concentrate on the skills agenda and new apprenticeship programmes. All teachers in College B were referred to as 'lecturer/assessors'. This reflected a change in approach to teaching and learning to provide the flexibility of staff to support learners in their workplaces. In some institutions 'assessors' are paid less than 'lecturers', but at College B all were paid lecturers' salaries. College D employed 'tutors', 'academic support tutors' (to work with students on all courses) and 'study skills and learning support tutors' for work with students with learning difficulties.

Before making a job application it is important to consider the curriculum, the approaches to learning and the culture prevailing in the college. It is advisable to read college literature with care; to explore their website; and, if practicable, to visit beforehand. Researching the institution's history, ambitions and status will enable an applicant to assess whether they would be comfortable there. To be positive and optimistic is recommended – but it is vital to be realistic and constructively critical in conducting a job search.

Job applications

The Internet has made job searching easier, and specialist websites exist. Job seekers can explore the number and geographical distribution of opportunities, identify what employers are asking for, and carefully consider the terms and conditions of employment. The *Guardian* newspaper (Tuesday is education jobs day) and the *Times Educational Supplement* (TES), available each Friday, are sources of information.

The first time a potential employer has contact with an applicant is normally when they receive a request for an application form and further details, usually nowadays through email or web download. A job description and person specification will usually be included in the application pack. Both require careful consideration. The job description details the post, enabling the potential applicant to check that this is the job they want. The person specification will include essential and desirable criteria.

To be successful an applicant must meet the 'essentials' and many of the desirable criteria. The application will require hours of preparation. Applicants should not underestimate their abilities and experience; they should consider their skills and strengths and match them to the job description and person specification. A positive and optimistic approach to self-appraisal is good, but an applicant should not be untruthful. In the unlikely event a post was secured this way, gaps in experience and ability would soon be exposed.

Appointments are normally subject to a satisfactory enhanced disclosure being sought from the DBS, as well as health checks for suitability to teach. This is also the case for entry to full-time teacher training courses. Job application forms will ask for details of any convictions, cautions, reprimands or warnings and for successful applicants this will, in due course, be checked through the DBS. The Rehabilitation of Offenders Act 1974 provides that certain criminal convictions become 'spent' after the passage of time. However, the Rehabilitation of Offenders Act 1974 (Exemptions) Order 1975 contains certain classes of employment where a person can be asked to disclose spent convictions. This will invariably apply to teaching jobs. A criminal record will not necessarily bar a person from teaching; this will be contingent on the nature of the position, the circumstances of and background to the offence, and the passage of time. Any successful applicant who had failed to disclose information would almost certainly have their job offer withdrawn. Potential applicants with concerns regarding these issues may wish to seek informal advice from the college before applying.

The essential criteria for a post will include qualifications, and candidates are expected to produce their original certificates either at interview or on appointment. College managers stressed the importance of presenting a good, well written application. College B preferred candidates to identify useful 'selling points'. In the case of recently qualified teachers these might include staff development undertaken on teaching practice and extra-curricular activities. College B also liked to know what else an applicant may have been involved with outside teaching. For example, membership of a parent-teachers' association, school or college governorship, or having been a student representative at university. Applicants to vocational posts in College D were expected to hold at least NVQ level 3 qualifications. College D provided guidance notes with the application form, as well as equal opportunities and related information. The information for applicants pack made it clear that no CV should be included.

The second time that an applicant contacts a college is when they are formally entering the application process. This requires time and care. Often the prospective employer will require a letter in support of an application. Grammar and spelling should be correct. The 'further particulars' supplied by the college should be carefully studied. Such information builds a picture of what the job is all about. It can assist discussions on the interview day or perhaps during the interview itself. Applicants should be well informed and knowledgeable – not only about their subject, but also about the job and the college.

The interview

A letter inviting attendance at a job interview is encouraging. It should be read carefully. Candidates are usually met by a member of the senior management team who will provide an overview of the college and clarify the logistics of the day. There may be a brief tour of the college or of the department. This provides an opportunity to see the facilities and generally assess the environment. Candidates should remember that the selection process begins from the moment they report to reception. Punctuality is essential. Whatever form of transport is chosen, a candidate should ensure that they have time to find the college. Where the interview is some distance from home colleges will normally pay for overnight accommodation, as well as reasonable travel expenses. It is surprising how many candidates get basic details like times and locations wrong. It is important to plan, be punctual, be prepared and to be positive.

It is usual for the interview process to include a presentation, or even for candidates to be required to teach a class. Formal interviews are an important part of the selection process, but a 'micro-teaching' scenario allows the applicant to be assessed in a more realistic environment. Where applicants are asked to teach or present for, say, 15 or 20 minutes they need to think carefully about what they are going to do. The presentation should be engaging, and any resources to be used should be remembered. Several (say six) copies of any materials should be available for the panel. Applicants should be prepared to answer questions or contribute to any discussion about the presentation. Colleges C and D used presentations as part of the selection process.

As five or six candidates may be called for interview and arrangements may involve a tour, presentations and formal interviews, interviewees need to be prepared to be in attendance all day. Inevitably this will involve some waiting. It is wise to resolve to use all parts of the day constructively. An interviewee may get the opportunity to talk to members of staff or chat to students. There may be times when a group of interviewees is left alone in a waiting area. Again, this time should be used effectively. Teaching can be a 'small world', and it is possible that fellow interviewees will meet again. The whole day should be treated as a learning experience – even if an interviewee does not get the job, they can learn what backgrounds other candidates have, gain insight into the workings of the organization, and build professional networks.

Candidates should keep a copy of their application as a reminder. An interviewee must show that they are familiar with the details of the post. These may, for example, include a teaching and learning policy. When answering a question on support for learners, an interviewee has an opportunity to show that they endorse the policy.

Personal appearance is crucial – interviewees should be smart and presentable. College managers expect interviewees to be dressed and groomed appropriately, demonstrating respect for the organization. Staff are expected to be appropriately dressed during the daily routine of their work, and to be role models for students in the respective vocational fields.

As previously mentioned, many colleges expect, as part of the selection process, to see candidates deliver a presentation. College A arranged for a group of students to be 'taught' by each candidate for 20 minutes. Students gave feedback on the session and academic staff made notes for the interviewing panel. The assessment criteria for this part of the process included subject knowledge and lesson planning (requiring a lesson plan for a full 90 minutes), presentation skills, interaction with the group and responsiveness to individuals.

College B set tasks as part of the selection process relating to the subject the post holder would teach. College B's HR manager explained that 'perhaps a rather mundane module will be selected by the curriculum manager and the candidates will be expected to give a short presentation on how they might approach teaching it in a creative and innovative way'. College C stressed that the interview panel wanted to see candidates 'in action' rather than merely theorizing.

Candidates should not be discouraged by letters of rejection. It is common, particularly in applying for a first post, to submit many applications. If an applicant has not been successful it is recommended that they should request college feedback that may be helpful in future applications. Much of the general research undertaken and personal details prepared for an application can be re-used in future applications.

The first post and career progression

Institutions in the LLS invest in professional development. Newly appointed full-time staff are generally inducted over several weeks, and are often allocated a mentor. At College A, mentors were allocated from a different but culturally similar curriculum area to that of the appointee. The intention was for the mentor to be someone who could be confided in. The process usually lasted for one year and might include observation of teaching. All staff at College A were observed teaching once a year, with new appointees visited in the classroom within six months of starting. These observations were carried out in the context of the annual staff review (see below). Similarly, new teachers at College C were observed teaching in the first term after appointment. Peer review of teaching, where individuals are annually observed and provided with feedback, is now standard practice – these normally relatively informal systems provide opportunities to receive (and provide) constructive feedback.

It is wise to take advantage of training opportunities offered by an employer and to apply for staff development funding for appropriate external events. At College A, staff were funded to attend meetings arranged by examinations boards. It is crucial that lecturers keep up to date with their specialist area and with wider developments in education. FE is fast moving; policy can change quickly making knowledge outdated.

Many colleges will financially support staff undertaking award bearing qualifications, including higher degrees. This may also include some release from teaching or other duties. It is, however, common practice that should an employee leave within two years of completing an award, they may be asked to repay some or all of the financial assistance given. Career-minded lecturers normally make the most of events and courses – even if, in the case of the latter, a lot of the work will be in their own time.

Part-time teaching and agencies

LLS institutions tend to employ more staff on a part-time and/or temporary or fractional basis than is the case in schools. On vocational courses the use of recent or current practitioners gives learning currency, and helps to foster valuable links with industry. Notwithstanding this, incorporation led colleges to utilize staff more intensively and to focus on productivity. One consequence of this has been an increased workload. Another has been intensified use of part-time, temporary and casually employed agency staff. Such practices, perhaps, peaked during the 1990s but the workforce is employed on more fluid and 'flexible' terms than was the case when colleges were under LA control.

College A rarely contacted teaching agencies. Inquiries for part-time or hourly paid teaching were kept in a 'pool' for possible contact. This college encouraged those who wanted to be considered for part-time employment to send a completed application form (not CV) around May or June. Rather than assume the college will contact them, those seeking work would probably benefit from making another inquiry in late August when student recruitment is underway. Unlike the schools sector, it is difficult for college managers to estimate recruitment numbers with accuracy until close to the beginning of term. The number and range of courses that can run is subject to student recruitment. Applicants should not be surprised if contacted just before a course begins and asked to teach at short notice. Those not employed at the start of the academic year may be approached later. Opportunities arise as staff change jobs or due to unforeseen circumstances, and some courses commence at different times of the year.

College B used teaching agencies for all its hourly paid 'lecturer/assessors'. Such an arrangement gave the College flexibility to respond to enrolments. The use of teaching agencies also offers colleges the advantage of the agency taking responsibility for DBS checks and allows the college to have reduced responsibilities under employment law. College B, however, otherwise treated its agency staff the same as those with permanent contracts. The College stated had often appointed full-time staff from those that had initially worked for it via the agency. Should a post become vacant agency staff were well placed to apply. All agency staff had access to College activities, including mentoring to support standards in teaching and learning, and had the same opportunities for CPD as staff employed directly.

College C did not use agency staff, employing all its part-time teachers directly. Although it had, in the past, considered using an agency, the College believed that direct employment offered a range of advantages – not least in ensuring continuity for students and encouraging harmonious staff relations. College D appointed 'associate staff' employed on variable contracts. These provided flexibility in relation to staffing requirements on a yearly basis, and they had the same employment rights as full-time staff at the College. They also had the same opportunities as full time staff regarding in-house professional development.

Creating and maintaining a curriculum vitae

Some colleges stipulate that a curriculum vitae (CV) should not be included with application forms and letters of application. Once appointed to post, whether part time or full time, it is wise to maintain a CV as a record of ongoing development, including additional qualifications, CPD activities, and teaching and management responsibilities.

Joining bodies such as the HEA (where this is appropriate) can provide practical benefits in terms of access to useful networks as well as professional profile enhancement. The same considerations apply to membership of subject/craft associations.

Their websites advise on how to join and the benefits offered. Following the demise of the IfL in the autumn of 2014, there was no longer a 'professional body' for the LLS, though ETF stressed its commitment to IfL's legacy and the support of teachers' and trainers' professional develolpment

While the colleges in this sample did not request a CV at the application stage, all highlighted the importance of maintaining one. Trainee teachers should construct a CV during their training and use it when completing application forms. In addition, many awarding bodies expect to see CVs from staff who teach and manage their courses. Universities and sector-wide bodies, such as the City and Guilds of London Institute (CGLI), normally specify the format to be used.

Staff appraisal and planning CPD

Most colleges have an appraisal system in which the appraiser (usually a line manager) and the appraisee discuss annual performance in relation to individual progress, challenges, professional development, agreed targets and career advancement. Such systems can be seen as part of a culture of performance management. However, there is a requirement to engage in CPD once in post. The former IfL had asked its members to record at least 30 hours a year of CPD which supported the needs of students. Orr (2008) argued that this requirement should be seen as an opportunity to engage in meaningful activities that enhance skills and knowledge.

College A conducted appraisals for all teaching staff at the start of the academic year with a mid-year review around January or February. The meetings usually lasted between one to two hours and included feedback from teaching observations, training analysis for the future, and agreed targets. The mid-year review provided the opportunity to see 'how things are going'. College B had an appraisal scheme for all staff with performance indicators. The form used by College B allowed appraisees to identify areas of success, areas that had not gone as well, and targets for the following twelve months. Where targets had been met, supporting evidence was to be produced. For example, the claim 'I am a really good teacher', would need to be supported with internal and external observations, including grades awarded. The appraisee was expected to compare their successes with national benchmarks. The college provided annual training for both appraisees and appraisers.

College A required new staff to attend in-service Certificate in Education or PGCE courses (if these awards were not held). As well as providing a teaching qualification, this enabled staff to keep abreast of developments and engage with broader debates. New appointments were advised regarding 'value added' issues, benchmarking and assessment and were inducted into the College's quality assurance systems, assessment criteria for their subject areas, and support for dealing with challenging behaviour in the classroom.

College B provided five days per year for CPD, two of which focused on cross-college development activities, while the remaining three days were designated for team development, for example, for team or directorate updating, training, developing new courses or working with employers. The college worked with three other institutions as part of its peer quality group collaborating in relation to issues of self-assessment and teaching observations.

In addition to ongoing activities, College C had an annual 'staff development week' in which current issues of priority were addressed. College D included the annual salary review in an appraisal process based on objectives (not competences) and on evidence as to how these were met.

Trade unions

Whether an individual joins a trade union is, of course, a matter of choice. As well as providing collective bargaining over terms and conditions, both at the institutional and national level, workplace union representatives can provide valuable services to their members and may be able to assist in disputes or difficulties. Unions such as the University and College Union (UCU) and the Association of Teachers and Lecturers (ATL) provide programmes of professional development and training. Furthermore, unions offer a range of free or discounted services, such as legal advice and insurance.

The relationship between college employers and trade unions has often been difficult. Although localized disputes sometimes took place under LA control, generally industrial relations were benign and LAs tended to cushion teachers from excessive exploitation. Work relations tended to be collegial; with college managers usually adopting a relatively low profile. Incorporation changed this situation: college principals and other managers were given increased responsibilities based on the belief that 'more forceful management organised on a decentralised basis and held accountable for performance would ensure greater control of costs and lead to better public services' (Winchester and Bach 1995: 304).

The early years of incorporation saw some well publicized instances of 'macho management' (Randle and Brady 1997). FE was marked by turbulent industrial relations and New Labour inherited a sector in crisis when it came to power in 1997. Although, as Williams (2003: 314) argued, many of the inherent conflicts of interest remained, a more conciliatory and pragmatic approach to running FE emerged under the New Labour administration. There was increased funding and a higher profile for the sector, including some impressive building projects that improved the image of FE. This perhaps derived from that government's identification of colleges as central to delivering the human and social capital deemed necessary for economic prosperity – a belief shared by the Coalition Government which followed it.

College A recognized two trade unions, UCU and ATL. The college claimed a good working relationship with union representatives and regular meetings were held between the unions and management. College B encouraged individual staff to join a union. College C recognized one trade union for teaching staff, UCU. College D had an employer forum of elected staff (one representative to 50 staff covering all areas, including academic, technical and administrative and estates). Any employee in the college who 'had an issue' could, if they wished, invite a union representative to these meetings.

Getting promotion

There are a number of options to consider in relation to promotion – one of which is moving into a management role. Colleges tend to have different structures and job titles can vary, but typically a main grade teacher may apply for a 'curriculum manager' or 'programme manager' post as a move into first-line management. In addition to retaining a strong element of teaching, normally such roles require the management of staff, budgets and resources as well as the curriculum. Before applying for such a job it is important to be aware that they are demanding. Those keen to gain further promotion may, after a few years as a curriculum manager, consider pursuing a head of school or faculty role, from which they can subsequently go on to more senior positions. Pay can be attractive in such roles, but they also carry considerable levels of responsibility and pressure. The further up the hierarchy, the less likely is contact with students.

College A expected staff wishing to move to senior posts to have gained complex knowledge regarding funding and budgetary systems. Aspiring managers were expected to know about income and expenditure to demonstrate readiness for posts with first- and second-line budgetary responsibilities. In addition, marketing, HR, sector-wide and government policies were all areas in which managers were expected to have expertise.

College B wanted ambitious lecturers to become involved with cross-college activities. The College designed its own 'Aspiring Manager Course' which covered themes such as managing meetings, managing staff and writing reports. Those who wished to pursue this were allocated a manager mentor. There was also the opportunity to work in other parts of the college. A 'lecturer/assessor' may, for example, work closely with a MIS colleague. Working on projects with managers across the College provided the opportunity for colleagues to present their work to the senior management team and to 'get noticed'. Few colleges look negatively on staff applying for promotion externally. Those seeking internal promotion indicate that they are interested in advancing. Either way, those keen to progress should display a willingness to take on additional responsibilities as opportunities arise.

For those that wish to retain more contact with learners the role of 'advanced practitioner' offers an alternative to entering a line manager's post. Being appointed as an advanced practitioner gives insight into quality assurance systems and assessing colleagues in preparation for Ofsted and other inspections. At College B, for example, appropriate staff were encouraged to become advanced practitioners, or mentors to new staff, and to be involved in developing new courses.

In transition

All learning is a process of transition, with the implication, but not the guarantee, of a positive trajectory. There is a sense in which this characteristic is amplified in the LLS, which itself is often a 'place between'. FE, in particular, bridges the worlds of school and work for some, and the worlds of school and HE for others. The LLS is diverse, complex and demanding. These factors make it a stimulating area of education in which to teach and to learn. Given the presence of both vocational and academic curricula, ranging from foundation level to HE, and the extraordinary diversity of its learners, lifelong learning is a field where the ability to constantly develop and adapt is important.

The disparate backgrounds of teachers and trainers working in FE have made it historically difficult for them to formulate a common professional identity

(Clow 2001) and, many, given the importance of vocational knowledge and practice 'retain strong allegiances to their first occupational identity' (Robson et al. 2004: 187). Gleeson et al.'s (2005: 449–50) study of FE professionalism found that

> [E]ntering FE is, for many, less a career choice or pathway than an opportunity at a particular moment in time. As Ruth notes: '. . . nobody leaves school saying, Oooh I want to be a basic skills teacher! It's something you come to via a variety of routes.' The transition into FE is not a smooth one. It often coincides with lifestyle changes, career breaks, redundancy, divorce and relocation, circumstances after divorce.

This is another sense in which colleges and training organizations can be experienced as liminal spaces, not only transitory zones for the students within them, but also for the staff who teach there. As Vähäsantanen and Eteläpelto (2009) have pointed out, teachers are positioned in roles which mediate between policy and practice – another aspect of being between sometimes conflicting forces. Sector and curriculum reform have an impact in the classroom and the staffroom, and in recent years these pressures have been intense. Negotiating these transitions and the associated tensions demands up-to-date knowledge and high level skills, optimism and tenacity. While it would be Utopian to claim that all teachers in this sector have a vocation in the other sense of that word – a 'calling' based on a commitment to particular values imbued with an ethos of human progress – there is no doubt that many have, and that this helps. The LLS, or 'FE and Skills Sector', is now highly monitored and controlled but at the same time it offers teachers and trainers the opportunity to make an important contribution, not only to improved educational standards in the abstract sense, but more concretely to individual learners. For those who find this an exciting prospect, a career in teaching or training, however carefully planned or however much a consequence of chance, is likely to offer a highly rewarding experience.

References

Abrams, D. and Houston, D. (2006) *Equality, Diversity and Prejudice in Britain: Results from the 2005 National Survey*, Report for the Cabinet Office Equalities Review. Canterbury: University of Kent.

Adler, P.S., Kwon, S-W., Heckscher, C. (2008) Professional work: the emergence of collaborative community, *Organizational Science*, 19(2): 359–76.

Ainley, P. (1994) *Degrees of Difference: Higher Education in the 1990s*. London: Lawrence and Wishart.

Ainley, P. (2001) From a national system locally administered to a national system nationally administered: the new leviathan in education and training in England, *Journal of Social Policy*, 30(3): 457–76.

Ainley, P. (2008) The cruellest con of all, *Times Higher Education Supplement*, 7 February.

Ainley, P. and Bailey, B. (1997) *The Business of Learning: Staff and Student Experiences of Further Education in the 1990s*. London: Cassell.

Alexander, C. (2004) Imagining the Asian gang: ethnicity, masculinity and youth after 'the riots', *Critical Social Policy*, 24(4): 526–49.

Allen, M. and Ainley, P. (2007) *Education Make you Fick, Innit?* London: Tuffnell.

Althusser, L. (1971) Ideology and ideological state apparatuses (notes towards an investigation), in L. Althusser *Lenin and Philosophy and Other Essays*. London: New Left Books.

Anderson, R. (2006) *British Universities Past and Present*. London: Hambledon Continuum.

Apple, M. (2006) *Educating the 'Right' Way: Markets, Standards, God and Inequality*. London: Routledge.

Apple, M. and Beane, J. (2007) *Democratic School: Lessons in Powerful Education*, 2nd edn. Portsmouth, NH: Heinemann.

Archer, M.S. (1979) *Social Origins of Educational Systems*. London: Sage.

AoC (2013) *About Colleges*. http://www.aoc.co.uk/en/about_colleges/index.cfm (accessed 27 January 2013.)

ARG (Assessment Reform Group) (2002) *Assessment for Learning: 10 Principles*. http://www.aaia.org.uk/afl/assessment-reform-group/ (accessed 20 February 2013).

Attwood, G., Croll, P. and Hamilton, J. (2003) Re-engaging with education, *Research Papers in Education*, 18(1): 75–95.

Ausubel, D.P. (1963) *The Psychology of Meaningful Verbal Learning*. New York: Grune and Stratton.

Avis, J. (1994) Teacher professionalism: one more time, *Education Review*, 46(1): 63–72.

Avis, J. (1995) Post-compulsory education: curricular forms, modernisation and social difference, *International Studies in the Sociology of Education*, 5(1): 57–75.

Avis, J. (1999) Shifting identity – new conditions and the transformation of practice: teaching
within post-compulsory education, *Journal of Vocational Education and Training*, 51(2):
245–64.

Avis, J. (2002) Imaginary friends: managerialism, globalisation and post-compulsory education
and training in England, *Discourse: Studies in the Cultural Politics of Education*, 23(1):
75–90.

Avis, J. (2003a) Re-thinking trust in a performative culture, *Journal of Education Policy*, 18(3):
315–32.

Avis, J. (2003b) Work-based knowledge, evidence informed practice and education, *British
Journal of Education Studies*, 51(4): 369–89.

Avis, J. (2007) Post-compulsory education and training: transformism and the struggle for
change, *International Studies in Sociology of Education*, 17(3): 195–209.

Avis, J. (2009a) *Education, Policy and Social Justice: Learning and Skills*, revised edn. London:
Continuum.

Avis, J (2009b) Further education: policy hysteria, competitiveness and performativity. *British
Journal of Sociology of Education*, 30(5): 653–62.

Avis, J. (2010) Workplace learning, knowledge, practice and transformation, *Journal for Critical
Education Policy Studies*, 8(2): 165–93.

Avis, J. (2011) More of the same? New Labour, the Coalition and education: markets, localism
and social justice, *Educational Review*, 63(4): 421–38.

Avis, J. and Bathmaker, A-M. (2004) The politics of care – emotional labour and trainee FE
lecturers, *Journal of Vocational Education and Training*, 56(1): 5–19.

Avis, J. and Bathmaker, A-M. (2006) From trainee to FE lecturer: trials and tribulations, *Journal
of Vocational Education and Training*, 58(2): 171–89.

Avis, J., Bathmaker, A-M. and Parsons, J. (2002a) Communities of practice and the construction
of learners in post-compulsory education and training, *Journal of Vocational Education
and Training*, 54(1): 27–50.

Avis, J., Bathmaker, A-M. and Parsons, J. (2002b) 'I think a lot of staff are dinosaurs': further
education trainee teachers' understandings of pedagogic relations, *Journal of Education
and Work*, 15(2): 181–200.

Avis, J. and Orr, K. (2014) The new professionalism: an exploration of vocational education and
Training Teachers, in S. Billett, C. Harteis, and H. Gruber, (eds), *International Handbook of
Research in Professional and Practice-based Learning*. New Jersey: Springer.

Ball, S. (1995) Education, majorism and the 'curriculum of the dead', in P. Murphy, M. Selinder,
J. Bourne and M. Briggs (eds), *Subject Learning in the Primary Curriculum*. London:
Routledge.

Ball, S.J. (2008) *The Education Debate*. Bristol: The Policy Press.

Barber, B. (1963) Some problems in the sociology of professions, *Daedalus*, 92(4): 669–88.

Barer, R. (2007) *Disabled Students in London: A Review of Higher and Further Education,
Including Students with Learning Difficulties*. London: GLA.

Barker, R. (2011) *Every Child Matters and the Coalition Government*. Whitley Bay: MCRT Ltd.

Barnett, R. (2003) *Beyond All Reason: Living with Ideology in the University*. Buckingham:
Open University Press.

Barnett, R. (2013) *Imagining the University*. London: Routledge.

Barton, D., Hamilton, M. and Ivanič, R. (2000) *Situated Literacies: Reading and Writing in
Context*. London: Routledge.

Barton, D. and Tusting, K. (eds) (2005) *Beyond Communities of Practice: Language, Power and
Social Context*. Cambridge: Cambridge University Press.

Bathmaker, A-M. and Avis, J. (2005) Becoming a lecturer in further education in England: the construction of professional identity and the role of communities of practice, *Journal of Education for Teaching*, 31(1): 47–66.

BBC (British Broadcasting Corporation) (2012) *Census Shows Rise in Foreign-born Residents*. http://www.bbc.co.uk/news/uk-20677515 (accessed 3 January 2013).

Beale, D. (2004) The impact of restructuring in further education colleges, *Employee Relations*, 26(5): 465–79.

Beck, U. (1992) *Risk Society: Towards a New Modernity*. London: Sage.

Beckett, D. and Hager, P (2000) Making judgements as the basis for workplace learning: towards an epistemology of practice, *International Journal of Lifelong Education*, 19(4): 300–11.

Becta (2006) *Safeguarding Children in a Digital World*. Coventry: Becta.

Becta (2008) *Technology Strategy for Further Education, Skills and Regeneration: Implementation Plan for 2008–2011*. Coventry: Becta.

Beetham, H. (2009) Academic values and web cultures: points of rupture. Paper presented to *ESRC Literacies in the Digital University* seminar, 16 October, Edinburgh University.

Bennett, E. (2012) *Learning from the Early Adopters: Web 2.0 Tools, Pedagogic Practices and the Development of the Digital Practitioner*. University of Huddersfield. http://eprints.hud.ac.uk/15997/ (accessed 24 September 2013).

Bennett, R. (2011) Formative assessment: a critical review, *Assessment in Education*, 18(1): 5–25.

Bhavnani, R., Mirza, H.S. and Meetoo, V. (2005) *Tackling the Roots of Racism: Lessons for Success*. Bristol: Policy Press.

Billett, S. (2001) Learning through work: workplace affordances and individual engagement, *Journal of Workplace Learning*, 13(5): 209–14.

Billett, S. (2002a) Workplace pedagogic practices: co-participation and learning, *British Journal of Educational Studies*, 50(4): 457–81.

Billett, S. (2002b) Toward a workplace pedagogy: guidance, participation and engagement, *Adult Education Quarterly*, 53(1): 27–43.

Billett, S. (2004) Learning through work: workplace participatory practices, in H. Rainbird, A. Fuller and A. Munro (eds), *Workplace Learning in Context*. London: Routledge.

Biott, C. and Eason, C. (1994) *Collaborative Learning in Staffrooms and Classrooms*. London: David Fulton.

BIS (Department of Business, Innovation and Skills) (2010a) *Skills for Sustainable Growth*. London: BIS.

BIS (2010b) *Investing in Skills for Sustainable Growth*. London: BIS.

BIS (2011a) *New Challenges, New Chances. Further Education and Skills System Reform Plan: Building a World Class Skills System*. London: BIS.

BIS (2011b) *Higher Education: Students at the Heart of the System*. London: BIS.

BIS (2012a) *Professionalism in Further Education: Final Report of the Independent Review Panel*. London: BIS.

BIS (2012b) *Professionalism in Further Education: Interim Report of the Independent Review Panel*. The Lingfield Review Interim Report. London: BIS.

BIS (2012c) *Developing a Guild for Further Education: Propectus*. London: BIS.

BIS (2012d) *Evaluation of FE Teachers' Qualifications (England) Regulations 2007*. BIS Research Paper No. 66. London: BIS.

BIS (2014) *Government Response to the recommendations from the Further Education Learning Technology Action Group (FELTAG)*. London: BIS.

Black, P. (2006) Assessment for learning: where is it now? Where is it going? in C. Rust (ed.) *Improving Student Learning through Assessment*. Oxford: Oxford Centre for Staff and Learning Development.

Black, P., Harrison, C., Lee, C., Marshall, B. and Wiliam, D. (2003) *Assessment for Learning: Putting it into Practice.* Maidenhead: Open University Press.

Black, P. and Wiliam, D. (1998) *Inside the Black Box: Raising Standards Through Classroom Assessment.* London: King's College.

Blair, T. (2002) *PM's Speech on Tackling Poverty and Social Exclusion.* London: HMSO.

Bloom, B. (ed.) (1956) *Taxonomy of Educational Objectives, Handbook 1: Cognitive Domain.* New York: Longman.

Bloomer, M. and Hodkinson, P. (2000) Learning careers: continuity and change in young people's dispositions to learning, *British Educational Research Journal*, 26(5): 583–98.

Blum, P. (2001) *A Teacher's Guide to Anger Management.* London: RoutledgeFalmer.

Board of Education (1944) *Teachers and Youth Leaders*, McNair Report. London: HMSO.

Boethel, M. and Dimock, V. (2000) *Constructing Knowledge with Technology.* Austin, TX: Southwest Educational Development Laboratory.

Boud, D., Cohen, R. and Walker, D. (1993) *Using Experience for Learning.* Buckingham: Society for Research into Higher Education and Open University Press.

Boud, D., Keogh, R. and Walker, D. (1985) *Reflection: Turning Experience into Learning.* London: Kogan Page.

Bourdieu, P. (1974) The school as a conservative force: scholastic and cultural inequalities, in J. Eggleston (ed.), *Contemporary Research in the Sociology of Education.* London: Methuen.

Bourdieu, P. (1989) Social space and symbolic power, *Sociological Theory*, 7(1): 14–25.

Bourdieu, P. (1990) *The Logic of Practice.* Cambridge: Polity Press.

Bourdieu, P. (1996) *The State Nobility: Elite Schools in the Field of Power.* Cambridge: Polity Press.

Bourdieu, P. and Passeron, J. (1990) *Reproduction in Education, Society and Culture*, 2nd edn. London: Sage.

Bowles, S. and Gintis, H. (1976) *Schooling in Capitalist America.* London: Routledge and Kegan Paul.

Brine, J. (2006) Lifelong learning and the knowledge economy: those that know and those that do not – the discourse of the European Union, *British Educational Research Journal*, 32(5): 649–65.

Brockbank, A. (2006) *Facilitating Reflective Learning Through Mentoring and Coaching.* London: Kogan Page.

Brookfield, S. (1995) *Becoming a Reflective Teacher.* San Francisco, CA: Jossey Bass.

Brookfield, S. D. (2005) *The Power of Critical Theory for Adult Learning and Teaching.* Maidenhead: Open University Press.

Brown, G. (2007) Speech to the nation, London's Imagination Gallery, London, 11 May.

Brown, P., Lauder, H., and Ashton, D. (2011) *The Global Auction: The Broken Promises of Eduation, Jobs, and Incomes.* Oxford: Oxford University Press.

Browne, R.B. (ed.) (2005) *Popular Culture Studies Across the Curriculum.* Jefferson: McFarlane and Company Inc., Publishers.

Browne, Lord, J. of Madingley (2010) *Securing a Sustainable Future for Higher Education: An Independent Review of Higher Education Funding and Student Finance.* London, TSO.

Bruner, J.S. (2006) *In Search of Pedagogy Vol. 1: The Selected Works of Jerome S. Bruner.* Abingdon: Routledge.

Buckingham, D. and Jones, K. (2001) New Labour's cultural turn: some tensions in contemporary educational and cultural policy, *Journal of Educational Policy*, 16(1): 1–14.

Bullying Matters (2009) *Is Your Business at Risk?* http://www.bullyingmatters. co.uk/index.php?pageid=12 (accessed 20 February 2009).

Burton, S. (2013) Safeguarding children from online danger, In J. Reid with S. Burton (eds), *Safeguarding and Protecting Children in the Early Years.* Abingdon: David Fulton.

Bush, T. and Middlewood, D. (2005) *Leading and Managing People in Education*. London: Sage Publications.

Butcher, J. (2002) A case for mentor challenge? The problem of learning to teach post-16, *Mentoring and Tutoring*, 10(3): 197–220.

Butcher, J. (2003) 'Sink or swim': learning to teach post-16 on an 11–18 Postgraduate Certificate of Education, *Teachers' Development*, 7(1): 31–57.

Cable, V. and Hayes, J. (2010) Foreword to BIS, *Skills for Sustainable Growth*. London: BIS.

Callaghan, J. (1976) Towards a national debate, *Education*, 148(17): 332–3.

Cantle, T. (2001) *Community Cohesion: A Report of the Independent Review Team*. London: Home Office.

Cantle, T. (2005) *Community Cohesion: A New Framework for Race Relations*. Basingstoke: Palgrave.

Carr, D. (2003) *Making Sense of Education*. London: RoutledgeFalmer.

Carr, W. (1995) *For Education: Towards a Critical Education Enquiry*. Buckingham: Open University Press.

Carr, W. and Kemmis, S. (1986) *Becoming Critical: Education Knowledge and Action Research*. London: Falmer.

Carter, M. and Francis, R. (2001) Mentoring and beginning teachers' workplace learning, *Asia-Pacific Journal of Teacher Education*, 29(3): 249–62.

Casanova, J. (1994) *Public Religions in the Modern World*. Chicago: University of Chicago Press.

Cassidy, S. (2004) Learning styles: an overview of theories, models, and measures, *Educational Psychology*, 24(4): 419–44.

Challis, M. (1993) *Introducing APEL*. London: Routledge.

Charlton, D., Gent, W. and Scammells, B. (1971) *The Administration of Technical Colleges*. Manchester: Manchester University Press.

Child, D. (2004) *Psychology and the Teacher*, 7th edn. London: Continuum.

Chin, C. and Brown, D. (2002) Student-generated questions: a meaningful aspect of learning in science. *International Journal of Science Education*, 24(5): 521–49.

Chitty, C. (2004) *Education Policy in Britain*. Basingstoke: Palgrave Macmillan.

City and Guilds Centre for Skills Development (2012) *The Role of Coaching in Vocational Education and Training*. London: City and Guilds of London Institute.

Clarke, P. (2012) *Education for Sustainability: Becoming Naturally Smart*. London: Routledge.

Clow, R. (2001) Further Education teachers' constructions of professionalism, *Journal of Vocational Education and Training*, 53(3): 407–19.

Clutterbuck, D. (2004) *Everyone Needs a Mentor*. London: CIPD.

Clutterbuck, D. (2005) *Coaching and Mentoring in Education*. Burnham: Clutterbuck Associates.

Coffield, F. (2005) *Learning Styles: Help or Hindrance*? London: Institute of Education.

Coffield, F. (2006) Running ever faster down the wrong road, inaugural lecture, London University Institute of Education, London, 5 December.

Coffield, F. and Edward, S. (2008) Rolling out 'good', 'best' and 'excellent' practice. What next? Perfect practice? *British Educational Research Journal*, iFirst Article: 1–20.

Coffield, F., Moseley, D., Hall, E. and Ecclestone, K. (2004) *Should We Be Using Learning Styles? What Research Has to Say to Practice*. Trowbridge: Learning and Skills Research Centre.

Colley, H. (2006) Learning to labour with feeling: class, gender and emotion in childcare education and training, *Contemporary Issues in Early Childhood*, 7(1): 15–29.

Colley, H. and James, D. (2005) Unbecoming tutors: towards a more dynamic notion of professional participation. Paper presented at the Changing teacher roles, identities and professionalism conference, King's College, London, 16 May.

Colley, H., James, D., Tedder, M. and Diment, K. (2003) Learning as becoming in vocational education and training: class, gender and the role of vocational habitus, *Journal of Vocational Education and Training*, 55(4): 471–97.

Colley, H., James, D. and Diment, K. (2007) Unbecoming teachers: towards a more dynamic notion of professional participation, *Journal of Education Policy*, 22(2): 173–93.

Collis, B. and Moonen, J.C. (2006) The contributing student: learners as co-developers of learning resources for reuse in Web environments, in D. Hung and M.S. Khine (eds), *Engaged Learning with Emerging Technologies*. Dordrecht, Nederland: Springer.

Commission for Black Staff in FE (2002) *Challenging Racism: Further Education Leading the Way*. London: Commission for Black Staff in FE.

Condie, R. and Munro, B. (2007) *The Impact of ICT in Schools: A Landscape Review*. Coventry: BECTA.

Connor, H., Tyers, C., Modood, T. and Hillage, J. (2004) *Why the Difference? A Closer Look at Higher Education Minority Ethnic Students and Graduates*, Research Report RR552. London: DfES.

Cornford, I. (2002) Reflective teaching: empirical research and some implications for teacher education, *Journal of Vocational Education and Training*, 54(2): 219–35.

Cosh, J. (1999) Peer observation: a reflective model, *ELT Journal*, 53(1): 22–7.

Cowan, K. (2006) *How to Monitor Sexual Orientation in the Workplace*. Stonewall Workplace Guides. www.stonewall.org.uk/education_for_all/research/1790.asp (accessed 14 January 2007).

Cowley, S. (2003) *Getting the Buggers to Behave 2*. London: Continuum.

Crawley, J. (2005) *In at the Deep End*. London: David Fulton Publishers.

CRE (Commission for Racial Equality) (1999) *Open Talk, Open Minds*. London: CRE.

Creanor, L. (2002) A tale of two courses: a comparative study of tutoring online, *Open Learning*, 17(1): 57–68.

Crombie White, R., Pring, R. and Brockington, D. (1995) *14–19 Education and Training: Implementing a Unified System of Learning*. London: RSA.

Cross, E.-J., Richardson, B., Douglas, T. and Vonkaenl-Flatt, J. (2009) *Virtual Violence: Protecting Children from Cyberbullying*. London: Beatbullying.

Cullimore, S. (2006) Joined-up training: improving the partnership links between a university PGCE (FE) course and its placement colleges, *Research in Post-Compulsory Education*, 11(3): 303–17.

Cullingford, C. (ed.) (1999) *An Inspector Calls: Ofsted and its Effect on School Standards*. London: Kogan Page.

Cullingford, C. (2007) Creativity and pupils' experience of school. *Education 3–13, 35*(2): 133–42.

Cummins, J., McNicholl, A., Love, D. and King, E. (2006) *Improving the Diversity Profile of the Learning and Skills Sector Workforce: Report for the DfES*. London: Office for Public Management Ltd.

Data Service (2012) *Post-16 Education and Skills: Learner Participation, Outcomes and Level of Highest Qualification Held*. Statistical First Release DS/SFR16. London: BIS.

Davies, J. and G. Biesta (2007) Coming to college or getting out of school? The experience of vocational learning of 14–16-year-olds in a further education college, *Research Papers in Education*, 22(1): 23–41.

Davies, P. (2000) The relevance of systematic reviews to educational policy and practice, *Oxford Review of Education*, 26(3/4): 365–78.

Davies, P., Slack, K., Hughes, A., Mangan, J. and Vigurs, K. (2008) *Knowing Where to Study? Fees, Bursaries and Fair Access*. Stoke-on-Trent: Institute for Educational Policy Research and Institute for Access Studies, Staffordshire University.

DBS (Disclosure and Barring Service) (2013) *DBS Services*. http://www.homeoffice.gov.uk/ agencies-public-bodies/dbs/services/ (accessed 14 February 2013).

DCSF (Department for Children, Schools and Families) (2007) *Targeted Youth Support: Integrated Support for Vulnerable Young People – A Guide*. London: TDA.

DCSF (Department for Children, Schools and Families) (2008) *Safer Children in a Digital World: The Report of the Byron Review*. Nottingham: DCSF.

DCSF (Department for Children, Schools and Families) (2009) *14–19 Education and Skills*. http://www.dcsf.gov.uk/14–19/index.cfm?go=site.home&sid=51&pid=421 &ctype=FAQ &ptype= Single (accessed 2 February 2009).

Deem, R., Hillyard, S. and Reed, M. (2007) *Knowledge, Higher Education and the New Managerialism: The Changing Management of UK Universities*. Oxford: Oxford University Press.

DES (Department of Education and Science) (1966) *The Supply and Training of Teachers for Further Education*, Russell Report. London: HMSO.

DES (Department of Education and Science) (1989) *Discipline in Schools*, Elton Report. London: HMSO.

DES (Department of Education and Science) (1991) *Education and Training for the 21st Century*. London: HMSO.

DfE (Department for Education) (2012a) *Teachers' Standards*. London: DfE.

DfE (Department for Education) (2012b) 2015 *Key Stage 4 Performance Tables: Inclusion of 14–16 Qualifications*.

DfE DoH (2014a) *Children and Families Act*.

DfE DoH (2014b) *Special Educational Needs (SEN) Code of Practice: for 0 to 25 years*. http://media.education.gov.uk/assets/files/pdf/q/2015%20ks4%20wolf%20list.pdf (accessed 2 February 2013).

Dewey, J. (1933) *How We Think*, 2nd edn. New York: D.C. Heath.

Dewey, J. (1938) *Experience and Education*. New York: Macmillan.

DfEE (Department for Education and Employment) (1999) *A Fresh Start: Improving Literacy and Numeracy*, Moser Report. London: DfEE.

DfEE (Department for Education and Employment) (2000a) *Opportunity for All: Skills for the New Economy*. London: DfEE.

DfEE (Department for Education and Employment) (2000) *Learning and Skills Act 2000*. London: HMSO.

DfEE (Department for Education and Employment) (2001) *Skills for Life: The National Strategy for Improving Adult Literacy and Numeracy Skills*. London: DfEE.

DfES (Department for Education and Skills) (2002a) *Success for All: Reforming Further Education and Training: A Discussion Document*. London: HMSO.

DfES (Department for Education and Skills) (2002b) *Success for All: Reforming Further Education and Training: Our Vision for the Future*. London: DfES.

DfES (Department for Education and Skills) (2003a) *Subject Specialism: Consultation Document*. London: DfES.

DfES (Department for Education and Skills) (2003b) *The Future of Initial Teacher Education for the Learning and Skills Sector: An Agenda for Reform – A Consultative Paper*. London: DfES.

DfES (Department for Education and Skills) (2003c) *Every Child Matters: Summary*. London: DfES.

DfES (Department for Education and Skills) (2004a) *Equipping our Teachers for the Future: Reforming Initial Teacher Training for the Learning and Skills Sector*. Nottingham: DfES Standards Unit.

DfES (Department for Education and Skills) (2004b) *14–19 Curriculum and Qualifications Reform: Final Report of the Working Group on 14–19 Reform*. Nottingham: DfES Publications.

DfES (Department for Education and Skills) (2005a) *14–19 Education and Skills.* London: HMSO.

DfES (Department for Education and Skills) (2005b) *Higher Standards, Better Schools for All: More Choice for Parents and Pupils.* London: DfES.

DfES (Department for Education and Skills) (2005c) *Skills: Getting on in Business, Getting on at Work.* Norwich: TSO.

DfES (Department for Education and Skills) (2006) *Further Education: Raising Skills, Improving Life Chances.* London: HMSO.

DfES (Department for Education and Skills) (2007) *Raising Expectations: Staying in Education and Training Post-16.* Norwich: HMSO.

DIUS/DWP (Department of Innovation, Universities and Skills/Department for Work and Pensions) (2007) *Opportunity, Employment and Progression: Making Skills Work.* Norwich: TSO.

Doherty, C. and Mayer, D. (2003) E-Mail as a 'Contact zone' for teacher-student Relationships, *Journal of Adolescent and Adult Literacy,* 46(7): 592–600.

Donald, J. (1992) *Sentimental Education: Schooling, Popular Culture and the Regulation of Liberty.* London: Verso.

Donovan, G. (2005) *Teaching 14–19: Everything You Need to Know About Teaching and Learning Across the Phases.* London: David Fulton.

Dreyfus, S. and Dreyfus, H. (1980) *A Five-stage Model of the Mental Activities Involved in Directed Skill Acquisition.* Berkeley, CA: Operations Research Center, University of California.

Drucker, P. (1993) *Post-Capitalist Society.* New York: HarperCollins.

Duckett, I. and Tatarkowsky, M. (2005) *Practical Strategies for Learning and Teaching on Vocational Programmes.* London: LSDA.

Eastwood, L., Coates, J., Dixon, L. et al. (2009) *A Toolkit for Creative Teaching in Post-Compulsory Education.* Maidenhead: Open University Press.

Ecclestone, K. (2004) From Freire to fear: the rise of the therapeutic culture in post-16 education, in J. Satterthwaite, E. Atkinson and W. Martin (eds), *The Disciplining of Education.* London: Trentham.

Ecclestone, K. and Hayes, D. (2009) *The Dangerous Rise of Therapeutic Education.* London: Routledge.

Edge Foundation (2012) *Six Steps for Change 2012.* London: Edge Foundation.

ECRE (European Council on Refugees and Exiles) (1999) *Good Practice Guide on Education for Refugees in the European Union.* London: World University Service.

ECU (Equality Challenge Unit) (2004) *Employing People in Higher Education: Sexual Orientation.* London: Equality Challenge Unit.

Education and Training Foundation (2014) *Professional Standards for Teachers and Trainers in England.* London: ETF

Education Group, CCCS (Centre for Contemporary Cultural Studies) (1981) *Unpopular Education: Schooling and Social Democracy in England Since 1944.* London: Hutchinson.

Edwards, R. (1980) *Contested Terrain: The Transformation of the Workplace in the Twentieth Century.* London: Heinemann.

Egan, G. (2002) *The Skilled Helper.* Pacific Grove, CA: Brooks-Cole, Thompson Learning.

Einstein, A. (1922) *The Meaning of Relativity.* London: Methuen.

Eisner, Elliot W. (1985) *The Art of Educational Evaluation: A Personal View.* London: Falmer Press.

Elliott, B. and Calderhead, J. (1993) Mentoring for teacher development: possibilities and caveats, in D. McIntyre, H. Hagger and N. Wilkin (eds), *Mentoring: Perspectives on School-based Teacher Education.* London: Kogan Page.

Elliott, G. (1998) Lecturing in post-compulsory education: profession, occupation or reflective practice? *Teachers and Training: Theory and Practice,* 4(1): 161–75.

ENTO (Employment National Training Organisation) (2006) *National Occupational Standards for Coaching and Mentoring in a Work Environment.* Leicester: ENTO.

EPPI (Evidence for Policy and Practice Information) (2001) *Review Group Manual.* London: EPPI-centre.

Eraut, M. (2000) Non-formal learning and tacit knowledge in professional work, *British Journal of Educational Psychology*, 70(1): 113–36.

ETF (Educational and Training Foundation) *Professional Standards for Teachers and Trainers in Education and Training – England.* http://www.et-foundation.co.uk (accessed 6 July 2014).

Evans, L. (2008) Professionalism, professionality and the development of education professionals, *British Journal of Educational Studies*, 56(1): 20–38.

Evans, J. and Benefield, P. (2001) Systematic reviews of educational research: does the medical model fit, *British Educational Research Journal*, 27(5): 527–41.

Evans, K., Hodkinson, P., Rainbird, H. and Unwin, L. (2006) *Improving Workplace Learning.* London: Routledge.

FELTAG (Further Education Learning Technology Action Group) (2014) *Paths forward to a digital future for Further Education and Skills.* http://feltag.org.uk (accessed 4 July 2014).

FENTO (Further Education National Training Organisation) (1999) *Standards for Teaching and Supporting Learning in Further Education in England and Wales.* London: FENTO.

Fidler, B. and Atton, T. (1999) *Poorly Performing Staff in Schools and How to Manage Them.* London: Routledge.

Fielding, M. (2001) Ofsted, inspection and the betrayal of democracy, *Journal of Philosophy of Education*, 35(4): 695–709.

Fisher, R. (2004) From *Business Education Council* to *Edexcel Foundation* 1969–1996: the short but winding road from technician education to instrumentalist technicism, *Journal of Education and Work*, 17(3): 237–55.

Fisher, R. (2010) Management, measurement and cultural change in the English further education college: 1963–1993, *Education, Knowledge and Economy*, 4(2):119–30.

Fisher, P. and Fisher, R. (2007) The subversive autodidact, the pursuit of knowledge and the politics of change, *Discourse: Studies in the Cultural Politics of Education*, 28(4): 515–29.

Fisher, R. and Simmons, R. (2012) Liberal Conservatism, vocationalism and further education in England, *Globalisation, Societies and Education*, 10(1): 31–51.

Fisher, R. and Webb, K. (2006) Subject specialist pedagogy and initial teacher training for the learning and skills sector in England: the context, a response and some critical issues, *Journal of Further and Higher Education*, 30(4): 337–49.

Flinders, D. and Thornton, S. (2004) *The Curriculum Studies Reader.* London: Routledge.

Foster, A. (2005) *Realising the Potential: A Review of the Role of Further Education Colleges.* London: DfES Publications.

Foucault, M. (1980) Truth and power, in C. Gordon (ed.), *Power/Knowledge: Selected Interviews and Other Writings 1972–1977.* New York: Pantheon.

Foucault, M. (1991) *Discipline and Punish: The Birth of the Prison.* Harmondsworth: Penguin.

Fox, R. (2001) Constructivism examined, *Oxford Review of Education*, 27(1) 23–35.

Fuller, A. and Unwin, L. (2004) Expansive learning environments: integrating organizational and personal development, in H. Rainbird, A. Fuller and A. Munro (eds), *Workplace Learning in Context*, London: Routledge.

Fryer, R.H. (1997) *Learning for the Twenty-first century: First Report of the National Advisory Group for Continuing Education and Lifelong Learning.* www.lifelonglearning. co.uk/nagcell2/index.htm (accessed 11 August 2009).

Fukuyama, F. (1992) *The End of History and the Last Man.* London: Penguin Books.

Furedi, F. (1997) *Culture of Fear: Risk-taking and the Morality of Low Expectation*. London: Cassell.

Furedi, F. (2003) *Therapy Culture*. London: Routledge.

Furlong, J. and Maynard, T. (1993) Learning to teach and models of mentoring, in D. McIntyre, H. Hagger and N. Wilkin (eds), *Mentoring: Perspectives on School-based Teacher Education*. London: Kogan Page.

Gagné, R.M. (1977) *The Conditions of Learning*, 3rd edn. New York: Holt, Rinehart and Winston.

Garber, M. (2003) *Academic Instincts*. Princeton: Princeton University Press.

Gee, J. (2003) *What Video Games Have to Teach us About Learning and Literacy*. Basingstoke: Palgrave Macmillan.

Gee, J. (2004) *Situated Language and Learning: A Critique of Traditional Schooling*. London: Routledge.

Gee, J.P. (1996) *Social Linguistics and Literacies: Ideology in Discourses*, 2nd edn. London: RoutledgeFalmer.

Gibbs, G. (1995) *Discussion with More Students*. Oxford: Oxford Centre for Staff and Learning Development, Oxford Brookes University.

Giddens, A. (1998) *The Third Way: The Renewal of Social Democracy*. Oxford: Polity.

Giddens, A. and Pierson, C. (1998) Interview 3: structuration theory, in *Conversations With Anthony Giddens: Making Sense of Modernity*. Cambridge: Polity Press.

Gillard D (2011) *Education in England: A Brief History*. www.educationengland.org.uk/history (accessed 2 February 2013).

Gilliat-Ray, S. (2000) *Religion in Higher Education: The Politics of the Multi-faith Campus*. Aldershot: Ashgate.

GLA (Greater London Authority) (2006) *Towards Joined Up Lives: Disabled and Deaf Londoners' Experience of Housing, Employment and Post-16 Education from a Social Model Perspective*. London: GLA.

Gleeson, D. (1983) Further education, tripartism and the labour market, in D. Gleeson (ed.), *Youth Training and the Search for Work*. London: RKP.

Gleeson, D. and Shain, F. (1999) Managing ambiguity: between markets and managerialism – a case study of 'middle' managers in further education, *Sociological Review*, 57(3): 461–90.

Gleeson, D., Davies, J. and Wheeler, E. (2005) On the making and taking of professionalism in the further education (FE) workplace, *British Journal of Sociology of Education*, 26(4): 445–60.

Golby, M. (1989) Curriculum traditions, in B. Moon, P. Murphy and J. Raynor (eds), *Policies for the Curriculum*. London: Hodder and Stoughton.

Goldsmith, M. (2008) Better coaching, *Leadership Excellence*, 25(5): 9.

Goodson, I.F. (1994) *Studying Curriculum: Cases and Methods*. Buckingham: Open University Press.

Goodson, I.F. (2003) *Professional Knowledge, Professional Lives: Studies in Education and Change*. Maidenhead: Open University Press.

Gorard, S. (2001) *A Changing Climate for Educational Research? The Role of Research Capability – building*. http://www.leeds.ac.uk/educol/documents/00001897.htm (accessed 24 September 2013).

Grace, G. (1987) Teachers and the state in Britain, in M. Lawn and G. Grace (eds), *Teachers: the Cultures and Politics of Work*. London: Falmer.

Grace, G. (1995) *School Leadership: Beyond Education Management*. London: Falmer.

Gramsci, A. (1971) *Selections from the Prison Notebooks*. London: Lawrence and Wishart.

Grayling, A.C. (2007) *The Ties that Bind*. www.equalityhumanrights.com/en/newsandcomment/ (accessed 26 March 2008).

Green, A. (1990) *Education and State Formation: The Rise of Education Systems in England, France and the USA*. London: Macmillan.

Green, A. (1991) The peculiarities of English education, in Education Group 2, Cultural Studies, Birmingham, *Education Limited: Schooling and Training and the New Right Since 1979*. London: Unwin Hyman.

Green, B. (2006) English, literacy, rhetoric: changing the project? *English in Education*, 40(1): 7–19.

Gregory, J. (2002) Principles of experiential education, in P. Jarvis (ed.), *The Theory and Practice of Teaching*. London: Kogan Page.

Grindrod, F. and Murray, I, (2011) Making quality count: the A union view, in T. Dolphin and T. Lanning (eds), *Rethinking Apprenticeships*. London: IPPR.

Gronlund, N.E. (1970) *Stating Behavioural Objectives for Classroom Instruction*. London: Collier-Macmillan.

GTC (General Teaching Council) (2003) *Department for Education and Skills Subject Specialism: Consultation Document: The Response of the General Teaching Council for England*. London: GTC.

GTC (General Teaching Council) (2006) *The Statement of Professional Values and Practice for Teachers*. London: GTC.

Haidar, E. (2007) Coaching and mentoring nursing students, *Nursing Management – UK*, 14(8): 32–5.

Halai, A. (2006) Mentoring in-service teachers: issues of role diversity, *Teaching and Teacher Education*, 22: 700–10.

Hall, D. and Raffo, C. (2004) Re-engaging 14–16-year-olds with their schooling through work-related learning, *Journal of Vocational Education and Training*, 56(1): 69–80.

Halsey, A.H., Lauder, H., Brown, P. and Stuart, A. (eds) (1997) *Education, Culture, Economy Society*. Oxford: Oxford University Press.

Hammersley, M. (ed.) (2007) *Educational Research and Evidence-based Practice*. London: Sage.

Hankey, J. (2004) The good, the bad and other considerations: reflections on mentoring trainee teachers in post-compulsory education, *Research in Post Compulsory Education*, 9(3): 389–400.

Hargreaves, D. (2005) *About Learning*. London: Demos.

Harkin, J. (2006) Treated like adults: 14–16-year-olds in further education, *Research in Post-Compulsory Education*, 11(3): 319–39.

Hart, R. (2010) Classroom behaviour management: educational psychologists' views on effective practice, *Emotional and Behavioural Difficulties*, 15(4): 353–71.

Harvey, B. and Harvey, J. (2013) *Creative Teaching Approaches in the Lifelong Learning Sector*. Maidenhead: Open University Press.

Harwood T., Garry, T. and Broderick, A. (2008) *Relationship Marketing: Perspectives, Dimensions and Contexts*. London: McGraw-Hill.

Hattie, J. (2009) *Visible Learning: A Synthesis of Over 800 Meta-analyses Relating to Achievement*. Abingdon: Routledge.

HSE (Health and Safety Executive) (2006a) *HSC Tells Health and Safety Pedants to 'Get a Life': Statement by Bill Callaghan, Chair of the Health and Safety Commission*. http://www.hse.gov.uk/risk/statement.htm (accessed 20 February 2009).

HSE (Health and Safety Executive) (2011a) *Five Steps to Risk Assessment*. Sudbury: HSE.

HSE (Health and Safety Executive) (2011b) *Health and Safety Checklist for Classrooms*. Sudbury: HSE.

Healey, M. and Jenkins, A. (draft 2001) Discipline-based educational development. A later version appeared in R. MacDonald and H. Eggins (eds) (2003), *The Scholarship of Academic Development*. Buckingham: Open University Press.

HM Government (2003) *Every Child Matters*. Norwich: The Stationery Office.

HM Government (2005) *Youth Matters*. Norwich: The Stationery Office.

HM Government (2007a) *The Further Education Teachers' Qualifications (England) Regulations 2007*. Statutory Instrument 2007 No. 2264. London: HMSO.

HM Government (2007b) *The Further Education Teachers' Continuing Professional Development and Registration (England) Regulations 2007*. Statutory Instrument 2007 No. 2116. London: HMSO.

HM Government (2012) *The Education (School Teachers) (Qualifications and Appraisal) (Miscellaneous Amendments) (England) Regulations 2012*. Statutory Instrument 2012 No. 431. London: HMSO.

Heron, J. (1989) *The Facilitator's Handbook*. London: Kogan Page.

Hewstone, M., Tausch, N., Hughes, J. and Cairns, E. (2007) Prejudice, intergroup contact and identity, in M. Wetherell, M. Lafleche and R. Berkley (eds), *Identity, Ethnic Diversity and Community Cohesion*. London: Sage.

HEA (Higher Education Academy) (2008) *Quality Enhancement and Assurance: A Changing Picture*. York: HEA.

HEA (Higher Education Academy) (2011) *The UK Professional Standards Framework for Teaching and Supporting Learning in Higher Education*. York: HEA.

HEFCE (Higher Education Funding Council for England) (2005) *HEFCE Strategy for E-learning*. http://www.hefce.ac.uk/pubs/hefce/2005/05_12/05_12.pdf (accessed 1 February 2009).

Hodkinson, P. (2004) Research as a form of work: expertise, community and methodological objectivity, *British Educational Research Journal*, 30(1): 9–26.

Hodkinson, P. (2008) 'What works' does not work! Researching lifelong learning in the culture of audit. Valedictory Lecture, Lifelong Learning Institute, the University of Leeds, June.

Hodkinson, H. (2009) Improving schoolteachers' workplace learning, S. Gewirtz, P. Mahony, I. Hextall, and A. Cribb, A. (eds), *Changing Teacher Professionalism*. London: Routledge.

Hodkinson, H. and Hodkinson, P. (2005) Improving schoolteachers' workplace learning, *Research Papers in Education* 20(2) 109–31.

Hodkinson, P. and James, D. (2003) Transforming learning cultures in further education, *Journal of Vocational Education and Training*, 55(4): 389–406.

Holmberg, B. (1989) *Theory and Practice of Distance Education*. Routledge: London.

House of Commons Education Committee (2012) *Great Teachers: Attracting, Training and Retaining the Best. Ninth Report of Session 2012–12 Volume 1*. London: The Stationery Office.

Hoyle, D. (2008) *Problematizing Every Child Matters, The Encyclopaedia of Informal Education*. http://www.infed.org (accessed 11 August 2008).

Huddleston, P. and Oh, S-A. (2004) The magic roundabout: work-related learning within the 14–19 curriculum, *Oxford Review of Education*, 30(1): 83–103.

Hunt, R. and Jensen, J. (2006) *The School Report: The Experiences of Young Gay People in Britain's Schools*. Stonewall. http://stonewall.org.uk/education_for_all/research/1790.asp (accessed 14 January 2007).

Husu, J., Toom, A. and Patrikainen, S. (2008) Guided reflection as a means to demonstrate and develop student teachers' competencies, *Reflective Practice*, 9(1): 37–51.

Hyland, T. and Merrill, B. (2003) *The Changing Face of Further Education: Lifelong Learning, Inclusion and Community Values in Further Education*. London: RoutledgeFalmer.

Information Authority (2012) *Further Education Public Information (FEPI) Update*. http://www.theia.org.uk (accessed 4 February 2013).

IfL (Institute for Learning) (2008) *Promote: The Code of Professional Practice*. London: IfL.

Jackson, A. and Wallis, B. (2006) No pain, no gain? Learning from inspection, *Research in Post-Compulsory Education*, 11(3): 251–66.

Jacques, D. and Salmon, G. (2007) *Learning in Groups*, 4th edn. Abingdon: Routledge.

James, D. and Biesta, G. (eds) (2007) *Improving Learning Cultures in Further Education*. London: Routledge.

James, D. and Bloomer, M. (2001) Cultures of learning and the learning of cultures. Paper presented at the Cultures of Learning Conference, University of Bristol, April.

Jameson, J. (2012) Coaching as a pedagogical approach, in City and Guilds Centre for Skills Development, *The Role of Coaching in Vocational Education and Training*. London: City and Guilds of London Institute.

Jarvis, P. (2004) *Adult Education and Lifelong Learning: Theory and Practice*, 3rd edn. London: RoutledgeFalmer.

Jeffrey, B. and Craft, A. (2001) The universalization of creativity, in A. Craft, B. Jeffrey and M. Leibling (eds), *Creativity in Education*. London: Continuum.

Jenkins, R. (1992) *Pierre Bourdieu*. London: Routledge.

JISC (Joint Information Systems Committee) (2003) *Duty of Care in the Further and Higher Education Sectors*. http://www.jisclegal.ac.uk/publications/Dutyofcare.htm (accessed 31 May 2013).

JISC (Joint Information Systems Committee) (2004) *Effective Practice with E-learning: A Good Practice Guide in Designing for Learning*. Bristol: University of Bristol JISC Development Group.

JISC (Joint Information Systems Committee) InfoNet (2008) *Exploring Tangible Benefits of E-learning: Does Investment Yield Interest?* Newcastle: Northumbria University.

JISC (Joint Information Systems Committee) (2011) Digital literacy anatomised: access, skills and practices. In JISC (ed.), *Digital Literacy Workshops*. Bristol: JISC.

Johnson, D. and Johnson, F. (2006) *Joining Together: Group Theory and Group Skills*, 9th edn. London: Pearson Education.

Johnson, T. (1972) *Professions and Power*. London: Macmillan.

Jones, K. (2003) *Education in Britain: 1944 to the Present*. Cambridge: Polity Press.

Jones, P., Selby, D. and Sterling, S. (eds) (2010) *Sustainability Education: Perspectives and Practice Across Higher Education*. Oxford: Earthscan.

Jones, R., Hughes, M. and Kingston, K. (2008) *An Introduction to Sports Coaching: From Science and Theory to Practice*. London: Routledge.

Joseph Rowntree Foundation (2007) *Experiences of Poverty and Disadvantage*. http://www.jrf. org.uk/knowledge/findings/socialpolicy/2123.asp (accessed 28 May 2013).

Kael, P. (1970) On 'Before the Revolution', *The New Yorker*, October 25.

Kandola, R. and Fullerton, J. (1998) *Diversity in Action: Managing the Mosaic*, 2nd edn. London: Institute of Personnel and Development.

Keep, E. (2006) State control of the English education and training system – playing with the biggest train set in the world, *Journal of Vocational Education and Training*, 58(1): 47–64.

Kelly, A.V. (2009) *The Curriculum: Theory and Practice*, 6th edn. London: Sage.

Kennedy, H. (1997) *Learning Works: Widening Participation in Further Education*. Coventry: Further Education Funding Council.

Kerfoot, D. and Whitehead, S. (1998) 'Boys own' stuff: masculinity and the management of further education, *Sociological Review*, 46(3): 436–57.

Kessler, S. and Bayliss, F. (1998) *Contemporary British Industrial Relations*, 3rd edn. London: Macmillan.

King, A. (1992) Facilitating elaborative learning through guided student-generated questioning, *Educational Psychologist*, 27(1): 111–126.

Kirkpatrick, D. (1998) *Evaluating Training Programmes: The Four Levels*. San Francisco, CA: Berrett-Koehler Publishers.

Klein, P. (2003) Rethinking the multiplicity of cognitive resources and curricular representations: alternatives to 'learning styles' and 'multiple intelligences', *Journal of Curriculum Studies*, 35(1): 45–81.

Knight, P. (1995) *Assessment for Learning in Higher Education*. London: Kogan Page.

Knight, P. and Yorke, M. (2003) *Assessment, Learning and Employability*. Maidenhead: Society for Research into Higher Education and Open University Press.

Knowles, M., Holton, E. and Swanson, R. (2005) *The Adult Learner*, 6th edn. London: Elsevier.

Kolb, D.A. (1984) *Experiential Learning: Experience as the Source of Learning and Development*. Englewood Cliffs, NJ: Prentice Hall.

Kundnani, A. (2002) *The Death of Multiculturalism*. London: Institute of Race Relations. http://www.irr.org.uk/2002/april/ak000001.html (accessed 28 May 2013).

Larivee, B. (2000) Transforming teaching practice: becoming the critically reflective teacher, *Reflective Practice*, 1(3): 293–307.

Lauder, H., Brown, P., Dillabough, J-A. and Halsey, A. (2006) *Education, Globalization and Social Change*. Oxford: Oxford University Press.

Laurillard, D. (2002) *Rethinking University Teaching: A Framework for the Effective Use of Learning Technologies*, 2nd edn. Abingdon: RoutledgeFalmer.

Lave, J. and Wenger, E. (1991) *Situated Learning: Legitimate Peripheral Participation*. Cambridge: Cambridge University Press.

Law, J. (2003) *Making a Mess with Method*. Lancaster: Centre for Science Studies, Lancaster University. http://www.lancs.ac.uk/fass/sociology/papers/law-making-a-messwith-method.pdf (accessed 28 June 2009).

Leadbeater, C. (2005) *Learning About Personalisation: How Can We Put the Learner at the Heart of the Education System?* Nottingham: DfES.

Le Cornu, R. (2005) Peer mentoring: engaging pre-service teachers in mentoring one another, *Mentoring and Tutoring*, 13(3): 355–66.

Leitch Review of Skills (2006) *Prosperity for All in the Global Economy – World Class Skills*. Norwich: HMSO.

Little, S.G. and Akin-Little, K.A. (2008) Psychology's contributions to classroom management, *Psychology in the Schools*, 45: 227–34.

LLUK (Lifelong Learning UK) (2005) *Further Education Workforce Data for England: An Analysis of the Staff Individualised Record (SIR) for 2003–04*. London: LLUK.

LLUK (Lifelong Learning UK) (2007a) *New Overarching Professional Standards for Teachers, Tutors and Trainers in the Lifelong Learning Sector*. London: LLUK.

LLUK (Lifelong Learning UK) (2007b) *Addressing Literacy, Language, Numeracy and ICT Needs in Education and Training: Defining the Minimum Core of Teachers' Knowledge, Understanding and Personal Skills*. London: LLUK.

LLUK (Lifelong Learning UK) (2007c) *Inclusive Learning Approaches for Literacy, Language, Numeracy and ICT*. London: LLUK.

LLUK (Lifelong Learning UK) (2009) *Overview of About LLUK*. http://www. lluk.org/3169.htm (accessed 3 February 2009).

Loughran, J. (2006) A response to 'Reflecting on the self', *Reflective Practice*, 7(1): 43–53.

Loughran, J. and Berry, A. (2005) Modelling by teacher educators, *Teaching and Teacher Education*, 21: 193–203.

Lovell, T. (2000) Thinking feminism within and against Bourdieu, in B. Fowler (ed.), *Reading Bourdieu on Society and Change*. Oxford: Blackwell.

LSC (Learning and Skills Council) (2001) *Mentoring Towards Excellence*. London: LSC.

LSC (Learning and Skills Council) (2007a) *Further Education, Work-based Learning, Train to Gain and Adult and Community Learning – Learner Numbers in England: 2006/07* (DIUS Statistical First Release, Ref. ILR/SFR14). Coventry: LSC.

LSC (Learning and Skills Council) (2007b) *Framework for Excellence: Raising Standards and Informing Choice*. Coventry: Learning and Skills Council.

LSDA (Learning and Skills Development Agency) (2007) *What's Your Problem? Working with Learners with Challenging Behaviour*. London: LSN.

LSIS (Learning and Skills Improvement Service) (2009) *About Subject Learning Coaches*. http:// www.subjectlearningcoaches. net/SLC_role.html (accessed 19 February 2009).

LSIS [Learning and Skills Improvement Service] (2013) *Further Education and Skills in England: New Qualifications for Teachers and Trainers Phase Two – Findings Report*. Coventry: LSIS.

Lucas, N. (1995) Challenges facing teacher education: a view from a post-16 perspective, *Forum*, 37(1): 11–13.

Lucas, N. (2004) *Teaching in Further Education: New Perspectives for a Changing Context*. London: Bedford Way Papers.

Lucas, N. (2007) Rethinking initial teacher education for further education teachers: from a standards-led to a knowledge-based approach, *Teaching Education*, 18(2): 93–106.

Lucas, N. and Unwin, L. (2009) Developing teacher expertise at work: in-service trainee teachers in colleges of further education in England, *Journal of Further and Higher Education*, 33(4): 423–33.

Lucas, N., Nasta, T. and Rogers, L. (2012) From fragmentation to chaos? The regulation of initial teacher training in further education, *British Educational Research Journal*, 38(4): 677–95.

Luckin, R., Clark, W., Logan, K. et al. (2009) Do Web 2.0 tools really open the door to learning? Practices, perceptions and profiles of 11–16 year olds learners, *Learning, Media and Technology*, 34(2): 87–104.

Luke, C. and Gore, J. (1992) *Feminisms and Critical Pedagogy*. London: Routledge.

Lumby, J. (2001) *Managing Further Education: Learning Enterprise*. London: Paul Chapman Publishing.

Lumby, J. and Foskett, N. (2007) Turbulence masquerading as change: exploring 14–19 policy, in D. Raffe and K. Spours (eds), *Policy-making and Policy Learning in 14–19 Education*. London: Institute of Education, University of London.

Lumby, J., Harris, A., Morrison, M. et al. (2005) *Leadership, Development and Diversity in the Learning and Skills Sector*. London: LSRC.

Lunenberg, M., Korthagen, F. and Swennen, A. (2007) The teacher educator as a role model, *Teaching and Teacher Education*, 23(5): 586–601.

Lyotard, J.-F. (1984) *The Postmodern Condition: A Report on Knowledge*. Manchester: University of Manchester Press.

MacDonald, J. and McAteer, E. (2003) New approaches to supporting students: strategies for blended learning in distance and campus based environments, *Journal of Educational Media*, 28(2–3): 129–46.

Macpherson, W. (1999) *The Stephen Lawrence Inquiry: Report of an Inquiry by Sir William Macpherson of Cluny*, Cm 4262. London: The Stationery Office.

Maker, C. (1982) *Curriculum Development for the Gifted*. Rockville, MD: Aspen.

Marriott, G. (2001) *Observing Teachers at Work*. Oxford: Heinemann Educational Publishers.

Martinez, P. and Munday, F. (1998) *9000 Voices: Student Persistence and Dropout in Further Education*. London: Further Education Development Agency.

Marton, F. and Säljö, R. (1976) On qualitative differences in learning: I – Outcome and process, *British Journal of Educational Psychology*, 46: 4–11.

Marx, K. (1968) The eighteenth brumaire of Louis Bonaparte, in K. Marx and F. Engels (eds), *Marx and Engels Selected Works*. London: Lawrence and Wishart.

Maslow, A. (1970) *Motivation and Personality*, 2nd edn. New York: Harper and Row.

Masterman, L. and Vogel, M. (2007) Practices and processes of design for learning, in H. Beetham and R. Sharpe (eds), *Rethinking Pedagogy for a Digital Age: Designing and Delivering E-learning*. Abingdon: Routledge.

May, S. (ed.) (1999) *Critical Multiculturalism: Rethinking Multicultural and Anti-racist Education*. London: Falmer.

Maynard, T. (2000) Learning to teach or learning to manage mentors? Experiences of school-based teacher training, *Mentoring and Tutoring*, 8(1): 17–30.

McLaren, P. (2013) *Critical Pedagogy and Marxism*. London: Continuum.

McCrone, T., Wade, P. and Golden, S. (2007) *The Impact of 14–16 Year Olds on Further Education Colleges*. Slough: NFER.

McDowell, L., Wakelin, D., Montgomery, C. and King, S. (2011) Does assessment for learning make a difference? The development of a questionnaire to explore the student response, *Assessment & Evaluation in Higher Education*, 36(7): 749–765.

McGhee, D. (2005) *Intolerant Britain: Hate, Citizenship and Difference*. Maidenhead: Open University Press.

McLuhan, M. (2001) *Understanding Media: The Extensions of Man*. London: Routledge Classics.

McNally, P. and Martin, S. (1998) Support and challenge in learning to teach: the role of the mentor, *Asia-Pacific Journal of Teacher Education*, 26(1): 39–50.

Medway, P. (2005) Literacy and the idea of English, *Changing English*, 12(1): 19–29.

Megginson, D. and Clutterbuck, D. (1999) *Mentoring Executives and Directors*. Oxford: Butterworth Heinemann.

Meighan, R. and Siraj-Blatchford, I. (1997) *A Sociology of Educating*. London: Cassell.

MHF (Mental Health Foundation) (2009) *Mental Health Problems*. http://www.mental health.org. uk/information/ (accessed 8 March 2009).

Millerson, G. (1964) *The Qualifying Associations*. London: Routledge Kegan and Paul.

Minton, D. (1991) *Teaching Skills in Further and Adult Education*. London: Palgrave MacMillan.

Modood, T. (2005) *Multicultural Politics: Racism, Ethnicity and Muslims in Britain*. Edinburgh: Edinburgh University Press.

Modood, T., Berthoud, R., Lakey, J. et al. (1997) *Ethnic Minorities in Britain: Diversity and Disadvantage*. London: PSI.

MoE (Ministry of Education) (1959) *15–18: A Report of the Central Advisory Council for Education*, Crowther Report. London: HMSO.

Moon, J. (1999) *Reflection in Learning and Professional Development*. London: Kogan Page.

Moore, A. (1999) Beyond reflection: contingency, idiosyncrasy and reflexivity in initial teacher education, in M. Hammersley (ed.), *Researching School Experience*. London: Falmer.

Moore, M.G. (1980) Independent study, in R. Boyd and J. Apps (eds), *Redefining the Discipline of Adult Education*. Washington, DC: Jossey Bass.

Morgan-Klein, B. and Osborne, M. (2007) *The Concepts and Practices of Lifelong Learning*. London: Routledge

Morrison, K. and Ridley, K. (1989) Ideological contexts for curriculum planning, in M. Preedy (ed.), *Approaches to Curriculum Management*. Milton Keynes: Open University Press.

Muijs, D. and Reynolds, D. (2011) *Effective Teaching: Evidence and Practice*, 3rd edn. London: SAGE Publications.

Mumford, A. (1995) Learning styles and mentoring, *Industrial and Commercial Training*, 27(8): 4–7.

Munro, E. (2011) *The Munro Review of Child Protection. Final Report. A Child-Centred System*. London: The Stationery Office.

Nasta, T. (2007) Translating national standards into practice for the initial training of further education (FE) teachers, *Research in Post-Compulsory Education*, 12(1): 1–17.

NACCCE (National Advisory Committee on Creative and Cultural Education) (1999) *All Our Futures: Creativity, Culture and Education*. London: DfEE.

National Audit Office (2007) *Staying the Course: The Retention of Students in Higher Education*. London: The Stationery Office.

NCE (National Commission on Education) (1993) *Learning to Succeed*. London: Heinemann.

Nayak, A. (1999) White English ethnicities: racism, anti-racism and student perspectives, *Race, Ethnicity and Education*, 2(2): 177–202.

NCET (National Council for Educational Technology) (1993) *Differentiation: A Practical Handbook of Classroom Strategies*. Coventry: NCET.

NCIHE (National Committee of Inquiry into Higher Education) (1997) *Higher Education in the Learning Society: Report of the National Committee*, Dearing Report. London: NCIHE.

NIACE (National Institute of Adult Continuing Education) (2006) *More Than a Language: NIACE Committee of Enquiry on English for Speakers of Other Languages Executive Summary*. Leicester: NIACE.

Nicholas, D., Rowlands, I. and Huntington, P. (2008) *Information Behaviour of the Researcher of the Future: Executive Summary*. London: JISC.

Nicol, D. and Macfarlane-Dick, D. (2006) Formative assessment and self-regulated learning: a model and seven principles of good feedback practice, *Studies in Higher Education*, 31(2): 199–218.

Nixon, L., Gregson, M. and Spedding, T. (2007) Pedagogy and the intuitive appeal of learning styles in post-compulsory education in England, *Journal of Vocational Education and Training*, 59(1): 39–51.

Norton Grubb, W. (1999) Improvement or control? A US view of English inspection, in C. Cullingford (ed.), *An Inspector Calls. Ofsted and its Effect on School Standards*. London: Kogan Page.

NUT (National Union of Teachers) (2003) *Risk Assessment: NUT Health and Safety Briefings*. London: NUT. http://www.teachers.org.uk/resources/pdf/risk.pdf (accessed on 20 February 2009).

Oblinger, D. and Oblinger, J. (2005) Is it age or IT?: first steps toward understanding the net generation, in D. Oblinger and J. Oblinger (eds), *Educating the Net Generation*. www.educause.edu/educatingthenetgen/ (accessed 24 January 2009).

O'Connell, B. (2005) *Creating an Outstanding College*. Cheltenham: Nelson Thornes.

Ofqual (2008) *Launch Brochure*. http://www.ofqual.gov.uk/.les/Ofqual_Launch Brochure.pdf (accessed 2 February 2009).

Ofqual (2011) *GCSE Subject Criteria for English Language*. Coventry: Ofqual.

Ofqual (2012a) *QCF, NQF and ECF*. http://www.ofqual.gov.uk/qualifications-and-assessments/qualification-frameworks/ (accessed 20 February 2013).

Ofqual (2012b) *Comparing Qualifications Levels*. http://www.ofqual.gov.uk/help-and-advice/comparing-qualifications/ (accessed 2 February 2013).

Ofsted (Office for Standards in Education) (2003) *The Initial Training of Further Education Teachers: A Survey*. London: Ofsted.

Ofsted (Office for Standards in Education) (2005a) *Race Equality in Further Education: A Report by HMI*. London: Ofsted.

Ofsted (2005b) *Managing Challenging Behaviour*. London: Ofsted.

Ofsted (Office for Standards in Education) (2009) *About Us*. http://www.ofsted.gov.uk/Ofsted-home/About-us (accessed 2 February 2009).

Ofsted (2012a) (Office for Standards in Education) *The Report of Her Majesty's Chief Inspector of Education, Children's Services and Skills: Learning and Skills*. Manchester: Ofsted.

Ofsted (2012b) *Handbook for the Inspection of Further Education and Skills*. Manchester: Ofsted.

Ofsted (2012c) *How Colleges Improve. A review of Effective Practice: What Makes an Impact and Why.* Manchester: Ofsted.

Ofsted (2012d) *Common Inspection Framework for Further Education and Skills.* Manchester: Ofsted.

Ofsted (2014) *Initial Teacher Education (ITE) Inspection Handbook: For Use From June 2014.* Manchester: Ofsted.

Ollin, R. and Tucker, J. (2012) *The Vocational Assessor Handbook,* 5th edn. London: Kogan Page.

Orr, K. (2008) Room for improvement? The impact of compulsory professional development for teachers in England's further education sector, *Journal of In-Service Education,* 34(1): 97–108.

Osborne, M., Houston, M. and Toman, N. (eds) (2007) *The Pedagogy of Lifelong Learning.* London: Routledge.

O'Toole, G. and Meyer, B. (2006) *Personalised Learning in the Post-16 Sector: A Preliminary Investigation.* London: Learning and Skills Network.

Ozga, J. and Lawn, M. (1981) *Teachers, Professionalism and Class.* London: Falmer.

Pahl, K. and Rowsell, J. (2005) *Literacy and Education: Understanding the New Literacy Studies in the Classroom.* London: Paul Chapman.

Papen, U. (2005) *Adult Literacy as Social Practice: More Than Skills.* London: Routledge.

Parker, S. (1997) *Reflective Teaching in the Postmodern World.* Buckingham: Open University Press.

Parsloe, E. and Leedham, M. (2009) *Coaching and Mentoring: Practical Conversations to Improve Learning.* London: Kogan Page.

Paul, R. and Elder, L. (2006) *The Thinker's Guide to the Art of Socratic Questioning.* Tomales, CA: The Critical Thinking Foundation.

Pearson, E. and Podeschi, R. (1999) Humanism and individualism: Maslow and his critics, *Adult Education Quarterly,* 50(1): 41–55.

Petty, G., (2009) *Evidence-based Teaching: A Practical Approach,* 2nd edn. Cheltenham: Nelson Thornes.

Piaget, J. and Inhelder, B. (1969) *The Psychology of the Child.* New York: Basic Books.

Pintrich, P. and Zusho, A. (2002) Student motivation and self-regulated learning in the college classroom, in J.C. Smart and W.G. Tierney (eds), *Higher Education: Handbook of Theory and Research,* Volume XVII. New York: Agathon Press.

Polanyi, M. (1983) *The Tacit Dimension.* Gloucester, MA: Peter Smith.

Pollard, A., Collins, J., Simco, N. et al. (2005) *Reflective Teaching,* 2nd edn. London: Continuum.

Pratt, J. (2000) The emergence of the colleges, in A. Smithers and P. Robinson (eds), *Further Education Re-formed.* London: Falmer.

Prensky, M. (2001) Digital natives, digital immigrants, *On the Horizon* (NCB University Press), 9(5): 1–15.

Preston, J. (2003) White trash vocationalism? Formations of class and race in an Essex further education college, *Widening Participation and Lifelong Learning,* 5(2): 6–17.

Pring, R. (2000) *Philosophy of Educational Research.* London: Continuum.

Purdy, L. (2007) Educating gifted children, in R. Curren (ed.), *Philosophy of Education: An Anthology.* Oxford: Blackwell.

Putnam, R. (2000) *Bowling Alone.* London: Touchstone Books.

QAA (Quality Assurance Agency) (2008) *The Framework for Higher Education Qualifications in England, Wales and Northern Ireland* (FHEQ). Gloucester: QAA.

QCA (Qualifications and Curriculum Authority) (2000) *National Standards for Adult Literacy and Numeracy.* London: QCA.

QCA (Qualifications and Curriculum Authority) (2007) *Functional Skills.* http://www.qca.org.uk/qca_6062.aspx (accessed 12 June 2008).

Ramsden, P. (1992) *Learning to Teach in Higher Education.* London: Routledge.

Randle, K. and Brady, N. (1997) Managerialism and professionalism in the 'Cinderella Service', *Journal of Vocational Education and Training*, 49(1): 121–40.

Rebbeck, G., and Ecclesfield, N. (2008) *E-Maturity and Staff Development Needs: Relating Individual and Organisational Perspectives* www.excellencegateway.org.uk/download. aspx?o=266707(accessed

Reeves, F. (1995) *The Modernity of FE: The Direction of Change in FE Colleges*. Bilston: Bilston College Publications.

Rennie, S. (2003) *Stories from the Front Line: The Impact of Inspection on Practitioners*. London: LSDA.

Rennie, S. (2006) *Promoting Equality and Diversity in Consortium for PCET Teacher Training Courses*. Huddersfield: Consortium for Post-Compulsory Education and Training.

Richardson, W. (2007) In search of the further education of young people in post-war England, *Journal of Vocational Education and Training*, 59(3): 385–418.

Ritchie, D. (2001) *Oldham Independent Review – One Oldham, One Future*. Manchester: Government Office for the Northwest.

Ritzer, G. (2008) *The McDonaldization of Society*. Los Angeles, CA: Pine Forge Press.

Robson, J. (2006) *Teacher Professionalism in Further and Higher Education: Challenges to Culture and Practice*. London: Routledge.

Robson, J. and Bailey, B. (2009) 'Bowing from the heart': an investigation into discourses of professionalism and the work of caring for students in further education, *British Educational Research Journal*, 35(1): 99–117.

Robson, J., Bailey, B. and Larkin, S. (2004) Adding value: investigating the discourse of professionalism adopted by vocational teachers in further education colleges, *Journal of Education and Work*, 17(2): 183–95.

Rodd, J. (2006) *Leadership in Early Childhood*. Maidenhead: Open University Press.

Rogers, A. (2002) *Teaching Adults*. Buckingham: Open University Press.

Rogers, B. (2004) *Cracking the Challenging Class*. Hendon: Books Education.

Rogers, C. (1983) *Freedom to Learn for the 1980s*. Columbus, OH: Charles E. Merrill Publishing Company.

Rogers, C. and Freiberg, J. (1994) *Freedom to Learn*, 3rd edn. New Jersey: Prentice Hall.

Rogers, J. (2007) *Adults Learning*, 5th edn. Maidenhead: Open University Press.

Rosenthal, L. (2004) Do school inspections improve school quality? Ofsted inspections and school examination results in the UK, *Economics of Education Review*, 23(2): 143–51.

Rothstein, D. and Santana, L. (2011) Teaching students to ask their own questions. *Harvard Education Letter*, 27(5): 1–2.

RSA (Royal Society for the Encouragement of Arts, Manufacture and Commerce) (2002) *Professional Values for the 21st Century*. London: RSA.

Ryle, G. (1949) *The Concept of Mind*. London: Hutchinson.

Sachdev, D. and Harries, B. (2006) *Learning and Skills Planning and Provision for Migrants from the Accession States: An Exploratory Study*. London: Learning and Skills Network.

Sadler, D. (1989) Formative assessment and the design of instructional systems, *Instructional Science*, 18(2): 119–44.

Saljö, R. (2009) Learning, theories of learning, and units of analysis in research. *Educational Psychologist*, 44(3): 202–8.

Salmon, G. (2003) *E-moderating: The Key to Teaching and Learning Online*, 2nd edn. London: RoutledgeFalmer.

Scarman, Lord (1981) *A Report into the Brixton Disturbances of 11/12 April 1981*. London: Home Office.

Schön, D.A. (1983) *The Reflective Practitioner: How Professionals Think in Action*. London: Temple Smith

Schön, D.A. (1987) *Educating the Reflective Practitioner: Towards a New Design for Teaching and Learning in the Professions*. San Francisco, CA: Jossey Bass.

Scriven, M. (1967) The methodology of evaluation, in R.E. Stake (ed.), *Perspectives of Curriculum Evaluation* (Vol. 1). Chicago: Rand McNally.

SEC (Secondary Examinations Council) (1985) *Working Paper 2: Coursework Assessment in GCSE*. London: SEC.

Seifert, T. (2004) Understanding student motivation, *Educational Research*, 46(2): 137–49.

Selwyn, N. (2009) The digital native: myth and reality, *Aslib Proceedings*, 61(4): 364–79.

Sfard, A. (1998) On two metaphors for learning and the dangers of choosing just one, *Educational Researcher*, 27(2): 4–13.

Shain, F. and Gleeson, D. (1999) Under new management: changing conceptions of teacher professionalism and policy in the further education sector, *Journal of Educational Policy*, 14(4): 445–62.

Shaw, R. and Colimore, K. (1988) Humanistic psychology as ideology: an analysis of Maslow's contradictions, *Journal of Humanistic Psychology*, 28(3): 51–74.

Shildrick, T., MacDonald, R., Webster, C. and Garthwaite, K. (2012) *Poverty and Insecurity: Life in Low-pay, No-pay Britain*. Bristol: Policy Press.

Simkins, T. and Lumby, J. (2002) Cultural transformation in further education? Mapping the debate, *Research in Post-compulsory Education*, 7(1): 9–25.

Simmons, R. (2008) Raising the age of compulsory education in England: a NEET solution? *British Journal of Educational Studies*, 56(4): 420–39.

Simmons, R. (2009) The long goodbye: how local authorities lost control of further education, *Research in Post-Compulsory Education*, 14(3): 287–97.

Simmons, R. and Thompson, R. (2007) Aiming higher? How will universities respond to changes in initial teacher training for the post-compulsory sector in England? *Journal of Further and Higher Education*, 31(2): 171–82.

Simmons, R. and Thompson, R. (2008) Creativity and performativity: the case of further education, *British Educational Research Journal*, 34(5): 601–18.

Simmons, R. and Thompson, R. (2011) *NEET Young People and Training for Work: Learning on the Margins*. Stoke-on-Trent: Trentham Books.

Simon, B. (1991) *Education and the Social Order 1940–1990*. London: Lawrence and Wishart.

Sivanandan, A. (2005) *Its Anti-racism that was Failed, Not Multiculturalism that Failed*. http://www.irr.org.uk/2005/october/ak000021.html (accessed 20 November 2005).

Smith, A. (2004) 'Off-campus support' in distance learning – how do our students define quality? *Quality Assurance in Education*, 12(1): 28–38.

Smith, E. and Gorard, S. (2005) 'They don't give us our marks': The role of formative feedback in student progress, *Assessment in Education: Principles, Policy & Practice*, 12(1): 21–38.

Smith, G. (2000) Research and inspection: HMI and Ofsted, 1981–1996 a commentary, *Oxford Review of Education*, 26(3/4): 333–52.

Smithers, A. (1993) *All Our Futures: Britain's Education Revolution*. London: Channel 4 (Dispatches Report).

Smyth, S., Houghton, C., Cooney, A. and Casey, D. (2012) Students' experiences of blended learning across a range of postgraduate programmes, *Nurse Education Today*, 32(4): 464.

Social Exclusion Unit (1999) *Bridging the Gap: New Opportunities for 16–18-year-olds Not in Education, Employment or Training*. London: HMSO.

Solomos, J. (2003) *Race and Racism in Britain*, 3rd edn. Basingstoke: Palgrave Macmillan.

Sparrow, S. (2008) Spot the difference, *Training and Coaching Today*, March: 18.

Standing, G. (2011) *The Precariat: The New Dangerous Class*. London: Bloomsbury.

Stanton, G. and Fletcher, M. (2006) 14–19 institutional arrangements in England: a research perspective on collaboration, competition and patterns of post-16 provision, *Nuffield Review of 14–19 Education and Training*, Working Paper 38.

Stanulis, R. and Russell, D. (2000) Jumping in: trust and communication in mentoring student teachers, *Teaching and Teacher Education*, 16(1): 65–80.

Starr, J. (2003) *The Coaching Manual: The Definitive Guide to the Process and Skills of Personal Coaching*. Harlow: Pearson Education.

Stenhouse, L. (1981) *An Introduction to Curriculum Research and Development*. London: Heinemann.

Strayer, J. F. (2012). How learning in an inverted classroom influences cooperation, innovation and task orientation. *Learning Environments Research*, 15(2): 171–93.

Stredwick, J. (2005) *Introduction to Human Resource Management*, 2nd edn. Oxford: Butterworth Heinemann.

SFA (Skills Funding Agency) (2010) *Fact Sheet: Foundation Learning Curriculum for Adults*. Coventry: SFA.

Suter, M. (2007) Constructing the reflective practitioner. Unpublished doctoral thesis, Manchester Metropolitan University.

Swaffield, S. (2011) Getting to the heart of authentic assessment for learning, *Assessment in Education: Principles, Policy & Practice*, 18(4): 433–49.

Sweeney, J., O'Donoghue, T. and Whitehead, C. (2004) Traditional face-to-face and web-based tutorials: a study of university students' perspectives on the roles of tutorial participants, *Teaching in Higher Education*, 9(3): 311–23.

Taylor, R. (2002) Shaping the culture of learning communities, *Principal Leadership*, 3(4): 42–5.

Taylor, P.H. and Richards, C. (1979) *An Introduction to Curriculum Studies*. Windsor: NFER.

Taylor, E., Gillborn, D. and Ladson-Billings, G. (2009) *Foundations of Critical Race Theory in Education*. London: Routledge.

Thomas, P. (2006) The impact of community cohesion on youth work: a case study from Oldham, *Youth and Policy*, 93: 41–60.

Thompson, E.P. (1980) *The Making of the English Working Class*. London: Penguin Books.

Thompson, M. (2007) A critique of the impact of policy and funding, in G. Conole and M. Oliver (eds), *Contemporary Perspectives in E-learning Research*. London: Routledge.

Thompson, R. (2009) Social class and participation in further education: evidence from the youth cohort study of England and Wales, *British Journal of Sociology of Education*, 30(1): 29–42.

Thompson, R. (2010) Teaching on the margins: tutors, discourse and pedagogy in work-based learning for young people, *Journal of Vocational Education and Training*, 62(2): 123–37.

Thompson, R. (2014) *Initial Teacher Education for the Education and Training Sector in England: Development and Change in Generic and Subject Specialist Provision*. London: Gatsby Foundation (in press).

Thompson, R. and Robinson, D. (2008) Changing step or marking time? Teacher education reforms for the learning and skills sector in England, *Journal of Further and Higher Education*, 32(2): 161–73.

Thornton, M. (1998) *Subject Specialists: Primary Schools*, UCET Occasional Papers No.10. London: UCET.

Tomlinson, M. (2004) *14–19 Curriculum and Qualifications Reform: Final Report of the Working Group on 14–19 Reform*. Annesley: DfES publications.

Tomlinson, S. (2008a) *Education in a Post-welfare Society*, 2nd edn. Maidenhead: Open University Press.

Tomlinson, S. (2008b) Gifted, talented and high ability: selection for education in a one-dimensional world, *Oxford Review of Education*, 34(1): 59–74.

Tooley, J. and Darby, D. (1998) *Educational Research: A Critique*. London: Ofsted.

Torrance, H. and Pryor, J. (1998) *Investigating Formative Assessment: Teaching and Learning in the Classroom.* Buckingham: Open University Press.

Tripp, D. (1993) *Critical Incidents in Teaching.* London: Routledge.

Troman, G. (2003) Teacher stress in the low-trust society, in L. Kydd, L. Anderson and W. Newton (eds), *Leading People and Teams in Education.* London: Paul Chapman Publishing.

Troyna, B. (1984) Fact or artefact? The 'educational underachievement' of black pupils, *British Journal of Sociology of Education,* 5(2): 153–66.

Tuckman, B. and Jensen, M. (1977) Stages of small-group development revisited, *Group and Organization Management,* 2(4): 419–27.

Tummons, J. (2011) *Assessing Learning in the Lifelong Learning Sector.* Exeter: Learning Matters.

Tummons, J. (2008) Assessment, and the literacy practices of trainee PCET teachers, *International Journal of Educational Research,* 47(3): 184–91.

Twining, P., Broadie, R., Cook, D. et al. (2006) *Educational Change and ICT: The Current Landscape and Implementation Issues.* Coventry: BECTA.

Tyler, R. (1949) *Basic Principles of Curriculum and Instruction.* Chicago: Chicago University Press.

UKBA (United Kingdom Border Agency) (2012) *Tier 4 UKBA Sponsor Guide.* http://www.ukba.homeoffice.gov.uk/sitecontent/documents/employersand sponsors/pbsguidance/ (accessed 7 May 2013).

UKCISA (UK Council for International Student Affairs) (2013) *International Students in UK Higher Education: Key Statistics.* http://www.ukcisa.org.uk/about/statistics_he.php (accessed 3 January 2013).

Vähäsantanen, K. and Eteläpelto, A. (2009) Vocational teachers in the face of a major educational reform: individual ways of negotiating professional identities, *Journal of Education and Work,* 22(1): 15–33.

Vaizey, J. (1962) *Education for Tomorrow.* Harmondsworth: Penguin.

Van Lieshout, M., Egyedl, T.M. and Dijker, W.E. (2001) *Social Learning Technologies: The Introduction of Multimedia in Education.* Aldershot: Ashgate.

Van Maanen, J. (1995) *Representation in Ethnography.* Thousand Oaks, CA: Sage.

Vicars, M. (2007) *Sexual Orientation: A Practical Guide to Equality.* The East Coast Centre for Diversity. http://www.grimsby.ac.uk/Eccd/documents/ LSCDiversity-LGBT-final.pdf (accessed 12 June 2008).

Villeneuve-Smith, F., Munoz, S. and McKenzie, E. (2008) *FE Colleges: The Frontline Under Pressure? A Staff Satisfaction Survey of FE Colleges in England.* London: Learning and Skills Network.

Vizard, D. (2007) *How to Manage Behaviour in Further Education.* London: Paul Chapman Publishing.

Vogel, M. (2010) *Engaging Academics in Professional Development for Technology-enhanced Learning: A Synthesis Project for the UK's Higher Education Academy.* York: Higher Education Academy.

von Glasersfeld, E. (1995) A constructivist approach to teaching, in L.P. Steffe and J. Gale (eds), *Constructivism in Education.* Hillsdale, NJ: Lawrence Erlbaum Associates.

Wacquant, L. (1989) Towards a reflexive sociology: a workshop with Pierre Bourdieu, *Sociological Theory,* 7(1): 26–63.

Waitt, I. (ed.) (1980) *College Administration.* London: NATFHE.

Walhberg, M. and Gleeson, D. (2003) 'Doing the business': paradox and irony in vocational education – GNVQ business studies as a case in point, *Journal of Vocational Education and Training,* 55(4): 423–46.

Wallace, S. (2002a) No good surprises: intending lecturers' preconceptions and initial experiences of further education, *British Educational Research Journal,* 28(1): 79–93.

Wallace, S. (2002b) *Managing Behaviour and Motivating Students in Further Education.* Exeter: Learning Matters.

Wallace, S. and Gravells, J. (2007) *Mentoring.* Exeter: Learning Matters.

Wallis, J. (ed.) (1996) *Liberal Adult Education: The End of an Era?* Nottingham: University of Nottingham.

Warren Little, J. (1992) *Stretching the Subject: The Subject Organisation of High Schools and the Transformation of Work Education.* Berkeley, CA: National Center for Research in Vocational Education, University of California at Berkeley. http://vocserve. berkeley.edu/ AllInOne/MDS-471.html (accessed 7 March 2009).

Watson, J. and Rayner, R. (1920) Conditioned emotional reactions, *Journal of Experimental Psychology*, 3(1): 1–14.

Weeden, P., with Winter, J. and Broadfoot, P. (2000) *The LEARN Project Phase 2: Guidance for Schools on Assessment for Learning.* Bristol: CLIO Centre for Assessment Studies, University of Bristol.

Weiner, M.J. (1981) *English Culture and the Decline of the Industrial Spirit, 1850–1980.* Cambridge: Cambridge University Press.

Weller, M. (2007) *Virtual Learning Environments: Using, Choosing and Developing Your VLE.* London: Routledge.

Wenger, E. (1998) *Communities of Practice: Learning, Meaning and Identity.* Cambridge: Cambridge University Press.

Wheeler, S. (2007) The influence of communication technologies and approaches to study on transactional distance in blended learning, *ALT-j, Research in Learning Technology*, 15(2): 103–17.

White, E. (2011) Working towards explicit modelling: experiences of a new teacher educator, *Professional Development in Education*, 37(4): 483–97.

Williams, S. (2003) Conflict in the colleges: industrial relations in FE since incorporation, *Journal of Further and Higher Education*, 27(3): 307–15.

Willis, P. (1977) *Learning to Labour: How Working Class Kids Get Working Class Jobs.* Farnham: Ashgate.

Winchester, D. and Bach, S. (1995) The State: the public sector, in P. Edwards (ed.), *Industrial Relations: Theory and Practice in Britain.* Oxford: Blackwell.

Wittgenstein, L. (1953) *Philosophical Investigations.* Oxford: Blackwell.

Witz, A. (1992) *Professions and Patriarchy.* London: Routledge.

Wolak, J., Finkelhor, D., Mitchell, K.J. and Ybarra, M.L. (2010) Online "predators" and their victims, *Psychology of Violence*, 1: 13–35.

Wood, E. and Geddis, A. (1999) Self-conscious narrative and teacher education: representing practice in professional course work, *Teaching and Teacher Education*, 15: 107–19.

Woodrow, M. (1993) Franchising: the quiet revolution, *Higher Education Quarterly*, 47(3): 207–20.

Wolf, A. (2011) *Review of Vocational Education: The Wolf Report.* London: Department for Education.

Yammer (2013) *Product Outline.* https://www.yammer.com/product/ (Accessed 15 February 2013).

Yeomans, R. (1986) Hearing secret harmonies; becoming a primary staff member. Paper presented at the British educational research association annual conference, Bristol University, 4–September.

Yilmaz, K. (2008) Constructivism: its theoretical underpinnings, variations, and implications for classroom instruction. *Educational Horizons*, Spring: 161–72.

Yorke, M. and Longden, B. (2004) *Retention and Student Success in Higher Education.* Maidenhead: Open University Press.

Young, M. (ed.) (1971) *Knowledge and Control: New Directions for the Sociology of Education.* London: Collier-Macmillan.

Young, M. (2003) Curriculum studies and the problem of knowledge: updating the Enlightenment? *Policy Futures in Education,* 1(3): 553–64.

Young, M., Lucas, N., Sharp, G. and Cunningham, B. (1995) *Teacher Education for the Further Education Sector: Training the Lecturer of the Future.* London: Association for Colleges / Institute of Education Post-16 Education Centre.

Young, P. (2000) 'I might as well give up': self-esteem and mature students' feelings about feedback on assignments, *Journal of Further and Higher Education,* 24(3): 409–18.

Youth Cohort Study (2009) *Youth Cohort Study & Longitudinal Study of Young People in England: The Activities and Experiences of 17 year olds: England 2008.* London: DCSF.

Youth Cohort Study (2011) *Youth Cohort Study & Longitudinal Study of Young People in England: The Activities and Experiences of 19 year olds: England 2010.* London:, DfE.

Yuval-Davis, N. (1997) Ethnicity, gender relations and multiculturalism, in T. Modood and P. Werbner (eds), *Debating Cultural Hybridity.* London: Zed Books.

Zimmer, R. and Alexander, G. (1996) The Rogerian interface: for open warm empathy in computer-mediated communication, *Innovations in Education and Teaching International,* 33(1): 13–21.

Index

Locators shown in *italics* refer to figures, tables and boxes.

14–19 education
  situation of learners aged, 106–7
  see also further education
15–18 (Crowther Report), 19

ability, exceptional
  priorities and situation of learners with,
    105–6
accreditation of prior experiential learning
  (APEL), 186–7, *187*
achievement, educational
  assessment strategies for gauging, 175–6,
    176
  need for harmony with bodies controlling,
    245–6
  theories about, 32–3
activities, learning
  developing transitions between, 128–9,
    129
  selection and use, 132–5, *133, 134*
administration
  and management of courses, 240–6
adult learners
  characteristics, 101–2
  practices of, 103
  theories of, 102
Adult Learning Inspectorate (ALI), 15, 255
Adult Literacy, Language and Numeracy
  (ALLaN), 125
affective learning, 82, *83*
affordance

of e-based tools for teaching and learning,
  160–1, *161*
agency
  need for commitment to in education
    practice, 38–9
aims and objectives
  significance and use in learning session
    planning, 129–32, *130, 132*
  significance as feature of curricula design
    and development, 116
  ALI (Adult Learning Inspectorate), 15, 255
ALLaN (Adult Literacy, Language and
  Numeracy), 125
ALT (Association of Law Teachers), 196
anti-racism
  definition and characteristics, 66–7
  importance of policy, 67
  problems with notion of, 67–8
  see also cohesion, community; integration,
    community; multiculturalism
anti-sexism
  significance for equality and diversity, 70–1
APCT (Association of Painting Crafts
  Teachers), 196
applications, job, 261–2
appraisal, staff
  and planning of CPD, 266–7
apprenticeships, 122–3
approachability
  need for in mentoring of teachers, 215–16
ARG (Assessment Reform Group), 180–1

assessment
  examples of strategies for, 175–6, *176*
  nature and purpose, 171–2
  of risk in education, 234
  planning and designing, 173–7, *174, 176, 177*
  significance as feature of curricula design and development, 117
  types of task involved, 172–3, *173*
  validity and reliability of, 183–6, *185*
  see also evaluation
  see also elements and factors to consider e.g feedback; moderation and standardisation
  see also outcomes e.g. accreditation of prior experiential learning; achievement, educational
  see also tools e.g. guidelines; specifications, tables of
  see also types e.g. competence-based assessment; criterion-referenced assessment; formative assessment; ipsative assessment; norm-referenced assessment; summative assessment; written assessment
Assessment Reform Group (ARG), 180–1
Associate Teacher Learning and Skills (ATLS), 24, 25
Association of Law Teachers (ALT), 196
Association of Painting Crafts Teachers (APCT), 196
Association of Teachers and Lecturers (ATL), 267
associations, subject
  engagement with as means to enhance specialism, 195–6
assurance, quality
  definition and features of educational, 248–9
ATL (Association of Teachers and Lecturers), 267
ATLS (Associate Teacher Learning and Skills), 24, 25
audiovisuals
  value and use in learning sessions, 141
audit, quality
  development and key features, 248–9
  see also methods e.g. inspections
authorities, awarding
  importance and need for harmony, 245–6

autonomous learning, 9
autonomy, professional
  development and key features, 248–9
awards, teacher
  need for harmony with bodies controlling, 245–6
  significance of framework of, 24–5
  situation following Lingfield review, 25–6

BEC (Business Education Council), 193–4
behaviour, learner
  management of, 149–52, *152*
behaviourism
  interpretations of learning process, 87–9, *88*
bisexuality
  significance for equality and diversity, 71–2
blended learning, 158–9
Blooms taxonomy of learning domains, 185
BNP (British National Party), 69
bodies, awarding
  importance and need for harmony, 245–6
Boud, D., 98–9, *98*
Bourdieu, P.
  theories in relation to work-based learning, 51–3
British National Party (BNP), 69
Brookfield, S., 205
BTEC (Business and Technology Education Council), 119, 193–4
bullying
  types and need for policies, 235
Business, Enterprise and Regulatory Reform, Department of (DBERR), 12–13
Business, Innovation and Skills, Department of,
  role in managing and monitoring lifelong learning, 12–13
Business and Technology Education Council (BTEC), 119, 193–4
Business Education Council (BEC), 193–4

Cantle Report (2001), 68–9
care, duty of, 232
careers, teacher
  appraisal and promotion options, 266–8
  characteristics and challenges of FE, 259–60
  employment and roles in FE, 260–1

usefulness of part time and agency work,
     264–5
see also aspects e.g. applications, job;
     curriculum vitae; development,
     continuing professional
case studies and examples
   assessment strategies for gauging
     achievement, 175–6, *176*
   designing for learning with technology,
     165, 166–8
   use of specification tables, 184–5
Centre for Learning and Performance
     Technologies, 160
Centre of Excellence in Leadership (CEL), 16
Centres of Excellence in Teacher Training
     (CETTs), 27
Certificate in Education (Cert Ed), 20, 25
challenge
   need for in mentoring of teachers, 216–17,
     217
Children, Schools and Families, Department
     of (DCSF), 12–13
CHME (Council for Hospitality Management
     Education), 195–6
class, social
   significance for equality, 75–6
   theories of approach to lifelong learning,
     33
coaches and coaching
   characteristics of experiential, 210–11
   definition and characteristics, 208–10, *209*
   social and situated theories, 211–12, *212*
   see also mentors and mentoring;
     relationships, coaching
   see also tools e.g. observation
coaching-mentoring continuum (Parsloe), *209*
Coalition government
   and education reform, 6–7, 8, 11, 12, 20
   and teacher qualifications, 25–6
   and vocational education, 18–19
   approach to teacher professionalism, 44–5
   approach to widening participation, 101
   inclusion of English and mathematics in
     Skills for Life, 125
   interest in subject specialist pedagogy,
       91–4
         st in widening education
            ipation, 101
               tion of socio-economic and
                  ontexts 32–3

reduction in prominence of *Every Child
     Matters*, 237–8, 238–9
   significance of context for ideas of, 32
   wish to return to traditional academic
     models, 175
   see also initiatives e.g. apprenticeships;
     'English Baccalaureate'; higher
     apprenticeships
   see also organisations e.g. Education,
     Department of
   see also reports of e.g. Lingfield Report
codes, conduct
   teacher professional values and, 43–5
cognitive learning, 82, *83*
cognitivism
   interpretations of learning process, 90–1, *91*
cohesion, community
   criticisms, 69–70
   significance for anti-racism, 68–9
collaboration, inter-professional
   need for in lifelong learning, 45
colleagues
   engagement with as means to enhance
     specialism, 195
college higher education
   development and role, 123
Commission for Black Staff in Further
     Education, 61
Commission for Social Care Inspection
     (CSCI), 255
committees
   membership of course, 246
Common Inspection Framework for post-16
     education, 129, 250
communities, cohesion of
   criticisms, 69–70
   significance for anti-racism, 68–9
'communities of practice,' 53–7, 158–9
Community Cohesion (Cantle Report), 68–9
competence-based assessment; 183
competitiveness
   stance of New Labour towards, 31–2
complexity, education
   policy scholarship approach to
     understanding, 33–6
   computers
   measures to ensure security of, 236–7
conditioning
   classical, 87–8, *88*
   operant, 88

conduct, codes of
    teacher professional values and, 43–5
conferences
    engagement with as means to enhance
        specialism, 196
connectedness, feelings of
    applicability to students online, 158–9
'connoisseurship' model of curricula
    evaluation (Eisner), 252
constructivism
    interpretations of learning process, 91–4, *93*
content
    significance as feature of curricula design
        and development, 117
contingency, education
    policy scholarship approach to
        understanding, 33–6
continuing professional development *see*
    development, continuing professional
Council for Hospitality Management
    Education (CHME), 195–6
courses
    management and administration, 240–6
    see also aspects e.g. assessment; curricula;
        learners and learning; teachers and
        teaching
CPD *see* development, continuing professional
creativity
    significance in developing curricula, 118–19
criterion-referenced assessment, 182–3
critical incident analysis (Tripp), 204–5
critical-organizational reflection, 201–2, *203*
'critical reflection' (Brookfield), 205
Crowther Report (1959), 19
CSCI (Commission for Social Care
    Inspection), 255
cultures, education
    policy scholarship approach to
        understanding, 33–6
currency, subject
    need for teachers to maintain within
        specialism, 194–6
curricula
    definition and characteristics, 109–10
    design and development, 116–17
    management of, 242
    significance of creativity in developing,
        118–19
    situation of in 14–19 education, 121–2
    theories and models, 110–16, *111, 112, 114*

see also approaches to e.g. apprenticeships;
    higher apprenticeships
see also factors impacting e.g. esteem,
    parity of; vocationalism
see also subjects e.g. English for Speakers
    of Other Languages; literacy and
    numeracy
see also venues e.g. further education
curriculum vitae (CVs), 265–6
cycles, experiential (Kolb), 96–7, *97*
cycles, learning, 129, *129*

DBERR (Business, Enterprise and Regulatory
    Reform, Department of), 12–13
    DBS (Disclosure and Barring Service),
        235–6
DCSF (Children, Schools and Families,
    Department of), 12–13
Dearing Report (1997), 28
deep learning, 85
deregulation
    as political focus of education reform, 6
design
    and development of curricula, 116–17
    and planning of assessment, 173–7, *174,
        176, 177*
    of technology for learning, 164–8, *165,
        166–8*
determinism
    applicability to notion of e-learning
        technology, 160
development
    aims and objectives, 129–32, *130, 132*
    and design of curricula, 116–17
    and design of technology for learning,
        164–8, *165, 166–8*
    and planning of learning session, 127–9,
        128, 129
development, continuing professional
    context of FE, 259–60
    engagement with as means to enhance
        specialism, 196
    importance for career progression, 264
    staff appraisal and planning of, 266–7
    see also results e.g. promotion, teacher
differentiation and inclusivity
    role and significance in learning, 142–3
    significance for teaching practice,
        73–4
diplomas, academic, 122

disabilities and disabled
  priorities and situation of learners with,
    62–3, 104–5
  see also factors impacting e.g. inclusivity
    and differentiation
Discipline in Schools (Elton Report), 149
disciplines, specialist
  definition and significance, 190–4
  need for teachers to maintain subject
    currency, 194–6
  significance of interdisciplinarity in, 196–7
Disclosure and Barring Service (DBS),
  235–6
disruption, learner
  management of, 149–52, 152
diversity, learner
  definition and interpretation of concept,
    58–9
  implications for ensuring in teaching, 73–5
  practices of in lifelong learning, 59–64, 61
  see also aspects e.g. bisexuality; gays;
    lesbians; transgender issues
  see also factors impacting e.g. class, social;
    mental health
  see also factors to ensure e.g. anti-racism;
    anti-sexism
  see also targets of e.g. cohesion,
    community; faith and religion, learner;
    integration, community; multiculturalism

EDL (English Defence League), 69
education
  impact of markets and globalisation, 3–5
  need for commitment to agency and social
    practice, 38–9
  need for expansiveness of practice of, 36–8
  socio-economic and political context, 31–6
  see also institutions, education;
    relationships, educational; research,
    educational
  see also factors affecting e.g. diversity,
    learner; equality, learner; faith and
    religion, learner; health and safety; risks
  see also players and elements e.g. learners
    and learning; teachers and teaching
  also types e.g. further education;
    long learning; teacher education
    , Department of
      naging and monitoring lifelong
      13

Education and Training Foundation (ETF), 6,
  13–14, 16, 22, 27, 28, 44, 45, 193, 196, 250,
  266
Education Funding Agency, 10, 14, 15
Education Maintenance Allowances (EMAs),
  101
e-learning
  developing teacher practices of, 157–9
  importance for teaching and learning,
    160–1, 161
  importance of teacher in facilitating and
    shaping, 162–4, 164
  value as method of learning, 156–7
e-mail
  usefulness in learning using technology,
    167
e-technology see technology and
  technologies
Elton Report (1989), 149
EMAs (Education Maintenance Allowances),
  101
English Baccalaureate, 122
English Defence League (EDL), 69
English for Speakers of Other Languages
  (ESOL), 123–5
environments, virtual learning
  drivers shaping in education, 162–4, 164
  see also e-learning
EQF (European Qualifications framework),
  110
equality, learner
  definition and interpretation, 58–9
  practice of in lifelong learning, 59–64, 61
  implications for ensuring in teaching,
    73–5
  see also inclusivity and differentiation
  see also aspects and groups affected e.g..
    bisexuality; gays; lesbians; minorities,
    ethnic; transgender issues
  see also factors impacting e.g. class, social;
    gender; mental health
  see also factors to ensure e.g. anti-racism;
    anti-sexism
  see also targets of e.g. cohesion,
    community; faith and religion, learner;
    integration, community; multiculturalism
equality, race
  situation of in lifelong learning, 60–2
Equality and Human Rights Commission,
  70

ESOL (English for Speakers of Other
    Languages), 123–5
    Establishments, educational *see*
    institutions, educational
esteem, parity of
    significance as consideration for curricula,
    119–21
ethnicity
    situation of in lifelong learning, 60–2
    see also equality, learner; inclusivity and
    differentiation
European Qualifications framework (EQF),
    110
evaluation
    annual course, 241–2
    definition, characteristics and influences,
    250–1
    of curricula, 252–4
    of learner retention, 254–5
    of learners, 250–1
    of teachers, 250–2
    see also assessment
    see also factors affecting e.g. audit, quality;
    autonomy, professional
    see also organisations involved e.g. Ofsted
    see also particular e.g. inspections
    Every Child Matters (2003)
    significance for child health and safety,
    237–8
examples and case studies
    assessment strategies, 175–6, *176*
    designing for learning with technology,
    165, 166–8
    use of specification tables, 184–5
expectation
    importance as factor influencing learning,
    87
experiential learning, 95–8, *96, 97*
experiential mentoring and coaching, 210–11
expository learning, 90–1

faith and religion, learner
    accommodation of in lifelong learning, 64–6
Family Learning initiative 10
FE *see* further education
FEDA (Further Education Development
    Association), 27–8
feedback
    importance as element of assessment,
    179–82

FEFCE (Further Education Funding Council
    for England), 14, 255–6
FHEQ (Framework for Higher Education
    Qualifications), 25, 110, *111*
field (Bourdieu)
    role in interpreting work-based learning,
    51–3
flipcharts
    value and use in learning sessions, 141
'flipped classrooms,' 165
Foundation Learning Curriculum (FLC), 126
formative assessment, 178–9
'formative' model of curricula evaluation
    (Scriven), 252
'four level' model of curricula evaluation
    (Kirkpatrick), 252
Framework for Higher Education
    Qualifications (FHEQ), 25, 110, *111*
frameworks
    teacher qualifications, 24–5
    teacher qualifications following Lingfield,
    25–6
friendliness
    need for in mentoring of teachers, 215–16
Fryer Reports (1997 & 1999), 18, 33
functionalism
    interpretation of teacher professionalism,
    40–1
further education (FE)
    context of as element of career planning
    and CPD, 259–60
    creating and maintaining suitable CVs,
    265–6
    employment and roles in, 260–1
    job application and interview processes,
    261–4
    recommended standards for subject
    specialisms, 193–4
    significance for lifelong learning policy
    agenda, 9–10
    situation of curricula in, 121–2
    staff appraisal and promotion in, 266–8
    use of part-time and agency teachers, 264–5
    see also aspects e.g. college higher
    education
    see also initiatives involving e.g.
    apprenticeships; diplomas, academic;
    'English Baccalaureate'; higher
    apprenticeships; English for Speakers of
    Other Languages; Skills for Life

Further Education Covenant, 6
Further Education Development Association
    (FEDA), 27–8
Further Education Funding Council for
    England (FEFCE), 14, 255–6
Further Education Guild, 6, 13
Further Education National Training
    Organization (FENTO), 6, 20, 21

gays
    significance for equality and diversity,
        71–2
GCSE English
    example of achievement and assessment
        strategies, 175
gender
    situation of in lifelong learning, 60–1, 62,
        62
    see also equality, learner; inclusivity and
        differentiation
General Teaching Council for England, 43
gifted and talented programme, 105–6
globalisation
    impact on education, 4–5
group teaching, 148–9
'Grow, Reality, Options, Way Forward' model
    of coaching, 214
guidelines
    written assessment tasks, *177*

HA (Historical Association), 195
habitats (Bourdieu)
    role in interpreting work-based learning,
        51–3
handouts
    value and use in learning sessions, 139–40
harm
    potential of technology for socio-moral and
        personal, 168–9
    harassment
    types and need for policies, 235
HEA (Higher Education Academy), 16, 27–8,
    44, 196
ᵗʰ, mental
    ᵗˡenge to ensuring diversity and
        ⁷²–3

        ᵖlace, 232–4
        , 231–2
        d youth, 237–9

see also aspects and issues e.g. bullying;
    harassment; risks; security
Help Children Achieve More initiative,
    237–9
hierarchies, institution
    need for trainee teachers to understand, 226
    development of performativity and
        managerialism, 227–8
    see also locations e.g. staffrooms
higher apprenticeships, 122–3
higher education
    recommended standards for subject
        specialisms in, 192–3
    reviews of, 257
    significance for lifelong learning policy
        agenda, 11–12
    see also college higher education
    see also organisations supporting e.g.
        Framework for Higher Education
        Qualifications; Institute for Learning and
        Teaching in Higher Education); Quality
        Assurance Agency for Higher Education
Higher Education Academy (HEA), 16, 27–8,
    44, 196
Higher Education in the Learning Society
    (Dearing Report), 28
Historical Association (HA), 195
HMI Court Administration (HMICA), 255
humanism
    interpretations of learning process, 94–5
humans, needs of
    Maslow's hierarchy, 85–6, *86*

IFL (Institute for Learning), 16, 24, 25, 27–8,
    29, 44, 265–6
ILTHE (Institute for Learning and Teaching in
    Higher Education), 27–8
inclusivity and differentiation
    role and significance in learning sessions,
        142–3
    significance for teaching practice, 73–4
    see also equality, learner
*Independent Review of Professionalism in
    Further Education* (Lingfield, 2012), 6,
    13, 19, 22, 25–6, 27, 45
individualism
    impact on education, 4–5
information technology *see* technology and
    technologies
initial teacher education (ITE)

growth of 19–21
need for perspective on, 16
New Labour ideas, 18–19
role and conduct of observation, 219–20
see also organisations supporting e.g.
    Centres of Excellence in Teacher
    Training
inspections
purpose and impact of issues arising from,
    256–7
Institute for Learning (IFL), 16, 24, 25, 27–8,
    29, 44, 265–6
Institute for Learning and Teaching in Higher
    Education (ILTHE), 27–8
institutions, educational
drivers shaping VLE's in, 162–4, *164*
factors to consider in initial teacher trainee
    visits, 225–6
impact of markets and globalisation, 3–5
need for trainees to understand structure
    and hierarchies, 226
see also aspects of e.g. managerialism;
    networks, informal; performativity
see also elements e.g. staffrooms
see also factors affecting e.g. achievement,
    educational; audit, quality; health and
    safety; inspections; retention, learner;
    risks
see also particular e.g. Education and
    Training Foundation; National College
    for Teaching and Leadership; Office of
    Qualifications and Examinations
    Regulator
Integrated Quality and Enhancement Reviews
    (IQERs), 257
integration, community
significance for anti-racism, 68–9
interdisciplinaarity
significance for subject specialisms,
    196–7
international learners
learning situation of, 103–4
interprofessionality
need for in lifelong learning, 45
interviews, job
processes and pitfalls, 262–4
ipsative assessment, 179
IQERs (Integrated Quality and Enhancement
    Reviews), 257
ITE *see* initial teacher education

jobs
processes and pitfalls of applications, 261–2
processes and pitfalls of interviews, 262–4
see also organisations supporting e.g.
    trade unions
Joint Information Systems Committee (JISC),
    156–7, 231–2

Kennedy report (1997), 18, 100
'knowing in action' (Schön), 203
Kolb, D., 96–7, *97*

learners and learning
approach of policy science and scholarship,
    29–31
debates over learning styles, 99–100
definitions, 79–82
evaluation of, 250–1
factors influencing, 85–7, *86*
significance of methods, 117
socio-economic and political context of
    theorising about, 31–6
theories of, 87–99, *88, 91, 93, 96–7, 98,*
    211–2, *212*
types, 82–5, *83–4*
widening participation in, 100–1
see also assessment; evaluation; 'not in
    education, employment or training';
    retention, learner; sessions, learning;
    teachers and teaching
see also aspects e.g.. bisexuality; gays;
    lesbians; transgender issues
see also factors affecting e.g. disabilities
    and disabled; diversity, learner; equality,
    learner; faith and religion, learner;
    learning difficulties
see also learner types e.g. adult learners;
    international students; talented and
    gifted
see also sites of e.g. further education;
    higher education; local authorities;
    providers, private; services, public;
    workplaces
see also specific type of learning e.g. 14–19
    education; affective learning;
    autonomous learning; blended learning;
    cognitive learning; deep learning;
    expository learning; lifelong learning;
    online learning; programmed learning;
    psychomotor learning; reception

learning; reflective learning; strategic
learning; surface learning; work-based
learning
see also tools e.g. technology and
technologies
Learning and Skills Council (LSC), 14–15,
255–6
Learning and Skills Improvement Service
(LSIS), 16, 26
Learning and Teaching Support Network
(LTSN), 28
learning difficulties
priorities and situation of learners with,
104–5
Learning for the Twenty-First Century
(Fryer Reports), 18, 33
Learning Works (Kennedy Report), 18, 100
lesbians
significance for equality and diversity,
71–2
lifelong learning
definition and importance of subject
specialism, 190–4
development of standards for, 21–4, *22, 23*
growth of teacher education for 19–21
historical development, 6–12
key institutions managing and monitoring,
12–16
need for inter-professionality and
collaboration, 45
need for perspective on changes in, 16–17
reform of, 5–6
significance of interdisciplinarity in, 196–7
see also players e.g. learners and learning;
mentors and mentoring; teachers and
teaching
see also priorities e.g. diversity, learner;
equality, learner
see also sites of e.g. further education;
higher education; local authorities;
providers, private; services, public
see also situations impacting e.g.
disabilities and disabled; gender;
minorities, ethnic
lifelong learning Sector (LLS) *see* lifelong
learning
Lifelong Learning UK (LLUK), 6–7, 16, 21–2,
22, 23, 24, 26, 28, 45, 192, 250
Lingfield review (2012), 6, 13, 19, 22, 25–6,
27, 45

listening
need for in mentoring of teachers, 216
literacy, digital, 163–4, *164*
Literacy, Language and Numeracy (LLN), 125
literacy and numeracy
role and curricula development, 123–5
LLS (lifelong learning Sector) *see* lifelong
learning
LLUK (Lifelong Learning UK), 6–7, 16, 21–2,
22, 23, 24, 26, 28, 45, 192, 250
local authorities
duties in relation to safeguarding, 237
involvement in measuring local cohesion,
68–9
removal of FE establishments from control
of, 260
role in providing 'adequate' FE, 7–8
significance for lifelong learning policy
agenda, 10
see also organisations supporting e.g.
Skills Funding Agency
LSC (Learning and Skills Council), 14–15,
255–6
LSIS (Learning and Skills Improvement
Service), 16, 26
LTSN (Learning and Teaching Support
Network), 28

Macpherson inquiry (1999), 67
McNair Report (1944), 19
management
and administration of courses, 240–6
organisations involved in LLS, 12–16
managerialism
development and forms in FE, 227–8
markets and marketing
impact on education, 4–5
methods in relation to course recruitment,
244
marking, double, 188–9
Maslow, A., 85–6, 86
mental health
as challenge to ensure diversity and
equality, 72–3
mentors and mentoring
characteristics for successful teacher,
215–18
characteristics of experiential, 210–11
definition and characteristics, 208–10, *209*
importance in WBE of teachers, 26–7

role in mentoring process, 218, *219*
see also coaches and coaching
see also tools e.g. observation
metaphors
learning acquisition and participation, *80*
methods, teaching and learning
significance as feature of curricula design
and development, 117
minorities, ethnic
situation of in lifelong learning, 60–2
see also equality, learner; inclusivity and
differentiation
modalities, learning
identification through VAK analysis, 99
modelling
role and use in learning sessions, 14 7–8
moderation and standardisation
importance as element of learning
assessment, 188
see also tools ensuring e.g. marking,
double
monitoring
of organisations involved in LLS, 12–16
motivation
importance as factor influencing learning,
85–6
multiculturalism
significance for anti-racism, 68–9

National Apprenticeship Service (NAS), 15,
122–3
National College for Teaching and Leadership,
13
National Open College Network (NOCN), 10
National Qualification Framework (NQF),
110, *111*, 124, 125
National Vocational Qualifications (NVQs),
176, *176*
need, humans
Maslow's hierarchy, 85–6, *86*
NEET ('not in education, employment or
training')
priorities and situation of young people as,
106–7
negligence, 232
neo-liberalism
impact on nature of education, 5
networks and networking
engagement with as means to enhance
specialism, 196

significance for trainee teachers of
informal, 227
usefulness in designing learning with
technology, 168
see also harm
New Labour
and community cohesion, 69–70
and education reform, 5–6, 8, 11, 19
and teacher qualifications, 25–6
interest in creative and cultural curricula,
118–19
interest in subject specialist pedagogy, 191–4
interest in widening education
participation, 101, 106
interest in work-based learning and
learning, 48, 106, 125
stance towards competitiveness, 31–2
support for *Every Child Matters* and *Help
Children Achieve More*, 237–9
see also initiatives e.g. apprenticeships;
diplomas, academic; Gifted and Talented
Programme; higher apprenticeships;
Skills for Life; standards
*see also organisations implementing
policies e.g.* Business, Innovation and
Skills, Department of
NOCN (National Open College Network), 10
norm-referenced assessment, 182–3
'not in education, employment or training'
(NEET)
priorities and situation of young people as,
106–7
NQF (National Qualification Framework),
110, *111*, 124, 125
numeracy and literacy
role and curricula development, 123–5
NVQs (National Vocational Qualifications),
176, *176*

objective model of curricula evaluation
(Tyler), 252
objectives and aims
significance and use in learning session
planning, 129–32, *130, 132*
significance as feature of curricula design
and development, 116
observances, religious
accommodation of in lifelong learning, 64–6
observation, mentee
role, usefulness and requirements, 218–21

Office for Standards in Education, Children's
    Services and Skills (Ofsted)
    history of development, 255–6
    impact and issues arising from work of,
        256–7
    influence on teaching and learning
        evaluation, 250–1, 253
    purpose of inspections of, 256
Office of Qualifications and Examinations
    Regulator (Ofqual), 14, 22, 25, 26–7, 62,
    99, 126, 193, 220, 233, 239, 249, 250, 253,
    255–6
online learning, 158–9
operant conditioning, 88
    organisations, educational *see* institutions,
        educational
organisations, professional teaching
    engagement with as means to enhance
        specialism, 196

Parsloe, E., *209*
participation, learner
    metaphors of, *80*
    widening of, 100–1
Partnerships for Schools, 14
Pavlov, I., 87–8, *88*
PCET (post-compulsory education and
    training) *see* lifelong learning
pedagogy
    definition and importance of specialist in,
        190–4
    peers
    role, use and focus of observation by, 221
    performativity
    development and forms in FE, 227–8
personal learning environments (PLEs), 163
personal learning networks (PLNs), 163
plagiarism
    impact on liability and validity of
        assessment, 186
planning
    and design of assessment methods, 173–7,
        174, 176, 177
    and development of learning sessions,
        127–9, *128, 129*
    use of aims and objectives in, 129–32, *130,
        132*
plans, lesson
    format and use, 143, *144, 145*
PLEs (personal learning environments), 163

PLNs (personal learning networks), 163
policy and policies
    approach to educational research, 46–7
    health and safety, 237–9
    history of lifelong learning, 6–12
    importance of anti-racist, 67
    recognition of need for teacher education,
        18–19
    see also scholarship, policy; science, policy
    *see also particular policies e.g. Every Child
        Matters;* Family Learning initiative;
        National Open College Network; *Youth
        Matters*
    see also tools ensuring e.g. conduct, codes
        of
post-compulsory education and training
    (PCET) *see* lifelong learning
practice, communities of
    and notion of work-based learning, 53–4
    applicability to students online, 158–9
    involving teachers in FE, 54–7
practice, education
    need for commitment to agency and social
        practice, 38–9
    need for expansiveness of, 36–8
    see also factors affecting e.g. relationships,
        educational
    see also players and elements e.g. learners
        and learning; teachers and teaching
practice, reflective
    criticisms of, 206–7
    definitions, 198–9
    importance in learning process, 98–9, *98*
    need for in teacher mentoring, 216
    process of, 199–200, *199*
    theories of, 202–5, *203*
    types and levels of, 200–2, *200–1, 202*
practice, social
    need for commitment to in education,
        38–9
presentations, software for
    value and use in learning sessions, 140–1
Professional Standards for Teachers and
    Trainers in Education and Training
    – England
    applicability to professional practice,
        xxvii–xxviii
professionalism, teacher
    historical development and theories
        defining, 40–3

see also collaboration, inter-professional; values, professional
see also organisations promoting e.g. Higher Education Academy
Professionalism in Further Education (Lingfield Review), 6, 13, 19, 22, 25–6, 27, 45
programmed learning, 89
'progressive' conceptions of curriculum, 113–16, *114*
projectors
   value and use in learning sessions, 140–1
promotion, teacher
   options to consider, 267–8
protocols, mentee, 219
providers, private
   significance for lifelong learning, 11
psychological constructivism, 92
psychomotor learning, 82, *84*

QAA (Quality Assurance Agency for Higher Education), 15–16, 110, 241, 257
QCF (Qualifications and Credit Framework), 24, 110, *111*, 122, 126, 176
QCDA (Qualifications and Curriculum Development Agency), 13
qualifications, teacher
   need for harmony with bodies controlling, 245–6
   significance of framework of, 24–5
   situation following Lingfield review, 25–6
Qualifications and Credit Framework (QCF), 24, 110, *111*, 122, 126, 176
Qualifications and Curriculum Development Agency (QCDA), 13
Qualified Teacher Learning and Skills (QTLS), 24–5, 28
quality, educational
   development and key features of audit of, 248–9
Quality Assurance Agency for Higher Education (QAA), 15–16, 110, 241, 257
questions and questioning
   need for in mentoring of teachers, 216
   use and purpose in learning sessions, 135–8, *138*
QTLS (Qualified Teacher Learning and Skills), 24–5, 28

race equality
   situation of in lifelong learning, 60–2
radical constructivism, 92
rapport
   need for in mentoring of teachers, 215–16
rationale
   significance for curricula design and development, 116
RCHEs (Reviews of College Higher Education), 255
reception learning, 90–1
records, course
   importance of maintenance of, 240–1
recruitment, course
   methods of marketing for, 244
reflection *see* practice, reflective
'reflection on action' (Schön), 204
reflexes, conditioned, 87–8, *88*
reform
   need for perspective on lifelong learning, 16–17
   of lifelong learning sector, 5–6
reinforcement
   importance as factor influencing learning, 86–7
relationships, coaching
   requirements for successful, 212–14, *213*
relationships, educational
   contingency and complexity of, 33–6
reliability
   need for in assessment, 185–6
religion and faith, learner
   accommodation of in lifelong learning, 64–6
research, educational
   engagement with as means to enhance specialism, 195
   policies on approach to, 46–7
resources
   range and use in learning, 138–9
   significance for curricula design and development, 117
   see also particular e.g. audiovisuals; flipcharts; handouts; projectors; software, presentation; whiteboards
retention, learner
   evaluation of, 254–5
Reviews of College Higher Education (RCHEs), 255

Review of Vocational Education (Wolf
    report), 61, 106
risks
    persons responsible for assessments of, 234
    place and significance in education, 231
    see also health and safety
    see also tools in management of e.g.
    Disclosure and Barring Service
Russell Report (1966), 19–20

safety *see* health and safety
schemes, of work, 143, 146–7, *146*
scholarship, educational
    engagement with as means to enhance
        specialism, 195
    policies on approach to, 46–7
scholarship, policy
    approach to educational complexity and
        contingency, 33–6
    approach to teaching and learning, 29–31
    definition and scope, 29
Schön, D., 202–4
science, policy
    approach to teaching and learning, 29–31
    definition and scope, 29
sector, lifelong learning *see* lifelong learning
    security
    types and relevance, 236–7
services, public
    significance for lifelong learning policy
        agenda, 11
sessions, learning
    developing transitions between activities,
        128–9, *129*
    planning and development of, 127–9, *128,*
        129
    role and significance of differentiation,
        142–3
    selection and use of activities, 132–5, *133,*
        134
    use of physical resources, 138–41
    use of questions, 135–8, *138*
    see also factors impacting e.g. aims and
        objectives; behaviour, learner
    see also forms e.g. group teaching; support;
        tutorials
    see also tools to enhance e.g. modelling;
        plans, lessons; schemes, of work
sexism (anti-sexism)
    significance for equality and diversity, 70–1

simplification
    as political focus of education reform, 6
Skills for Life,
    role and curricula development of, 125–6
Skills Funding Agency (SFA), 14–15, 255–6
SMART objectives of learning, 131
social constructivism, 92
software, presentation
    value and use in learning sessions, 140–1
specialisms, subject
    definition and significance, 190–4
    need for teachers to maintain subject
        currency, 194–6
    significance of interdisciplinarity, 196–7
specifications, tables of
    role in aiding assessment validity, 184–5
staff, administrative
    need for positive relations with, 245
staffrooms
    as 'communities of practice,' 55–7
    significance for trainee teachers, 228–30
standardisation and moderation
    importance as element of learning
        assessment, 188
    see also tools ensuring e.g. marking, double
standards
    contribution of policy to teaching, 43–4
    development of lifelong learning, 20, 21–4,
        22, 23
    subject specialism in lifelong learning,
        192–3
Standards Verification UK (SVUK), 16
strategic learning, 85
strategies, assessment *see* assessments
strategies, teaching and learning *see* learners
    and learning; teachers and teaching
streamlining
    as political focus of education reform, 6
structures, institution
    need for trainee teachers to understand, 226
    development of performativity and
        managerialism, 227–8
    see also particular e.g. staffrooms
students *see* learners and learning
styles, learning
    debates over, 99–100
    importance as factor influencing learning,
        87
subjects, specialisms of
    definition and significance, 190–4

need for teachers to maintain subject
currency, 194–6
significance of interdisciplinarity in, 196–7
summative assessment; 178
*Supply and Training of Teachers for Further
Education* (Russell Report), 19–20
support
need for in mentoring of teachers, 216–17,
217
value and use of pastoral, 152–4
surface learning, 85
SVUK (Standards Verification UK), 16

TA (Teaching Agency), 13
tables, specification
role in aiding assessment validity, 184–5
talented and gifted programme, 105–6
teacher education
policy recognition of the need for, 18–19
recent growth in, 19–21
see also sites of e.g. workplaces
teachers and teaching
approach of policy science and scholarship
to, 29–31
evaluation of, 250–2
management of in relation to courses, 243
need for commitment to in education
practice, 38–9
significance of methods, 117
socio-economic and political context of
theorising about, 31–6
work-based mentor training of, 26–7
see also careers, teacher; coaches and
coaching; mentors and mentoring;
qualifications, teacher; sessions,
learning; standards; trainees, teacher
*see also aspects requiring attention from
e.g.* differentiation and inclusiviety;
diversity, learner; equality, learner; faith
and religion, learner; multiculturalism
see also factors impacting e.g. behaviour,
learner
see also features of e.g. assessment;
organisations, professional teaching;
professionalism, teacher; specialism,
subject; support; technology and
technologies
see also forms e.g. coaches and coaching;
group teaching; mentors and mentoring;
tutorials; work-based learning

*see also particular organisations
supporting e.g.* Higher Education
Academy; Institute for Learning
Teachers and Youth Leaders (McNair Report),
19
Teaching Agency (TA), 13
Teaching Quality Enhancement Fund (TQEF),
28
technical reflection, 201–2, *202*
technologies, information *see* technology and
technologies
technology and technologies
concepts and terminology for learning with,
159–60, *159*
design of for learning engagement, 164–8,
165, 166–8
development of teacher skills in use of
e-learning, 157–9
perceptions about use of, 155–6
potential for socio-moral and personal
harm, 168–9
socio-cultural shaping of, 162–4, *164*
types available for learning, 160–2, *161,
162*
value of learning with, 156–7
see also particular e.g. computers
TECs (Training and Enterprise Councils),
14
TDLB (Training and Development Lead
Body), 20
terminology
of learning with technology, 159–60, *159*
'The Foundation' 6, 13–14, 16, 22, 27, 28, 44,
45, 193, 196, 250, 266
theft
measures to prevent, 236
theories and theorising
adult learning, 102
defining teacher professionalism, 40–3
educational achievement, 32–3
of learning, 211–12, *212*
process of learning, 87–99, *88, 91, 93, 96–7,
98*
reflective practice, 202–5, *203*
socio-economic and political context of
education, 31–6
vocational learning, 31–2
work-based learning, 48, 51–3
see also aspects e.g. complexities;
contingency

see also factors affected e.g. relationships, educational
see also particular e.g. functionalism; neoliberalism; trait approach
three stage model of reflective learning, 98–9, *98*
TLC ('Transforming Learning Cultures') project, 36, 51
total quality management (TQM), 244
TQEF (Teaching Quality Enhancement Fund), 28
trade unions
   significance for teacher careers, 267
'traditional' conceptions of curriculum, 113–16, *114*
   Train to Gain (TTG), 62
   trainees, teacher
   education visits of, 225–6
   need for understanding of hierarchies and structures, 226
   significance of informal networks, 227
   significance of staffrooms, 228–30
   see also institutional styles impacting e.g. managerialism; performativity
training, teacher *see* teacher education
Training and Development Agency for Schools, 13
Training and Development Lead Body (TDLB), 20
Training and Enterprise Councils (TECs), 14
trait approach
   interpretation of teacher professionalism, 40
'Transforming Learning Cultures' (TLC) project, 36, 51
transgender issues
   significance for equality and diversity, 71–2
Tripp, D., 204–5
   TTG (Train to Gain), 62
tutors and tutoring *see* teachers and teaching
tutorials
   value and use as learning session type, 152–4

UCU (University and College Union), 267
UK Council for Child Internet Safety (UKCCIS), 237
UK Resource Centre for Women in Science, Engineering and Technology, 70
unions
   significance for teacher careers, 267
University and College Union (UCU), 267

VAK (visual, auditory, kinaesthetic) learning styles, 99
validity
   need for in assessment, 183–6, *185*
values, professional
   and codes of conduct, 43–5
virtual learning environments (VLEs)
   drivers shaping in education, 162–4, *164*
   see also e-learning
visits, trainee
   factors to consider for educational, 225–6
visual, auditory, kinaesthetic (VAK) learning styles, 99
VLEs (virtual learning environments)
   drivers shaping in education, 162–4, *164*
   see also e-learning
vocationalism
   significance as consideration for curricula: 119–21
   theories about learning involving, 31–2

Warnock Report (1978), 142
WBL *see* work-based learning
whiteboards
   value and use in learning sessions, 139, 140–1
Wolf report (2011), 61, 106
work, schemes of, 143, 146–7, *146*
work-based learning (WBL)
   as socially situated practice for teachers, 48–51
   Bourdieu's theories in relation to, 51–3
   notion of 'communities of practice' and, 53–4
   theories in relation to, 48, 51–3
workplaces
   mentoring and teacher education in, 26–7
workshops
   as 'communities of practice,' 55–7
written assessment, *177*

Youth Matters
   significance for child health and safety, 238
Young People's Learning Agency (YPLA), 10, 14, 15, 255–6
Youth Training Scheme (YTS), 108

zone of proximal development (Vygotsky), 93–4, *93*